BIG BOOK OF IPv6 ADDRESSING RFCs

Big Book of IPv6 Addressing RFCs

Compiled by
Peter H. Salus

Morgan Kaufmann
An Imprint of ACADEMIC PRESS
A Harcourt Science and Technology Company
San Diego San Francisco New York Boston
London Sydney Tokyo

This book is printed on acid-free paper. ∞

ACADEMIC PRESS
A Harcourt Science and Technology Company
525 B Street, Suite 1900, San Diego, CA 92101-4495 USA
http://www.academicpress.com

Academic Press
Harcourt Place, 32 Jamestown Road, London NW1 7BY, UK
http://www.hbuk.co.uk/ap/

Morgan Kaufmann Publishers
340 Pine Street, Sixth Floor, San Francisco, CA 94104-3205
http://www.mkp.com

Library of Congress Catalog Number: 99-69848
International Standard Book Number: 0-12-616770-2

Printed in the United States of America
00 01 02 03 04 IP 9 8 7 6 5 4 3 2 1

For Dr. Ruth Coman of the British Library

Table of Contents

Foreword

Computer Science folk theory suggests that the important problems of Computer Science can be decomposed into naming, recursion and very little else. To what degree this characterization is accurate can be debated, but it does capture the central importance of naming as a fundamental abstraction.

Computer networking uses naming in a number of different ways. For example, it's difficult to imagine the process for establishing a communication between two parties without some mechanism to designate the conversants. Designation implies distinction, so the subtle notion of identity is involved as well.

To understand a network architecture, one must understand how it uses naming. A very particular form of naming characteristic of computer networks is the "address". While it is quite tricky to define the notion of "address" precisely, the general notion is (surprisingly) understood with sufficient commonality.

IP version 4 has a complex and subtle set of naming mechanisms and IPv6 has a somewhat more complex set. To its credit, IPv6 replaces some of the obscure subtleties of IPv4 with more explicit, comprehensible mechanisms.

So to understand IP version 6 to any significant depth, one must understand how it uses naming, and in particular, how it uses various forms of addressing in pivotal ways.

Peter Salus has performed a significant public service producing this volume. Until now, the only way to assemble this information was to laboriously visit the RFC FTP sites, download the files, and materially shorten the life of a laser printer. Peter also includes material which provides needed context framing the RFCs both technically and historically. This assistance can make some design decisions easier to understand.

In closing, it is interesting to note that there is no equivalent set of RFCs for IP version 4 focussed on addressing, much less an equivalent book.

Michael D. O'Dell
Senior Vice President & Chief Scientist
UUNET Technologies

CHAPTER 1 | Historical Introduction

You would never drop an envelope into the mailbox without an address on it. Similarly, each node on the Internet—router or end system (often called *host* or *server*)—has an identifier attached to it. This identifier is its address. Any packet sent between nodes must use the destination address to tell the intervening routers where it should go.

Just as the postal service allots ZIP codes and recognizes house numbers, destination addresses must be shared out, too. Early on, this was done by consensus, but over the past decade the process has become more bureaucratic.

The source of all knowledge where the Internet is concerned is the set of RFCs (Requests for Comment) and the IETF (Internet Engineering Task Force) drafts. There are now well over 2800 RFCs and many drafts, but only a few people track history, evolution, and outright paradigm shift. But some of the history is necessary, as it illuminates our future path.

In RFC 1 (April 1969), Steve Crocker (then a graduate student, recently a vice president at Cybercash) laid out a scheme that allotted 5 bits to address space: enough for 32 addresses. By September 1969, when IMP #1 (Interface Message Processor, a Honeywell 516 that was, effectively, the first router) was installed in Leonard Kleinrock's lab at UCLA, this had grown to 6 bits (63 addresses, because 0 wasn't employed). By 1972 it had become clear that this would be insufficient, and the address space was enlarged to 8 bits (255 addresses). In fact, the ARPANET finally hit 63 hosts only in January 1976. But this was already a lot in terms of the host.txt tables (the routing *phone book*) that were distributed to every site. By August 1983, there were 213 hosts and we were pushing the 8-bit address barrier.

Vinton Cerf (now a vice president at MCI) and Bob Kahn (the president of CNRI) came up with the original version of TCP (Transmission Control

Protocol, RFC 675; December 1974), and Jon Postel with that of IP (Internet Protocol, RFC 760; January 1980). These increased this *address space* to 32 bits, but the structure of the ARPANET was *classless*, that is, the hierarchic distributed database we are familiar with only came about with Mills' conceptualization of the Domain Naming System (DNS; RFC 799; September 1981), and its implementation by Paul Mockapetris (RFCs 882 and 883; November 1983). Mockapetris' implementation was called *Jeeves*; *BIND*, (Berkeley Internet Name Domain; written by Kevin Dunlap; capably maintained by Paul Vixie) is currently the most used.

And so we achieved 32-bit addressing and a hierarchical array of classes of networks: A, B, C, D, and E. There are 128 Class A addresses, each of which can have 16,777,216 unique host identifiers. There are thus 16,384 Class B addresses, with 65,536 unique identifiers; 2,097,192 Class C addresses; and over 268 million Class D groups. Class E addresses have never been available for general use.

Using the IP addressing scheme, DNS allowed for about 4 billion hosts on 16.7 million networks. This seemed like a very large number of addresses of various kinds. But the expansion of the use of the Internet over the past decade has been explosive.

In August 1990, during the Vancouver IETF meeting, Frank Solensky, Phill Gross, and Sue Hares projected that the current rate of assignment would exhaust the Class B space by March of 1994.

Classless Inter-Domain Routing (CIDR, RFCs 1518 and 1519; September 1993) was introduced to improve both routing scalability and address space utilization in the Internet. By eliminating the notion of network classes, CIDR allows a better match between address requirements and address allocation. Eliminating the notion of network classes allows expansion of the scope of hierarchical address allocation. This results in expanding the scope of hierarchical routing, which in turn improved scaling properties of the Internet routing system. CIDR has proven to be the palliative that has enabled the Internet to continue functioning while growth continues.

Even with this, it was revealed at the July 1994 Toronto meeting of the IETF that, using the current allocation statistics, the Internet would exhaust the IPv4 address space between 2005 and 2011. With several more years of experience, which has also brought greater uncertainty as to gross numbers, we can push these dates out a bit, but exhaustion will come.

As the Internet has waxed, and with it the number of intranets (what we used to think of as internal corporate networks) as well as the number of different uses to which they are put, the pressures mounted.

The Toronto IETF meeting set up an IPng (Internet Protocol Next Generation), or IPv6, task force, cochaired by Scott Bradner and Allison Mankin. Recommendations from that task force were released in October 1994 for discussion at the December 1994 IETF meeting. The basic goal was to have something in place before 2000, so that the time limit would not be pushed. Unfortunately, as Bradner and Mankin put it in their recommendation, "Some people pointed out that this type of projection makes an assumption of no paradigm shifts in IP usage. If someone were to develop a new 'killer application,'(for example cable-TV set top boxes), the resultant rise in the demand for IP addresses could make this an over-estimate of the time available."

IPv6 provides for 128-bit addressing. This is a gigantic number: larger than the estimated total number of molecules in the universe. Just how this will work is still unclear: as I write, the new protocol has yet to be widely deployed. Among other things, going from 32 to 128 bits will entail renumbering a large number of addresses already in use. Some organizations will have to renumber in order to use the address space more efficiently. One of the ways of doing this is through the use of NATs (Network Address Translators), which allow you to consume address space more slowly so that an organization can have one external address and many private addresses (net 10 is often used) internally (these need not be globally unique). The 128 bits can be thought of as 64 (external) and 64 (internal).

However, it is absurd to state that address space depletion is the only driving force behind IPv6. Although the address space now provided for is enormous, it's not everything. A number of other abilities "have been developed in direct response to current business requirements for more scalable network architectures, mandatory security and data integrity, an additional field for quality-of-service (QoS), autoconfiguration, and more efficient network route aggregation at the global backbone level."

A business or private user might well say "So what?" to this, thinking that IPv6 support for a large diversity of network devices just isn't an end-user or business concern.

Over the next few years, conventional computers on the Internet will be joined by a variety of new devices, including palm-top personal data assistants (PDA), hybrid mobile phone technology with data processing capabilities, smart set-top boxes with integrated Web browsers, and embedded network components in equipment ranging from office copy machines to kitchen appliances. Some of the new devices requiring IP addresses and connectivity will be consumer-oriented, like your coffee machine, dishwasher, etc.

IPv6's 128-bit address space will allow businesses to deploy a huge array of new desktop, mobile, and embedded network devices in a cost-effective, manageable manner. Further, IPv6's autoconfiguration features will make it feasible for large numbers of devices to attach dynamically to the network, without incurring unsupportable costs for the administration for an ever-increasing number of adds, moves, and changes. The business requirement for IPv6 will be driven by end-user applications.

It isn't true, either, that IPv6 is primarily relevant to routers, not end-user applications. It is true that IPv6 address aggregation allows efficient routing hierarchies that limit the growth of routing tables. But many of these IPv6 features also bring direct benefits to end-user applications. Applications will have available the mandatory IPv6 encryption and authentication services as an integral part of the IP stack. For mobile users and organizations, the automatic configuration components allow the efficient assignment of IP addresses without delays and costs associated with manual address administration.

IPv6 is very much both an end-user concern and a business concern.

A truly excellent job of making the case for IPv6 is the Internet Architecture Board draft by Steve King and a half dozen colleagues (draft-iab-case-for-ipv6-05.txt), which I quoted from earlier. Other works in progress deal with the adjustments to OSPF, multicasting, mobility, etc.

The period from 1981 through 1983—the conversion to DNS—was painful to all concerned. Over the past 15 years we have learned a lot: But the switch from IPv4 to IPv6 may be yet more painful. The drafts tell the tale of those who are striving to make things easier. There has been a lot of discussion about various kinds of transition mechanisms and some of these may be less painful (more automated) than we might think at first. Remember, this pain is not because of the innate difficulty of altering a scheme, but causing a ship carrying under 250 passengers to veer is far easier than when the vessel carries 200 million and more.

Even though there are few implementations of IPv6 and scant deployment, this book is intended to make the transition over the next 5–10 years less painful to both users and network administrators.

To that end, a number of RFCs form the bulk of this volume.

RFC 1

Network Working Group
Request for Comments: 1

Steve Crocker
UCLA
7 April 1969

Title: Host Software
Author: Steve Crocker
Installation: UCLA
Date: 7 April 1969
Network Working Group Request for Comment: 1

CONTENTS

Introduction

The software for the ARPA Network exists partly in the IMPs and partly in the respective HOSTs. BB&N has specified the software of the IMPs and it is the responsibility of the HOST groups to agree on HOST software.

During the summer of 1968, representatives from the initial four sites met several times to discuss the HOST software and initial experiments on the network. There emerged from these meetings a working group of three, Steve Carr from Utah, Jeff Rulifson from SRI, and Steve Crocker of UCLA, who met during the fall and winter. The most recent meeting was in the last week of March in Utah. Also present was Bill Duvall of SRI who has recently started working with Jeff Rulifson.

Somewhat independently, Gerard DeLoche of UCLA has been working on the HOST-IMP interface.

I present here some of the tentative agreements reached and some of the open questions encountered. Very little of what is here is firm and reactions are expected.

I. A Summary of the IMP Software

Messages

Information is transmitted from HOST to HOST in bundles called messages. A message is any stream of not more than 8080 bits, together with its header. The header is 16 bits and contains the following information:

Destination	5 bits
Link	8 bits
Trace	1 bit
Spare	2 bits

The destination is the numerical code for the HOST to which the message should be sent. The trace bit signals the IMPs to record status information about the message and send the information back to the NMC (Network Measurement Center, i.e., UCLA). The spare bits are unused.

Links

The link field is a special device used by the IMPs to limit certain kinds of congestion. They function as follows. Between every pair of HOSTs there are 32 logical full-duplex connections over which messages may be passed in either direction. The IMPs place the restriction on these links that no HOST can send two successive messages over the same link before the IMP at the destination has sent back a special message called an RFNM (Request for Next Message). This arrangement limits the congestion one HOST can cause another if the sending HOST is attempting to send too much over one link. We note, however, that since the IMP at the destination does not have enough capacity to handle all 32 links simultaneously, the links serve their purpose only if the overload is coming from one or two links. It is necessary for the HOSTs to cooperate in this respect.

The links have the following primitive characteristics. They are always functioning and there are always 32 of them.

By "always functioning," we mean that the IMPs are always prepared to transmit another message over them. No notion of beginning or ending a conversation is contained in the IMP software. It is thus not possible to query an IMP about the state of a link (although it might be possible to query an IMP about the recent history of a link – quite a different matter!).

The other primitive characteristic of the links is that there are always 32 of them, whether they are in use or not. This means that each IMP must maintain 18 tables, each with 32 entries, regardless of the actual traffic.

The objections to the link structure notwithstanding, the links are easily programmed within the IMPs and are probably a better alternative to more complex arrangements just because of their simplicity.

IMP Transmission and Error Checking

After receiving a message from a HOST, an IMP partitions the message into one or more packets. Packets are not more than 1010 bits long and are the unit of data transmission from IMP to IMP. A 24 bit cyclic checksum is computed by the transmission hardware and is appended to an outgoing packet. The checksum is recomputed by the receiving hardware and is checked against the transmitted checksum. Packets are reassembled into messages at the destination IMP.

Open Questions on the IMP Software

1. An 8 bit field is provided for link specification, but only 32 links are provided, why?

2. The HOST is supposed to be able to send messages to its IMP. How does it do this?

3. Can a HOST, as opposed to its IMP, control RFNMs?

4. Will the IMPs perform code conversion? How is it to be controlled?

II. Some Requirements Upon the Host-to-Host Software

Simple Use

As with any new facility, there will be a period of very light usage until the community of users experiments with the network and begins to depend upon it. One of our goals must be to stimulate the immediate and easy use by a wide class of users. With this goal, it seems natural to provide the ability to use any remote HOST as if it had been dialed up from a TTY (teletype) terminal. Additionally, we would like some ability to transmit a file in a somewhat different manner perhaps than simulating a teletype.

Deep Use

One of the inherent problems in the network is the fact that all responses from a remote HOST will require on the order of a half-second or so, no matter how simple. For teletype use, we could shift to a half-duplex local-echo arrangement, but this would destroy some of the usefulness of the network. The 940 Systems, for example, have a very specialized echo.

When we consider using graphics stations or other sophisticated terminals under the control of a remote HOST, the problem becomes more severe. We must look for some method which allows us to use our most sophisticated equipment as much as possible as if we were connected directly to the remote computer.

Error Checking

The point is made by Jeff Rulifson at SRI that error checking at major software interfaces is always a good thing. He points to some experience at SRI where it has saved much dispute and wasted effort. On these grounds, we would like to see some HOST to HOST checking. Besides checking the software interface, it would also check the HOST-IMP transmission hardware. (BB&N claims the HOST-IMP hardware will be as reliable as the internal registers of the HOST. We believe them, but we still want the error checking.)

III. The Host Software

Establishment of a Connection

The simplest connection we can imagine is where the local HOST acts as if it is a TTY and has dialed up the remote HOST. After some consideration of the problems of initiating and terminating such a connection , it has been decided to reserve link 0 for communication between HOST operating systems. The remaining 31 links are thus to be used as dial-up lines.

Each HOST operating system must provide to its user level programs a primitive to establish a connection with a remote HOST and a primitive to break the connection. When these primitives are invoked, the operating system must select a free link and send a message over link 0 to the remote HOST requesting a connection on the selected link. The operating system in the remote HOST must agree and send back an accepting message over link 0. In the event both HOSTs select the same link to initiate a connection and both send request messages at essentially the same time, a simple priority scheme will be invoked in which the HOST of lower priority gives way and selects another free link. One usable priority scheme is simply the ranking of HOSTS by their identification numbers. Note that both HOSTs are aware that simultaneous requests have been made, but they take complementary actions: The higher priority HOST disregards the request while the lower priority HOST sends both an acceptance and another request.

The connection so established is a TTY-like connection in the pre-log-in state. This means the remote HOST operating system will initially treat the link as if a TTY had just called up. The remote HOST will generate the same echos, expect the same log-in sequence and look for the same interrupt characters.

High Volume Transmission

Teletypes acting as terminals have two special drawbacks when we consider the transmission of a large file. The first is that some characters are special interrupt characters. The second is that special buffering techniques are often employed, and these are appropriate only for low-speed character at time transmission.

We therefore define another class of connection to be used for the transmission of files or other large volumes of data. To initiate this class of link, user level programs at both ends of an established TTY-like link must request the establishment of a file-like connection parallel to the TTY-like link. Again the priority scheme comes into play, for the higher priority HOST sends a message over link 0 while the lower priority HOST waits for it. The user level programs are, of course, not concerned with this. Selection of the free link is done by the higher priority HOST.

File-like links are distinguished by the fact that no searching for interrupt characters takes place and buffering techniques appropriate for the higher data rates takes place.

A Summary of Primitives

Each HOST operating systems must provide at least the following primitives to its users. This list knows not to be necessary but not sufficient.

a) Initiate TTY-like connection with HOST x.

b) Terminate connection.

c) Send/Receive character(s) over TTY-like connection.

d) Initiate file-like connection parallel to TTY-like connection.

e) Terminate file-like connection.

f) Send/Receive over file-like connection.

Error Checking

We propose that each message carry a message number, bit count, and a checksum in its body, that is transparent to the IMP. For a checksum we suggest a 16-bit end-around-carry sum computed on 1152 bits and then circularly shifted right one bit. The right circular shift every 1152 bits is designed to catch errors in message reassembly by the IMPs.

Closer Interaction

The above described primitives suggest how a user can make simple use of a remote facility. They shed no light on how much more intricate use of the network is to be carried out. Specifically, we are concerned with the fact that as some sites a great deal of work has gone into making the computer highly responsive to a sophisticated console. Culler's consoles at UCSB and Englebart's at SRI are at least two examples. It is clear that delays of a half-second or so for trivial echo-like responses degrade the interaction to the point of making the sophistication of the console irrelevant.

We believe that most console interaction can be divided into two parts, an essentially local, immediate and trivial part and a remote, more lengthy and significant part. As a simple example, consider a user at a console consisting of a keyboard and refreshing display screen. The program the user is talking typing into accumulates a string of characters until a carriage return is encountered and then it processes the string. While characters are being typed, it displays the characters on the screen. When a rubout character is typed, it deletes the previous non-rubout character. If the user types H E L L O <- <- P <CR> where <- is rubout and <CR> is carriage-return, he has made nine keystrokes. If each of these keystrokes causes a message to be sent which in return invokes instructions to our display station we will quickly become bored.

A better solution would be to have the front-end of the remote program – that is the part scanning for <- and <CR> – be resident in our computer. In that case, only one five character message would be sent, i.e., H E L P <CR>, and the screen would be managed locally.

We propose to implement this solution by creating a language for console control. This language, current named DEL, would be used by subsystem designers to specify what components are needed in a terminal and how the terminal is to respond to inputs from its keyboard, Lincoln Wand, etc. Then, as a part of the initial protocol, the remote HOST would send to the local HOST, the source language text of the program which controls the console. This program would have been by the subsystem designer in DEL, but will be compiled locally.

The specifications of DEL are under discussion. The following diagrams show the sequence of actions.

A. Before Link Establishment

```
          /                                                        \
         |     +-----------+                    +-----------+       |
         |     |           |                    |           |       |
         |     |           |                    |           |       |
         |     | terminal  |                    | terminal  |       |
         |     |           |                    |           |       |
         |     |           |                    |           |       |
         |     +-----+-----+                    +-----+-----+       |
         |           |                                |             |
         |           |                                |             |
         |           |                                |             |
         |     +-----+-----+                    +-----------+       |
         |     |     |     | Request connection |     |     |       |
   UCLA {      |     |     | -> over link 25    |     |     |       } SRI
         |     |  +-+-+    |  +-+        +-+    |  +-+-+    |       |
         |     |  | OS|---+-=|I|----------|I|=-+---| OS|    |       |
         |     |  +-+-+    |  +-+        +-+    |  +---+    |       |
         |     |           |                    |           |       |
         |     |           |                    |           |       |
         |     +-----------+                    +-----------+       |
         |      HOST: UCLA                       HOST: SRI          |
          \                                                        /
```

b. After Link Establishment and Log-in

```
         /                                                      \
        |     +-----------+                     +-----------+    |
        |     |           |                     |           |    |
        |     |           |                     |           |    |
        |     | terminal  |                     | terminal  |    |
        |     |           |                     |           |    |
        |     |           |                     |           |    |
        |     +-----+-----+                     +-----+-----+    |
        |           |                                 |          |
        |           |                                 |          |
        |           |                                 |          |
        |     +-----+-----+ "Please send front"+-----------+    |
        |     |     |     | end control"        |     |     |    |
   UCLA {     |     |     |       ->            |     |     |    } SRI ___
        |     |  +-+-+    | +-+         +-+     | +--+---+  |    |    /    |
        |     |  | OS|---+-=|I|----------|I|=-+--|OS|NLS|  +----+---|     |
        |     |  +-+-+    | +-+         +-+     | +------+  |    |   |___/
        |     |           |      DEL prog.      |           |    |   |    |
        |     |           |       <-            |           |    |   |____|
        |     +-----------+                     +-----------+    |
        |      HOST: UCLA                        HOST:SRI        |
         \                                                      /
```

c. After Receipt and Compilation of the DEL program

```
         /                                                      \
         |    +-----------+                    +-----------+     |
         |    |           |                    |           |     |
         |    |           |                    |           |     |
         |    | terminal  |                    | terminal  |     |
         |    |           |                    |           |     |
         |    |           |                    |           |     |
         |    +-----+-----+                    +-----+-----+     |
         |          |Trivial                         |           |
         |          |Responses                       |           |
         |          |                                |           |
         |    +-----+------+                    +-----+------+   |
         |    |     |      |                    |     |      |   |
   UCLA  {    |     |      | Major Responses    |     |      |   } SRI ___
         |    |  +--+--+   | +-+           +-+  |  +--+---+  |   |    /   |
         |    |  |DEL  |---+-=|I|-----------|I|=-+--|OS|NLS|  +---+---|    |
         |    |  |front|   | +-+           +-+  |  +------+  |   |   |___/
         |    |  | end |   |                    |            |   |   |    |
         |    |  |prog.|   |                    |            |   |   |____|
         |    |  +-----+   |                    |            |   |
         |    |  | OS  |   |                    |            |   |
         |    |  +-----+   |                    |            |   |
         |    |            |                    |            |   |
         |    +------------+                    +------------+   |
         |     HOST: UCLA                         HOST: SRI      |
         \                                                      /
```

Open Questions

1. If the IMPs do code conversion, the checksum will not be correct.

2. The procedure for requesting the DEL front end is not yet specified.

IV. Initial Experiments

Experiment One

SRI is currently modifying their on-line retrieval system which will be the major software component on the Network Documentation Center so that it can be operated with model 35 teletypes. The control of the teletypes will be written in DEL. All sites will write DEL compilers and use NLS through the DEL program.

Experiment Two

SRI will write a DEL front end for full NLS, graphics included. UCLA and UTAH will use NLS with graphics.

[This RFC was put into machine readable form for entry]
[into the online RFC archives by Celeste Anderson 3/97]

CHAPTER 2 | The IAB, the IESG, and the IETF

One of the great complaints heard concerns the overwhelming number of acronyms with which we are afflicted. If you are an acronymophobe, stop here. I persist in using many acronyms to explain just where the standards must come from.

The group responsible for the TCP/IP protocol suite—for design, engineering, and management—is the Internet Architecture Board (IAB). The IAB does not manage the Internet, but it serves two basic needs:

1. Providing a forum for communication and collaboration among network operators. The participants may include anyone who has run networks; typically this means regional networks.
2. Specifying and recommending technology. (Cerf 1992, quoted in Quarterman & Wilhelm 1993)

The IAB is a truly worldwide organization and is self-perpetuating: the new chair is elected to serve for two years by the members, who were appointed by the IAB chair with the advice and consent of other members.

There are two taskforces of the IAB: the Internet Research Task Force (IRTF) and the Internet Engineering Task Force (IETF). The IRTF, in turn, sponsors the Internet Research Steering Group (IRSG), and the IETF sponsors the Internet Engineering Steering Group (IESG).

The IRSG has a number of research groups (e.g., Privacy and Security, Autonomous Networks). The IESG has a vast number of working groups, which I'll go into later. I'll abandon the IRTF and the IRSG here, though.

The IAB doesn't do any technical work: It makes architectural and policy recommendations. The IETF does the work of designing and specifying protocols. It has a number of Working Groups that handle the various projects, grouped by Areas. There were about 10 Areas and 60 Working Groups (WGs) in 1997.

A year later, there were 112, divided up as:

Applications area, 27 Working Groups
General, 1 WG
Internet, 16 WGs
Operations & Management, 20 WGs
Routing, 15 WGs
Security, 12 WGs
Transport, 17 WGs
User Services, 4 WGs

If you are interested in minutes, proposals, etc., see http://www.ietf.org.

It is of great importance to note that none of these is a formal governmental structure. In fact, like Topsy in *Uncle Tom's Cabin*, it "jes' growed." When, on the suggestion of Elmer Shapiro, the graduate students who would become the founders of the Internet met at Christmas 1968, they called themselves the NWG (Network Working Group). Most RFCs still carry that designation. All of the structures have evolved from the NWG.

CHAPTER 3 | Net Growth

Though the daily newspapers are filled with estimates of the numbers of Internet users, it's important to discuss just what has been going on and how the estimates are made.

Perhaps it is not so strange to realize that there are wildly variant opinions as to what it might mean to be "on the net." It is not like the telephone where, if you have a number, that's it. The stringent end of the definition holds that if one cannot use the basic tools (here defined as ftp and telnet), you are not on the net (John Quarterman may be the best example of this view). The liberal end, typified by Lyman Chapin, would hold that if you can send and receive mail and have access to news and bulletin boards, you are on the net.

In *Matrix News* for October 1994, Quarterman stated "The core Internet consists of computers that are reachable with ICMP ECHO (ping) and at least some of the basic TCP/IP application services, such as FTP, the File Transfer Protocol." Thus, to him, the millions of users who were connected via store-and-forward networks like BITNET were not part of the Internet, nor were those who subscribed to America OnLine or Compuserve until a short time ago. To Chapin, all these individuals are Matrix users. My personal feeling is that the information highway of the Corporation for National Research Initiatives (CNRI) is there, whether you choose to bicycle on it, or zip along in a sports car.

ARPANET Hosts

In the early years, the numbers of hosts and the estimates of users were quite straightforward. The number of hosts was ascertainable by just counting the entries in the host table. In January 1992, Mark Lottor put together RFC 1296, which enumerated the number of hosts from August 1981 to January 1992.

Though the Domain Name System was introduced in 1984, it wasn't fully implemented until 1988.

Recall, the Host–Host Program permitted 63 hosts; the NCP permitted 255; the IP permits many millions, especially in its current (IPv4) version. The earliest numbers (which I have derived from the BBN Reports) are easy:

Date	Hosts
12/69	4
01/71	13
04/72	23
01/73	35
10/74	49
01/76	63

In October 1975, BBN had modified the Network Control Center's program so that it would be able to handle more than 63 IMPs. In January 1976 they made it possible for more than 63 IMPs to be on the net and more than four hosts on an IMP. This brought the possible number of hosts to 255. Over the next decade, which included the shift to TCP/IP and then to DNS, the numbers reported by Lottor are:

Date	Hosts	
08/81	213	Host table #152
05/82	235	Host table #166
08/83	562	Host table #300
10/84	1024	Host table #392
10/85	1961	Host table #485
02/86	2308	Host table #515

The great switch occurred on January 1, 1983. It was none too soon: The 562 hosts of August 1983 just wouldn't have been manageable under the older protocols and the older scheme. But even more growth was at hand.

Date	Hosts
11/86	5089
12/87	28,174
07/88	33,000
10/88	56,000
01/89	80,000
07/89	130,000
10/89	159,000

10/90	313,000
01/91	376,000
07/91	535,000
10/91	617,000
01/92	727,000

In doing a user-calculation, it is important to recognize that many hosts have more than one IP address, and that most IP addresses have more than one user. Lottor's numbers on numbers of IP addresses for January 1, 1992 were (only the first 10 entries are shown)

Addresses	**Hosts**
1	715,143
2	9015
3	1027
4	556
5	314
6	213
7	100
8	85
9	58
10	71

The *Internet Domain Survey* of Network Wizards (July 1998), showed

Hosts found (number of PTR records):	36,739,000
Hosts pingable: [estimated by pinging 1% of total hosts found]	6,529,000
Number of classless in-addr.arpa delegations: [missed on previous survey; see RFC-2317]	1,841,000

Top 10 hostnames:

777518	www	13318	a
142865	host	1176	ftp
56380	mail	1168	gw
20219	router	10099	user
14315	ns	8298	server

How Many?

Just what the median number of users per IP address is has been repeatedly estimated. The highest number I have seen is 10 (this is the number that *TIME* and *Newsweek* used in early 1994 to arrive at "over 30 million" Internet users). The more sensible one, used by both Craig Partridge and by John Quarterman, is 5. This would mean that as of 1992, there were about 3.6 million users.

More recent pollings of hosts have shown that the number has doubled nearly every year since Lottor's RFC, to about 1.5 million in 1993 and 3.1 million in 1994. Again, the 3.1 million is the figure that the news weeklies multiplied by 10 to get their "over 30 million." If we use the more conservative figure, we would get about 16 million users in 1994, plus the several million "second-class citizens" who are on BITNET or subscribe to the various online services.

In the *Third Annual MIDS Internet Demographic Survey* (*Matrix News* 6.1 [January 1996]), Quarterman estimated 16.9 million core Internet users; 26.4 million Consumer Internet users; and 39 million Matrix users—just about 40 million folks.

By January 1997, MIDS was estimating 71 million users of the Matrix (*Matrix News* 7.1 [January 1997]); and by February 1998, Lottor and *Matrix News* were estimating about 30 million Internet hosts, worldwide. But the growth rate began to slow. From a high of 2.1/year, it waned to 1.5/year in 1998–1999. At 5 users/host, this would be 150 million users.

(In an interview with Katie Hafner in September 1994, Cerf said there would be 300 million users by 2000; two months later, he had raised the number to 400 million. Quarterman has pointed out that if we plot the UN's population curve against the Internet's, they cross around 2010, at which time we might have more computer connections than people on the planet. As with many such projections, this was intended to be tongue-in-cheek. However, there were 70 million hosts in January 2000, with (perhaps) 350 million users.)

Domains

Let me use one more set of Lottor's figures: hosts per top-level domain. That is, in an address, which .xxx occur the most frequently? On New Year's Day 1992, the top 10 were

243020	edu	[educational institution]
18136	com	[commercial business]
46463	gov	[government]
3162	au	[Australia]
31016	de	[Germany]
27492	mil	[military]
27052	ca	[Canada]
19117	org	[organization]
18984	uk	[United Kingdom]
18473	se	[Sweden]

In July 1998, Lottor found the following:

Top 10 TLDs (number of hosts):

com	10301570
net	7054863
edu	4464216
mil	1359153
jp	1352200
us	1302204
uk	1190663
de	1154340
ca	1027571
au	750327

In 75 months, the number of .com domains had risen from under 200,000 to over 10 million!

Lottor's numbers also revealed the following:

Top 10 second-level domains (number of hosts):

1146825	aol.com	491517	co.uk
955215	ans.net	485529	or.jp
677596	af.mil	378249	ac.jp
649687	ac.uk	314885	edu.au
601225	uu.net	293972	navy.mil

And:

Top 10 third-level domains (number of hosts):

926726	dialup.ans.net	243174	saturn.bbn.com
739133	ipt.aol.com	240404	demon.co.uk
580582	da.uu.net	226060	dial-access.att.net
398682	iptr.aol.com	206739	k12.ca.us
260897	pub-ip.psi.net	170399	us.ibm.net

Businesses have discovered the value of communicating electronically, and there has been no notable increase in the number of educational institutions. This explains (at least in part) the changes. Furthermore, the Internet has expanded a great deal outside of North America. Note that Japan now has more domains than the US Government had a mere five years ago.

On January 1, 1970, there were four hosts; in July 1998, Lottor found 36,739,000. By the end of 1999, Quarterman was estimating 70 million. That's a lot of addresses.

CHAPTER 4 | Protocol Overview and IPv4

Computers can't communicate with one another, but we can install software that enables them to both communicate and do other things. We call such a software program a *protocol*. Simply, protocols are programs that enable the rituals of computer communication.

In 1969, the ARPANET had but two protocols (called *programs* at that time): rlogin (which permitted logging in to a remote machine) and ftp (now the File Transfer Protocol). Over the 30 years since then, the number of protocols has escalated. By and large, when TCP/IP (Transmission Control Protocol/Internet Protocol) is referred to, it is shorthand for a full suite of protocols. This suite can be represented as shown in Figure 4.1.

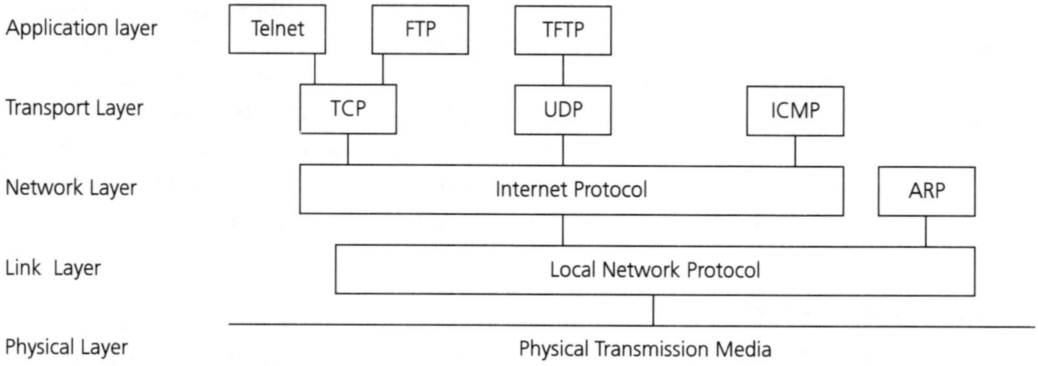

FIGURE 4.1

Although some of the protocols in the Transport and Application Layers will be mentioned in this book, the Network Layer will be the focus. (ARP is the Address Resolution Protocol, RFC 826, refined in RFCs 903, 1293, and 1735. It will not be discussed in this book.)

The representation of everything from the wires to the end use in layers is conceptually derived from the OSI (Open Systems Interconnection) model, but does not agree with it. The TCP/IP stack has five layers, and OSI has a seven-layer cake that looks like

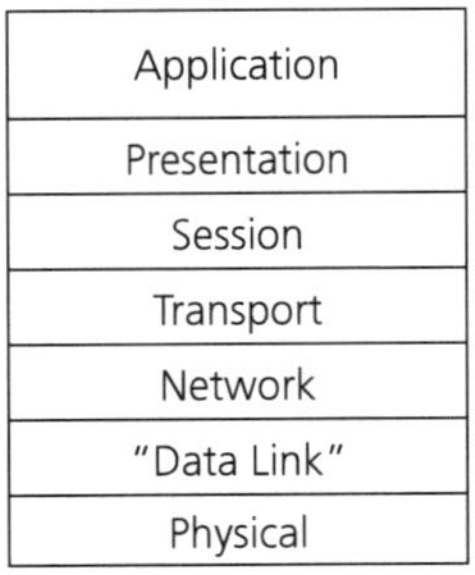

Although the Open Systems Interconnection is the only internationally accepted set of standards for communication, it is hardly used and few manufacturers have implemented it. OSI came into being disregarding the fact that TCP/IP was already in use and that TCP/IP was popular within the technical community. The war between the various advocates was over years ago, but representing different aspects of a transaction as a *stack* is quite useful.

Protocols can thus be described in terms of the services provided to the next-higher layer and those it uses from the next-lower layer. There is no necessity for protocols to have separate program modules for each layer—layering is a conceptual aid, not a rule of implementation.

Narrowing in on the focus of this book, IP is the protocol of the Internet layer. TCP is the transport protocol; X.25, FDDI, Ethernet, etc., are the network standards. IP is the most important of the protocols because it provides addressing and routing within a common address space across many lower level protocols. IP is thus the tool that permits the Internet to function.

How Does It Work?

Let's go back to Figure 4.1. The physical layer comprises things like unshielded twisted pair, coaxial cable, and infrared and radio frequency. These are entities upon which everything else rides.

The link layer is a set of protocols (Ethernet, Frame Relay, PPP, for instance) that distances the user from the physical layer: If you are involved in an

Ethernet, it is irrelevant what kind of cable is being used. Having said this, let's actually look at the link header for Ethernet (RFC 894) in Figure 4.2.

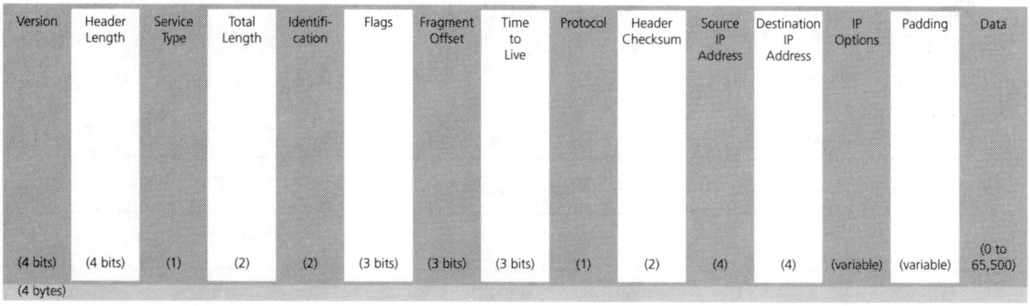

FIGURE 4.2

The destination and the source addresses are called hardware addresses. They are made up of six octets and are generally called MAC (media access control) addresses (in truth, they should be referred to as LAN addresses, but we don't generally use that term). We still use hardware addresses.

Let's consider the basic connection on a network as one between a host (or server) and a client. As I noted earlier, merely connecting these entries physically isn't enough. They need a way to talk to each other: a communication protocol.

But let's imagine that one machine is a PC running Windows (a Microsoft operating system) and the other is running Solaris (from Sun Microsystems). There may well be incompatibilities between them. At the beginning of the ARPANET, this problem was solved by having an IMP (Interface Message Processor; a Honeywell 516, serving as what we would today call a router) at each site. The IMPs communicated with each other, and each site communicated with its local IMP (the first four sites in 1969 were running a DEC-10, an IBM 360, an SDS, and a Sigma 7; each running a different operating system).

The IMPs were the first routers. And as new sites were connected to the ARPANET, the list (host table) grew longer. IP addresses are the descendants of the host tables.

IP is a connectionless datagram delivery protocol: It provides for the delivery of packets between machines that are not connected directly. Each datagram/packet contains information including from whence it has come, where it is going, control information, and any data passed on from the host layer.

The mechanism that directs hosts and gateways as to how to route packets is based on the destination address built into each one. (RFC 792 supplies the structural definition of the address structure.) Every packet begins with a packet header, and the IP scans this to locate the destination address.

Figure 4.3 shows the make-up of the IPv4 header. It is made up of 32 bits.

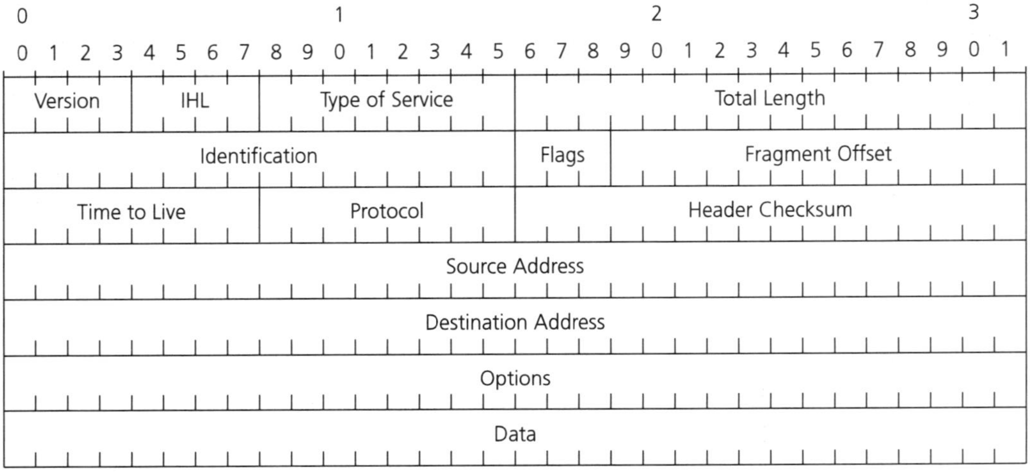

FIG. 4.3

The first four bits of the header tell the Internet module how to parse the rest of the header. RFC 1700 supplies the Assigned Internet Version Numbers for IPv4 (Table 4.1):

Decimal	Keyword	Version
0		Reserved
1–3		Unassigned
4	IP	Internet Protocol
5	ST	ST Datagram Mode
6	SIP	Simple Internet Protocol
7	TP/IX	TP/IX: The Next Internet
8	PIP	The P Internet Protocol
9	TUBA	TUBA
10–14		Unassigned
15		Reserved

TABLE 4.1

This is already passé, as you will see in the next chapter.

The next four bits identify the beginning and end of the header, as this is not a constant length.

The "type of service" bits fall into two fields—precedence (the three high-order bits) and type (five-bits; delay, throughput, reliability, and cost). The low-order bit seven is reserved, and rarely used.

Total length includes header and data: It is 16 bits, allowing for over 65K. Identification (16 bits) is for a unique idetifier for the datagram. Flags (3 bits) control fragmentation. The two low-order bits are "don't fragment" and "more fragments." Fragment offset (13 bits) controls the reassembly of fragments. Time to Live (8 bits) is really an indicator of the number of hops a datagram is permitted to travel before it is dropped (*purged*). Protocol (8 bits) stands for the next higher protocol in the data portion of the datagram. These are mandated by the Assigned Numbers RFC (RFC 1700). The first 20 are shown in Table 4.2.

Decimal	Keyword	Protocol
0	Reserved	
1	ICMP	Internet Control Message
2	IGMP	Internet Group Management
3	GGP	Gateway-to-Gateway
4	IP	IP in IP (encapsulation)
5	ST	Stream
6	TCP	Transmission Control
7	UCL	UCL
8	EGP	Exterior Gateway
9	IGP	Any private interior gateway
10	BBN-RCC-MON	BBN RCC Monitoring
17	UDP	User Datagram
18	MUX	Multiplexing
27	RDP	Reliable Data
29	ISO-TP4	ISO Transport Class 4
46	RSVP	Reservation
88	IGRP	IGRP
89	OSPFIGP	OSPFIGP
101–254		Unassigned
255		Reserved

TABLE 4.2

The trouble with this 32-bit scheme is that it doesn't provide for many of the uses that have been newly discovered, nor the others we'll see in the future.

Mobility, hand-held appliances, voice-over IP, streaming video, video-on-demand, have put ever-greater strains on our current system.

Vint Cerf wears a pin "IP on Everything!" Someday fairly soon we will have smart refrigerators and smart stoves that will be addressable. It's IPv6 that will make this all feasible.

CHAPTER 5 | Why 128-bit Addressing?

One of the most obvious questions asked about IPv6 is "Why?"

Even though the growth of the Internet itself is a reason for enlarging address space from 32 to 128 bits, that growth isn't as important as the growth in uses to which the Internet is being put. Mobile computing, for example, as well as the graphics on the web contribute to the need for more space.

There are a number of good arguments as to why this is so, most of which are discussed in the Internet Architecture Board draft *The Case for IPv6* (draft 1, 13 March 1998; draft 5, 22 October 1999). The *Case* addresses both the business and technical reasons for IPv6. Some of this chapter draws on that work.

Because it is intended to replace IPv4, IPv6 is of great importance to commercial and individual users, and to access providers of all sizes (ISPs). IPv6 is expected to improve IPv4's scalability, security, ease-of-configuration, and network management; these issues are central to the competitiveness and performance of all types of businesses. On the other hand, IPv6 intentionally aims at preserving existing investment as much as possible.

"IPv6 has been designed to enable high-performance, scalable internetworks that should operate as needed well into the next century. Much of this design process involved correcting the inadequacies of IPv4. Some of the qualities of IPv6 are found in enhanced features, such as the larger address space and streamlined packet design" (*Case for IPv6,* draft 1).

IPv6 provides a framework for resolving several problems that currently exist both inside and among enterprises. On the global level, IPv6 allows backbone engineers to create a flexible and expandable routing hierarchy. The Internet backbone (where enterprises and ISP networks come together) makes the maintenance of a hierarchical addressing system necessary, analogous to the national (and international) telephone systems. IPv4 uses the address hierarchy to sort traffic towards networks attached to the backbone.

"Without an address hierarchy, backbone routers would be forced to store routing table information on the reachability of every network in the world. Given the current number of IP subnets in the world and the growth of the Internet, it is not feasible to manage routing tables and updates for so many routes" (*Case*). This is precisely the problem that drove the switch to DNS over 15 years ago—the ever-increasing length and complexity of host lists (from 213 in August 1981 to 68 million at the end of 1999). With a hierarchy, backbone routers can use IP address prefixes to determine the way that traffic is to be routed through the backbone. IPv4 uses a technique called Classless InterDomain Routing (CIDR, RFC 1219), which specifies variable-length network prefixes. CIDR permits *route aggregation* at various levels of the hierarchy, so that backbone routers can store a single routing table entry providing reachability to a large number of lower level networks.

Unfortunately, CIDR guarantees neither efficiency nor scalability. To avoid maintaining a separate entry for each route, it is vital for routes at lower levels of the routing hierarchy (because they have longer prefixes) to be aggregated (*summarized*) into more general routes at higher levels of the routing hierarchy (which have shorter prefixes).

Legacy IPv4 address assignments originating before CIDR and the current access provider hierarchy do not make summarization feasible. The lack of uniformity of the current system, together with the rationing of IPv4 addresses, means that Internet addressing and routing have become unnecessarily complicated at every level. "Renumbering IPv4 sites when changing from one ISP to another, to maintain address/route aggregation, is unnecessarily complicated [in IPv4] compared to IPv6's ease, and thus low cost, of site renumbering"(*Case*).

Large enterprises and even small business users encounter the same problems. The inability of a large entity to conveniently summarize its addresses through the use of a small number of prefixes makes it increasingly difficult to support the backbone routing tables.

Private address spaces with nonunique addresses generally require gateways and Network Address Translators (NATs) to manage external connectivity. This, in turn, means that several services are unavailable. A NAT allows an enterprise to have any internal address structure it wishes, without concern for integrating internal addresses with the global Internet. (In fact, though 128-bit addressing has been mentioned here repeatedly, the global Internet will utilize 64 of the bits, the other 64 being more "local.") The NAT is the interface between the enterprise's net and the Internet, converting private internal addresses to a smaller pool of unique addresses that are passed to the backbone (Figure 5.1).

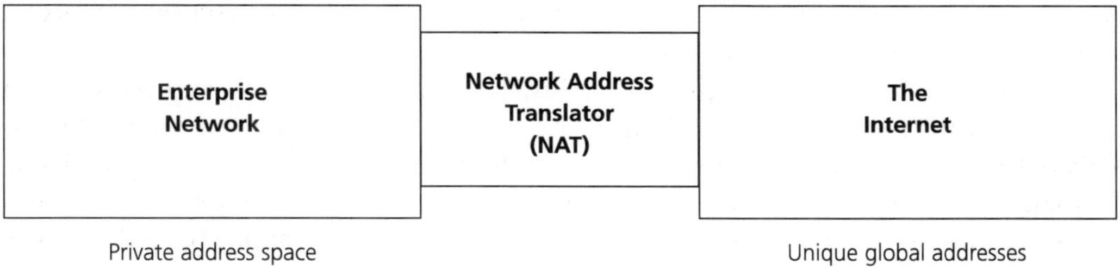

FIGURE 5.1

Employing a NAT may be the right thing for some organizations, especially if only limited connectivity with the outside world is desired. However, if a company needs a truly robust interactive connection with the Internet, a NAT will be an obstacle. This is because a NAT swaps address fields on every packet as it departs or as it arrives. Because this procedure is very demanding, it frequently results in a bottleneck. In a small internal network, a NAT may keep up with address conversion; but with increased Internet access, the NAT's performance has to increase.

NAT translators also run into trouble when applications embed their IP addresses in the packet payload, above the Network Layer. This is the case for a number of applications, including some ftp programs, Mobile IP, and the Windows Internet Name Service (WINS) registration process of Windows 95 and Windows NT. Unless a NAT parses every packet all the way to the application level, it may fail to translate embedded addresses, which can result in application failures. NATs can also break Domain Name Servers, because they work above the Network Layer. NATs also prevent the use of IP-level security from end-to-end of a transaction. The result is that NAT services are valuable for certain scenarios, but they aren't advantageous for wide-spread Internet use.

IPv4 also has problems managing mobile computers. Among the reasons for this are

- A mobile computer needs to make use of a forwarding address at each new point of attachment to the Internet, and it isn't so easy to get such an address with IPv4.
- Informing any agent in the routing infrastructure about the mobile node's new location requires good authentication facilities, which are not commonly deployed in IPv4 nodes.
- In IPv4, it is often more difficult for mobile nodes to find out whether they are still attached to the same network or not.
- It is unlikely in IPv4 that mobile nodes would be able to inform their communication partners about any change in location.

The solutions to the mobile computing problems are resolved by aspects of the design of the IPv6 protocols.

IPv4 is limited, too, in that some enterprises need to renumber devices (assign new IP numbers) frequently. For example, if a company changes ISPs, it may have to either renumber all of its addresses to match a new prefix, or implement NATs.

A unique IP address means that any user, large or small, can gain direct connectivity to other users. It thus simplifies a wide range of interactive applications, of which telecommuting is the most obvious instance. The hierarchy of limited and poorly allocated IPv4 addresses has already caused problems, which will continue. In fact, as more devices of varying demands and capabilities are demanded by the customers of the Internet, service can only degrade further.

Address shortages and routing problems threaten the networking of large corporate entities, but they similarly threaten small sites. Small networks can be dropped from backbone routing tables if they do not adhere to the address hierarchy. At the same time, some larger networks may not renumber, thereby causing larger routing problems for the backbone providers. Today, many ISPs with dial-up user accounts can't allocate IP addresses easily. The result is that large numbers of dial-up users employ addresses allocated on a temporary basis. In other cases, small sites are forced to share an address among several systems.

With over a third of a duodecillion addresses, no one will have to share for several more decades.

Network Working Group
Request for Comments: 1338

V. Fuller
BARRNet
T. Li
cisco
J. Yu
MERIT
K. Varadhan
OARnet

June 1992

Supernetting: an Address Assignment and Aggregation Strategy

Status of this Memo

This memo provides information for the Internet community. It does not specify an Internet standard. Distribution of this memo is unlimited.

Abstract

This memo discusses strategies for address assignment of the existing IP address space with a view to conserve the address space and stem the explosive growth of routing tables in default-route-free routers run by transit routing domain providers.

Table of Contents

Acknowledgements

The authors wish to express their appreciation to the members of the ROAD group with whom many of the ideas contained in this document were inspired and developed.

1. Problem, Goal, and Motivation

As the Internet has evolved and grown over in recent years, it has become painfully evident that it is soon to face several serious scaling problems. These include:

1. Exhaustion of the class-B network address space. One fundamental cause of this problem is the lack of a network class of a size which is appropriate for mid-sized organization; class-C, with a maximum of 254 host addresses, is too small while class-B, which allows up to 65534 addresses, is to large to be widely allocated.

2. Growth of routing tables in Internet routers beyond the ability of current software (and people) to effectively manage.

3. Eventual exhaustion of the 32-bit IP address space.

It has become clear that the first two of these problems are likely to become critical within the next one to three years. This memo attempts to deal with these problems by proposing a mechanism to slow the growth of the routing table and the need for allocating new IP network numbers. It does not attempt to solve the third problem, which is of a more long-term nature, but instead endeavors to ease enough of the short to mid-term difficulties to allow the Internet to continue to function efficiently while progress is made on a longer-term solution.

The proposed solution is to hierarchically allocate future IP address assignment, by delegating control of segments of the IP address space to the various network service providers.

It is proposed that this scheme of allocating IP addresses be undertaken as soon as possible. It is also believed that the scheme will suffice as a short term strategy, to fill the gap between now and the time when a viable long term plan can be put into place and deployed effectively. It is believed that this scheme would be viable for at least three (3) years, in which time frame, a suitable long term solution would be expected to be deployed.

Note that this plan neither requires nor assumes that already assigned addresses will be reassigned, though if doing so were possible, it would further reduce routing table sizes. It is assumed that routing technology will be capable of dealing with the current routing table size and with some reasonably-small rate of growth. The emphasis of this plan is on significantly slowing the rate of this growth.

This scheme will not affect the deployment of any specific long term plan, and therefore, this document will not discuss any long term plans for routing and address architectures.

2. Scheme Plan

There are two basic components of this addressing and routing scheme: one, to distribute the allocation of Internet address space and two, to provide a mechanism for the aggregation of routing information.

2.1. Aggregation and its limitations

One major goal of this addressing plan is to allocate Internet address space in such a manner as to allow aggregation of routing information along topological lines. For simple, single-homed clients, the allocation of their address space out of a service provider's space will accomplish this automatically - rather than advertise a separate route for each such client, the service provider may advertise a single, aggregate, route which describes all of the destinations contained within it. Unfortunately, not all sites are singly-connected to the network, so some loss of ability to aggregate is realized for the non simple cases.

There are two situations that cause a loss of aggregation efficiency.

- o Organizations which are multi-homed. Because multi-homed organizations must be advertised into the system by each of their service providers, it is often not feasible to aggregate their routing information into the address space any one of those providers. Note that they still may receive their address allocation out of a service provider's address space (which has other advantages), but their routing information must still be explicitly advertised by most of their service providers (the exception being that if the site's allocation comes out of its least-preferable service provider, then that service provider need not advertise the explicit route - longest-match will insure that its aggregated route is used to get to the site on a non-primary basis). For this reason, the routing cost for these organizations will typically be about the same as it is today.

- Organizations which move from one service provider to another. This has the effect of "punching a hole" in the aggregation of the original service provider's advertisement. This plan will handle the situation by requiring the newer service provider to advertise a specific advertisement for the new client, which is preferred by virtue of being the longest match. To maintain efficiency of aggregation, it is recommended that organizations which do change service providers plan to eventually migrate their address assignments from the old provider's space to that of the new provider. To this end, it is recommended that mechanisms to facilitate such migration, including improved protocols and procedures for dynamic host address assignment, be developed.

Note that some aggregation efficiency gain can still be had for multi-homed sites (and, in general, for any site composed of multiple, logical IP network numbers) - by allocating a contiguous block of network numbers to the client (as opposed to multiple, independently represented network numbers) the client's routing information may be aggregated into a single (net, mask) pair. Also, since the routing cost associated with assigning a multi-homed site out of a service provider's address space is no greater than the current method of a random allocation by a central authority, it makes sense to allocate all address space out of blocks assigned to service providers.

It is also worthwhile to mention that since aggregation may occur at multiple levels in the system, it may still be possible to aggregate these anomalous routes at higher levels of whatever hierarchy may be present. For example, if a site is multi-homed to two NSFNet regional networks both of whom obtain their address space from the NSFNet, then aggregation by the NSFNet of routes from the regionals will include all routes to the multi-homed site.

Finally, it should also be noted that deployment of the new addressing plan described in this document may (and should) begin almost immediately but effective use of the plan to aggregate routing information will require changes to some Inter-Domain routing protocols. Likewise, deploying the supernet-capable Inter-Domain protocols without deployment of the new address plan will not allow useful aggregation to occur (in other words, the addressing plan and routing protocol changes are both required for supernetting, and its resulting reduction in table growth, to be effective.) Note, however, that during the period of time between deployment of the addressing plan and deployment of the new protocols, the size of routing tables may temporarily grow very rapidly. This must be considered when planning the deployment of the two plans.

Note: in the discussion and examples which follow, the network+mask notation is used to represent routing destinations. This is used for illustration only and does not require that routing protocols use this representation in their updates.

2.2. Distributed allocation of address space

The basic idea of the plan is to allocate one or more blocks of Class-C network numbers to each network service provider. Organizations using the network service provider for Internet connectivity are allocated bitmask-oriented subsets of the provider's address space as required.

Note that in contrast to a previously described scheme of subnetting a class-A network number, this plan should not require difficult host changes to work around domain system limitations - since each sub-allocated piece of the address space looks like a class-C network number, delegation of authority for the IN-ADDR.ARPA domain works much the same as it does today - there will just be a lot of class-C network numbers whose IN-ADDR.ARPA delegations all point to the same servers (the same will be true of the root delegating a large block of class-Cs to the network provider, unless the delegation just happens to fall on a byte boundary). It is also the case that this method of aggregating class-C's is somewhat easier to deploy, since it does not require the ability to split a class-A across a routing domain boundary (i.e., non-contiguous subnets).

It is also worthy to mention that once Inter-Domain protocols which support classless network destinations are widely deployed, the rules described by the "supernetting" plan generalize to permit arbitrary super/subnetting of the remaining class-A and class-B address space (the assumption being that classless Inter-Domain protocols will either allow for non-contiguous subnets to exist in the system or that all components of a sub-allocated class-A/B will be contained within a single routing domain). This will allow this plan to continue to be used in the event that the class-C space is exhausted before implementation of a long-term solution is deployed (there may, however, be further implementation considerations before doing this).

Hierarchical sub-allocation of addresses in this manner implies that clients with addresses allocated out of a given service provider are, for routing purposes, part of that service provider and will be routed via its infrastructure. This implies that routing information about multi-homed organizations, i.e., organizations connected to more than one network service provider, will still need to be known by higher levels in the hierarchy.

The advantages of hierarchical assignment in this fashion are

a) It is expected to be easier for a relatively small number of service providers to obtain addresses from the central authority, rather than a much larger, and monotonically increasing, number of individual clients. This is not to be considered as a loss of part of the service providers' address space.

b) Given the current growth of the Internet, a scalable and delegatable method of future allocation of network numbers has to be achieved.

For these reasons, and in the interest of providing a consistent procedure for obtaining Internet addresses, it is recommended that most, if not all, network numbers be distributed through service providers.

3. Cost-benefit analysis

This new method of assigning address through service providers can be put into effect immediately and will, from the start, have the benefit of distributing the currently centralized process of assigning new addresses. Unfortunately, before the benefit of reducing the size of globally-known routing destinations can be achieved, it will be necessary to deploy an Inter-Domain routing protocol capable of handling arbitrary network+mask pairs. Only then will it be possible to aggregate individual class-C networks into larger blocks represented by single routing table entries.

This means that upon introduction, the new addressing plan will not in and of itself help solve the routing table size problem. Once the new Inter-Domain routing protocol is deployed, however, an immediate drop in the number of destinations which clients of the new protocol must carry will occur. A detailed analysis of the magnitude of this expected drop and the permanent reduction in rate of growth is given in the next section.

In should also be noted that the present method of flat address allocations imposes a large bureaucratic cost on the central address allocation authority. For scaling reasons unrelated to address space exhaustion or routing table overflow, this should be changed. Using the mechanism proposed in this paper will have the happy side effect of distributing the address allocation procedure, greatly reducing the load on the central authority.

3.1. Present Allocation Figures

A back-of-the-envelope analysis of "network-contacts.txt" (available from the DDN NIC) indicates that as of 2/25/92, 46 of 126 class-A network numbers have been allocated (leaving 81) and 5467 of 16256 class-B numbers have been allocated, leaving 10789. Assuming that recent trends continue, the number of allocated class-B's will continue to double approximately once a year. At this rate of grown, all class-B's will be exhausted within about 15 months.

3.2. Historic growth rates

MM/YY	ROUTES ADVERTISED	MM/YY	ROUTES ADVERTISED
Feb-92	4775	Apr-90	1525
Jan-92	4526	Mar-90	1038
Dec-91	4305	Feb-90	997
Nov-91	3751	Jan-90	927
Oct-91	3556	Dec-89	897
Sep-91	3389	Nov-89	837
Aug-91	3258	Oct-89	809
Jul-91	3086	Sep-89	745
Jun-91	2982	Aug-89	650
May-91	2763	Jul-89	603
Apr-91	2622	Jun-89	564
Mar-91	2501	May-89	516
Feb-91	2417	Apr-89	467
Jan-91	2338	Mar-89	410
Dec-90	2190	Feb-89	384
Nov-90	2125	Jan-89	346
Oct-90	2063	Dec-88	334
Sep-90	1988	Nov-88	313
Aug-90	1894	Oct-88	291
Jul-90	1727	Sep-88	244
Jun-90	1639	Aug-88	217
May-90	1580	Jul-88	173

Table I : Growth in routing table size, total numbers
Source for the routing table size data is MERIT

3.3. Detailed Analysis

There is no technical cost and minimal administrative cost associated with deployment of the new address assignment plan. The administrative cost is basically that of convincing the NIC, the IANA, and the network service providers to agree to this plan, which is not expected to be too difficult. In addition, administrative cost for the central numbering authorities (the NIC and the IANA) will be greatly decreased by the deployment of this plan. To take advantage of aggregation of routing information, however, it is necessary that the capability to represent routes as arbitrary network+mask fields (as opposed to the current class-A/B/C distinction) be added to the common Internet inter-domain routing protocol(s).

3.3.1. Benefits of the new addressing plan

There are two benefits to be had by deploying this plan:

- o The current problem with depletion of the available class-B address space can be ameliorated by assigning more-appropriately sized blocks of class-C's to mid-sized organizations (in the 200-4000 host range).

- o When the improved inter-domain routing protocol is deployed, an immediate decrease in the number routing table entries followed by a significant reduction in the rate growth of routing table size should occur (for default-free routers).

3.3.2. Growth rate projections

Currently, a default-free routing table (for example, the routing tables maintained by the routers in the NSFNET backbone) contains approximately 4700 entries. This number reflects the current size of the NSFNET routing database. Historic data shows that this number, on average, has doubled every 10 months between 1988 and 1991. Assuming that this growth rate is going to persist in the foreseeable future (and there is no reason to assume otherwise), we expect the number of entries in a default-free routing table to grow to approximately 30000 in two(2) years time. In the following analysis, we assume that the growth of the Internet has been, and will continue to be, exponential.

It should be stressed that these projections do not consider that the current shortage of class-B network numbers may increase the number of instances where many class-C's are used rather than a class-B. Using an assumption that new organizations which formerly obtained class-B's will now obtain somewhere between 4 and 16 class-C's, the rate of routing table growth can conservatively be expected to at least double and probably quadruple. This means the number of entries in a default-free routing table may well exceed 10,000 entries within six months and 20,000 entries in less than a year.

Under the proposed plan, growth of the routing table in a default-free router is greatly reduced since most new address assignment will come from one of the large blocks allocated to the service providers. For the sake of this analysis, we assume prompt implementation of this proposal and deployment of the revised routing protocols. We make the initial assumption that any initial block given to a provider is sufficient to satisfy its needs for two years.

Since under this plan, multi-homed networks must continue to be explicitly advertised throughout the system (according to Rule#1 described in section 4.2), the number multi-homed routes is expected to be the dominant factor in future growth of routing table size, once the supernetting plan is applied.

Presently, it is estimated that there are fewer than 100 multi-homed organizations connected to the Internet. Each such organization's network is comprised of one or more network numbers. In many cases (and in all future cases under this plan), the network numbers used by an organization are consecutive, meaning that aggregation of those networks during route advertisement may be possible. This means that the number of routes advertised within the Internet for multi-homed networks may be approximated as the total number of multi-homed organizations. Assuming that the number of multi-homed organization will double every year (which may be a over-estimation, given that every connection costs money), the number of routes for multi-homed networks would be expected to grow to approximately 800 in three years.

If we further assume that there are approximately 100 service providers, then each service provider will also need to advertise its block of addresses. However, due to aggregation, these advertisements will be reduced to only 100 additional routes. We assume that after the initial two years, new service providers combined with additional requests from existing providers will require an additional 50 routes per year. Thus, the total is 4700 + 800 + 150 = 5650. This represents an annual grown rate of approximately 6%. This is in clear contrast to the current annual growth of 150%. This analysis also assumes an immediate deployment of this plan with full compliance. Note that this analysis assumes only a single level of route aggregation in the current Internet - intelligent address allocation should significantly improve this.

Clearly, this is not a very conservative assumption in the Internet environment nor can 100% adoption of this proposal be expected. Still, with only a 90% participation in this proposal by service providers, at the end of the target three years, global routing table size will be "only" 4700 + 800 + 145 + 7500 = 13145 routes – without any action, the routing table will grow to approximately 75000 routes during that time period.

4. Changes to Inter-Domain routing protocols

In order to support supernetting efficiently, it is clear that some changes will need to be made to both routing protocols themselves and to the way in which routing information is interpreted. In the case of "new" inter-domain protocols, the actual protocol syntax changes should be relatively minor. This mechanism will not work with older inter-domain protocols such as EGP2; the only ways to interoperate with old systems using such protocols are either to use existing mechanisms for providing "default" routes or b) require that new routers talking to old routers "explode" supernet information into individual network numbers. Since the first of these is trivial while the latter is cumbersome (at best – consider the memory requirements it imposes on the receiver of the exploded information), it is recommended that the first approach be used – that older systems to continue to the mechanisms they currently employ for default handling.

Note that a basic assumption of this plan is that those organizations which need to import "supernet" information into their routing systems must run IGPs (such as OSPF[RFC1267]) which support classless routes. Systems running older IGPs may still advertise and receive "supernet" information, but they will not be able to propagate such information through their routing domains.

4.1. Protocol-independent semantic changes

There are two fundamental changes which must be applied to Inter-Domain routing protocols in order for this plan to work. First, the concept of network "class" needs to be deprecated - this plan assumes that routing destinations are represented by network+mask pairs and that routing is done on a longest-match basis (i.e., for a given destination which matches multiple network+mask pairs, the match with the longest mask is used). Second, current Inter-Domain protocols generally do not support the concept of route aggregation, so the new semantics need to be implemented mechanisms that routers use to interpret routing information returned by the Inter-Domain protocols. In particular, when doing aggregation, dealing with multi-homed sites or destinations which change service providers is difficult. Fortunately, it is possible to define several fairly simple rules for dealing with such cases.

4.2. Rules for route advertisement

1. Routing to all destinations must be done on a longest-match basis only. This implies that destinations which are multi-homed relative to a routing domain must always be explicitly announced into that routing domain - they cannot be summarized

(this makes intuitive sense - if a network is multi-homed, all of its paths into a routing domain which is "higher" in the hierarchy of networks must be known to the "higher" network).

2. A routing domain which performs summarization of multiple routes must discard packets which match the summarization but do not match any of the explicit routes which makes up the summarization. This is necessary to prevent routing loops in the presence of less-specific information (such as a default route). Implementation note - one simple way to implement this rule would be for the border router to maintain a "sink" route for each of its aggregations. By the rule of longest match, this would cause all traffic destined to components of the aggregation which are not explicitly known to be discarded.

Note that during failures, partial routing of traffic to a site which takes its address space from one service provider but which is actually reachable only through another (i.e., the case of a site which has change service providers) may occur because such traffic will be routed along the path advertised by the aggregated route. Rule #2 will prevent any real problem from occurring by forcing such traffic to be discarded by the advertiser of the aggregated route, but the output of "traceroute" and other similar tools will suggest that a problem exists within the service provider advertising the aggregate, which may be confusing to network operators (see the example in section 5.2 for details). Solutions to this problem appear to be challenging and not likely to be implementable by current Inter-Domain protocols within the time-frame suggested by this document. This decision may need to be revisited as Inter-Domain protocols evolve.

An implementation following these rules should also make the implementation be generalized, so that arbitrary network number and mask are accepted for all routing destinations. The only outstanding constraint is that the mask must be left contiguous. Note that the degenerate route 0.0.0.0 mask 0.0.0.0 is used as a default route and MUST be accepted by all implementations. Further, to protect against accidental advertisements of this route via the inter-domain protocol, this route should never be advertised unless there is specific configuration information indicating to do so.

Systems which process route announcements must also be able to verify that information which they receive is correct. Thus, implementations of this plan which filter route advertisements must also allow masks in the filter elements. To simplify administration, it would be useful if filter elements automatically allowed more specific network numbers and masks to pass in filter elements given for a more general mask. Thus, filter elements which looked like:

```
accept 128.32.0.0
accept 128.120.0.0
accept 134.139.0.0
accept 36.0.0.0
```

would look something like:

```
accept 128.32.0.0 255.255.0.0
accept 128.120.0.0 255.255.0.0
accept 134.139.0.0 255.255.0.0
deny 36.2.0.0 255.255.0.0
accept 36.0.0.0 255.0.0.0
```

This is merely making explicit the network mask which was implied by the class-A/B/C classification of network numbers.

4.3. How the rules work

Rule #1 guarantees that the routing algorithm used is consistent across implementations and consistent with other routing protocols, such as OSPF. Multi-homed networks are always explicitly advertised by every service provider through which they are routed even if they are a specific subset of one service provider's aggregate (if they are not, they clearly must be explicitly advertised). It may seem as if the "primary" service provider could advertise the multi-homed site implicitly as part of its aggregate, but the assumption that longest-match routing is always done causes this not to work.

Rule #2 guarantees that no routing loops form due to aggregation. Consider a mid-level network which has been allocated the 2048 class-C networks starting with 192.24.0.0 (see the example in section 5 for more on this). The mid-level advertises to a "backbone" 192.24.0.0/255.248.0.0. Assume that the "backbone", in turn, has been allocated the block of networks 192.0.0.0/255.0.0.0. The backbone will then advertise this aggregate route to the mid-level. Now, if the mid-level loses internal connectivity to the network 192.24.1.0/255.255.255.0 (which is part of its aggregate), traffic from the "backbone" to the mid-level to destination 192.24.1.1 will follow the mid-level's advertised route. When that traffic gets to the mid-level, however, the mid-level *must not* follow the route

192.0.0.0/255.0.0.0 it learned from the backbone, since that would result in a routing loop. Rule #2 says that the mid-level may not follow a less-specific route for a destination which matches one of its own aggregated routes. Note that handling of the "default" route (0.0.0.0/0.0.0.0) is a special case of this rule - a network must not follow the default to destinations which are part of one of it's aggregated advertisements.

4.4. Responsibility for and configuration of aggregation

The AS which owns a range of addresses has the sole authority for aggregation of its address space. In the usual case, the AS will install manual configuration commands in its border routers to aggregate some portion of its address space. As AS can also delegate aggregation authority to another AS. In this case, aggregation is done in the other AS by one of its border routers.

When an inter-domain border router performs route aggregation, it needs to know the range of the block of IP addresses to be aggregated. The basic principle is that it should aggregate as much as possible but not to aggregate those routes which cannot be treated as part of a single unit due to multi-homing, policy, or other constraints.

One mechanism is to do aggregation solely based on dynamically learned routing information. This has the danger of not specifying a precise enough range since when a route is not present, it is not always possible to distinguish whether it is temporarily unreachable or that it does not belong in the aggregate. Purely dynamic routing also does not allow the flexibility of defining what to aggregate within a range. The other mechanism is to do all aggregation based on ranges of blocks of IP addresses preconfigured in the router. It is recommended that preconfiguration be used, since it more flexible and allows precise specification of the range of destinations to aggregate.

Preconfiguration does require some manually-maintained configuration information, but not excessively more so than what router administrators already maintain today. As an addition to the amount of information that must be typed in and maintained by a human, preconfiguration is just a line or two defining the range of the block of IP addresses to aggregate. In terms of gathering the information, if the advertising router is doing the aggregation, its administrator knows the information because the aggregation ranges are assigned to its domain. If the receiving domain has been granted the authority to and task of performing aggregation, the information would be known as part of the agreement to delegate aggregation. Given that it is common practice that a network administrator learns from its neighbor which routes it should be willing to accept, preconfiguration of aggregation information does not introduce additional administrative overhead.

5. Example of new allocation and routing

5.1. Address allocation

Consider the block of 2048 class-C network numbers beginning with 192.24.0.0 (0xC0180000 and ending with 192.31.255.0 (0xC01FFF00) allocated to a single network provider, "RA". A "supernetted" route to this block of network numbers would be described as 192.24.0.0 with mask of 255.248.0.0 (0xFFF80000).

Assume this service provider connects six clients in the following order (significant because it demonstrates how temporary "holes" may form in the service provider's address space):

"C1" requiring fewer than 2048 addresses (8 class-C networks)

"C2" requiring fewer than 4096 addresses (16 class-C networks)

"C3" requiring fewer than 1024 addresses (4 class-C networks)

"C4" requiring fewer than 1024 addresses (4 class-C networks)

"C5" requiring fewer than 512 addresses (2 class-C networks)

"C6" requiring fewer than 512 addresses (2 class-C networks)

In all cases, the number of IP addresses "required" by each client is assumed to allow for significant growth. The service provider allocates its address space as follows:

C1: allocate 192.24.0 through 192.24.7. This block of networks is described by the "supernet" route 192.24.0.0 and mask 255.255.248.0

C2: allocate 192.24.16 through 192.24.31. This block is described by the route 192.24.16.0, mask 255.255.240.0

C3: allocate 192.24.8 through 192.24.11. This block is described by the route 192.24.8.0, mask 255.255.252.0

C4: allocate 192.24.12 through 192.24.15. This block is described by the route 192.24.12.0, mask 255.255.252.0

C5: allocate 192.24.32 and 192.24.33. This block is described by the route 192.24.32.0, mask 255.255.254.0

C6: allocate 192.24.34 and 192.24.35. This block is described by the route 192.24.34.0, mask 255.255.254.0

Note that if the network provider uses an IGP which can support classless networks, he can (but doesn't have to) perform "supernetting" at the point where he connects to his clients and therefore only maintain six distinct routes for the 36 class-C network numbers. If not, explicit routes to all 36 class-C networks will have to be carried by the IGP.

To make this example more realistic, assume that C4 and C5 are multi-homed through some other service provider, "RB". Further assume the existence of a client "C7" which was originally connected to "RB" but has moved to "RA". For this reason, it has a block of network numbers which are allocated out "RB"'s block of (the next) 2048 class-C network numbers:

C7: allocate 192.32.0 through 192.32.15. This block is described by the route 192.32.0, mask 255.255.240.0

For the multi-homed clients, we will assume that C4 is advertised as primary via "RA" and secondary via "RB"; C5 is primary via "RB" and secondary via "RA". To connect this mess together, we will assume that "RA" and "RB" are connected via some common "backbone" provider "BB".

Graphically, this simple topology looks something like this:

```
                                 C1
192.24.0.0 - 192.24.7.0 \                _ 192.32.0.0 - 192.32.15.0
192.24.0.0/255.255.248.0 \              /  192.32.0.0/255.255.240.0
                          \            /            C7
                           C2  +----+                               +----+
192.24.16.0 - 192.24.31.0 \|    |                               |    |
192.24.16.0/255.255.240.0  |    | _ 192.24.12.0 - 192.24.15.0 _ |    |
                           |    | / 192.24.12.0/255.255.252.0  \ |    |
                        C3 -|   |/            C4                \|    |
192.24.8.0 - 192.24.11.0   | RA |                                | RB |
192.24.8.0/255.255.252.0   |    |___ 192.24.32.0 - 192.24.33.0 ___|    |
                          /|    |    192.24.32.0/255.255.254.0    |    |
                        C6 |    |             C5                  |    |
192.24.34.0 - 192.24.35.0  |    |                                 |    |
192.24.34.0/255.255.254.0  |    |                                 |    |
                           +----+                                 +----+
                              \\                                      \\
192.24.12.0/255.255.252.0 (C4) ||   192.32.12.0/255.255.252.0 (C4) ||
192.24.32.0/255.255.254.0 (C5) ||   192.32.32.0/255.255.192.0 (C5) ||
192.32.0.0/255.255.240.0  (C7) ||   192.32.0.0/255.248.0.0 (RB)     ||
192.24.0.0/255.248.0.0 (RA)    ||                                   ||
                               VV                                   VV
                +-------------- BACKBONE PEER  BB --------------+
```

5.2. Routing advertisements

To follow rule #1, RA will need to advertise the block of addresses that it was given and C7. Since C4 and C5 are multi-homed, they must also be advertised.

Advertisements from "RA" to "BB" will be:

```
192.24.12.0/255.255.252.0 primary    (advertises C4)
192.24.32.0/255.255.254.0 secondary  (advertises C5)
192.32.0.0/255.255.240.0 primary     (advertises C7)
192.24.0.0/255.248.0.0 primary       (advertises remainder of RA)
```

For RB, the advertisements must also include C4 and C5 as well as it's block of addresses. Further, RB may advertise that C7 is unreachable.

Advertisements from "RB" to "BB" will be:

```
192.24.12.0/255.255.252.0 secondary  (advertises C4)
192.24.32.0/255.255.254.0 primary    (advertises C5)
192.32.0.0/255.248.0.0 primary       (advertises remainder of RB)
```

To illustrate the problem alluded to by the "note" in section 4.2, consider what happens if RA loses connectivity to C7 (the client which is allocated out of RB's space). In a stateful protocol, RA will announce to BB that 192.32.0.0/255.255.240.0 has become unreachable. Now, when BB flushes this information out of its routing table, any future traffic sent through it for this destination will be forwarded to RB (where it will be dropped according to Rule #2) by virtue of RB's less specific match 192.32.0.0/255.248.0.0. While this does not cause an operational problem (C7 is unreachable in any case), it does create some extra traffic across "BB" (and may also prove confusing to a network manager debugging the outage with "traceroute"). A mechanism to cache such unreachability information would help here, but is beyond the scope of this document (such a mechanism is also not implementable in the near-term).

6. Transitioning to a long term solution

This solution does not change the Internet routing and addressing architectures. Hence, transitioning to a more long term solution is not affected by the deployment of this plan.

7. Conclusions

We are all aware of the growth in routing complexity, and the rapid increase in allocation of network numbers. Given the rate at which this growth is being observed, we expect to run out in a few short years.

If the inter-domain routing protocol supports carrying network routes with associated masks, all of the major concerns demonstrated in this paper would be eliminated.

One of the influential factors which permits maximal exploitation of the advantages of this plan is the number of people who agree to use it. It is hoped that having the IAB and the Internet society bless this plan would go a long way in the wide deployment, and hence benefit of this plan.

If service providers start charging networks for advertising network numbers, this would be a very great incentive to share the address space, and hence the associated costs of advertising routes to service providers.

8. Recommendations

The NIC should begin to hand out large blocks of class-C addresses to network service providers. Each block must fall on bit boundaries and should be large enough to serve the provider for two years.

Further, the NIC should distribute very large blocks to continental and national network service organizations to allow additional levels of aggregation to take place at the major backbone networks.

Service providers will further allocate power-of-two blocks of class-C addresses from their address space to their subscribers.

All organizations, including those which are multi-homed, should obtain address space from their provider (or one of their providers, in the case of the multi-homed). These blocks should also fall on bit boundaries to permit easy route aggregation.

To allow effective use of this new addressing plan to reduce propagated routing information, appropriate IETF WGs will specify the modifications needed to Inter-Domain routing protocols. Implementation and deployment of these modifications should occur as quickly as possible.

9. Bibliography

[RFC1247] Moy, J, "The OSPF Specification Version 2", January 1991.

10. Security Considerations

Security issues are not discussed in this memo.

11. Authors' Addresses

Vince Fuller
BARRNet
Pine Hall 115
Stanford, CA, 94305-4122

EMail: vaf@Stanford.EDU

Tony Li
cisco Systems, Inc.
1525 O'Brien Drive
Menlo Park, CA 94025

EMail: tli@cisco.com

Jessica (Jie Yun) Yu
Merit Network, Inc.
1071 Beal Ave.
Ann Arbor, MI 48109

EMail: jyy@merit.edu

Kannan Varadhan
Internet Engineer, OARnet
1224, Kinnear Road,
Columbus, OH 43212

EMail: kannan@oar.net

Network Working Group
Request for Comments: 1519
Obsoletes: 1338
Category: Standards Track

V. Fuller
BARRNet
T. Li
cisco
J. Yu
MERIT
K. Varadhan
OARnet

September 1993

Classless Inter-Domain Routing (CIDR): an Address Assignment and Aggregation Strategy

Status of this Memo

This RFC specifies an Internet standards track protocol for the Internet community, and requests discussion and suggestions for improvements. Please refer to the current edition of the "Internet Official Protocol Standards" for the standardization state and status of this protocol. Distribution of this memo is unlimited.

Abstract

This memo discusses strategies for address assignment of the existing IP address space with a view to conserve the address space and stem the explosive growth of routing tables in default-route-free routers.

Table of Contents

Acknowledgements

The authors wish to express their appreciation to the members of the ROAD group with whom many of the ideas contained in this document were inspired and developed.1. Problem, Goal, and Motivation

As the Internet has evolved and grown over in recent years, it has become evident that it is soon to face several serious scaling problems. These include:

1. Exhaustion of the class B network address space. One fundamental cause of this problem is the lack of a network class of a size which is appropriate for mid-sized organization; class C, with a maximum of 254 host addresses, is too small, while class B, which allows up to 65534 addresses, is too large for most organizations.

2. Growth of routing tables in Internet routers beyond the ability of current software, hardware, and people to effectively manage.

3. Eventual exhaustion of the 32-bit IP address space.

It has become clear that the first two of these problems are likely to become critical within the next one to three years. This memo attempts to deal with these problems by proposing a mechanism to slow the growth of the routing table and the need for allocating new IP network numbers. It does not attempt to solve the third problem, which is of a more long-term nature, but instead endeavors to ease enough of the short to mid-term difficulties to allow the Internet to continue to function efficiently while progress is made on a longer-term solution.

The proposed solution is to topologically allocate future IP address assignment, by allocating segments of the IP address space to the transit routing domains.

This plan for allocating IP addresses should be undertaken as soon as possible. We believe that this will suffice as a short term strategy, to fill the gap between now and the time when a viable long term plan can be put into place and deployed effectively. This plan should be viable for at least three (3) years, after which time, deployment of a suitable long term solution is expected to occur.

This plan is primarily directed at the first two problems listed above. We believe that the judicious use of variable-length subnetting techniques should help defer the onset of the last problem problem, the exhaustion of the 32-bit address space. Note also that improved tools for performing address allocation in a "supernetted" and variably-subnetted world would greatly help the user community in accepting these sometimes confusing techniques. Efforts to create some simple tools for this purpose should be encouraged by the Internet community.

Note that this plan neither requires nor assumes that already assigned addresses will be reassigned, though if doing so were possible, it would further reduce routing table sizes. It is assumed that routing technology will be capable of dealing with the current routing table size and with some reasonably small rate of growth. The emphasis of this plan is on significantly slowing the rate of this growth.

Note that this plan does not require domains to renumber if they change their attached transit routing domain. Domains are encouraged to renumber so that their individual address allocations do not need to be advertised.

This plan will not affect the deployment of any specific long term plan, and therefore, this document will not discuss any long term plans for routing and address architectures.

2. CIDR address allocation

There are two basic components of this addressing and routing plan: one, to distribute the allocation of Internet address space and two, to provide a mechanism for the aggregation of routing information.

2.1 Aggregation and its limitations

One major goal of this addressing plan is to allocate Internet address space in such a manner as to allow aggregation of routing information along topological lines. For simple, single-homed clients, the allocation of their address space out of a transit routing domain's space will accomplish this automatically - rather than advertise a separate route for each such client, the transit domain may advertise a single aggregate route which describes all of the destinations connected to it. Unfortunately, not all sites are singly-connected to the network, so some loss of ability to aggregate is realized for the non-trivial cases.

There are two situations that cause a loss of aggregation efficiency.

- o Organizations which are multi-homed. Because multi-homed organizations must be advertised into the system by each of their service providers, it is often not feasible to aggregate their routing information into the address space any one of those providers. Note that they still may receive their address allocation out of a transit domain's address space (which has other advantages), but their routing information must still be explicitly advertised by most of their service providers (the exception being that if the site's allocation comes out of its least-preferable service provider, then that service provider need not advertise the explicit route - longest-match will insure that its aggregated route is used to get to the site on a backup basis). For this reason, the routing cost for these organizations will typically be about the same as it is today.

- o Organizations which change service provider but do not renumber. This has the effect of "punching a hole" in the aggregation of the original service provider's advertisement.

  This plan will handle the situation by requiring the newer service provider to advertise a specific advertisement for the new client, which is preferred by virtue of being the longest match. To maintain efficiency of aggregation, it is recommended that organizations which do change service providers plan to eventually migrate their address assignments from the old provider's space to that of the new provider. To this end, it is recommended that mechanisms to facilitate such migration, including improved protocols and procedures for dynamic host address assignment, be developed.

Note that some aggregation efficiency gain can still be had for multi-homed sites (and, in general, for any site composed of multiple, logical IP network numbers) - by allocating a contiguous power-of-two block of network numbers to the client (as opposed to multiple, independent network numbers) the client's routing information may be aggregated into a single (net, mask) pair. Also, since the routing cost associated with assigning a multi-homed site out of a service provider's address space is no greater than the current method of a random allocation by a central authority, it makes sense to allocate all address space out of blocks assigned to service providers.

It is also worthwhile to mention that since aggregation may occur at multiple levels in the system, it may still be possible to aggregate these anomalous routes at higher levels of whatever hierarchy may be present. For example, if a site is multi-homed to two NSFNET regional networks both of whom obtain their address space from the NSFNET, then aggregation by the NSFNET of routes from the regionals will include all routes to the multi-homed site.

Finally, it should also be noted that deployment of the new addressing plan described in this document may (and should) begin almost immediately but effective use of the plan to aggregate routing information will require changes to some Inter-Domain routing protocols. Likewise, deploying classless Inter-Domain protocols without deployment of the new address plan will not allow useful aggregation to occur (in other words, the addressing plan and routing protocol changes are both required for supernetting, and its resulting reduction in table growth, to be effective.) Note, however, that during the period of time between deployment of the addressing plan and deployment of the new protocols, the size of routing tables may temporarily grow very rapidly. This must be considered when planning the deployment of the two plans.

Note: in the discussion and examples which follow, the network and mask notation is used to represent routing destinations. This is used for illustration only and does not require that routing protocols use this representation in their updates.

2.2 Distributed allocation of address space

The basic idea of the plan is to allocate one or more blocks of Class C network numbers to each network service provider. Organizations using the network service provider for Internet connectivity are allocated bitmask-oriented subsets of the provider's address space as required.

It is also worthwhile to mention that once inter-domain protocols which support classless network destinations are widely deployed, the rules described by this plan generalize to permit arbitrary super/subnetting of the remaining class A and class B address space (the assumption being that classless inter-domain protocols will either allow for non-contiguous subnets to exist in the system or that all components of a sub-allocated class A/B will be contained within a single routing domain). This will allow this plan to continue to be used in the event that the class C space is exhausted before implementation of a long-term solution is deployed. This alternative is discussed further below in section 6.

Hierarchical sub-allocation of addresses in this manner implies that clients with addresses allocated out of a given service provider are, for routing purposes, part of that service provider and will be routed via its infrastructure. This implies that routing information about multi-homed organizations, i.e., organizations connected to more than one network service provider, will still need to be known by higher levels in the hierarchy.

The advantages of hierarchical assignment in this fashion are

a) It is expected to be easier for a relatively small number of service providers to obtain addresses from the central authority, rather than a much larger, and monotonically increasing, number of individual clients. This is not to be considered as a loss of part of the service providers' address space.

b) Given the current growth of the Internet, a scalable and delegatable method of future allocation of network numbers has to be achieved.

For these reasons, and in the interest of providing a consistent procedure for obtaining Internet addresses, it is recommended that most, if not all, network numbers be distributed through service providers. These issues are discussed in much greater length in [2].

3. Cost-benefit analysis

This new method of assigning address through service providers can be put into effect immediately and will, from the start, have the benefit of distributing the currently centralized process of assigning new addresses. Unfortunately, before the benefit of reducing the size of globally-known routing destinations can be achieved, it will be necessary to deploy an Inter-Domain routing protocol capable of handling arbitrary network and mask pairs. Only then will it be possible to aggregate individual class C networks into larger blocks represented by single routing table entries.

This means that upon introduction, the new addressing allocation plan will not in and of itself help solve the routing table size problem. Once the new Inter-Domain routing protocol is deployed, however, an immediate drop in the number of destinations which clients of the new protocol must carry will occur. A detailed analysis of the magnitude of this expected drop and the permanent reduction in rate of growth is given in the next section.

In should also be noted that the present method of flat address allocations imposes a large bureaucratic cost on the central address allocation authority. For scaling reasons unrelated to address space exhaustion or routing table overflow, this should be changed. Using the mechanism proposed in this paper will have the fortunate side effect of distributing the address allocation procedure, greatly reducing the load on the central authority.

3.1 Present Allocation Figures

An informal analysis of "network-contacts.txt" (available from the DDN NIC) indicates that as of 2/25/92, 46 of 126 class A network numbers have been allocated (leaving 81) and 5467 of 16382 class B numbers have been allocated, leaving 10915. Assuming that recent trends continue, the number of allocated class B's will continue to double approximately once a year. At this rate of growth, all class B's will be exhausted within about 15 months. As of 1/13/93, 52 class A network numbers have been allocated and 7133 class B's have been allocated. We suggest that the change in the class B allocation rate is due to the initial deployment of this address allocation plan.

3.2 Historic growth rates

MM/YY	ROUTES ADVERTISED	MM/YY	ROUTES ADVERTISED
Dec-92	8561	Sep-90	1988
Nov-92	7854	Aug-90	1894
Oct-92	7354	Jul-90	1727
Sep-92	6640	Jun-90	1639
Aug-92	6385	May-90	1580
Jul-92	6031	Apr-90	1525
Jun-92	5739	Mar-90	1038
May-92	5515	Feb-90	997
Apr-92	5291	Jan-90	927
Mar-92	4976	Dec-89	897
Feb-92	4740	Nov-89	837
Jan-92	4526	Oct-89	809
Dec-91	4305	Sep-89	745
Nov-91	3751	Aug-89	650
Oct-91	3556	Jul-89	603
Sep-91	3389	Jun-89	564
Aug-91	3258	May-89	516
Jul-91	3086	Apr-89	467
Jun-91	2982	Mar-89	410
May-91	2763	Feb-89	384
Apr-91	2622	Jan-89	346
Mar-91	2501	Dec-88	334
Feb-91	2417	Nov-88	313
Jan-91	2338	Oct-88	291
Dec-90	2190	Sep-88	244
Nov-90	2125	Aug-88	217
Oct-90	2063	Jul-88	173

Table I : Growth in routing table size, total numbers
Source for the routing table size data is MERIT

3.3 Detailed Analysis

There is a small technical cost and minimal administrative cost associated with deployment of the new address assignment plan. The administrative cost is basically that of convincing the NIC, the IANA, and the network service providers to agree to this plan, which is not expected to be too difficult. In addition, administrative cost for the central numbering authorities (the NIC and the IANA) will be greatly decreased by the deployment of this plan. To take advantage of aggregation of routing information, however, it is necessary that the capability to represent routes as arbitrary network and mask fields (as opposed to the current class A/B/C distinction) be added to the common Internet inter-domain routing protocol(s). Thus, the technical cost is in the implementation of classless interdomain routing protocols.

3.3.1 Benefits of the new addressing plan

There are two benefits to be had by deploying this plan:

- The current problem with depletion of the available class B address space can be ameliorated by assigning more-appropriately sized blocks of class C's to mid-sized organizations (in the 200-4000 host range).

- When the improved inter-domain routing protocol is deployed, an immediate decrease in the number routing table entries should occur, followed by a significant reduction in the rate growth of routing table size (for default-free routers).

3.3.2 Growth rate projections

As of Jan '92, a default-free routing table (for example, the routing tables maintained by the routers in the NSFNET backbone) contained approximately 4700 entries. This number reflects the current size of the NSFNET routing database. Historic data shows that this number, on average, has doubled every 10 months between 1988 and 1991. Assuming that this growth rate is going to persist in the foreseeable future (and there is no reason to assume otherwise), we expect the number of entries in a default-free routing table to grow to approximately 30000 in two years time. In the following analysis, we assume that the growth of the Internet has been, and will continue to be, exponential.

It should be stressed that these projections do not consider that the current shortage of class B network numbers may increase the number of instances where many class C's are used rather than a class B.

Using an assumption that new organizations which formerly obtained class B's will now obtain somewhere between 4 and 16 class C's, the rate of routing table growth can conservatively be expected to at least double and probably quadruple. This means the number of entries in a default-free routing table may well exceed 10,000 entries within six months and 20,000 entries in less than a year.

As of Dec '92, the routing table contains 8500 routes. The original growth curves would predict over 9400 routes. At this time, it is not clear if this would indicate a significant change in the rate of growth.

Under the proposed plan, growth of the routing table in a default-free router is greatly reduced since most new address assignment will come from one of the large blocks allocated to the service providers. For the sake of this analysis, we assume prompt implementation of this proposal and deployment of the revised routing protocols. We make the initial assumption that any initial block given to a provider is sufficient to satisfy its needs for two years.

Since under this plan, multi-homed networks must continue to be explicitly advertised throughout the system (according to Rule #1 described in section 4.2), the number multi-homed routes is expected to be the dominant factor in future growth of routing table size, once the supernetting plan is applied.

Presently, it is estimated that there are fewer than 100 multi-homed organizations connected to the Internet. Each such organization's network is comprised of one or more network numbers. In many cases (and in all future cases under this plan), the network numbers used by an organization are consecutive, meaning that aggregation of those networks during route advertisement may be possible. This means that the number of routes advertised within the Internet for multi-homed networks may be approximated as the total number of multi-homed organizations. Assuming that the number of multi-homed organization will double every year (which may be a over-estimation, given that every connection costs money), the number of routes for multi-homed networks would be expected to grow to approximately 800 in three years.

If we further assume that there are approximately 100 service providers, then each service provider will also need to advertise its block of addresses. However, due to aggregation, these advertisements will be reduced to only 100 additional routes. We assume that after the initial two years, new service providers combined with additional requests from existing providers will require an additional 50 routes per year. Thus, the total is 4700 + 800 + 150 = 5650. This represents an annual growth rate of approximately 6%. This is in clear contrast to the current annual growth of 130%. This analysis also assumes an immediate deployment of this plan with full compliance. Note that this analysis assumes only a single level of route aggregation in the current Internet - intelligent address allocation should significantly improve this.

Clearly, this is not a very conservative assumption in the Internet environment nor can 100% adoption of this proposal be expected. Still, with only a 90% participation in this proposal by service providers, at the end of the target three years, global routing table size will be "only" 4700 + 800 + 145 + 7500 = 13145 routes – without any action, the routing table will grow to approximately 75000 routes during that time period.

4. Changes to inter-domain routing protocols and practices

In order to support supernetting efficiently, it is clear that some changes will need to be made to both routing protocols themselves and to the way in which routing information is interpreted. In the case of "new" inter-domain protocols, the actual protocol syntax changes should be relatively minor. This mechanism will not work with older inter-domain protocols such as EGP2; the only ways to interoperate with old systems using such protocols are either to use existing mechanisms for providing "default" routes or b) require that new routers talking to old routers "explode" supernet information into individual network numbers. Since the first of these is trivial while the latter is cumbersome (at best – consider the memory requirements it imposes on the receiver of the exploded information), it is recommended that the first approach be used – that older systems to continue to the mechanisms they currently employ for default handling.

Note that a basic assumption of this plan is that those organizations which need to import "supernet" information into their routing systems must run IGPs (such as OSPF [1]) which support classless routes. Systems running older IGPs may still advertise and receive "supernet" information, but they will not be able to propagate such information through their routing domains.

4.1 Protocol-independent semantic changes

There are two fundamental changes which must be applied to Inter-Domain routing protocols in order for this plan to work. First, the concept of network "class" needs to be deprecated - this plan assumes that routing destinations are represented by network and mask pairs and that routing is done on a longest-match basis (i.e., for a given destination which matches multiple network+mask pairs, the match with the longest mask is used). Second, current inter-domain protocols generally do not support the concept of route aggregation, so the new semantics need to be implemented in a new set of inter-domain protocols. In particular, when doing aggregation, dealing with multi-homed sites or destinations which change service providers is difficult. Fortunately, it is possible to define several fairly simple rules for dealing with such cases.

4.2. Rules for route advertisement

1. Routing to all destinations must be done on a longest-match basis only. This implies that destinations which are multi-homed relative to a routing domain must always be explicitly announced into that routing domain - they cannot be summarized (this makes intuitive sense - if a network is multi-homed, all

of its paths into a routing domain which is "higher" in the hierarchy of networks must be known to the "higher" network).

2. A routing domain which performs summarization of multiple routes must discard packets which match the summarization but do not match any of the explicit routes which makes up the summarization. This is necessary to prevent routing loops in the presence of less-specific information (such as a default route). Implementation note - one simple way to implement this rule would be for the border router to maintain a "sink" route for each of its aggregations. By the rule of longest match, this would cause all traffic destined to components of the aggregation which are not explicitly known to be discarded.

Note that during failures, partial routing of traffic to a site which takes its address space from one service provider but which is actually reachable only through another (i.e., the case of a site which has change service providers) may occur because such traffic will be routed along the path advertised by the aggregated route.

Rule #2 will prevent any real problem from occurring by forcing such traffic to be discarded by the advertiser of the aggregated route, but the output of "traceroute" and other similar tools will suggest that a problem exists within the service provider advertising the aggregate, which may be confusing to network operators (see the example in section 5.2 for details). Solutions to this problem appear to be challenging and not likely to be implementable by current Inter-Domain protocols within the time-frame suggested by this document. This decision may need to be revisited as Inter-Domain protocols evolve.

An implementation following these rules should also be generalized, so that an arbitrary network number and mask are accepted for all routing destinations. The only outstanding constraint is that the mask must be left contiguous. Note that the degenerate route 0.0.0.0 mask 0.0.0.0 is used as a default route and MUST be accepted by all implementations. Further, to protect against accidental advertisements of this route via the inter-domain protocol, this route should never be advertised unless there is specific configuration information indicating to do so.

Systems which process route announcements must also be able to verify that information which they receive is correct. Thus, implementations of this plan which filter route advertisements must also allow masks in the filter elements. To simplify administration, it would be useful if filter elements automatically allowed more specific network numbers and masks to pass in filter elements given for a more general mask. Thus, filter elements which looked like:

```
accept 128.32.0.0
accept 128.120.0.0
accept 134.139.0.0
deny 36.2.0.0
accept 36.0.0.0
```

would look something like:

```
accept 128.32.0.0 255.255.0.0
accept 128.120.0.0 255.255.0.0
accept 134.139.0.0 255.255.0.0
deny 36.2.0.0 255.255.0.0
accept 36.0.0.0 255.0.0.0
```

This is merely making explicit the network mask which was implied by the class A/B/C classification of network numbers.

4.3. How the rules work

Rule #1 guarantees that the routing algorithm used is consistent across implementations and consistent with other routing protocols, such as OSPF. Multi-homed networks are always explicitly advertised by every service provider through which they are routed even if they are a specific subset of one service provider's aggregate (if they are not, they clearly must be explicitly advertised). It may seem as if the "primary" service provider could advertise the multi-homed site implicitly as part of its aggregate, but the assumption that longest-match routing is always done causes this not to work.

Rule #2 guarantees that no routing loops form due to aggregation. Consider a mid-level network which has been allocated the 2048 class C networks starting with 192.24.0.0 (see the example in section 5 for more on this). The mid-level advertises to a "backbone" 192.24.0.0/255.248.0.0. Assume that the "backbone", in turn, has been allocated the block of networks 192.0.0.0/255.0.0.0. The backbone will then advertise this aggregate route to the mid-level. Now, if the mid-level loses internal connectivity to the network 192.24.1.0/255.255.255.0 (which is part of its aggregate), traffic from the "backbone" to the mid-level to destination 192.24.1.1 will follow the mid-level's advertised route. When that traffic gets to the mid-level, however, the mid-level *must not* follow the route 192.0.0.0/255.0.0.0 it learned from the backbone, since that would result in a routing loop. Rule #2 says that the mid-level may not follow a less-specific route for a destination which matches one of its own aggregated routes. Note that handling of the "default" route (0.0.0.0/0.0.0.0) is a special case of this rule - a network must not follow the default to destinations which are part of one of it's aggregated advertisements.

4.4. Responsibility for and configuration of aggregation

The domain which has been allocated a range of addresses has the sole authority for aggregation of its address space. In the usual case, the AS will install manual configuration commands in its border routers to aggregate some portion of its address space. An domain can also delegate aggregation authority to another domain. In this case, aggregation is done in the other domain by one of its border routers.

When an inter-domain border router performs route aggregation, it needs to know the range of the block of IP addresses to be aggregated. The basic principle is that it should aggregate as much as possible but not to aggregate those routes which cannot be treated as part of a single unit due to multi-homing, policy, or other constraints.

One mechanism is to do aggregation solely based on dynamically learned routing information. This has the danger of not specifying a precise enough range since when a route is not present, it is not always possible to distinguish whether it is temporarily unreachable or that it does not belong in the aggregate. Purely dynamic routing also does not allow the flexibility of defining what to aggregate within a range. The other mechanism is to do all aggregation based on ranges of blocks of IP addresses preconfigured in the router. It is recommended that preconfiguration be used, since it more flexible and allows precise specification of the range of destinations to aggregate.

Preconfiguration does require some manually-maintained configuration information, but not excessively more so than what router administrators already maintain today. As an addition to the amount of information that must be typed in and maintained by a human, preconfiguration is just a line or two defining the range of the block of IP addresses to aggregate. In terms of gathering the information, if the advertising router is doing the aggregation, its administrator knows the information because the aggregation ranges are assigned to its domain. If the receiving domain has been granted the authority to and task of performing aggregation, the information would be known as part of the agreement to delegate aggregation. Given that it is common practice that a network administrator learns from its neighbor which routes it should be willing to accept, preconfiguration of aggregation information does not introduce additional administrative overhead.

Implementation note: aggregates which encompass the class D address space (multicast addresses) are currently not well understood. At present, it appears that the optimal strategy is to consider aggregates to never encompass class D space, even if they do so numerically.

4.5 Intra-domain protocol considerations

While no changes need be made to internal routing protocols to support the advertisement of aggregated routing information between autonomous systems, it is often the case that external routing information is propagated within interior protocols for policy reasons or to aid in the propagation of information through a transit network. At the point when aggregated routing information starts to appear in the new exterior protocols, this practice of importing external information will have to be modified. A transit network which imports external information will have to do one of:

a) use an interior protocol which supports aggregated routing

b) find some other method of propagating external information which does not involve flooding it through the interior protocol (i.e., by the use of internal BGP, for example).

c) stop the importation of external information and flood a "default" route through the internal protocol for discovery of paths to external destinations.

For case (a), the modifications necessary to a routing protocol to allow it to support aggregated information may not be simple. For protocols such as OSPF and IS-IS, which represent routing information as either a destination+mask (OSPF) or as a prefix+prefix-length (IS-IS) changes to support aggregated information are conceptually fairly simple; for protocols which are dependent on the class-A/B/C nature of networks or which support only fixed-sized subnets, the changes are of a more fundamental nature. Even in the "conceptually simple" cases of OSPF and IS-IS, an implementation may need to be modified to support supernets in the database or in the forwarding table.

5. Example of new allocation and routing

5.1 Address allocation

Consider the block of 2048 class C network numbers beginning with 192.24.0.0 (0xC0180000 and ending with 192.31.255.0 (0xC01FFF00) allocated to a single network provider, "RA". A "supernetted" route to this block of network numbers would be described as 192.24.0.0 with mask of 255.248.0.0 (0xFFF80000).

Assume this service provider connects six clients in the following order (significant because it demonstrates how temporary "holes" may form in the service provider's address space):

"C1" requiring fewer than 2048 addresses (8 class C networks)

"C2" requiring fewer than 4096 addresses (16 class C networks)

"C3" requiring fewer than 1024 addresses (4 class C networks)

"C4" requiring fewer than 1024 addresses (4 class C networks)

"C5" requiring fewer than 512 addresses (2 class C networks)

"C6" requiring fewer than 512 addresses (2 class C networks)

In all cases, the number of IP addresses "required" by each client is assumed to allow for significant growth. The service provider allocates its address space as follows:

C1: allocate 192.24.0 through 192.24.7. This block of networks is described by the "supernet" route 192.24.0.0 and mask 255.255.248.0

C2: allocate 192.24.16 through 192.24.31. This block is described by the route 192.24.16.0, mask 255.255.240.0

C3: allocate 192.24.8 through 192.24.11. This block is described by the route 192.24.8.0, mask 255.255.252.0

C4: allocate 192.24.12 through 192.24.15. This block is described by the route 192.24.12.0, mask 255.255.252.0

C5: allocate 192.24.32 and 192.24.33. This block is described by the route 192.24.32.0, mask 255.255.254.0

C6: allocate 192.24.34 and 192.24.35. This block is described by the route 192.24.34.0, mask 255.255.254.0

Note that if the network provider uses an IGP which can support classless networks, he can (but doesn't have to) perform "supernetting" at the point where he connects to his clients and therefore only maintain six distinct routes for the 36 class C network numbers. If not, explicit routes to all 36 class C networks will have to be carried by the IGP.

To make this example more realistic, assume that C4 and C5 are multi-homed through some other service provider, "RB". Further assume the existence of a client "C7" which was originally connected to "RB" but has moved to "RA". For this reason, it has a block of network numbers which are allocated out "RB"'s block of (the next) 2048 class C network numbers:

C7: allocate 192.32.0 through 192.32.15. This block is described by the route 192.32.0, mask 255.255.240.0

For the multi-homed clients, we will assume that C4 is advertised as primary via "RA" and secondary via "RB"; C5 is primary via "RB" and secondary via "RA". To connect this mess together, we will assume that "RA" and "RB" are connected via some common "backbone" provider "BB".

Graphically, this simple topology looks something like this:

```
                       C1
192.24.0.0 - 192.24.7.0  \         _ 192.32.0.0 - 192.32.15.0
192.24.0.0/255.255.248.0  \       /  192.32.0.0/255.255.240.0
                           \     /             C7
                        C2 +----+                                 +----+
192.24.16.0 - 192.24.31.0 \|    |                                 |    |
192.24.16.0/255.255.240.0  |    |  _ 192.24.12.0 - 192.24.15.0 _  |    |
                           |    | /  192.24.12.0/255.255.252.0  \ |    |
                       C3 -|    |/              C4               \|    |
192.24.8.0 - 192.24.11.0   | RA |                                 | RB |
192.24.8.0/255.255.252.0   |    |___ 192.24.32.0 - 192.24.33.0 ___|    |
                          /|    |    192.24.32.0/255.255.254.0    |    |
                       C6  |    |               C5                |    |
192.24.34.0 - 192.24.35.0  |    |                                 |    |
192.24.34.0/255.255.254.0  |    |                                 |    |
                           +----+                                 +----+
                              \\                                      \\
192.24.12.0/255.255.252.0 (C4) ||      192.24.12.0/255.255.252.0 (C4) ||
192.32.0.0/255.255.240.0  (C7) ||      192.24.32.0/255.255.254.0 (C5) ||
192.24.0.0/255.248.0.0 (RA)    ||      192.32.0.0/255.248.0.0 (RB)    ||
                               ||                                     ||
                               VV                                     VV
                     +--------------- BACKBONE PEER  BB ---------------+
```

5.2 Routing advertisements

To follow rule #1, RA will need to advertise the block of addresses that it was given and C7. Since C4 is multi-homed and primary through RA, it must also be advertised. C5 is multi-homed and primary through RB. It need not be advertised since longest match by BB will automatically select RB as primary and the advertisement of

RA's aggregate will be used as a secondary.

Advertisements from "RA" to "BB" will be:

```
192.24.12.0/255.255.252.0 primary    (advertises C4)
192.32.0.0/255.255.240.0 primary     (advertises C7)
192.24.0.0/255.248.0.0 primary       (advertises remainder of RA)
```

For RB, the advertisements must also include C4 and C5 as well as it's block of addresses. Further, RB may advertise that C7 is unreachable.

Advertisements from "RB" to "BB" will be:

```
192.24.12.0/255.255.252.0 secondary  (advertises C4)
192.24.32.0/255.255.254.0 primary    (advertises C5)
192.32.0.0/255.248.0.0 primary       (advertises remainder of RB)
```

To illustrate the problem alluded to by the "note" in section 4.2, consider what happens if RA loses connectivity to C7 (the client which is allocated out of RB's space). In a stateful protocol, RA will announce to BB that 192.32.0.0/255.255.240.0 has become unreachable. Now, when BB flushes this information out of its routing table, any future traffic sent through it for this destination will be forwarded to RB (where it will be dropped according to Rule #2) by virtue of RB's less specific match 192.32.0.0/255.248.0.0. While this does not cause an operational problem (C7 is unreachable in any case), it does create some extra traffic across "BB" (and may also prove confusing to a network manager debugging the outage with "traceroute"). A mechanism to cache such unreachability information would help here, but is beyond the scope of this document (such a mechanism is also not implementable in the near-term).

6. Extending CIDR to class A addresses

At some point, it is expected that this plan will eventually consume all of the remaining class C address space. As of this writing, the upper half of the class A address space has already been reserved for future expansion. This section describes how the CIDR plan can be used to utilize this portion of the class A space efficiently. It is expected that this contingency would only be used if no long term solution has become apparent by the time that the class C address space is consumed.

Fundamentally, there are two differences between using a class A address and a block of class C's. First, the configuration of DNS becomes somewhat more complicated than it is without the aggregation of class A subnets. The second difference is that the routers within the class A address would need to support and use a classless IGP.

Maintenance of DNS with a subnetted class A is somewhat painful. As part of the mechanism for providing reverse address lookups, DNS maintains a "IN-ADDR.ARPA" reverse domain. This is configured by reversing the dotted decimal network number, appending "IN-ADDR.ARPA" and using this as a type of pseudo-domain. Individual hosts then end up pointing back to a host name. Thus, for example, 131.108.1.111 has a DNS record "111.1.108.131.IN-ADDR.ARPA." Since the pseudo-domains can only be delegated on a byte boundary, this becomes painful if a stub domain receives a block of address space that does not fall on a byte boundary. The solution in this case is to enumerate all of the possible byte combinations involved. This is painful, but workable. This is discussed further below.

Routing within a class A used for CIDR is also an interesting challenge. The usual case will be that a domain will be assigned a portion of the class A address space. The domain can either use an IGP which allows variable length subnets or it can pick a single subnet mask to be used throughout the domain. In the latter case, difficulties arise because other domains have been allocated other parts of the class A address space and may be using a different subnet mask. If the domain is itself a transit, it may also need to allocate some portion of its space to a client, which might also use a different subnet mask. The client would then need routing information about the remainder of the class A.

If the client's IGP does not support variable length subnet masks, this could be done by advertising the remainder of the class A's address space in appropriately sized subnets. However, unless the client has a very large portion of the class A space, this is likely to result in a large number of subnets (for example, a mask of 255.255.255.0 would require a total of 65535 subnets, including those allocated to the client). For this reason, it may be preferable to simply use an IGP that supports variable length subnet masks within the client's domain.

Similarly, if a transit has been assigned address space from a class A network number, it is likely that it was not assigned the entire class A, and that other transit domains will get address space from this class A. In this case, the transit would also have to inject routing information about the remainder of the class A into it's IGP. This is analogous to the situation above, with the same complications. For this reason, we recommend that the use of a class A for CIDR only be attempted if IGP's with variable length subnet mask support be used throughout the class A. Note that the IGP's need not support supernetting, as discussed above.

Note that the technique here could also apply to class B addresses. However, the limited number of available class B addresses and their usage for multihomed networks suggests that this address space should only be reserved for those large single organizations that warrant this type of address. [2]

7. Domain Service considerations

One aspect of Internet services which will be notably affected by a move to either "supernetted" class-C network numbers or subdivided class-A's will be the mechanism used for address-to-name translation: the IN-ADDR.ARPA zone of the domain system. Because this zone is delegated on octet boundaries only, any address allocation plan which uses bitmask-oriented addressing will cause some degree of difficulty for those which maintain parts of the IN-ADDR.ARPA zone.

7.1 Procedural changes for class-C "supernets"

At the present time, parts of the IN-ADDR.ARPA zone are delegated only on network boundaries which happen to fall on octet boundaries. To aid in the use of blocks of class-C networks, it is recommended that this policy be relaxed and allow the delegation of arbitrary, octet-oriented pieces of the IN-ADDR.ARPA zone.

As an example of this policy change, consider a hypothetical large network provider named "BigNet" which has been allocated the 1024 class-C networks 199.0.0 through 199.3.255. Under current policies, the root domain servers would need to have 1024 entries of the form:

```
        0.0.199.IN-ADDR.ARPA.   IN      NS      NS1.BIG.NET.

        1.0.199.IN-ADDR.ARPA.   IN      NS      NS1.BIG.NET.

                ....

        255.3.199.IN-ADDR.ARPA. IN      NS      NS1.BIG.NET.
```

By revising the policy as described above, this is reduced only four delegation records:

```
        0.199.IN-ADDR.ARPA.     IN      NS      NS1.BIG.NET.

        1.199.IN-ADDR.ARPA.     IN      NS      NS1.BIG.NET.

        2.199.IN-ADDR.ARPA.     IN      NS      NS1.BIG.NET.

        3.199.IN-ADDR.ARPA.     IN      NS      NS1.BIG.NET.
```

The provider would then maintain further delegations of naming authority for each individual class-C network which it assigns, rather than having each registered separately. Note that due to the way the DNS is designed, it is still possible for the root nameservers to maintain the delegation information for individual networks for which the provider is unwilling or unable to do so. This should greatly reduce the load on the domain servers for the "top" levels of the IN-ADDR.ARPA domain. The example above illustrates only the records for a single nameserver. In the normal case, there are usually several nameservers for each domain, thus the size of the examples will double or triple in the common cases.

7.2 Procedural changes for class-A subnetting

Should it be the case the class-A network numbers are subdivided into blocks allocated to transit network providers, it will be similarly necessary to relax the restriction on how IN-ADDR.ARPA naming works for them. As an example, take a provider is allocated the 19-bit portion of address space which matches 10.8.0.0 with mask 255.248.0.0. This represents all addresses which begin with the prefixes 10.8, 10.9, 10.10, 10.11, 10.12, 10.13, 10.14, an 10.15 and requires the following IN-ADDR.ARPA delegations:

```
        8.10.IN-ADDR.ARPA.       IN      NS      NS1.MOBY.NET.

        9.10.IN-ADDR.ARPA.       IN      NS      NS1.MOBY.NET.

                ....

        15.10.IN-ADDR.ARPA.      IN      NS      NS1.MOBY.NET.
```

To further illustrate how IN-ADDR.ARPA sub-delegation will work, consider a company named "FOO" connected to this provider which has been allocated the 14-bit piece of address space which matches 10.10.64.0 with mask 255.255.192.0. This represents all addresses in the range 10.10.64.0 through 10.10.127.255 and will require that the provider implement the following IN-ADDR.ARPA delegations:

```
        64.10.10.IN-ADDR.ARPA.  IN      NS      NS1.FOO.COM.

        65.10.10.IN-ADDR.ARPA.  IN      NS      NS1.FOO.COM.

                ....

        127.10.10.IN-ADDR.ARPA. IN      NS      NS1.FOO.COM.
```

with the servers for "FOO.COM" containing the individual PTR records for all of the addresses on each of these subnets.

8. Transitioning to a long term solution

This solution does not change the Internet routing and addressing architectures. Hence, transitioning to a more long term solution is not affected by the deployment of this plan.

9. Conclusions

We are all aware of the growth in routing complexity, and the rapid increase in allocation of network numbers. Given the rate at which this growth is being observed, we expect to run out in a few short years.

If the inter-domain routing protocol supports carrying network routes with associated masks, all of the major concerns demonstrated in this paper would be eliminated.

One of the influential factors which permits maximal exploitation of the advantages of this plan is the number of people who agree to use it.

If service providers start charging networks for advertising network numbers, this would be a very great incentive to share the address space, and hence the associated costs of advertising routes to service providers.

10. Recommendations

The NIC should begin to hand out large blocks of class C addresses to network service providers. Each block must fall on bit boundaries and should be large enough to serve the provider for two years. Further, the NIC should distribute very large blocks to continental and national network service organizations to allow additional levels of aggregation to take place at the major backbone networks. In addition, the NIC should modify its procedures for the IN-ADDR.ARPA domain to permit delegation along arbitrary octet boundaries.

Service providers will further allocate power-of-two blocks of class C addresses from their address space to their subscribers.

All organizations, including those which are multi-homed, should obtain address space from their provider (or one of their providers, in the case of the multi-homed). These blocks should also fall on bit boundaries to permit easy route aggregation.

To allow effective use of this new addressing plan to reduce propagated routing information, appropriate IETF WGs will specify the modifications needed to Inter-Domain routing protocols.

Implementation and deployment of these modifications should occur as quickly as possible.

11 References

[1] Moy, J, "The OSPF Specification Version 2", RFC 1247, Proteon, Inc., January 1991.

[2] Rekhter, Y., and T. Li, "An Architecture for IP Address Allocation with CIDR", RFC 1518, T.J. Watson Research Center, IBM Corp., cisco Systems, September 1993.

12. Security Considerations

Security issues are not discussed in this memo.

13. Authors' Addresses

Vince Fuller
BARRNet
Pine Hall 115
Stanford, CA, 94305-4122

EMail: vaf@Stanford.EDU

Tony Li
cisco Systems, Inc.
1525 O'Brien Drive
Menlo Park, CA 94025

EMail: tli@cisco.com

Jessica (Jie Yun) Yu
Merit Network, Inc.
1071 Beal Ave.
Ann Arbor, MI 48109

EMail: jyy@merit.edu

Kannan Varadhan
Internet Engineer, OARnet
1224, Kinnear Road,
Columbus, OH 43212

EMail: kannan@oar.net

Network Working Group
Request for Comments: 1886
Category: Standards Track

S. Thomson
Bellcore
C. Huitema
INRIA

December 1995

DNS Extensions to support IP version 6

Status of this Memo

This document specifies an Internet standards track protocol for the Internet community, and requests discussion and suggestions for improvements. Please refer to the current edition of the "Internet Official Protocol Standards" (STD 1) for the standardization state and status of this protocol. Distribution of this memo is unlimited.

Abstract

This document defines the changes that need to be made to the Domain Name System to support hosts running IP version 6 (IPv6). The changes include a new resource record type to store an IPv6 address, a new domain to support lookups based on an IPv6 address, and updated definitions of existing query types that return Internet addresses as part of additional section processing. The extensions are designed to be compatible with existing applications and, in particular, DNS implementations themselves.

1. INTRODUCTION

Current support for the storage of Internet addresses in the Domain Name System (DNS)[1,2] cannot easily be extended to support IPv6 addresses[3] since applications assume that address queries return 32-bit IPv4 addresses only.

To support the storage of IPv6 addresses we define the following extensions:

- o A new resource record type is defined to map a domain name to an IPv6 address.
- o A new domain is defined to support lookups based on address.
- o Existing queries that perform additional section processing to locate IPv4 addresses are redefined to perform additional section processing on both IPv4 and IPv6 addresses.

The changes are designed to be compatible with existing software. The existing support for IPv4 addresses is retained. Transition issues related to the co-existence of both IPv4 and IPv6 addresses in DNS are discussed in [4].

2. NEW RESOURCE RECORD DEFINITION AND DOMAIN

A new record type is defined to store a host's IPv6 address. A host that has more than one IPv6 address must have more than one such record.

2.1 AAAA record type

The AAAA resource record type is a new record specific to the Internet class that stores a single IPv6 address.

The value of the type is 28 (decimal).

2.2 AAAA data format

A 128 bit IPv6 address is encoded in the data portion of an AAAA resource record in network byte order (high-order byte first).

2.3 AAAA query

An AAAA query for a specified domain name in the Internet class returns all associated AAAA resource records in the answer section of a response.

A type AAAA query does not perform additional section processing.

2.4 Textual format of AAAA records

The textual representation of the data portion of the AAAA resource record used in a master database file is the textual representation of a IPv6 address as defined in [3].

2.5 IP6.INT Domain

A special domain is defined to look up a record given an address. The intent of this domain is to provide a way of mapping an IPv6 address to a host name, although it may be used for other purposes as well.

The domain is rooted at IP6.INT.

An IPv6 address is represented as a name in the IP6.INT domain by a sequence of nibbles separated by dots with the suffix ".IP6.INT". The sequence of nibbles is encoded in reverse order, i.e. the low-order nibble is encoded first, followed by the next low-order nibble and so on. Each nibble is represented by a hexadecimal digit. For example, the inverse lookup domain name corresponding to the address

    4321:0:1:2:3:4:567:89ab

would be

b.a.9.8.7.6.5.0.4.0.0.0.3.0.0.0.2.0.0.0.1.0.0.0.0.0.0.0.1.2.3.4.IP6.INT.

3. MODIFICATIONS TO EXISTING QUERY TYPES

All existing query types that perform type A additional section processing, i.e. name server (NS), mail exchange (MX) and mailbox (MB) query types, must be redefined to perform both type A and type AAAA additional section processing. These new definitions mean that a name server must add any relevant IPv4 addresses and any relevant

IPv6 addresses available locally to the additional section of a response when processing any one of the above queries.

4. SECURITY CONSIDERATIONS

Security issues are not discussed in this memo.

5. REFERENCES

[1] Mockapetris, P., "Domain Names - Concepts and Facilities", STD 13, RFC 1034, USC/Information Sciences Institute, November 1987.

[2] Mockapetris, P., "Domain Names - Implementation and Specification", STD 13, RFC 1035, USC/Information Sciences Institute, November 1987.

[3] Hinden, R., and S. Deering, Editors, "IP Version 6 Addressing Architecture", RFC 1884, Ipsilon Networks, Xerox PARC, December 1995.

[4] Gilligan, R., and E. Nordmark, "Transition Mechanisms for IPv6 Hosts and Routers", Work in Progress.

Authors' Addresses

Susan Thomson
Bellcore
MRE 2P343
445 South Street
Morristown, NJ 07960
U.S.A.

Phone: +1 201-829-4514
EMail: set@thumper.bellcore.com

Christian Huitema
INRIA, Sophia-Antipolis
2004 Route des Lucioles
BP 109
F-06561 Valbonne Cedex
France

Phone: +33 93 65 77 15
EMail: Christian.Huitema@MIRSA.INRIA.FR

RFC 2460 1

Network Working Group
Request for Comments: 2460
Obsoletes: 1883
Category: Standards Track

S. Deering
Cisco
R. Hinden
Nokia
December 1998

Internet Protocol, Version 6 (IPv6) Specification

Status of this Memo

This document specifies an Internet standards track protocol for the Internet community, and requests discussion and suggestions for improvements. Please refer to the current edition of the "Internet Official Protocol Standards" (STD 1) for the standardization state and status of this protocol. Distribution of this memo is unlimited.

Copyright Notice

Abstract

This document specifies version 6 of the Internet Protocol (IPv6), also sometimes referred to as IP Next Generation or IPng.

Table of Contents

1. Introduction

IP version 6 (IPv6) is a new version of the Internet Protocol, designed as the successor to IP version 4 (IPv4) [RFC-791]. The changes from IPv4 to IPv6 fall primarily into the following categories:

- o Expanded Addressing Capabilities

  IPv6 increases the IP address size from 32 bits to 128 bits, to support more levels of addressing hierarchy, a much greater number of addressable nodes, and simpler auto-configuration of addresses. The scalability of multicast routing is improved by adding a "scope" field to multicast addresses. And a new type of address called an "anycast address" is defined, used to send a packet to any one of a group of nodes.

- o Header Format Simplification

  Some IPv4 header fields have been dropped or made optional, to reduce the common-case processing cost of packet handling and to limit the bandwidth cost of the IPv6 header.

- o Improved Support for Extensions and Options

  Changes in the way IP header options are encoded allows for more efficient forwarding, less stringent limits on the length of options, and greater flexibility for introducing new options in the future.

- o Flow Labeling Capability

  A new capability is added to enable the labeling of packets belonging to particular traffic "flows" for which the sender requests special handling, such as non-default quality of service or "real-time" service.

o Authentication and Privacy Capabilities

Extensions to support authentication, data integrity, and (optional) data confidentiality are specified for IPv6.

This document specifies the basic IPv6 header and the initially-defined IPv6 extension headers and options. It also discusses packet size issues, the semantics of flow labels and traffic classes, and the effects of IPv6 on upper-layer protocols. The format and semantics of IPv6 addresses are specified separately in [ADDRARCH]. The IPv6 version of ICMP, which all IPv6 implementations are required to include, is specified in [ICMPv6].

2. Terminology

node - a device that implements IPv6.

router - a node that forwards IPv6 packets not explicitly addressed to itself. [See Note below].

host - any node that is not a router. [See Note below].

upper layer - a protocol layer immediately above IPv6. Examples are transport protocols such as TCP and UDP, control protocols such as ICMP, routing protocols such as OSPF, and internet or lower-layer protocols being "tunneled" over (i.e., encapsulated in) IPv6 such as IPX, AppleTalk, or IPv6 itself.

link - a communication facility or medium over which nodes can communicate at the link layer, i.e., the layer immediately below IPv6. Examples are Ethernets (simple or bridged); PPP links; X.25, Frame Relay, or ATM networks; and internet (or higher) layer "tunnels", such as tunnels over IPv4 or IPv6 itself.

neighbors - nodes attached to the same link.

interface - a node's attachment to a link.

address - an IPv6-layer identifier for an interface or a set of interfaces.

packet - an IPv6 header plus payload.

link MTU - the maximum transmission unit, i.e., maximum packet size in octets, that can be conveyed over a link.

path MTU - the minimum link MTU of all the links in a path between a source node and a destination node.

Note: it is possible, though unusual, for a device with multiple interfaces to be configured to forward non-self-destined packets arriving from some set (fewer than all) of its interfaces, and to discard non-self-destined packets arriving from its other interfaces. Such a device must obey the protocol requirements for routers when receiving packets from, and interacting with neighbors over, the former (forwarding) interfaces. It must obey the protocol requirements for hosts when receiving packets from, and interacting with neighbors over, the latter (non-forwarding) interfaces.

3. IPv6 Header Format

```
+-+-+-+-+-+-+-+-+-+-+-+-+-+-+-+-+-+-+-+-+-+-+-+-+-+-+-+-+-+-+-+-+
|Version| Traffic Class |           Flow Label                  |
+-+-+-+-+-+-+-+-+-+-+-+-+-+-+-+-+-+-+-+-+-+-+-+-+-+-+-+-+-+-+-+-+
|         Payload Length        |  Next Header  |   Hop Limit   |
+-+-+-+-+-+-+-+-+-+-+-+-+-+-+-+-+-+-+-+-+-+-+-+-+-+-+-+-+-+-+-+-+
|                                                               |
+                                                               +
|                                                               |
+                         Source Address                        +
|                                                               |
+                                                               +
|                                                               |
+-+-+-+-+-+-+-+-+-+-+-+-+-+-+-+-+-+-+-+-+-+-+-+-+-+-+-+-+-+-+-+-+
|                                                               |
+                                                               +
|                                                               |
+                      Destination Address                      +
|                                                               |
+                                                               +
|                                                               |
+-+-+-+-+-+-+-+-+-+-+-+-+-+-+-+-+-+-+-+-+-+-+-+-+-+-+-+-+-+-+-+-+
```

Version 4-bit Internet Protocol version number = 6.

Traffic Class 8-bit traffic class field. See section 7.

Flow Label 20-bit flow label. See section 6.

Payload Length 16-bit unsigned integer. Length of the IPv6 payload, i.e., the rest of the packet following this IPv6 header, in octets. (Note that any extension headers [section 4] present are considered part of the payload, i.e., included in the length count.)

Next Header	8-bit selector. Identifies the type of header immediately following the IPv6 header. Uses the same values as the IPv4 Protocol field [RFC-1700 et seq.].
Hop Limit	8-bit unsigned integer. Decremented by 1 by each node that forwards the packet. The packet is discarded if Hop Limit is decremented to zero.
Source Address	128-bit address of the originator of the packet. See [ADDRARCH].
Destination Address	128-bit address of the intended recipient of the packet (possibly not the ultimate recipient, if a Routing header is present). See [ADDRARCH] and section 4.4.

4. IPv6 Extension Headers

In IPv6, optional internet-layer information is encoded in separate headers that may be placed between the IPv6 header and the upper-layer header in a packet. There are a small number of such extension headers, each identified by a distinct Next Header value. As illustrated in these examples, an IPv6 packet may carry zero, one, or more extension headers, each identified by the Next Header field of the preceding header:

```
+---------------+------------------------
|  IPv6 header  | TCP header + data
|               |
| Next Header = |
|      TCP      |
+---------------+------------------------

+---------------+----------------+------------------------
|  IPv6 header  | Routing header | TCP header + data
|               |                |
| Next Header = |  Next Header = |
|    Routing    |      TCP       |
+---------------+----------------+------------------------

+---------------+----------------+-----------------+-----------------
|  IPv6 header  | Routing header | Fragment header | fragment of TCP
|               |                |                 |  header + data
| Next Header = |  Next Header = |  Next Header =  |
|    Routing    |    Fragment    |       TCP       |
+---------------+----------------+-----------------+-----------------
```

With one exception, extension headers are not examined or processed by any node along a packet's delivery path, until the packet reaches the node (or each of the set of nodes, in the case of multicast) identified in the Destination Address field of the IPv6 header. There, normal demultiplexing on the Next Header field of the IPv6 header invokes the module to process the first extension header, or the upper-layer header if no extension header is present. The contents and semantics of each extension header determine whether or not to proceed to the next header. Therefore, extension headers must be processed strictly in the order they appear in the packet; a receiver must not, for example, scan through a packet looking for a particular kind of extension header and process that header prior to processing all preceding ones.

The exception referred to in the preceding paragraph is the Hop-by-Hop Options header, which carries information that must be examined and processed by every node along a packet's delivery path, including the source and destination nodes. The Hop-by-Hop Options header, when present, must immediately follow the IPv6 header. Its presence is indicated by the value zero in the Next Header field of the IPv6 header.

If, as a result of processing a header, a node is required to proceed to the next header but the Next Header value in the current header is unrecognized by the node, it should discard the packet and send an ICMP Parameter Problem message to the source of the packet, with an ICMP Code value of 1 ("unrecognized Next Header type encountered") and the ICMP Pointer field containing the offset of the unrecognized value within the original packet. The same action should be taken if a node encounters a Next Header value of zero in any header other than an IPv6 header.

Each extension header is an integer multiple of 8 octets long, in order to retain 8-octet alignment for subsequent headers. Multi-octet fields within each extension header are aligned on their natural boundaries, i.e., fields of width n octets are placed at an integer multiple of n octets from the start of the header, for n = 1, 2, 4, or 8.

A full implementation of IPv6 includes implementation of the following extension headers:

```
Hop-by-Hop Options
Routing (Type 0)
Fragment
Destination Options
Authentication
Encapsulating Security Payload
```

The first four are specified in this document; the last two are specified in [RFC-2402] and [RFC-2406], respectively.

4.1 Extension Header Order

When more than one extension header is used in the same packet, it is recommended that those headers appear in the following order:

```
IPv6 header
Hop-by-Hop Options header
Destination Options header (note 1)
Routing header
Fragment header
```

Authentication header (note 2)
Encapsulating Security Payload header (note 2)
Destination Options header (note 3)
upper-layer header

note 1: for options to be processed by the first destination that appears in the IPv6 Destination Address field plus subsequent destinations listed in the Routing header.

note 2: additional recommendations regarding the relative order of the Authentication and Encapsulating Security Payload headers are given in [RFC-2406].

note 3: for options to be processed only by the final destination of the packet.

Each extension header should occur at most once, except for the Destination Options header which should occur at most twice (once before a Routing header and once before the upper-layer header).

If the upper-layer header is another IPv6 header (in the case of IPv6 being tunneled over or encapsulated in IPv6), it may be followed by its own extension headers, which are separately subject to the same ordering recommendations.

If and when other extension headers are defined, their ordering constraints relative to the above listed headers must be specified.

IPv6 nodes must accept and attempt to process extension headers in any order and occurring any number of times in the same packet, except for the Hop-by-Hop Options header which is restricted to appear immediately after an IPv6 header only. Nonetheless, it is strongly advised that sources of IPv6 packets adhere to the above recommended order until and unless subsequent specifications revise that recommendation.

4.2 Options

Two of the currently-defined extension headers – the Hop-by-Hop Options header and the Destination Options header – carry a variable number of type-length-value (TLV) encoded "options", of the following format:

```
+-+-+-+-+-+-+-+-+-+-+-+-+-+-+-+-+- - - - - - - - -
|  Option Type  |  Opt Data Len |  Option Data
+-+-+-+-+-+-+-+-+-+-+-+-+-+-+-+-+- - - - - - - - -
```

Option Type — 8-bit identifier of the type of option.

Opt Data Len — 8-bit unsigned integer. Length of the Option Data field of this option, in octets.

Option Data — Variable-length field. Option-Type-specific data.

The sequence of options within a header must be processed strictly in the order they appear in the header; a receiver must not, for example, scan through the header looking for a particular kind of option and process that option prior to processing all preceding ones.

The Option Type identifiers are internally encoded such that their highest-order two bits specify the action that must be taken if the processing IPv6 node does not recognize the Option Type:

00 - skip over this option and continue processing the header.

01 - discard the packet.

10 - discard the packet and, regardless of whether or not the packet's Destination Address was a multicast address, send an ICMP Parameter Problem, Code 2, message to the packet's Source Address, pointing to the unrecognized Option Type.

11 - discard the packet and, only if the packet's Destination Address was not a multicast address, send an ICMP Parameter Problem, Code 2, message to the packet's Source Address, pointing to the unrecognized Option Type.

The third-highest-order bit of the Option Type specifies whether or not the Option Data of that option can change en-route to the packet's final destination. When an Authentication header is present in the packet, for any option whose data may change en-route, its entire Option Data field must be treated as zero-valued octets when computing or verifying the packet's authenticating value.

0 - Option Data does not change en-route

1 - Option Data may change en-route

The three high-order bits described above are to be treated as part of the Option Type, not independent of the Option Type. That is, a particular option is identified by a full 8-bit Option Type, not just the low-order 5 bits of an Option Type.

The same Option Type numbering space is used for both the Hop-by-Hop Options header and the Destination Options header. However, the specification of a particular option may restrict its use to only one of those two headers.

Individual options may have specific alignment requirements, to ensure that multi-octet values within Option Data fields fall on natural boundaries. The alignment requirement of an option is specified using the notation xn+y, meaning the Option Type must appear at an integer multiple of x octets from the start of the header, plus y octets. For example:

```
2n    means any 2-octet offset from the start of the header.
8n+2  means any 8-octet offset from the start of the header,
      plus 2 octets.
```

There are two padding options which are used when necessary to align subsequent options and to pad out the containing header to a multiple of 8 octets in length. These padding options must be recognized by all IPv6 implementations:

Pad1 option (alignment requirement: none)

```
+-+-+-+-+-+-+-+-+
|       0       |
+-+-+-+-+-+-+-+-+
```

NOTE! the format of the Pad1 option is a special case – it does not have length and value fields.

The Pad1 option is used to insert one octet of padding into the Options area of a header. If more than one octet of padding is required, the PadN option, described next, should be used, rather than multiple Pad1 options.

PadN option (alignment requirement: none)

```
+-+-+-+-+-+-+-+-+-+-+-+-+-+-+-+-+- - - - - - - - -
|       1       |  Opt Data Len |  Option Data
+-+-+-+-+-+-+-+-+-+-+-+-+-+-+-+-+- - - - - - - - -
```

The PadN option is used to insert two or more octets of padding into the Options area of a header. For N octets of padding, the Opt Data Len field contains the value N-2, and the Option Data consists of N-2 zero-valued octets.

Appendix B contains formatting guidelines for designing new options.

4.3 Hop-by-Hop Options Header

The Hop-by-Hop Options header is used to carry optional information that must be examined by every node along a packet's delivery path. The Hop-by-Hop Options header is identified by a Next Header value of 0 in the IPv6 header, and has the following format:

```
+-+-+-+-+-+-+-+-+-+-+-+-+-+-+-+-+-+-+-+-+-+-+-+-+-+-+-+-+-+-+-+-+
|  Next Header  |  Hdr Ext Len  |                               |
+-+-+-+-+-+-+-+-+-+-+-+-+-+-+-+-+                               +
|                                                               |
.                                                               .
.                            Options                            .
.                                                               .
|                                                               |
+-+-+-+-+-+-+-+-+-+-+-+-+-+-+-+-+-+-+-+-+-+-+-+-+-+-+-+-+-+-+-+-+
```

Next Header — 8-bit selector. Identifies the type of header immediately following the Hop-by-Hop Options header. Uses the same values as the IPv4 Protocol field [RFC-1700 et seq.].

Hdr Ext Len — 8-bit unsigned integer. Length of the Hop-by-Hop Options header in 8-octet units, not including the first 8 octets.

Options — Variable-length field, of length such that the complete Hop-by-Hop Options header is an integer multiple of 8 octets long. Contains one or more TLV-encoded options, as described in section 4.2.

The only hop-by-hop options defined in this document are the Pad1 and PadN options specified in section 4.2.

4.4 Routing Header

The Routing header is used by an IPv6 source to list one or more intermediate nodes to be "visited" on the way to a packet's destination. This function is very similar to IPv4's Loose Source and Record Route option. The Routing header is identified by a Next Header value of 43 in the immediately preceding header, and has the following format:

```
+-+-+-+-+-+-+-+-+-+-+-+-+-+-+-+-+-+-+-+-+-+-+-+-+-+-+-+-+-+-+-+-+
|  Next Header  |  Hdr Ext Len  |  Routing Type | Segments Left |
+-+-+-+-+-+-+-+-+-+-+-+-+-+-+-+-+-+-+-+-+-+-+-+-+-+-+-+-+-+-+-+-+
|                                                               |
.                                                               .
.                       type-specific data                      .
.                                                               .
|                                                               |
+-+-+-+-+-+-+-+-+-+-+-+-+-+-+-+-+-+-+-+-+-+-+-+-+-+-+-+-+-+-+-+-+
```

Next Header — 8-bit selector. Identifies the type of header immediately following the Routing header. Uses the same values as the IPv4 Protocol field [RFC-1700 et seq.].

Hdr Ext Len — 8-bit unsigned integer. Length of the Routing header in 8-octet units, not including the first 8 octets.

Routing Type — 8-bit identifier of a particular Routing header variant.

Segments Left — 8-bit unsigned integer. Number of route segments remaining, i.e., number of explicitly listed intermediate nodes still to be visited before reaching the final destination.

type-specific data — Variable-length field, of format determined by the Routing Type, and of length such that the complete Routing header is an integer multiple of 8 octets long.

If, while processing a received packet, a node encounters a Routing header with an unrecognized Routing Type value, the required behavior of the node depends on the value of the Segments Left field, as follows:

If Segments Left is zero, the node must ignore the Routing header and proceed to process the next header in the packet, whose type is identified by the Next Header field in the Routing header.

If Segments Left is non-zero, the node must discard the packet and send an ICMP Parameter Problem, Code 0, message to the packet's Source Address, pointing to the unrecognized Routing Type.

If, after processing a Routing header of a received packet, an intermediate node determines that the packet is to be forwarded onto a link whose link MTU is less than the size of the packet, the node must discard the packet and send an ICMP Packet Too Big message to the packet's Source Address.

The Type 0 Routing header has the following format:

```
+-+-+-+-+-+-+-+-+-+-+-+-+-+-+-+-+-+-+-+-+-+-+-+-+-+-+-+-+-+-+-+-+
|  Next Header  |  Hdr Ext Len  | Routing Type=0| Segments Left |
+-+-+-+-+-+-+-+-+-+-+-+-+-+-+-+-+-+-+-+-+-+-+-+-+-+-+-+-+-+-+-+-+
|                            Reserved                           |
+-+-+-+-+-+-+-+-+-+-+-+-+-+-+-+-+-+-+-+-+-+-+-+-+-+-+-+-+-+-+-+-+
|                                                               |
+                                                               +
|                                                               |
+                           Address[1]                          +
|                                                               |
+                                                               +
|                                                               |
+-+-+-+-+-+-+-+-+-+-+-+-+-+-+-+-+-+-+-+-+-+-+-+-+-+-+-+-+-+-+-+-+
|                                                               |
+                                                               +
|                                                               |
+                           Address[2]                          +
|                                                               |
+                                                               +
|                                                               |
+-+-+-+-+-+-+-+-+-+-+-+-+-+-+-+-+-+-+-+-+-+-+-+-+-+-+-+-+-+-+-+-+
.                               .                               .
.                               .                               .
.                               .                               .
+-+-+-+-+-+-+-+-+-+-+-+-+-+-+-+-+-+-+-+-+-+-+-+-+-+-+-+-+-+-+-+-+
|                                                               |
+                                                               +
|                                                               |
+                           Address[n]                          +
|                                                               |
+                                                               +
|                                                               |
+-+-+-+-+-+-+-+-+-+-+-+-+-+-+-+-+-+-+-+-+-+-+-+-+-+-+-+-+-+-+-+-+
```

Next Header — 8-bit selector. Identifies the type of header immediately following the Routing header. Uses the same values as the IPv4 Protocol field [RFC-1700 et seq.].

Hdr Ext Len — 8-bit unsigned integer. Length of the Routing header in 8-octet units, not including the first 8 octets. For the Type 0 Routing header, Hdr Ext Len is equal to two times the number of addresses in the header.

Routing Type — 0.

Segments Left	8-bit unsigned integer. Number of route segments remaining, i.e., number of explicitly listed intermediate nodes still to be visited before reaching the final destination.
Reserved	32-bit reserved field. Initialized to zero for transmission; ignored on reception.
Address[1..n]	Vector of 128-bit addresses, numbered 1 to n.

Multicast addresses must not appear in a Routing header of Type 0, or in the IPv6 Destination Address field of a packet carrying a Routing header of Type 0.

A Routing header is not examined or processed until it reaches the node identified in the Destination Address field of the IPv6 header. In that node, dispatching on the Next Header field of the immediately preceding header causes the Routing header module to be invoked, which, in the case of Routing Type 0, performs the following algorithm:

```
if Segments Left = 0 {
   proceed to process the next header in the packet, whose type is
   identified by the Next Header field in the Routing header
}
else if Hdr Ext Len is odd {
      send an ICMP Parameter Problem, Code 0, message to the Source
      Address, pointing to the Hdr Ext Len field, and discard the
      packet
}
else {
   compute n, the number of addresses in the Routing header, by
   dividing Hdr Ext Len by 2

   if Segments Left is greater than n {
      send an ICMP Parameter Problem, Code 0, message to the Source
      Address, pointing to the Segments Left field, and discard the
      packet
   }
   else {
      decrement Segments Left by 1;
      compute i, the index of the next address to be visited in
      the address vector, by subtracting Segments Left from n

      if Address [i] or the IPv6 Destination Address is multicast {
         discard the packet
      }
      else {
         swap the IPv6 Destination Address and Address[i]
         if the IPv6 Hop Limit is less than or equal to 1 {
            send an ICMP Time Exceeded — Hop Limit Exceeded in
            Transit message to the Source Address and discard the
            packet
         }
         else {
            decrement the Hop Limit by 1

            resubmit the packet to the IPv6 module for transmission
            to the new destination
         }
      }
   }
}
```

As an example of the effects of the above algorithm, consider the case of a source node S sending a packet to destination node D, using a Routing header to cause the packet to be routed via intermediate nodes I1, I2, and I3. The values of the relevant IPv6 header and Routing header fields on each segment of the delivery path would be as follows:

As the packet travels from S to I1:

```
     Source Address = S                  Hdr Ext Len = 6
     Destination Address = I1            Segments Left = 3
                                         Address[1] = I2
                                         Address[2] = I3
                                         Address[3] = D
```

As the packet travels from I1 to I2:

```
     Source Address = S                  Hdr Ext Len = 6
     Destination Address = I2            Segments Left = 2
                                         Address[1] = I1
                                         Address[2] = I3
                                         Address[3] = D
```

As the packet travels from I2 to I3:

```
     Source Address = S                  Hdr Ext Len = 6
     Destination Address = I3            Segments Left = 1
                                         Address[1] = I1
                                         Address[2] = I2
                                         Address[3] = D
```

As the packet travels from I3 to D:

```
     Source Address = S                  Hdr Ext Len = 6
     Destination Address = D             Segments Left = 0
                                         Address[1] = I1
                                         Address[2] = I2
                                         Address[3] = I3
```

4.5 Fragment Header

The Fragment header is used by an IPv6 source to send a packet larger than would fit in the path MTU to its destination. (Note: unlike IPv4, fragmentation in IPv6 is performed only by source nodes, not by routers along a packet's delivery path - see section 5.) The Fragment header is identified by a Next Header value of 44 in the immediately preceding header, and has the following format:

```
+-+-+-+-+-+-+-+-+-+-+-+-+-+-+-+-+-+-+-+-+-+-+-+-+-+-+-+-+-+-+-+-+
|  Next Header  |   Reserved    |      Fragment Offset    |Res|M|
+-+-+-+-+-+-+-+-+-+-+-+-+-+-+-+-+-+-+-+-+-+-+-+-+-+-+-+-+-+-+-+-+
|                         Identification                        |
+-+-+-+-+-+-+-+-+-+-+-+-+-+-+-+-+-+-+-+-+-+-+-+-+-+-+-+-+-+-+-+-+
```

Next Header — 8-bit selector. Identifies the initial header type of the Fragmentable Part of the original packet (defined below). Uses the same values as the IPv4 Protocol field [RFC-1700 et seq.].

Reserved — 8-bit reserved field. Initialized to zero for transmission; ignored on reception.

Fragment Offset — 13-bit unsigned integer. The offset, in 8-octet units, of the data following this header, relative to the start of the Fragmentable Part of the original packet.

Res — 2-bit reserved field. Initialized to zero for transmission; ignored on reception.

M flag — 1 = more fragments; 0 = last fragment.

Identification — 32 bits. See description below.

In order to send a packet that is too large to fit in the MTU of the path to its destination, a source node may divide the packet into fragments and send each fragment as a separate packet, to be reassembled at the receiver.

For every packet that is to be fragmented, the source node generates an Identification value. The Identification must be different than that of any other fragmented packet sent recently* with the same Source Address and Destination Address. If a Routing header is present, the Destination Address of concern is that of the final destination.

* "recently" means within the maximum likely lifetime of a packet, including transit time from source to destination and time spent awaiting reassembly with other fragments of the same packet. However, it is not required that a source node know the maximum packet lifetime. Rather, it is assumed that the requirement can be met by maintaining the Identification value as a simple, 32-bit, "wrap-around" counter, incremented each time a packet must be fragmented. It is an implementation choice whether to maintain a single counter for the node or multiple counters, e.g., one for each of the node's possible source addresses, or one for each active (source address, destination address) combination.

The initial, large, unfragmented packet is referred to as the "original packet", and it is considered to consist of two parts, as illustrated:

original packet:

```
+------------------+----------------------//-----------------------+
|  Unfragmentable  |                Fragmentable                   |
|       Part       |                    Part                       |
+------------------+----------------------//-----------------------+
```

The Unfragmentable Part consists of the IPv6 header plus any extension headers that must be processed by nodes en route to the destination, that is, all headers up to and including the Routing header if present, else the Hop-by-Hop Options header if present, else no extension headers.

The Fragmentable Part consists of the rest of the packet, that is, any extension headers that need be processed only by the final destination node(s), plus the upper-layer header and data.

The Fragmentable Part of the original packet is divided into fragments, each, except possibly the last ("rightmost") one, being an integer multiple of 8 octets long. The fragments are transmitted in separate "fragment packets" as illustrated:

original packet:

```
+------------------+--------------+--------------+--//--+----------+
|  Unfragmentable  |    first     |    second    |      |   last   |
|       Part       |   fragment   |   fragment   | .... | fragment |
+------------------+--------------+--------------+--//--+----------+
```

fragment packets:

```
+------------------+--------+--------------+
|  Unfragmentable  |Fragment|    first     |
|       Part       | Header |   fragment   |
+------------------+--------+--------------+

+------------------+--------+--------------+
|  Unfragmentable  |Fragment|    second    |
|       Part       | Header |   fragment   |
+------------------+--------+--------------+
                      o
                      o
                      o
+------------------+--------+----------+
|  Unfragmentable  |Fragment|   last   |
|       Part       | Header | fragment |
+------------------+--------+----------+
```

Each fragment packet is composed of:

(1) The Unfragmentable Part of the original packet, with the Payload Length of the original IPv6 header changed to contain the length of this fragment packet only (excluding the length of the IPv6 header itself), and the Next Header field of the last header of the Unfragmentable Part changed to 44.

(2) A Fragment header containing:

The Next Header value that identifies the first header of the Fragmentable Part of the original packet.

A Fragment Offset containing the offset of the fragment, in 8-octet units, relative to the start of the Fragmentable Part of the original packet. The Fragment Offset of the first ("leftmost") fragment is 0.

An M flag value of 0 if the fragment is the last ("rightmost") one, else an M flag value of 1.

The Identification value generated for the original packet.

(3) The fragment itself.

The lengths of the fragments must be chosen such that the resulting fragment packets fit within the MTU of the path to the packets' destination(s).

At the destination, fragment packets are reassembled into their original, unfragmented form, as illustrated:

reassembled original packet:

```
+------------------+---------------------//-----------------------+
|  Unfragmentable  |                 Fragmentable                  |
|       Part       |                     Part                      |
+------------------+---------------------//-----------------------+
```

The following rules govern reassembly:

An original packet is reassembled only from fragment packets that have the same Source Address, Destination Address, and Fragment Identification.

The Unfragmentable Part of the reassembled packet consists of all headers up to, but not including, the Fragment header of the first fragment packet (that is, the packet whose Fragment Offset is zero), with the following two changes:

The Next Header field of the last header of the Unfragmentable Part is obtained from the Next Header field of the first fragment's Fragment header.

The Payload Length of the reassembled packet is computed from the length of the Unfragmentable Part and the length and offset of the last fragment. For example, a formula for computing the Payload Length of the reassembled original packet is:

```
PL.orig = PL.first - FL.first - 8 + (8 * FO.last) + FL.last

where
PL.orig  = Payload Length field of reassembled packet.
PL.first = Payload Length field of first fragment packet.
FL.first = length of fragment following Fragment header of
           first fragment packet.
FO.last  = Fragment Offset field of Fragment header of
           last fragment packet.
FL.last  = length of fragment following Fragment header of
           last fragment packet.
```

The Fragmentable Part of the reassembled packet is constructed from the fragments following the Fragment headers in each of the fragment packets. The length of each fragment is computed by subtracting from the packet's Payload Length the length of the headers between the IPv6 header and fragment itself; its relative position in Fragmentable Part is computed from its Fragment Offset value.

The Fragment header is not present in the final, reassembled packet.

The following error conditions may arise when reassembling fragmented packets:

If insufficient fragments are received to complete reassembly of a packet within 60 seconds of the reception of the first-arriving fragment of that packet, reassembly of that packet must be abandoned and all the fragments that have been received for that packet must be discarded. If the first fragment (i.e., the one with a Fragment Offset of zero) has been received, an ICMP Time Exceeded -- Fragment Reassembly Time Exceeded message should be sent to the source of that fragment.

If the length of a fragment, as derived from the fragment packet's Payload Length field, is not a multiple of 8 octets and the M flag of that fragment is 1, then that fragment must be discarded and an ICMP Parameter Problem, Code 0, message should be sent to the source of the fragment, pointing to the Payload Length field of the fragment packet.

If the length and offset of a fragment are such that the Payload Length of the packet reassembled from that fragment would exceed 65,535 octets, then that fragment must be discarded and an ICMP Parameter Problem, Code 0, message should be sent to the source of the fragment, pointing to the Fragment Offset field of the fragment packet.

The following conditions are not expected to occur, but are not considered errors if they do:

The number and content of the headers preceding the Fragment header of different fragments of the same original packet may differ. Whatever headers are present, preceding the Fragment header in each fragment packet, are processed when the packets arrive, prior to queueing the fragments for reassembly. Only those headers in the Offset zero fragment packet are retained in the reassembled packet.

The Next Header values in the Fragment headers of different fragments of the same original packet may differ. Only the value from the Offset zero fragment packet is used for reassembly.

4.6 Destination Options Header

The Destination Options header is used to carry optional information that need be examined only by a packet's destination node(s). The Destination Options header is identified by a Next Header value of 60 in the immediately preceding header, and has the following format:

```
+-+-+-+-+-+-+-+-+-+-+-+-+-+-+-+-+-+-+-+-+-+-+-+-+-+-+-+-+-+-+-+-+
|  Next Header  |  Hdr Ext Len  |                               |
+-+-+-+-+-+-+-+-+-+-+-+-+-+-+-+-+                               +
|                                                               |
.                                                               .
.                            Options                            .
.                                                               .
|                                                               |
+-+-+-+-+-+-+-+-+-+-+-+-+-+-+-+-+-+-+-+-+-+-+-+-+-+-+-+-+-+-+-+-+
```

Next Header — 8-bit selector. Identifies the type of header immediately following the Destination Options header. Uses the same values as the IPv4 Protocol field [RFC-1700 et seq.].

Hdr Ext Len — 8-bit unsigned integer. Length of the Destination Options header in 8-octet units, not including the first 8 octets.

Options — Variable-length field, of length such that the complete Destination Options header is an integer multiple of 8 octets long. Contains one or more TLV-encoded options, as described in section 4.2.

The only destination options defined in this document are the Pad1 and PadN options specified in section 4.2.

Note that there are two possible ways to encode optional destination information in an IPv6 packet: either as an option in the Destination Options header, or as a separate extension header. The Fragment header and the Authentication header are examples of the latter approach. Which approach can be used depends on what action is desired of a destination node that does not understand the optional information:

- o If the desired action is for the destination node to discard the packet and, only if the packet's Destination Address is not a multicast address, send an ICMP Unrecognized Type message to the packet's Source Address, then the information may be encoded either as a separate header or as an option in the

Destination Options header whose Option Type has the value 11 in its highest-order two bits. The choice may depend on such factors as which takes fewer octets, or which yields better alignment or more efficient parsing.

- o If any other action is desired, the information must be encoded as an option in the Destination Options header whose Option Type has the value 00, 01, or 10 in its highest-order two bits, specifying the desired action (see section 4.2).

4.7 No Next Header

The value 59 in the Next Header field of an IPv6 header or any extension header indicates that there is nothing following that header. If the Payload Length field of the IPv6 header indicates the presence of octets past the end of a header whose Next Header field contains 59, those octets must be ignored, and passed on unchanged if the packet is forwarded.

5. Packet Size Issues

IPv6 requires that every link in the internet have an MTU of 1280 octets or greater. On any link that cannot convey a 1280-octet packet in one piece, link-specific fragmentation and reassembly must be provided at a layer below IPv6.

Links that have a configurable MTU (for example, PPP links [RFC-1661]) must be configured to have an MTU of at least 1280 octets; it is recommended that they be configured with an MTU of 1500 octets or greater, to accommodate possible encapsulations (i.e., tunneling) without incurring IPv6-layer fragmentation.

From each link to which a node is directly attached, the node must be able to accept packets as large as that link's MTU.

It is strongly recommended that IPv6 nodes implement Path MTU Discovery [RFC-1981], in order to discover and take advantage of path MTUs greater than 1280 octets. However, a minimal IPv6 implementation (e.g., in a boot ROM) may simply restrict itself to sending packets no larger than 1280 octets, and omit implementation of Path MTU Discovery.

In order to send a packet larger than a path's MTU, a node may use the IPv6 Fragment header to fragment the packet at the source and have it reassembled at the destination(s). However, the use of such fragmentation is discouraged in any application that is able to adjust its packets to fit the measured path MTU (i.e., down to 1280 octets).

A node must be able to accept a fragmented packet that, after reassembly, is as large as 1500 octets. A node is permitted to accept fragmented packets that reassemble to more than 1500 octets. An upper-layer protocol or application that depends on IPv6 fragmentation to send packets larger than the MTU of a path should not send packets larger than 1500 octets unless it has assurance that the destination is capable of reassembling packets of that larger size.

In response to an IPv6 packet that is sent to an IPv4 destination (i.e., a packet that undergoes translation from IPv6 to IPv4), the originating IPv6 node may receive an ICMP Packet Too Big message reporting a Next-Hop MTU less than 1280. In that case, the IPv6 node is not required to reduce the size of subsequent packets to less than 1280, but must include a Fragment header in those packets so that the IPv6-to-IPv4 translating router can obtain a suitable Identification value to use in resulting IPv4 fragments. Note that this means the payload may have to be reduced to 1232 octets (1280 minus 40 for the IPv6 header and 8 for the Fragment header), and smaller still if additional extension headers are used.

6. Flow Labels

The 20-bit Flow Label field in the IPv6 header may be used by a source to label sequences of packets for which it requests special handling by the IPv6 routers, such as non-default quality of service or "real-time" service. This aspect of IPv6 is, at the time of writing, still experimental and subject to change as the requirements for flow support in the Internet become clearer. Hosts or routers that do not support the functions of the Flow Label field are required to set the field to zero when originating a packet, pass the field on unchanged when forwarding a packet, and ignore the field when receiving a packet.

Appendix A describes the current intended semantics and usage of the Flow Label field.

7. Traffic Classes

The 8-bit Traffic Class field in the IPv6 header is available for use by originating nodes and/or forwarding routers to identify and distinguish between different classes or priorities of IPv6 packets.

At the point in time at which this specification is being written, there are a number of experiments underway in the use of the IPv4 Type of Service and/or Precedence bits to provide various forms of "differentiated service" for IP packets, other than through the use of explicit flow set-up. The Traffic Class field in the IPv6 header is intended to allow similar functionality to be supported in IPv6.

It is hoped that those experiments will eventually lead to agreement on what sorts of traffic classifications are most useful for IP packets. Detailed definitions of the syntax and semantics of all or some of the IPv6 Traffic Class bits, whether experimental or intended for eventual standardization, are to be provided in separate documents.

The following general requirements apply to the Traffic Class field:

- o The service interface to the IPv6 service within a node must provide a means for an upper-layer protocol to supply the value of the Traffic Class bits in packets originated by that upper-layer protocol. The default value must be zero for all 8 bits.

- o Nodes that support a specific (experimental or eventual standard) use of some or all of the Traffic Class bits are permitted to change the value of those bits in packets that they originate, forward, or receive, as required for that specific use. Nodes should ignore and leave unchanged any bits of the Traffic Class field for which they do not support a specific use.

- o An upper-layer protocol must not assume that the value of the Traffic Class bits in a received packet are the same as the value sent by the packet's source.

8. Upper-Layer Protocol Issues

8.1 Upper-Layer Checksums

Any transport or other upper-layer protocol that includes the addresses from the IP header in its checksum computation must be modified for use over IPv6, to include the 128-bit IPv6 addresses instead of 32-bit IPv4 addresses. In particular, the following illustration shows the TCP and UDP "pseudo-header" for IPv6:

```
+-+-+-+-+-+-+-+-+-+-+-+-+-+-+-+-+-+-+-+-+-+-+-+-+-+-+-+-+-+-+-+-+
|                                                               |
+                                                               +
|                                                               |
+                         Source Address                        +
|                                                               |
+                                                               +
|                                                               |
+-+-+-+-+-+-+-+-+-+-+-+-+-+-+-+-+-+-+-+-+-+-+-+-+-+-+-+-+-+-+-+-+
|                                                               |
+                                                               +
|                                                               |
+                      Destination Address                      +
|                                                               |
+                                                               +
|                                                               |
+-+-+-+-+-+-+-+-+-+-+-+-+-+-+-+-+-+-+-+-+-+-+-+-+-+-+-+-+-+-+-+-+
|                   Upper-Layer Packet Length                   |
+-+-+-+-+-+-+-+-+-+-+-+-+-+-+-+-+-+-+-+-+-+-+-+-+-+-+-+-+-+-+-+-+
|                      zero                     |  Next Header  |
+-+-+-+-+-+-+-+-+-+-+-+-+-+-+-+-+-+-+-+-+-+-+-+-+-+-+-+-+-+-+-+-+
```

- o If the IPv6 packet contains a Routing header, the Destination Address used in the pseudo-header is that of the final destination. At the originating node, that address will be in the last element of the Routing header; at the recipient(s), that address will be in the Destination Address field of the IPv6 header.

- o The Next Header value in the pseudo-header identifies the upper-layer protocol (e.g., 6 for TCP, or 17 for UDP). It will differ from the Next Header value in the IPv6 header if there are extension headers between the IPv6 header and the upper-layer header.

- o The Upper-Layer Packet Length in the pseudo-header is the length of the upper-layer header and data (e.g., TCP header plus TCP data). Some upper-layer protocols carry their own length information (e.g., the Length field in the UDP header); for such protocols, that is the length used in the pseudo-header. Other protocols (such as TCP) do not carry their own length information, in which case the length used in the pseudo-header is the Payload Length from the IPv6 header, minus the length of any extension headers present between the IPv6 header and the upper-layer header.

- o Unlike IPv4, when UDP packets are originated by an IPv6 node, the UDP checksum is not optional. That is, whenever originating a UDP packet, an IPv6 node must compute a UDP checksum over the packet and the pseudo-header, and, if that computation yields a result of zero, it must be changed to hex FFFF for placement in the UDP header. IPv6 receivers must discard UDP packets containing a zero checksum, and should log the error.

The IPv6 version of ICMP [ICMPv6] includes the above pseudo-header in its checksum computation; this is a change from the IPv4 version of ICMP, which does not include a pseudo-header in its checksum. The reason for the change is to protect ICMP from misdelivery or corruption of those fields of the IPv6 header on which it depends, which, unlike IPv4, are not covered by an internet-layer checksum. The Next Header field in the pseudo-header for ICMP contains the value 58, which identifies the IPv6 version of ICMP.

8.2 Maximum Packet Lifetime

Unlike IPv4, IPv6 nodes are not required to enforce maximum packet lifetime. That is the reason the IPv4 "Time to Live" field was renamed "Hop Limit" in IPv6. In practice, very few, if any, IPv4 implementations conform to the requirement that they limit packet lifetime, so this is not a change in practice. Any upper-layer protocol that relies on the internet layer (whether IPv4 or IPv6) to limit packet lifetime ought to be upgraded to provide its own mechanisms for detecting and discarding obsolete packets.

8.3 Maximum Upper-Layer Payload Size

When computing the maximum payload size available for upper-layer data, an upper-layer protocol must take into account the larger size of the IPv6 header relative to the IPv4 header. For example, in IPv4, TCP's MSS option is computed as the maximum packet size (a default value or a value learned through Path MTU Discovery) minus 40 octets (20 octets for the minimum-length IPv4 header and 20 octets for the minimum-length TCP header). When using TCP over IPv6, the MSS must be computed as the maximum packet size minus 60 octets, because the minimum-length IPv6 header (i.e., an IPv6 header with no extension headers) is 20 octets longer than a minimum-length IPv4 header.

8.4 Responding to Packets Carrying Routing Headers

When an upper-layer protocol sends one or more packets in response to a received packet that included a Routing header, the response packet(s) must not include a Routing header that was automatically derived by "reversing" the received Routing header UNLESS the integrity and authenticity of the received Source Address and Routing header have been verified (e.g., via the use of an Authentication header in the received packet). In other words, only the following kinds of packets are permitted in response to a received packet bearing a Routing header:

- o Response packets that do not carry Routing headers.

- o Response packets that carry Routing headers that were NOT derived by reversing the Routing header of the received packet (for example, a Routing header supplied by local configuration).

- o Response packets that carry Routing headers that were derived by reversing the Routing header of the received packet IF AND ONLY IF the integrity and authenticity of the Source Address and Routing header from the received packet have been verified by the responder.

Appendix A. Semantics and Usage of the Flow Label Field

A flow is a sequence of packets sent from a particular source to a particular (unicast or multicast) destination for which the source desires special handling by the intervening routers. The nature of that special handling might be conveyed to the routers by a control protocol, such as a resource reservation protocol, or by information within the flow's packets themselves, e.g., in a hop-by-hop option. The details of such control protocols or options are beyond the scope of this document.

There may be multiple active flows from a source to a destination, as well as traffic that is not associated with any flow. A flow is uniquely identified by the combination of a source address and a non-zero flow label. Packets that do not belong to a flow carry a flow label of zero.

A flow label is assigned to a flow by the flow's source node. New flow labels must be chosen (pseudo-)randomly and uniformly from the range 1 to FFFFF hex. The purpose of the random allocation is to make any set of bits within the Flow Label field suitable for use as a hash key by routers, for looking up the state associated with the flow.

All packets belonging to the same flow must be sent with the same source address, destination address, and flow label. If any of those packets includes a Hop-by-Hop Options header, then they all must be originated with the same Hop-by-Hop Options header contents (excluding the Next Header field of the Hop-by-Hop Options header). If any of those packets includes a Routing header, then they all must be originated with the same contents in all extension headers up to and including the Routing header (excluding the Next Header field in the Routing header). The routers or destinations are permitted, but not required, to verify that these conditions are satisfied. If a violation is detected, it should be reported to the source by an ICMP Parameter Problem message, Code 0, pointing to the high-order octet of the Flow Label field (i.e., offset 1 within the IPv6 packet).

The maximum lifetime of any flow-handling state established along a flow's path must be specified as part of the description of the state-establishment mechanism, e.g., the resource reservation protocol or the flow-setup hop-by-hop option. A source must not re-use a flow label for a new flow within the maximum lifetime of any flow-handling state that might have been established for the prior use of that flow label.

When a node stops and restarts (e.g., as a result of a "crash"), it must be careful not to use a flow label that it might have used for an earlier flow whose lifetime may not have expired yet. This may be accomplished by recording flow label usage on stable storage so that it can be remembered across crashes, or by refraining from using any flow labels until the maximum lifetime of any possible previously established flows has expired. If the minimum time for rebooting the node is known, that time can be deducted from the necessary waiting period before starting to allocate flow labels.

There is no requirement that all, or even most, packets belong to flows, i.e., carry non-zero flow labels. This observation is placed here to remind protocol designers and implementors not to assume otherwise. For example, it would be unwise to design a router whose performance would be adequate only if most packets belonged to flows, or to design a header compression scheme that only worked on packets that belonged to flows.

Appendix B. Formatting Guidelines for Options

This appendix gives some advice on how to lay out the fields when designing new options to be used in the Hop-by-Hop Options header or the Destination Options header, as described in section 4.2. These guidelines are based on the following assumptions:

- o One desirable feature is that any multi-octet fields within the Option Data area of an option be aligned on their natural boundaries, i.e., fields of width n octets should be placed at an integer multiple of n octets from the start of the Hop-by-Hop or Destination Options header, for n = 1, 2, 4, or 8.
- o Another desirable feature is that the Hop-by-Hop or Destination Options header take up as little space as possible, subject to the requirement that the header be an integer multiple of 8 octets long.
- o It may be assumed that, when either of the option-bearing headers are present, they carry a very small number of options, usually only one.

These assumptions suggest the following approach to laying out the fields of an option: order the fields from smallest to largest, with no interior padding, then derive the alignment requirement for the entire option based on the alignment requirement of the largest field (up to a maximum alignment of 8 octets). This approach is illustrated in the following examples:

Example 1

If an option X required two data fields, one of length 8 octets and one of length 4 octets, it would be laid out as follows:

```
                                +-+-+-+-+-+-+-+-+-+-+-+-+-+-+-+-+
                                | Option Type=X |Opt Data Len=12|
+-+-+-+-+-+-+-+-+-+-+-+-+-+-+-+-+-+-+-+-+-+-+-+-+-+-+-+-+-+-+-+-+
|                         4-octet field                         |
+-+-+-+-+-+-+-+-+-+-+-+-+-+-+-+-+-+-+-+-+-+-+-+-+-+-+-+-+-+-+-+-+
|                                                               |
+                         8-octet field                         +
|                                                               |
+-+-+-+-+-+-+-+-+-+-+-+-+-+-+-+-+-+-+-+-+-+-+-+-+-+-+-+-+-+-+-+-+
```

Its alignment requirement is 8n+2, to ensure that the 8-octet field starts at a multiple-of-8 offset from the start of the enclosing header. A complete Hop-by-Hop or Destination Options header containing this one option would look as follows:

```
+-+-+-+-+-+-+-+-+-+-+-+-+-+-+-+-+-+-+-+-+-+-+-+-+-+-+-+-+-+-+-+-+
|  Next Header  | Hdr Ext Len=1 | Option Type=X |Opt Data Len=12|
+-+-+-+-+-+-+-+-+-+-+-+-+-+-+-+-+-+-+-+-+-+-+-+-+-+-+-+-+-+-+-+-+
|                         4-octet field                         |
+-+-+-+-+-+-+-+-+-+-+-+-+-+-+-+-+-+-+-+-+-+-+-+-+-+-+-+-+-+-+-+-+
|                                                               |
+                         8-octet field                         +
|                                                               |
+-+-+-+-+-+-+-+-+-+-+-+-+-+-+-+-+-+-+-+-+-+-+-+-+-+-+-+-+-+-+-+-+
```

Example 2

If an option Y required three data fields, one of length 4 octets, one of length 2 octets, and one of length 1 octet, it would be laid out as follows:

```
                                                +-+-+-+-+-+-+-+-+
                                                | Option Type=Y |
+-+-+-+-+-+-+-+-+-+-+-+-+-+-+-+-+-+-+-+-+-+-+-+-+-+-+-+-+-+-+-+-+
|Opt Data Len=7 | 1-octet field |         2-octet field         |
+-+-+-+-+-+-+-+-+-+-+-+-+-+-+-+-+-+-+-+-+-+-+-+-+-+-+-+-+-+-+-+-+
|                         4-octet field                         |
+-+-+-+-+-+-+-+-+-+-+-+-+-+-+-+-+-+-+-+-+-+-+-+-+-+-+-+-+-+-+-+-+
```

Its alignment requirement is 4n+3, to ensure that the 4-octet field starts at a multiple-of-4 offset from the start of the enclosing header. A complete Hop-by-Hop or Destination Options header containing this one option would look as follows:

```
+-+-+-+-+-+-+-+-+-+-+-+-+-+-+-+-+-+-+-+-+-+-+-+-+-+-+-+-+-+-+-+-+
|  Next Header  | Hdr Ext Len=1 | Pad1 Option=0 | Option Type=Y |
+-+-+-+-+-+-+-+-+-+-+-+-+-+-+-+-+-+-+-+-+-+-+-+-+-+-+-+-+-+-+-+-+
|Opt Data Len=7 | 1-octet field |         2-octet field         |
+-+-+-+-+-+-+-+-+-+-+-+-+-+-+-+-+-+-+-+-+-+-+-+-+-+-+-+-+-+-+-+-+
|                         4-octet field                         |
+-+-+-+-+-+-+-+-+-+-+-+-+-+-+-+-+-+-+-+-+-+-+-+-+-+-+-+-+-+-+-+-+
| PadN Option=1 |Opt Data Len=2 |       0       |       0       |
+-+-+-+-+-+-+-+-+-+-+-+-+-+-+-+-+-+-+-+-+-+-+-+-+-+-+-+-+-+-+-+-+
```

Example 3

A Hop-by-Hop or Destination Options header containing both options X and Y from Examples 1 and 2 would have one of the two following formats, depending on which option appeared first:

```
+-+-+-+-+-+-+-+-+-+-+-+-+-+-+-+-+-+-+-+-+-+-+-+-+-+-+-+-+-+-+-+-+
|  Next Header  | Hdr Ext Len=3 | Option Type=X |Opt Data Len=12|
+-+-+-+-+-+-+-+-+-+-+-+-+-+-+-+-+-+-+-+-+-+-+-+-+-+-+-+-+-+-+-+-+
|                         4-octet field                         |
+-+-+-+-+-+-+-+-+-+-+-+-+-+-+-+-+-+-+-+-+-+-+-+-+-+-+-+-+-+-+-+-+
|                                                               |
+                         8-octet field                         +
|                                                               |
+-+-+-+-+-+-+-+-+-+-+-+-+-+-+-+-+-+-+-+-+-+-+-+-+-+-+-+-+-+-+-+-+
| PadN Option=1 |Opt Data Len=1 |       0       | Option Type=Y |
+-+-+-+-+-+-+-+-+-+-+-+-+-+-+-+-+-+-+-+-+-+-+-+-+-+-+-+-+-+-+-+-+
|Opt Data Len=7 | 1-octet field |         2-octet field         |
+-+-+-+-+-+-+-+-+-+-+-+-+-+-+-+-+-+-+-+-+-+-+-+-+-+-+-+-+-+-+-+-+
|                         4-octet field                         |
+-+-+-+-+-+-+-+-+-+-+-+-+-+-+-+-+-+-+-+-+-+-+-+-+-+-+-+-+-+-+-+-+
| PadN Option=1 |Opt Data Len=2 |       0       |       0       |
+-+-+-+-+-+-+-+-+-+-+-+-+-+-+-+-+-+-+-+-+-+-+-+-+-+-+-+-+-+-+-+-+

+-+-+-+-+-+-+-+-+-+-+-+-+-+-+-+-+-+-+-+-+-+-+-+-+-+-+-+-+-+-+-+-+
|  Next Header  | Hdr Ext Len=3 | Pad1 Option=0 | Option Type=Y |
+-+-+-+-+-+-+-+-+-+-+-+-+-+-+-+-+-+-+-+-+-+-+-+-+-+-+-+-+-+-+-+-+
|Opt Data Len=7 | 1-octet field |         2-octet field         |
+-+-+-+-+-+-+-+-+-+-+-+-+-+-+-+-+-+-+-+-+-+-+-+-+-+-+-+-+-+-+-+-+
|                         4-octet field                         |
+-+-+-+-+-+-+-+-+-+-+-+-+-+-+-+-+-+-+-+-+-+-+-+-+-+-+-+-+-+-+-+-+
| PadN Option=1 |Opt Data Len=4 |       0       |       0       |
+-+-+-+-+-+-+-+-+-+-+-+-+-+-+-+-+-+-+-+-+-+-+-+-+-+-+-+-+-+-+-+-+
|       0       |       0       | Option Type=X |Opt Data Len=12|
+-+-+-+-+-+-+-+-+-+-+-+-+-+-+-+-+-+-+-+-+-+-+-+-+-+-+-+-+-+-+-+-+
|                         4-octet field                         |
+-+-+-+-+-+-+-+-+-+-+-+-+-+-+-+-+-+-+-+-+-+-+-+-+-+-+-+-+-+-+-+-+
|                                                               |
+                         8-octet field                         +
|                                                               |
+-+-+-+-+-+-+-+-+-+-+-+-+-+-+-+-+-+-+-+-+-+-+-+-+-+-+-+-+-+-+-+-+
```

Security Considerations

The security features of IPv6 are described in the Security Architecture for the Internet Protocol [RFC-2401].

Acknowledgments

The authors gratefully acknowledge the many helpful suggestions of the members of the IPng working group, the End-to-End Protocols research group, and the Internet Community At Large.

Authors' Addresses

Stephen E. Deering
Cisco Systems, Inc.
170 West Tasman Drive
San Jose, CA 95134-1706
USA

Phone: +1 408 527 8213
Fax:
+1 408 527 8254
EMail: deering@cisco.com

Robert M. Hinden
Nokia
232 Java Drive
Sunnyvale, CA 94089
USA

Phone: +1 408 990-2004
Fax:
+1 408 743-5677
EMail: hinden@iprg.nokia.com

References

[RFC-2401] Kent, S. and R. Atkinson, "Security Architecture for the Internet Protocol", RFC 2401, November 1998.

[RFC-2402] Kent, S. and R. Atkinson, "IP Authentication Header", RFC 2402, November 1998.

[RFC-2406] Kent, S. and R. Atkinson, "IP Encapsulating Security Protocol (ESP)", RFC 2406, November 1998.

[ICMPv6] Conta, A. and S. Deering, "ICMP for the Internet Protocol Version 6 (IPv6)", RFC 2463, December 1998.

[ADDRARCH] Hinden, R. and S. Deering, "IP Version 6 Addressing Architecture", RFC 2373, July 1998.

[RFC-1981] McCann, J., Mogul, J. and S. Deering, "Path MTU Discovery for IP version 6", RFC 1981, August 1996.

[RFC-791] Postel, J., "Internet Protocol", STD 5, RFC 791, September 1981.

[RFC-1700] Reynolds, J. and J. Postel, "Assigned Numbers", STD 2, RFC 1700, October 1994. See also: http://www.iana.org/numbers.html

[RFC-1661] Simpson, W., "The Point-to-Point Protocol (PPP)", STD 51, RFC 1661, July 1994.

CHANGES SINCE RFC-1883

This memo has the following changes from RFC-1883. Numbers identify the Internet-Draft version in which the change was made.

02) Removed all references to jumbograms and the Jumbo Payload option (moved to a separate document).

02) Moved most of Flow Label description from section 6 to (new) Appendix A.

02) In Flow Label description, now in Appendix A, corrected maximum Flow Label value from FFFFFF to FFFFF (i.e., one less "F") due to reduction of size of Flow Label field from 24 bits to 20 bits.

02) Renumbered (relettered?) the previous Appendix A to be Appendix B.

02) Changed the wording of the Security Considerations section to avoid dependency loop between this spec and the IPsec specs.

02) Updated R. Hinden's email address and company affiliation.

----

01) In section 3, changed field name "Class" to "Traffic Class" and increased its size from 4 to 8 bits. Decreased size of Flow Label field from 24 to 20 bits to compensate for increase in Traffic Class field.

01) In section 4.1, restored the order of the Authentication Header and the ESP header, which were mistakenly swapped in the 00 version of this memo.

01) In section 4.4, deleted the Strict/Loose Bit Map field and the strict routing functionality from the Type 0 Routing header, and removed the restriction on number of addresses that may be carried in the Type 0 Routing header (was limited to 23 addresses, because of the size of the strict/loose bit map).

01) In section 5, changed the minimum IPv6 MTU from 576 to 1280 octets, and added a recommendation that links with configurable MTU (e.g., PPP links) be configured to have an MTU of at least 1500 octets.

01) In section 5, deleted the requirement that a node must not send fragmented packets that reassemble to more than 1500 octets without knowledge of the destination reassembly buffer size, and replaced it with a recommendation that upper-layer protocols or applications should not do that.

01) Replaced reference to the IPv4 Path MTU Discovery spec (RFC-1191) with reference to the IPv6 Path MTU Discovery spec (RFC-1981), and deleted the Notes at the end of section 5 regarding Path MTU Discovery, since those details are now covered by RFC-1981.

01) In section 6, deleted specification of "opportunistic" flow set-up, and removed all references to the 6-second maximum lifetime for opportunistically established flow state.

01) In section 7, deleted the provisional description of the internal structure and semantics of the Traffic Class field, and specified that such descriptions be provided in separate documents.

----

00) In section 4, corrected the Code value to indicate "unrecognized Next Header type encountered" in an ICMP Parameter Problem message (changed from 2 to 1).

00) In the description of the Payload Length field in section 3, and of the Jumbo Payload Length field in section 4.3, made it clearer that extension headers are included in the payload length count.

00) In section 4.1, swapped the order of the Authentication header and the ESP header. (NOTE: this was a mistake, and the change was undone in version 01.)

00) In section 4.2, made it clearer that options are identified by the full 8-bit Option Type, not by the low-order 5 bits of an Option Type. Also specified that the same Option Type numbering space is used for both Hop-by-Hop Options and Destination Options headers.

00) In section 4.4, added a sentence requiring that nodes processing a Routing header must send an ICMP Packet Too Big message in response to a packet that is too big to fit in the next hop link (rather than, say, performing fragmentation).

00) Changed the name of the IPv6 Priority field to "Class", and replaced the previous description of Priority in section 7 with a description of the Class field. Also, excluded this field from the set of fields that must remain the same for all packets in the same flow, as specified in section 6.

00) In the pseudo-header in section 8.1, changed the name of the "Payload Length" field to "Upper-Layer Packet Length". Also clarified that, in the case of protocols that carry their own length info (like non-jumbogram UDP), it is the upper-layer-derived length, not the IP-layer-derived length, that is used in the pseudo-header.

00) Added section 8.4, specifying that upper-layer protocols, when responding to a received packet that carried a Routing header, must not include the reverse of the Routing header in the response packet(s) unless the received Routing header was authenticated.

00) Fixed some typos and grammatical errors.

00) Authors' contact info updated.

Full Copyright Statement

Network Working Group
Request for Comments: 2461
Obsoletes: 1970
Category: Standards Track

T. Narten
IBM
E. Nordmark
Sun Microsystems
W. Simpson
Daydreamer
December 1998

Neighbor Discovery for IP Version 6 (IPv6)

Status of this Memo

This document specifies an Internet standards track protocol for the Internet community, and requests discussion and suggestions for improvements. Please refer to the current edition of the "Internet Official Protocol Standards" (STD 1) for the standardization state and status of this protocol. Distribution of this memo is unlimited.

Copyright Notice

Abstract

This document specifies the Neighbor Discovery protocol for IP Version 6. IPv6 nodes on the same link use Neighbor Discovery to discover each other's presence, to determine each other's link-layer addresses, to find routers and to maintain reachability information about the paths to active neighbors.

Table of Contents

1. INTRODUCTION

This specification defines the Neighbor Discovery (ND) protocol for Internet Protocol Version 6 (IPv6). Nodes (hosts and routers) use Neighbor Discovery to determine the link-layer addresses for neighbors known to reside on attached links and to quickly purge cached values that become invalid. Hosts also use Neighbor Discovery to find neighboring routers that are willing to forward packets on their behalf. Finally, nodes use the protocol to actively keep track of which neighbors are reachable and which are not, and to detect changed link-layer addresses. When a router or the path to a router fails, a host actively searches for functioning alternates.

Unless specified otherwise (in a document that covers operating IP over a particular link type) this document applies to all link types. However, because ND uses link-layer multicast for some of its services, it is possible that on some link types (e.g., NBMA links) alternative protocols or mechanisms to implement those services will be specified (in the appropriate document covering the operation of IP over a particular link type). The services described in this document that are not directly dependent on multicast, such as Redirects, Next-hop determination, Neighbor Unreachability Detection, etc., are expected to be provided as specified in this document. The details of how one uses ND on NBMA links is an area for further study.

The authors would like to acknowledge the contributions of the IPNGWG working group and, in particular, (in alphabetical order) Ran Atkinson, Jim Bound, Scott Bradner, Alex Conta, Stephen Deering,

Richard Draves, Francis Dupont, Robert Elz, Robert Gilligan, Robert Hinden, Allison Mankin, Dan McDonald, Charles Perkins, Matt Thomas, and Susan Thomson.

2. TERMINOLOGY

2.1. General

IP - Internet Protocol Version 6. The terms IPv4 and IPv6 are used only in contexts where necessary to avoid ambiguity.

ICMP - Internet Message Control Protocol for the Internet Protocol Version 6. The terms ICMPv4 and ICMPv6 are used only in contexts where necessary to avoid ambiguity.

node - a device that implements IP.

router - a node that forwards IP packets not explicitly addressed to itself.

host - any node that is not a router.

upper layer - a protocol layer immediately above IP. Examples are transport protocols such as TCP and UDP, control protocols such as ICMP, routing protocols such as OSPF, and internet or lower-layer protocols being "tunneled" over (i.e., encapsulated in) IP such as IPX, AppleTalk, or IP itself.

link - a communication facility or medium over which nodes can communicate at the link layer, i.e., the layer immediately below IP. Examples are Ethernets (simple or bridged), PPP links, X.25, Frame Relay, or ATM networks as well as internet (or higher) layer "tunnels", such as tunnels over IPv4 or IPv6 itself.

interface - a node's attachment to a link.

neighbors - nodes attached to the same link.

address - an IP-layer identifier for an interface or a set of interfaces.

anycast address
- an identifier for a set of interfaces (typically belonging to different nodes). A packet sent to an

anycast address is delivered to one of the interfaces identified by that address (the "nearest" one, according to the routing protocol's measure of distance). See [ADDR-ARCH].

Note that an anycast address is syntactically indistinguishable from a unicast address. Thus, nodes sending packets to anycast addresses don't generally know that an anycast address is being used. Throughout the rest of this document, references to unicast addresses also apply to anycast addresses in those cases where the node is unaware that a unicast address is actually an anycast address.

prefix - a bit string that consists of some number of initial bits of an address.

link-layer address - a link-layer identifier for an interface. Examples include IEEE 802 addresses for Ethernet links and E.164 addresses for ISDN links.

on-link - an address that is assigned to an interface on a specified link. A node considers an address to be on-link if:

- it is covered by one of the link's prefixes, or
- a neighboring router specifies the address as the target of a Redirect message, or
- a Neighbor Advertisement message is received for the (target) address, or
- any Neighbor Discovery message is received from the address.

off-link - the opposite of "on-link"; an address that is not assigned to any interfaces on the specified link.

longest prefix match - The process of determining which prefix (if any) in a set of prefixes covers a target address. A target address is covered by a prefix if all of the bits in the prefix match the left-most bits of the target address. When multiple prefixes cover an address, the longest prefix is the one that matches.

reachability
- whether or not the one-way "forward" path to a neighbor is functioning properly. In particular, whether packets sent to a neighbor are reaching the IP layer on the neighboring machine and are being processed properly by the receiving IP layer. For neighboring routers, reachability means that packets sent by a node's IP layer are delivered to the router's IP layer, and the router is indeed forwarding packets (i.e., it is configured as a router, not a host). For hosts, reachability means that packets sent by a node's IP layer are delivered to the neighbor host's IP layer.

packet - an IP header plus payload.

link MTU - the maximum transmission unit, i.e., maximum packet size in octets, that can be conveyed in one piece over a link.

target - an address about which address resolution information is sought, or an address which is the new first-hop when being redirected.

proxy - a router that responds to Neighbor Discovery query messages on behalf of another node. A router acting on behalf of a mobile node that has moved off-link could potentially act as a proxy for the mobile node.

ICMP destination unreachable indication
- an error indication returned to the original sender of a packet that cannot be delivered for the reasons outlined in [ICMPv6]. If the error occurs on a node other than the node originating the packet, an ICMP error message is generated. If the error occurs on the originating node, an implementation is not required to actually create and send an ICMP error packet to the source, as long as the upper-layer sender is notified through an appropriate mechanism (e.g., return value from a procedure call). Note, however, that an implementation may find it convenient in some cases to return errors to the sender by taking the offending packet, generating an ICMP error message, and then delivering it (locally) through the generic error handling routines.

random delay
- when sending out messages, it is sometimes necessary to delay a transmission for a random amount of time in order to prevent multiple nodes from transmitting at exactly the same time, or to prevent long-range periodic transmissions from synchronizing with each other [SYNC]. When a random component is required, a node calculates the actual delay in such a way that the computed delay forms a uniformly-distributed random value that falls between the specified minimum and maximum delay times. The implementor must take care to insure that the granularity of the calculated random component and the resolution of the timer used are both high enough to insure that the probability of multiple nodes delaying the same amount of time is small.

random delay seed
- If a pseudo-random number generator is used in calculating a random delay component, the generator should be initialized with a unique seed prior to being used. Note that it is not sufficient to use the interface token alone as the seed, since interface tokens will not always be unique. To reduce the probability that duplicate interface tokens cause the same seed to be used, the seed should be calculated from a variety of input sources (e.g., machine components) that are likely to be different even on identical "boxes". For example, the seed could be formed by combining the CPU's serial number with an interface token.

2.2. Link Types

Different link layers have different properties. The ones of concern to Neighbor Discovery are:

multicast - a link that supports a native mechanism at the link layer for sending packets to all (i.e., broadcast) or a subset of all neighbors.

point-to-point - a link that connects exactly two interfaces. A point-to-point link is assumed to have multicast capability and have a link-local address.

non-broadcast multi-access (NBMA)
- a link to which more than two interfaces can attach, but that does not support a native form of multicast or broadcast (e.g., X.25, ATM, frame relay, etc.).

Note that all link types (including NBMA) are expected to provide multicast service for IP (e.g., using multicast servers), but it is an issue for further study whether ND should use such facilities or an alternate mechanism that provides the equivalent ND services.

shared media - a link that allows direct communication among a number of nodes, but attached nodes are configured in such a way that they do not have complete prefix information for all on-link destinations. That is, at the IP level, nodes on the same link may not know that they are neighbors; by default, they communicate through a router. Examples are large (switched) public data networks such as SMDS and B-ISDN. Also known as "large clouds". See [SH-MEDIA].

variable MTU - a link that does not have a well-defined MTU (e.g., IEEE 802.5 token rings). Many links (e.g., Ethernet) have a standard MTU defined by the link-layer protocol or by the specific document describing how to run IP over the link layer.

asymmetric reachability
- a link where non-reflexive and/or non-transitive reachability is part of normal operation. (Non-reflexive reachability means packets from A reach B but packets from B don't reach A. Non-transitive reachability means packets from A reach B, and packets from B reach C, but packets from A don't reach C.) Many radio links exhibit these properties.

2.3. Addresses

Neighbor Discovery makes use of a number of different addresses defined in [ADDR-ARCH], including:

all-nodes multicast address
- the link-local scope address to reach all nodes. FF02::1

all-routers multicast address
- the link-local scope address to reach all routers. FF02::2

solicited-node multicast address
- a link-local scope multicast address that is computed as a function of the solicited target's address. The function is described in [ADDR-ARCH]. The function is chosen so that IP addresses which differ only in the high-order bits, e.g., due to multiple high-order prefixes associated with different providers, will map to the same solicited-node address thereby reducing the number of multicast addresses a node must join.

link-local address
- a unicast address having link-only scope that can be used to reach neighbors. All interfaces on routers MUST have a link-local address. Also, [ADDRCONF] requires that interfaces on hosts have a link-local address.

unspecified address
- a reserved address value that indicates the lack of an address (e.g., the address is unknown). It is never used as a destination address, but may be used as a source address if the sender does not (yet) know its own address (e.g., while verifying an address is unused during address autoconfiguration [ADDRCONF]). The unspecified address has a value of 0:0:0:0:0:0:0:0.

2.4. Requirements

The keywords MUST, MUST NOT, REQUIRED, SHALL, SHALL NOT, SHOULD, SHOULD NOT, RECOMMENDED, MAY, and OPTIONAL, when they appear in this document, are to be interpreted as described in [KEYWORDS].

This document also makes use of internal conceptual variables to describe protocol behavior and external variables that an implementation must allow system administrators to change. The specific variable names, how their values change, and how their settings influence protocol behavior are provided to demonstrate protocol behavior. An implementation is not required to have them in the exact form described here, so long as its external behavior is consistent with that described in this document.

3. PROTOCOL OVERVIEW

This protocol solves a set of problems related to the interaction between nodes attached to the same link. It defines mechanisms for solving each of the following problems:

Router Discovery: How hosts locate routers that reside on an attached link.

Prefix Discovery: How hosts discover the set of address prefixes that define which destinations are on-link for an attached link. (Nodes use prefixes to distinguish destinations that reside on-link from those only reachable through a router.)

Parameter Discovery: How a node learns such link parameters as the link MTU or such Internet parameters as the hop limit value to place in outgoing packets.

Address Autoconfiguration: How nodes automatically configure an address for an interface.

Address resolution: How nodes determine the link-layer address of an on-link destination (e.g., a neighbor) given only the destination's IP address.

Next-hop determination: The algorithm for mapping an IP destination address into the IP address of the neighbor to which traffic for the destination should be sent. The next-hop can be a router or the destination itself.

Neighbor Unreachability Detection: How nodes determine that a neighbor is no longer reachable. For neighbors used as routers, alternate default routers can be tried. For both routers and hosts, address resolution can be performed again.

Duplicate Address Detection: How a node determines that an address it wishes to use is not already in use by another node.

Redirect: How a router informs a host of a better first-hop node to reach a particular destination.

Neighbor Discovery defines five different ICMP packet types: A pair of Router Solicitation and Router Advertisement messages, a pair of Neighbor Solicitation and Neighbor Advertisements messages, and a Redirect message. The messages serve the following purpose:

Router Solicitation: When an interface becomes enabled, hosts may send out Router Solicitations that request routers to generate Router Advertisements immediately rather than at their next scheduled time.

Router Advertisement: Routers advertise their presence together with various link and Internet parameters either periodically, or in response to a Router Solicitation message. Router Advertisements contain prefixes that are used for on-link determination and/or address configuration, a suggested hop limit value, etc.

Neighbor Solicitation: Sent by a node to determine the link-layer address of a neighbor, or to verify that a neighbor is still reachable via a cached link-layer address. Neighbor Solicitations are also used for Duplicate Address Detection.

Neighbor Advertisement: A response to a Neighbor Solicitation message. A node may also send unsolicited Neighbor Advertisements to announce a link-layer address change.

Redirect: Used by routers to inform hosts of a better first hop for a destination.

On multicast-capable links, each router periodically multicasts a Router Advertisement packet announcing its availability. A host receives Router Advertisements from all routers, building a list of default routers. Routers generate Router Advertisements frequently enough that hosts will learn of their presence within a few minutes, but not frequently enough to rely on an absence of advertisements to detect router failure; a separate Neighbor Unreachability Detection algorithm provides failure detection.

Router Advertisements contain a list of prefixes used for on-link determination and/or autonomous address configuration; flags associated with the prefixes specify the intended uses of a particular prefix. Hosts use the advertised on-link prefixes to build and maintain a list that is used in deciding when a packet's destination is on-link or beyond a router. Note that a destination can be on-link even though it is not covered by any advertised on-link prefix. In such cases a router can send a Redirect informing the sender that the destination is a neighbor.

Router Advertisements (and per-prefix flags) allow routers to inform hosts how to perform Address Autoconfiguration. For example, routers can specify whether hosts should use stateful (DHCPv6) and/or autonomous (stateless) address configuration. The exact semantics and usage of the address configuration-related information is specified in [ADDRCONF].

Router Advertisement messages also contain Internet parameters such as the hop limit that hosts should use in outgoing packets and, optionally, link parameters such as the link MTU. This facilitates centralized administration of critical parameters that can be set on routers and automatically propagated to all attached hosts.

Nodes accomplish address resolution by multicasting a Neighbor Solicitation that asks the target node to return its link-layer address. Neighbor Solicitation messages are multicast to the solicited-node multicast address of the target address. The target returns its link-layer address in a unicast Neighbor Advertisement message. A single request-response pair of packets is sufficient for both the initiator and the target to resolve each other's link-layer addresses; the initiator includes its link-layer address in the Neighbor Solicitation.

Neighbor Solicitation messages can also be used to determine if more than one node has been assigned the same unicast address. The use of Neighbor Solicitation messages for Duplicate Address Detection is specified in [ADDRCONF].

Neighbor Unreachability Detection detects the failure of a neighbor or the failure of the forward path to the neighbor. Doing so requires positive confirmation that packets sent to a neighbor are actually reaching that neighbor and being processed properly by its IP layer. Neighbor Unreachability Detection uses confirmation from two sources. When possible, upper-layer protocols provide a positive confirmation that a connection is making "forward progress", that is, previously sent data is known to have been delivered correctly (e.g., new acknowledgments were received recently). When positive confirmation is not forthcoming through such "hints", a node sends unicast Neighbor Solicitation messages that solicit Neighbor Advertisements as reachability confirmation from the next hop. To reduce unnecessary network traffic, probe messages are only sent to neighbors to which the node is actively sending packets.

In addition to addressing the above general problems, Neighbor Discovery also handles the following situations:

Link-layer address change - A node that knows its link-layer address has changed can multicast a few (unsolicited) Neighbor Advertisement packets to all nodes to quickly update cached link-layer addresses that have become invalid. Note that the sending of unsolicited advertisements is a performance enhancement only (e.g., unreliable). The Neighbor Unreachability Detection algorithm ensures that all nodes will reliably discover the new address, though the delay may be somewhat longer.

Inbound load balancing - Nodes with replicated interfaces may want to load balance the reception of incoming packets across multiple network interfaces on the same link. Such nodes have multiple link-layer addresses assigned to the same interface. For example, a single network driver could represent multiple network interface cards as a single logical interface having multiple link-layer addresses.

Load balancing is handled by allowing routers to omit the source link-layer address from Router Advertisement packets, thereby forcing neighbors to use Neighbor Solicitation messages to learn link-layer addresses of routers. Returned Neighbor Advertisement messages can then contain link-layer addresses that differ depending on who issued the solicitation.

Anycast addresses - Anycast addresses identify one of a set of nodes providing an equivalent service, and multiple nodes on the same link may be configured to recognize the same Anycast address. Neighbor Discovery handles anycasts by having nodes expect to receive multiple Neighbor Advertisements for the same target. All advertisements for anycast addresses are tagged as being non-Override advertisements. This invokes specific rules to determine which of potentially multiple advertisements should be used.

Proxy advertisements - A router willing to accept packets on behalf of a target address that is unable to respond to Neighbor Solicitations can issue non-Override Neighbor Advertisements. There is currently no specified use of proxy, but proxy advertising could potentially be used to handle cases like mobile nodes that have moved off-link. However, it is not intended as a general mechanism to handle nodes that, e.g., do not implement this protocol.

3.1. Comparison with IPv4

The IPv6 Neighbor Discovery protocol corresponds to a combination of the IPv4 protocols ARP [ARP], ICMP Router Discovery [RDISC], and ICMP Redirect [ICMPv4]. In IPv4 there is no generally agreed upon protocol or mechanism for Neighbor Unreachability Detection, although Hosts Requirements [HR-CL] does specify some possible algorithms for Dead Gateway Detection (a subset of the problems Neighbor Unreachability Detection tackles).

The Neighbor Discovery protocol provides a multitude of improvements over the IPv4 set of protocols:

Router Discovery is part of the base protocol set; there is no need for hosts to "snoop" the routing protocols.

Router advertisements carry link-layer addresses; no additional packet exchange is needed to resolve the router's link-layer address.

Router advertisements carry prefixes for a link; there is no need to have a separate mechanism to configure the "netmask".

Router advertisements enable Address Autoconfiguration.

Routers can advertise an MTU for hosts to use on the link, ensuring that all nodes use the same MTU value on links lacking a well-defined MTU.

Address resolution multicasts are "spread" over 4 billion (2^32) multicast addresses greatly reducing address resolution related interrupts on nodes other than the target. Moreover, non-IPv6 machines should not be interrupted at all.

Redirects contain the link-layer address of the new first hop; separate address resolution is not needed upon receiving a redirect.

Multiple prefixes can be associated with the same link. By default, hosts learn all on-link prefixes from Router Advertisements. However, routers may be configured to omit some or all prefixes from Router Advertisements. In such cases hosts assume that destinations are off-link and send traffic to routers. A router can then issue redirects as appropriate.

Unlike IPv4, the recipient of an IPv6 redirect assumes that the new next-hop is on-link. In IPv4, a host ignores redirects specifying a next-hop that is not on-link according to the link's network mask. The IPv6 redirect mechanism is analogous to the XRedirect facility specified in [SH-MEDIA]. It is expected to be useful on non-broadcast and shared media links in which it is undesirable or not possible for nodes to know all prefixes for on-link destinations.

Neighbor Unreachability Detection is part of the base significantly improving the robustness of packet delivery in the presence of failing routers, partially failing or partitioned links and nodes that change their link-layer addresses. For instance, mobile nodes can move off-link without losing any connectivity due to stale ARP caches.

Unlike ARP, Neighbor Discovery detects half-link failures (using Neighbor Unreachability Detection) and avoids sending traffic to neighbors with which two-way connectivity is absent.

Unlike in IPv4 Router Discovery the Router Advertisement messages do not contain a preference field. The preference field is not needed to handle routers of different "stability"; the Neighbor Unreachability Detection will detect dead routers and switch to a working one.

The use of link-local addresses to uniquely identify routers (for Router Advertisement and Redirect messages) makes it possible for hosts to maintain the router associations in the event of the site renumbering to use new global prefixes.

Using the Hop Limit equal to 255 trick Neighbor Discovery is immune to off-link senders that accidentally or intentionally send ND messages. In IPv4 off-link senders can send both ICMP Redirects and Router Advertisement messages.

Placing address resolution at the ICMP layer makes the protocol more media-independent than ARP and makes it possible to use standard IP authentication and security mechanisms as appropriate [IPv6-AUTH, IPv6-ESP].

3.2. Supported Link Types

Neighbor Discovery supports links with different properties. In the presence of certain properties only a subset of the ND protocol mechanisms are fully specified in this document:

point-to-point - Neighbor Discovery handles such links just like multicast links. (Multicast can be trivially provided on point to point links, and interfaces can be assigned link-local addresses.) Neighbor Discovery should be implemented as described in this document.

multicast - Neighbor Discovery should be implemented as described in this document.

non-broadcast multiple access (NBMA)
- Redirect, Neighbor Unreachability Detection and next-hop determination should be implemented as described in this document. Address resolution, and the mechanism for delivering Router Solicitations and Advertisements on NBMA links is not specified in this document. Note that if

hosts support manual configuration of a list of default routers, hosts can dynamically acquire the link-layer addresses for their neighbors from Redirect messages.

shared media - The Redirect message is modeled after the XRedirect message in [SH-MEDIA] in order to simplify use of the protocol on shared media links.

This specification does not address shared media issues that only relate to routers, such as:

- How routers exchange reachability information on a shared media link.

- How a router determines the link-layer address of a host, which it needs to send redirect messages to the host.

- How a router determines that it is the first-hop router for a received packet.

The protocol is extensible (through the definition of new options) so that other solutions might be possible in the future.

variable MTU - Neighbor Discovery allows routers to specify a MTU for the link, which all nodes then use. All nodes on a link must use the same MTU (or Maximum Receive Unit) in order for multicast to work properly. Otherwise when multicasting a sender, which can not know which nodes will receive the packet, could not determine a minimum packet size all receivers can process.

asymmetric reachability
- Neighbor Discovery detects the absence of symmetric reachability; a node avoids paths to a neighbor with which it does not have symmetric connectivity.

The Neighbor Unreachability Detection will typically identify such half-links and the node will refrain from using them.

The protocol can presumably be extended in the future to find viable paths in environments that lack reflexive and transitive connectivity.

4. MESSAGE FORMATS

4.1. Router Solicitation Message Format

Hosts send Router Solicitations in order to prompt routers to generate Router Advertisements quickly.

```
 0                   1                   2                   3
 0 1 2 3 4 5 6 7 8 9 0 1 2 3 4 5 6 7 8 9 0 1 2 3 4 5 6 7 8 9 0 1
+-+-+-+-+-+-+-+-+-+-+-+-+-+-+-+-+-+-+-+-+-+-+-+-+-+-+-+-+-+-+-+-+
|     Type      |     Code      |          Checksum             |
+-+-+-+-+-+-+-+-+-+-+-+-+-+-+-+-+-+-+-+-+-+-+-+-+-+-+-+-+-+-+-+-+
|                            Reserved                           |
+-+-+-+-+-+-+-+-+-+-+-+-+-+-+-+-+-+-+-+-+-+-+-+-+-+-+-+-+-+-+-+-+
|   Options ...
+-+-+-+-+-+-+-+-+-+-+-+-
```

IP Fields:

Source Address
An IP address assigned to the sending interface, or the unspecified address if no address is assigned to the sending interface.

Destination Address
Typically the all-routers multicast address.

Hop Limit 255

Authentication Header
If a Security Association for the IP Authentication Header exists between the sender and the destination address, then the sender SHOULD include this header.

ICMP Fields:

Type 133

Code 0

Checksum The ICMP checksum. See [ICMPv6].

Reserved This field is unused. It MUST be initialized to zero by the sender and MUST be ignored by the receiver.

Valid Options:

Source link-layer address
The link-layer address of the sender, if known. MUST NOT be included if the Source Address is the unspecified address. Otherwise it SHOULD be included on link layers that have addresses.

Future versions of this protocol may define new option types. Receivers MUST silently ignore any options they do not recognize and continue processing the message.

4.2. Router Advertisement Message Format

Routers send out Router Advertisement message periodically, or in response to a Router Solicitation.

```
 0                   1                   2                   3
 0 1 2 3 4 5 6 7 8 9 0 1 2 3 4 5 6 7 8 9 0 1 2 3 4 5 6 7 8 9 0 1
+-+-+-+-+-+-+-+-+-+-+-+-+-+-+-+-+-+-+-+-+-+-+-+-+-+-+-+-+-+-+-+-+
|     Type      |     Code      |          Checksum             |
+-+-+-+-+-+-+-+-+-+-+-+-+-+-+-+-+-+-+-+-+-+-+-+-+-+-+-+-+-+-+-+-+
| Cur Hop Limit |M|O|  Reserved |       Router Lifetime         |
+-+-+-+-+-+-+-+-+-+-+-+-+-+-+-+-+-+-+-+-+-+-+-+-+-+-+-+-+-+-+-+-+
|                         Reachable Time                        |
+-+-+-+-+-+-+-+-+-+-+-+-+-+-+-+-+-+-+-+-+-+-+-+-+-+-+-+-+-+-+-+-+
|                          Retrans Timer                        |
+-+-+-+-+-+-+-+-+-+-+-+-+-+-+-+-+-+-+-+-+-+-+-+-+-+-+-+-+-+-+-+-+
|   Options ...
+-+-+-+-+-+-+-+-+-+-+-+-
```

IP Fields:

Source Address
MUST be the link-local address assigned to the interface from which this message is sent.

Destination Address
Typically the Source Address of an invoking Router Solicitation or the all-nodes multicast address.

Hop Limit 255

Authentication Header
If a Security Association for the IP Authentication Header exists between the sender and the destination address, then the sender SHOULD include this header.

ICMP Fields:

Type 134

Code 0

Checksum The ICMP checksum. See [ICMPv6].

Cur Hop Limit 8-bit unsigned integer. The default value that should be placed in the Hop Count field of the IP header for outgoing IP packets. A value of zero means unspecified (by this router).

M 1-bit "Managed address configuration" flag. When set, hosts use the administered (stateful) protocol for address autoconfiguration in addition to any addresses autoconfigured using stateless address autoconfiguration. The use of this flag is described in [ADDRCONF].

O 1-bit "Other stateful configuration" flag. When set, hosts use the administered (stateful) protocol for autoconfiguration of other (non-address) information. The use of this flag is described in [ADDRCONF].

Reserved A 6-bit unused field. It MUST be initialized to zero by the sender and MUST be ignored by the receiver.

Router Lifetime
16-bit unsigned integer. The lifetime associated with the default router in units of seconds. The maximum value corresponds to 18.2 hours. A Lifetime of 0 indicates that the router is not a default router and SHOULD NOT appear on the default router list. The Router Lifetime applies only to the router's usefulness as a default router; it does not apply to information contained in other message fields or options. Options that need time limits for their information include their own lifetime fields.

Reachable Time 32-bit unsigned integer. The time, in milliseconds, that a node assumes a neighbor is reachable after having received a reachability confirmation. Used by the Neighbor Unreachability Detection algorithm (see Section 7.3). A value of zero means unspecified (by this router).

Retrans Timer 32-bit unsigned integer. The time, in milliseconds, between retransmitted Neighbor Solicitation messages. Used by address resolution and the Neighbor Unreachability Detection algorithm (see Sections 7.2 and 7.3). A value of zero means unspecified (by this router).

Possible options:

Source link-layer address
The link-layer address of the interface from which the Router Advertisement is sent. Only used on link layers that have addresses. A router MAY omit this option in order to enable inbound load sharing across multiple link-layer addresses.

MTU SHOULD be sent on links that have a variable MTU (as specified in the document that describes how to run IP over the particular link type). MAY be sent on other links.

Prefix Information
These options specify the prefixes that are on-link and/or are used for address autoconfiguration. A router SHOULD include all its on-link prefixes (except the link-local prefix) so that multihomed hosts have complete prefix information about on-link destinations for the links to which they attach. If complete information is lacking, a multihomed host may not be able to choose the correct outgoing interface when sending traffic to its neighbors.

Future versions of this protocol may define new option types. Receivers MUST silently ignore any options they do not recognize and continue processing the message.

4.3. Neighbor Solicitation Message Format

Nodes send Neighbor Solicitations to request the link-layer address of a target node while also providing their own link-layer address to the target. Neighbor Solicitations are multicast when the node needs to resolve an address and unicast when the node seeks to verify the reachability of a neighbor.

```
 0                   1                   2                   3
 0 1 2 3 4 5 6 7 8 9 0 1 2 3 4 5 6 7 8 9 0 1 2 3 4 5 6 7 8 9 0 1
+-+-+-+-+-+-+-+-+-+-+-+-+-+-+-+-+-+-+-+-+-+-+-+-+-+-+-+-+-+-+-+-+
|     Type      |     Code      |          Checksum             |
+-+-+-+-+-+-+-+-+-+-+-+-+-+-+-+-+-+-+-+-+-+-+-+-+-+-+-+-+-+-+-+-+
|                           Reserved                            |
+-+-+-+-+-+-+-+-+-+-+-+-+-+-+-+-+-+-+-+-+-+-+-+-+-+-+-+-+-+-+-+-+
|                                                               |
+                                                               +
|                                                               |
+                       Target Address                          +
|                                                               |
+                                                               +
|                                                               |
+-+-+-+-+-+-+-+-+-+-+-+-+-+-+-+-+-+-+-+-+-+-+-+-+-+-+-+-+-+-+-+-+
|   Options ...
+-+-+-+-+-+-+-+-+-+-+-+-
```

IP Fields:

Source Address
Either an address assigned to the interface from which this message is sent or (if Duplicate Address Detection is in progress [ADDRCONF]) the unspecified address.

Destination Address
Either the solicited-node multicast address corresponding to the target address, or the target address.

Hop Limit 255

Authentication Header
If a Security Association for the IP Authentication Header exists between the sender and the destination address, then the sender SHOULD include this header.

ICMP Fields:

Type 135

Code 0

Checksum The ICMP checksum. See [ICMPv6].

Reserved This field is unused. It MUST be initialized to zero by the sender and MUST be ignored by the receiver.

Target Address
The IP address of the target of the solicitation. It MUST NOT be a multicast address.

Possible options:

Source link-layer address
The link-layer address for the sender. MUST NOT be included when the source IP address is the unspecified address. Otherwise, on link layers that have addresses this option MUST be included in multicast solicitations and SHOULD be included in unicast solicitations.

Future versions of this protocol may define new option types. Receivers MUST silently ignore any options they do not recognize and continue processing the message.

4.4. Neighbor Advertisement Message Format

A node sends Neighbor Advertisements in response to Neighbor Solicitations and sends unsolicited Neighbor Advertisements in order to (unreliably) propagate new information quickly.

```
 0                   1                   2                   3
 0 1 2 3 4 5 6 7 8 9 0 1 2 3 4 5 6 7 8 9 0 1 2 3 4 5 6 7 8 9 0 1
+-+-+-+-+-+-+-+-+-+-+-+-+-+-+-+-+-+-+-+-+-+-+-+-+-+-+-+-+-+-+-+-+
|     Type      |     Code      |          Checksum             |
+-+-+-+-+-+-+-+-+-+-+-+-+-+-+-+-+-+-+-+-+-+-+-+-+-+-+-+-+-+-+-+-+
|R|S|O|                     Reserved                            |
+-+-+-+-+-+-+-+-+-+-+-+-+-+-+-+-+-+-+-+-+-+-+-+-+-+-+-+-+-+-+-+-+
|                                                               |
+                                                               +
|                                                               |
+                       Target Address                          +
|                                                               |
+                                                               +
|                                                               |
+-+-+-+-+-+-+-+-+-+-+-+-+-+-+-+-+-+-+-+-+-+-+-+-+-+-+-+-+-+-+-+-+
|   Options ...
+-+-+-+-+-+-+-+-+-+-+-+-
```

IP Fields:

Source Address
: An address assigned to the interface from which the advertisement is sent.

Destination Address
: For solicited advertisements, the Source Address of an invoking Neighbor Solicitation or, if the solicitation's Source Address is the unspecified address, the all-nodes multicast address.

  For unsolicited advertisements typically the all-nodes multicast address.

Hop Limit 255

Authentication Header
: If a Security Association for the IP Authentication Header exists between the sender and the destination address, then the sender SHOULD include this header.

ICMP Fields:

Type 136

Code 0

Checksum The ICMP checksum. See [ICMPv6].

R Router flag. When set, the R-bit indicates that the sender is a router. The R-bit is used by Neighbor Unreachability Detection to detect a router that changes to a host.

S Solicited flag. When set, the S-bit indicates that the advertisement was sent in response to a Neighbor Solicitation from the Destination address. The S-bit is used as a reachability confirmation for Neighbor Unreachability Detection. It MUST NOT be set in multicast advertisements or in unsolicited unicast advertisements.

O Override flag. When set, the O-bit indicates that the advertisement should override an existing cache entry and update the cached link-layer address. When it is not set the advertisement will not update a cached link-layer address though it will update an existing Neighbor Cache entry for which no link-layer address is known. It SHOULD NOT be set in solicited advertisements for anycast addresses and in solicited proxy advertisements. It SHOULD be set in other solicited advertisements and in unsolicited advertisements.

Reserved 29-bit unused field. It MUST be initialized to zero by the sender and MUST be ignored by the receiver.

Target Address

For solicited advertisements, the Target Address field in the Neighbor Solicitation message that prompted this advertisement. For an unsolicited advertisement, the address whose link-layer address has changed. The Target Address MUST NOT be a multicast address.

Possible options:

Target link-layer address

The link-layer address for the target, i.e., the sender of the advertisement. This option MUST be included on link layers that have addresses when responding to multicast solicitations. When responding to a unicast Neighbor Solicitation this option SHOULD be included.

The option MUST be included for multicast solicitations in order to avoid infinite Neighbor Solicitation "recursion" when the peer node does not have a cache entry to return a Neighbor Advertisements message. When responding to unicast solicitations, the option can be omitted since the sender of the solicitation has the correct link-layer address; otherwise it would not have be able to send the unicast solicitation in the first place. However, including the link-layer address in this case adds little overhead and eliminates a potential race condition where the sender deletes the cached link-layer address prior to receiving a response to a previous solicitation.

Future versions of this protocol may define new option types. Receivers MUST silently ignore any options they do not recognize and continue processing the message.

4.5. Redirect Message Format

Routers send Redirect packets to inform a host of a better first-hop node on the path to a destination. Hosts can be redirected to a better first-hop router but can also be informed by a redirect that the destination is in fact a neighbor. The latter is accomplished by setting the ICMP Target Address equal to the ICMP Destination Address.

```
 0                   1                   2                   3
 0 1 2 3 4 5 6 7 8 9 0 1 2 3 4 5 6 7 8 9 0 1 2 3 4 5 6 7 8 9 0 1
+-+-+-+-+-+-+-+-+-+-+-+-+-+-+-+-+-+-+-+-+-+-+-+-+-+-+-+-+-+-+-+-+
|     Type      |     Code      |          Checksum             |
+-+-+-+-+-+-+-+-+-+-+-+-+-+-+-+-+-+-+-+-+-+-+-+-+-+-+-+-+-+-+-+-+
|                           Reserved                            |
+-+-+-+-+-+-+-+-+-+-+-+-+-+-+-+-+-+-+-+-+-+-+-+-+-+-+-+-+-+-+-+-+
|                                                               |
+                                                               +
|                                                               |
+                       Target Address                          +
|                                                               |
+                                                               +
|                                                               |
+-+-+-+-+-+-+-+-+-+-+-+-+-+-+-+-+-+-+-+-+-+-+-+-+-+-+-+-+-+-+-+-+
|                                                               |
+                                                               +
|                                                               |
+                     Destination Address                       +
|                                                               |
+                                                               +
|                                                               |
+-+-+-+-+-+-+-+-+-+-+-+-+-+-+-+-+-+-+-+-+-+-+-+-+-+-+-+-+-+-+-+-+
|   Options ...
+-+-+-+-+-+-+-+-+-+-+-+-
```

IP Fields:

Source Address
MUST be the link-local address assigned to the interface from which this message is sent.

Destination Address
The Source Address of the packet that triggered the redirect.

Hop Limit 255

Authentication Header
: If a Security Association for the IP Authentication Header exists between the sender and the destination address, then the sender SHOULD include this header.

ICMP Fields:

Type
: 137

Code
: 0

Checksum
: The ICMP checksum. See [ICMPv6].

Reserved
: This field is unused. It MUST be initialized to zero by the sender and MUST be ignored by the receiver.

Target Address
: An IP address that is a better first hop to use for the ICMP Destination Address. When the target is the actual endpoint of communication, i.e., the destination is a neighbor, the Target Address field MUST contain the same value as the ICMP Destination Address field. Otherwise the target is a better first-hop router and the Target Address MUST be the router's link-local address so that hosts can uniquely identify routers.

Destination Address
: The IP address of the destination which is redirected to the target.

Possible options:

Target link-layer address
: The link-layer address for the target. It SHOULD be included (if known). Note that on NBMA links, hosts may rely on the presence of the Target Link-Layer Address option in Redirect messages as the means for determining the link-layer addresses of neighbors. In such cases, the option MUST be included in Redirect messages.

Redirected Header
: As much as possible of the IP packet that triggered the sending of the Redirect without making the redirect packet exceed 1280 octets.

4.6. Option Formats

Neighbor Discovery messages include zero or more options, some of which may appear multiple times in the same message. All options are of the form:

```
 0                   1                   2                   3
 0 1 2 3 4 5 6 7 8 9 0 1 2 3 4 5 6 7 8 9 0 1 2 3 4 5 6 7 8 9 0 1
+-+-+-+-+-+-+-+-+-+-+-+-+-+-+-+-+-+-+-+-+-+-+-+-+-+-+-+-+-+-+-+-+
|     Type      |    Length     |              ...              |
+-+-+-+-+-+-+-+-+-+-+-+-+-+-+-+-+-+-+-+-+-+-+-+-+-+-+-+-+-+-+-+-+
~                              ...                              ~
+-+-+-+-+-+-+-+-+-+-+-+-+-+-+-+-+-+-+-+-+-+-+-+-+-+-+-+-+-+-+-+-+
```

Fields:

Type — 8-bit identifier of the type of option. The options defined in this document are:

Option Name	Type
Source Link-Layer Address	1
Target Link-Layer Address	2
Prefix Information	3
Redirected Header	4
MTU	5

Length — 8-bit unsigned integer. The length of the option (including the type and length fields) in units of 8 octets. The value 0 is invalid. Nodes MUST silently discard an ND packet that contains an option with length zero.

4.6.1. Source/Target Link-layer Address

```
 0                   1                   2                   3
 0 1 2 3 4 5 6 7 8 9 0 1 2 3 4 5 6 7 8 9 0 1 2 3 4 5 6 7 8 9 0 1
+-+-+-+-+-+-+-+-+-+-+-+-+-+-+-+-+-+-+-+-+-+-+-+-+-+-+-+-+-+-+-+-+
|     Type      |    Length     |    Link-Layer Address ...
+-+-+-+-+-+-+-+-+-+-+-+-+-+-+-+-+-+-+-+-+-+-+-+-+-+-+-+-+-+-+-+-+
```

Fields:

Type

1 for Source Link-layer Address
2 for Target Link-layer Address

Length The length of the option (including the type and length fields) in units of 8 octets. For example, the length for IEEE 802 addresses is 1 [IPv6-ETHER].

Link-Layer Address
The variable length link-layer address.

The content and format of this field (including byte and bit ordering) is expected to be specified in specific documents that describe how IPv6 operates over different link layers. For instance, [IPv6-ETHER].

Description

The Source Link-Layer Address option contains the link-layer address of the sender of the packet. It is used in the Neighbor Solicitation, Router Solicitation, and Router Advertisement packets.

The Target Link-Layer Address option contains the link-layer address of the target. It is used in Neighbor Advertisement and Redirect packets.

These options MUST be silently ignored for other Neighbor Discovery messages.

4.6.2. Prefix Information

```
 0                   1                   2                   3
 0 1 2 3 4 5 6 7 8 9 0 1 2 3 4 5 6 7 8 9 0 1 2 3 4 5 6 7 8 9 0 1
+-+-+-+-+-+-+-+-+-+-+-+-+-+-+-+-+-+-+-+-+-+-+-+-+-+-+-+-+-+-+-+-+
|     Type      |    Length     | Prefix Length |L|A| Reserved1 |
+-+-+-+-+-+-+-+-+-+-+-+-+-+-+-+-+-+-+-+-+-+-+-+-+-+-+-+-+-+-+-+-+
|                         Valid Lifetime                        |
+-+-+-+-+-+-+-+-+-+-+-+-+-+-+-+-+-+-+-+-+-+-+-+-+-+-+-+-+-+-+-+-+
|                       Preferred Lifetime                      |
+-+-+-+-+-+-+-+-+-+-+-+-+-+-+-+-+-+-+-+-+-+-+-+-+-+-+-+-+-+-+-+-+
|                           Reserved2                           |
+-+-+-+-+-+-+-+-+-+-+-+-+-+-+-+-+-+-+-+-+-+-+-+-+-+-+-+-+-+-+-+-+
|                                                               |
+                                                               +
|                                                               |
+                            Prefix                             +
|                                                               |
+                                                               +
|                                                               |
+-+-+-+-+-+-+-+-+-+-+-+-+-+-+-+-+-+-+-+-+-+-+-+-+-+-+-+-+-+-+-+-+
```

Fields:

Type 3

Length 4

Prefix Length 8-bit unsigned integer. The number of leading bits in the Prefix that are valid. The value ranges from 0 to 128.

L 1-bit on-link flag. When set, indicates that this prefix can be used for on-link determination. When not set the advertisement makes no statement about on-link or off-link properties of the prefix. For instance, the prefix might be used for address configuration with some of the addresses belonging to the prefix being on-link and others being off-link.

A 1-bit autonomous address-configuration flag. When set indicates that this prefix can be used for autonomous address configuration as specified in [ADDRCONF].

Reserved1 6-bit unused field. It MUST be initialized to zero by the sender and MUST be ignored by the receiver.

Valid Lifetime
32-bit unsigned integer. The length of time in seconds (relative to the time the packet is sent) that the prefix is valid for the purpose of on-link determination. A value of all one bits (0xffffffff) represents infinity. The Valid Lifetime is also used by [ADDRCONF].

Preferred Lifetime
32-bit unsigned integer. The length of time in seconds (relative to the time the packet is sent) that addresses generated from the prefix via stateless address autoconfiguration remain preferred [ADDRCONF]. A value of all one bits (0xffffffff) represents infinity. See [ADDRCONF].

Reserved2 This field is unused. It MUST be initialized to zero by the sender and MUST be ignored by the receiver.

Prefix An IP address or a prefix of an IP address. The Prefix Length field contains the number of valid leading bits in the prefix. The bits in the prefix after the prefix length are reserved and MUST be initialized to zero by the sender and ignored by the receiver. A router SHOULD NOT send a prefix option for the link-local prefix and a host SHOULD ignore such a prefix option.

Description

The Prefix Information option provide hosts with on-link prefixes and prefixes for Address Autoconfiguration.

The Prefix Information option appears in Router Advertisement packets and MUST be silently ignored for other messages.

4.6.3. Redirected Header

```
 0                   1                   2                   3
 0 1 2 3 4 5 6 7 8 9 0 1 2 3 4 5 6 7 8 9 0 1 2 3 4 5 6 7 8 9 0 1
+-+-+-+-+-+-+-+-+-+-+-+-+-+-+-+-+-+-+-+-+-+-+-+-+-+-+-+-+-+-+-+-+
|     Type      |    Length     |            Reserved           |
+-+-+-+-+-+-+-+-+-+-+-+-+-+-+-+-+-+-+-+-+-+-+-+-+-+-+-+-+-+-+-+-+
|                           Reserved                            |
+-+-+-+-+-+-+-+-+-+-+-+-+-+-+-+-+-+-+-+-+-+-+-+-+-+-+-+-+-+-+-+-+
|                                                               |
~                       IP header + data                        ~
|                                                               |
+-+-+-+-+-+-+-+-+-+-+-+-+-+-+-+-+-+-+-+-+-+-+-+-+-+-+-+-+-+-+-+-+
```

Fields:

Type 4

Length The length of the option in units of 8 octets.

Reserved These fields are unused. They MUST be initialized to zero by the sender and MUST be ignored by the receiver.

IP header + data

The original packet truncated to ensure that the size of the redirect message does not exceed 1280 octets.

Description

The Redirected Header option is used in Redirect messages and contains all or part of the packet that is being redirected.

This option MUST be silently ignored for other Neighbor Discovery messages.

4.6.4. MTU

```
 0                   1                   2                   3
 0 1 2 3 4 5 6 7 8 9 0 1 2 3 4 5 6 7 8 9 0 1 2 3 4 5 6 7 8 9 0 1
+-+-+-+-+-+-+-+-+-+-+-+-+-+-+-+-+-+-+-+-+-+-+-+-+-+-+-+-+-+-+-+-+
|     Type      |    Length     |           Reserved            |
+-+-+-+-+-+-+-+-+-+-+-+-+-+-+-+-+-+-+-+-+-+-+-+-+-+-+-+-+-+-+-+-+
|                              MTU                              |
+-+-+-+-+-+-+-+-+-+-+-+-+-+-+-+-+-+-+-+-+-+-+-+-+-+-+-+-+-+-+-+-+
```

Fields:

Type 5

Length 1

Reserved This field is unused. It MUST be initialized to zero by the sender and MUST be ignored by the receiver.

MTU 32-bit unsigned integer. The recommended MTU for the link.

Description

The MTU option is used in Router Advertisement messages to insure that all nodes on a link use the same MTU value in those cases where the link MTU is not well known.

This option MUST be silently ignored for other Neighbor Discovery messages.

In configurations in which heterogeneous technologies are bridged together, the maximum supported MTU may differ from one segment to another. If the bridges do not generate ICMP Packet Too Big messages, communicating nodes will be unable to use Path MTU to dynamically determine the appropriate MTU on a per-neighbor basis. In such cases, routers use the MTU option to specify the maximum MTU value that is supported by all segments.

5. CONCEPTUAL MODEL OF A HOST

This section describes a conceptual model of one possible data structure organization that hosts (and to some extent routers) will maintain in interacting with neighboring nodes. The described organization is provided to facilitate the explanation of how the Neighbor Discovery protocol should behave. This document does not mandate that implementations adhere to this model as long as their external behavior is consistent with that described in this document.

This model is only concerned with the aspects of host behavior directly related to Neighbor Discovery. In particular, it does not concern itself with such issues as source address selection or the selecting of an outgoing interface on a multihomed host.

5.1. Conceptual Data Structures

Hosts will need to maintain the following pieces of information for each interface:

Neighbor Cache
- A set of entries about individual neighbors to which traffic has been sent recently. Entries are keyed on the neighbor's on-link unicast IP address and contain such information as its link-layer address, a flag indicating whether the neighbor is a router or a host (called IsRouter in this document), a pointer to any queued packets waiting for address resolution to complete, etc.

  A Neighbor Cache entry also contains information used by the Neighbor Unreachability Detection algorithm, including the reachability state, the number of unanswered probes, and the time the next Neighbor Unreachability Detection event is scheduled to take place.

Destination Cache
- A set of entries about destinations to which traffic has been sent recently. The Destination Cache includes both on-link and off-link destinations and provides a level of indirection into the Neighbor Cache; the Destination Cache maps a destination IP address to the IP address of the next-hop neighbor. This cache is updated with

information learned from Redirect messages. Implementations may find it convenient to store additional information not directly related to Neighbor Discovery in Destination Cache entries, such as the Path MTU (PMTU) and round trip timers maintained by transport protocols.

Prefix List - A list of the prefixes that define a set of addresses that are on-link. Prefix List entries are created from information received in Router Advertisements. Each entry has an associated invalidation timer value (extracted from the advertisement) used to expire prefixes when they become invalid. A special "infinity" timer value specifies that a prefix remains valid forever, unless a new (finite) value is received in a subsequent advertisement.

The link-local prefix is considered to be on the prefix list with an infinite invalidation timer regardless of whether routers are advertising a prefix for it. Received Router Advertisements SHOULD NOT modify the invalidation timer for the link-local prefix.

Default Router List
- A list of routers to which packets may be sent. Router list entries point to entries in the Neighbor Cache; the algorithm for selecting a default router favors routers known to be reachable over those whose reachability is suspect. Each entry also has an associated invalidation timer value (extracted from Router Advertisements) used to delete entries that are no longer advertised.

Note that the above conceptual data structures can be implemented using a variety of techniques. One possible implementation is to use a single longest-match routing table for all of the above data structures. Regardless of the specific implementation, it is critical that the Neighbor Cache entry for a router is shared by all Destination Cache entries using that router in order to prevent redundant Neighbor Unreachability Detection probes.

Note also that other protocols (e.g., IPv6 Mobility) might add additional conceptual data structures. An implementation is at liberty to implement such data structures in any way it pleases. For example, an implementation could merge all conceptual data structures into a single routing table.

The Neighbor Cache contains information maintained by the Neighbor Unreachability Detection algorithm. A key piece of information is a neighbor's reachability state, which is one of five possible values. The following definitions are informal; precise definitions can be found in Section 7.3.2.

INCOMPLETE Address resolution is in progress and the link-layer address of the neighbor has not yet been determined.

REACHABLE Roughly speaking, the neighbor is known to have been reachable recently (within tens of seconds ago).

STALE The neighbor is no longer known to be reachable but until traffic is sent to the neighbor, no attempt should be made to verify its reachability.

DELAY The neighbor is no longer known to be reachable, and traffic has recently been sent to the neighbor. Rather than probe the neighbor immediately, however, delay sending probes for a short while in order to give upper layer protocols a chance to provide reachability confirmation.

PROBE The neighbor is no longer known to be reachable, and unicast Neighbor Solicitation probes are being sent to verify reachability.

5.2. Conceptual Sending Algorithm

When sending a packet to a destination, a node uses a combination of the Destination Cache, the Prefix List, and the Default Router List to determine the IP address of the appropriate next hop, an operation known as "next-hop determination". Once the IP address of the next hop is known, the Neighbor Cache is consulted for link-layer information about that neighbor.

Next-hop determination for a given unicast destination operates as follows. The sender performs a longest prefix match against the Prefix List to determine whether the packet's destination is on- or off-link. If the destination is on-link, the next-hop address is the same as the packet's destination address. Otherwise, the sender selects a router from the Default Router List (following the rules described in Section 6.3.6). If the Default Router List is empty, the sender assumes that the destination is on-link.

For efficiency reasons, next-hop determination is not performed on every packet that is sent. Instead, the results of next-hop determination computations are saved in the Destination Cache (which also contains updates learned from Redirect messages). When the sending node has a packet to send, it first examines the Destination Cache. If no entry exists for the destination, next-hop determination is invoked to create a Destination Cache entry.

Once the IP address of the next-hop node is known, the sender examines the Neighbor Cache for link-layer information about that neighbor. If no entry exists, the sender creates one, sets its state to INCOMPLETE, initiates Address Resolution, and then queues the data packet pending completion of address resolution. For multicast-capable interfaces Address Resolution consists of sending a Neighbor Solicitation message and waiting for a Neighbor Advertisement. When a Neighbor Advertisement response is received, the link-layer addresses is entered in the Neighbor Cache entry and the queued packet is transmitted. The address resolution mechanism is described in detail in Section 7.2.

For multicast packets the next-hop is always the (multicast) destination address and is considered to be on-link. The procedure for determining the link-layer address corresponding to a given IP multicast address can be found in a separate document that covers operating IP over a particular link type (e.g., [IPv6-ETHER]).

Each time a Neighbor Cache entry is accessed while transmitting a unicast packet, the sender checks Neighbor Unreachability Detection related information according to the Neighbor Unreachability Detection algorithm (Section 7.3). This unreachability check might result in the sender transmitting a unicast Neighbor Solicitation to verify that the neighbor is still reachable.

Next-hop determination is done the first time traffic is sent to a destination. As long as subsequent communication to that destination proceeds successfully, the Destination Cache entry continues to be used. If at some point communication ceases to proceed, as determined by the Neighbor Unreachability Detection algorithm, next-hop determination may need to be performed again. For example, traffic through a failed router should be switched to a working router. Likewise, it may be possible to reroute traffic destined for a mobile node to a "mobility agent".

Note that when a node redoes next-hop determination there is no need to discard the complete Destination Cache entry. In fact, it is generally beneficial to retain such cached information as the PMTU and round trip timer values that may also be kept in the Destination Cache entry.

Routers and multihomed hosts have multiple interfaces. The remainder of this document assumes that all sent and received Neighbor Discovery messages refer to the interface of appropriate context. For example, when responding to a Router Solicitation, the corresponding Router Advertisement is sent out the interface on which the solicitation was received.

5.3. Garbage Collection and Timeout Requirements

The conceptual data structures described above use different mechanisms for discarding potentially stale or unused information.

From the perspective of correctness there is no need to periodically purge Destination and Neighbor Cache entries. Although stale information can potentially remain in the cache indefinitely, the Neighbor Unreachability Detection algorithm ensures that stale information is purged quickly if it is actually being used.

To limit the storage needed for the Destination and Neighbor Caches, a node may need to garbage-collect old entries. However, care must be taken to insure that sufficient space is always present to hold the working set of active entries. A small cache may result in an excessive number of Neighbor Discovery messages if entries are discarded and rebuilt in quick succession. Any LRU-based policy that only reclaims entries that have not been used in some time (e.g., ten minutes or more) should be adequate for garbage-collecting unused entries.

A node should retain entries in the Default Router List and the Prefix List until their lifetimes expire. However, a node may garbage collect entries prematurely if it is low on memory. If not all routers are kept on the Default Router list, a node should retain at least two entries in the Default Router List (and preferably more) in order to maintain robust connectivity for off-link destinations.

When removing an entry from the Prefix List there is no need to purge any entries from the Destination or Neighbor Caches. Neighbor Unreachability Detection will efficiently purge any entries in these caches that have become invalid. When removing an entry from the Default Router List, however, any entries in the Destination Cache that go through that router must perform next-hop determination again to select a new default router.

6. ROUTER AND PREFIX DISCOVERY

This section describes router and host behavior related to the Router Discovery portion of Neighbor Discovery. Router Discovery is used to locate neighboring routers as well as learn prefixes and configuration parameters related to address autoconfiguration.

Prefix Discovery is the process through which hosts learn the ranges of IP addresses that reside on-link and can be reached directly without going through a router. Routers send Router Advertisements that indicate whether the sender is willing to be a default router. Router Advertisements also contain Prefix Information options that list the set of prefixes that identify on-link IP addresses.

Stateless Address Autoconfiguration must also obtain subnet prefixes as part of configuring addresses. Although the prefixes used for address autoconfiguration are logically distinct from those used for on-link determination, autoconfiguration information is piggybacked on Router Discovery messages to reduce network traffic. Indeed, the same prefixes can be advertised for on-link determination and address autoconfiguration by specifying the appropriate flags in the Prefix Information options. See [ADDRCONF] for details on how autoconfiguration information is processed.

6.1. Message Validation

6.1.1. Validation of Router Solicitation Messages

Hosts MUST silently discard any received Router Solicitation Messages.

A router MUST silently discard any received Router Solicitation messages that do not satisfy all of the following validity checks:

- The IP Hop Limit field has a value of 255, i.e., the packet could not possibly have been forwarded by a router.

- If the message includes an IP Authentication Header, the message authenticates correctly.

- ICMP Checksum is valid.

- ICMP Code is 0.

- ICMP length (derived from the IP length) is 8 or more octets.

- All included options have a length that is greater than zero.

- If the IP source address is the unspecified address, there is no source link-layer address option in the message.

The contents of the Reserved field, and of any unrecognized options, MUST be ignored. Future, backward-compatible changes to the protocol may specify the contents of the Reserved field or add new options; backward-incompatible changes may use different Code values.

The contents of any defined options that are not specified to be used with Router Solicitation messages MUST be ignored and the packet processed as normal. The only defined option that may appear is the Source Link-Layer Address option.

A solicitation that passes the validity checks is called a "valid solicitation".

6.1.2. Validation of Router Advertisement Messages

A node MUST silently discard any received Router Advertisement messages that do not satisfy all of the following validity checks:

- IP Source Address is a link-local address. Routers must use their link-local address as the source for Router Advertisement and Redirect messages so that hosts can uniquely identify routers.

- The IP Hop Limit field has a value of 255, i.e., the packet could not possibly have been forwarded by a router.

- If the message includes an IP Authentication Header, the message authenticates correctly.

- ICMP Checksum is valid.

- ICMP Code is 0.

- ICMP length (derived from the IP length) is 16 or more octets.

- All included options have a length that is greater than zero.

The contents of the Reserved field, and of any unrecognized options, MUST be ignored. Future, backward-compatible changes to the protocol may specify the contents of the Reserved field or add new options; backward-incompatible changes may use different Code values.

The contents of any defined options that are not specified to be used with Router Advertisement messages MUST be ignored and the packet processed as normal. The only defined options that may appear are the Source Link-Layer Address, Prefix Information and MTU options.

An advertisement that passes the validity checks is called a "valid advertisement".

6.2. Router Specification

6.2.1. Router Configuration Variables

A router MUST allow for the following conceptual variables to be configured by system management. The specific variable names are used for demonstration purposes only, and an implementation is not required to have them, so long as its external behavior is consistent with that described in this document. Default values are specified to simplify configuration in common cases.

The default values for some of the variables listed below may be overridden by specific documents that describe how IPv6 operates over different link layers. This rule simplifies the configuration of Neighbor Discovery over link types with widely differing performance characteristics.

For each multicast interface:

AdvSendAdvertisements
: A flag indicating whether or not the router sends periodic Router Advertisements and responds to Router Solicitations.

  Default: FALSE

  Note that AdvSendAdvertisements MUST be FALSE by default so that a node will not accidentally start acting as a router unless it is explicitly configured by system management to send Router Advertisements.

MaxRtrAdvInterval
: The maximum time allowed between sending unsolicited multicast Router Advertisements from the interface, in seconds. MUST be no less than 4 seconds and no greater than 1800 seconds.

  Default: 600 seconds

MinRtrAdvInterval
: The minimum time allowed between sending unsolicited multicast Router Advertisements from the interface, in seconds. MUST be no less than 3 seconds and no greater than .75 *

MaxRtrAdvInterval.

Default: 0.33 * MaxRtrAdvInterval

AdvManagedFlag
The TRUE/FALSE value to be placed in the "Managed address configuration" flag field in the Router Advertisement. See [ADDRCONF].

Default: FALSE

AdvOtherConfigFlag
The TRUE/FALSE value to be placed in the "Other stateful configuration" flag field in the Router Advertisement. See [ADDRCONF].

Default: FALSE

AdvLinkMTU
The value to be placed in MTU options sent by the router. A value of zero indicates that no MTU options are sent.

Default: 0

AdvReachableTime
The value to be placed in the Reachable Time field in the Router Advertisement messages sent by the router. The value zero means unspecified (by this router). MUST be no greater than 3,600,000 milliseconds (1 hour).

Default: 0

AdvRetransTimer
The value to be placed in the Retrans Timer field in the Router Advertisement messages sent by the router. The value zero means unspecified (by this router).

Default: 0

AdvCurHopLimit
The default value to be placed in the Cur Hop Limit field in the Router Advertisement messages sent by the router. The value should be set to that current diameter of the Internet. The value zero means unspecified (by this router).

Default: The value specified in the "Assigned Numbers" RFC [ASSIGNED] that was in effect at the time of implementation.

AdvDefaultLifetime

The value to be placed in the Router Lifetime field of Router Advertisements sent from the interface, in seconds. MUST be either zero or between MaxRtrAdvInterval and 9000 seconds. A value of zero indicates that the router is not to be used as a default router.

Default: 3 * MaxRtrAdvInterval

AdvPrefixList

A list of prefixes to be placed in Prefix Information options in Router Advertisement messages sent from the interface.

Default: all prefixes that the router advertises via routing protocols as being on-link for the interface from which the advertisement is sent. The link-local prefix SHOULD NOT be included in the list of advertised prefixes.

Each prefix has an associated:

AdvValidLifetime

The value to be placed in the Valid Lifetime in the Prefix Information option, in seconds. The designated value of all 1's (0xffffffff) represents infinity. Implementations MUST allow AdvValidLifetime to be specified in two ways:

- a time that decrements in real time, that is, one that will result in a Lifetime of zero at the specified time in the future, or

- a fixed time that stays the same in consecutive advertisements.

Default: 2592000 seconds (30 days), fixed (i.e., stays the same in consecutive advertisements).

AdvOnLinkFlag
The value to be placed in the on-link flag ("L-bit") field in the Prefix Information option.

Default: TRUE

Automatic address configuration [ADDRCONF] defines additional information associated with each the prefixes:

AdvPreferredLifetime
The value to be placed in the Preferred Lifetime in the Prefix Information option, in seconds. The designated value of all 1's (0xffffffff) represents infinity. See [ADDRCONF] for details on how this value is used. Implementations MUST allow AdvPreferredLifetime to be specified in two ways:

- a time that decrements in real time, that is, one that will result in a Lifetime of zero at a specified time in the future, or

- a fixed time that stays the same in consecutive advertisements.

Default: 604800 seconds (7 days), fixed (i.e., stays the same in consecutive advertisements).

AdvAutonomousFlag
The value to be placed in the Autonomous Flag field in the Prefix Information option. See [ADDRCONF].

Default: TRUE

The above variables contain information that is placed in outgoing Router Advertisement messages. Hosts use the received information to initialize a set of analogous variables that control their external behavior (see Section 6.3.2). Some of these host variables (e.g., CurHopLimit, RetransTimer, and ReachableTime) apply to all nodes including routers. In practice, these variables may not actually be present on routers, since their contents can be derived from the variables described above. However, external router behavior MUST be the same as host behavior with respect to these variables. In particular, this includes the occasional randomization of the ReachableTime value as described in Section 6.3.2.

Protocol constants are defined in Section 10.

6.2.2. Becoming An Advertising Interface

The term "advertising interface" refers to any functioning and enabled multicast interface that has at least one unicast IP address assigned to it and whose corresponding AdvSendAdvertisements flag is TRUE. A router MUST NOT send Router Advertisements out any interface that is not an advertising interface.

An interface may become an advertising interface at times other than system startup. For example:

- changing the AdvSendAdvertisements flag on an enabled interface from FALSE to TRUE, or

- administratively enabling the interface, if it had been administratively disabled, and its AdvSendAdvertisements flag is TRUE, or

- enabling IP forwarding capability (i.e., changing the system from being a host to being a router), when the interface's AdvSendAdvertisements flag is TRUE.

A router MUST join the all-routers multicast address on an advertising interface. Routers respond to Router Solicitations sent to the all-routers address and verify the consistency of Router Advertisements sent by neighboring routers.

6.2.3. Router Advertisement Message Content

A router sends periodic as well as solicited Router Advertisements out its advertising interfaces. Outgoing Router Advertisements are filled with the following values consistent with the message format given in Section 4.2:

- In the Router Lifetime field: the interface's configured AdvDefaultLifetime.

- In the M and O flags: the interface's configured AdvManagedFlag and AdvOtherConfigFlag, respectively. See [ADDRCONF].

- In the Cur Hop Limit field: the interface's configured CurHopLimit.

- In the Reachable Time field: the interface's configured AdvReachableTime.

- In the Retrans Timer field: the interface's configured AdvRetransTimer.

- In the options:

  o Source Link-Layer Address option: link-layer address of the sending interface. This option MAY be omitted to facilitate in-bound load balancing over replicated interfaces.

  o MTU option: the interface's configured AdvLinkMTU value if the value is non-zero. If AdvLinkMTU is zero the MTU option is not sent.

  o Prefix Information options: one Prefix Information option for each prefix listed in AdvPrefixList with the option fields set from the information in the AdvPrefixList entry as follows:

    - In the "on-link" flag: the entry's AdvOnLinkFlag.

    - In the Valid Lifetime field: the entry's AdvValidLifetime.

    - In the "Autonomous address configuration" flag: the entry's AdvAutonomousFlag.

    - In the Preferred Lifetime field: the entry's AdvPreferredLifetime.

A router might want to send Router Advertisements without advertising itself as a default router. For instance, a router might advertise prefixes for address autoconfiguration while not wishing to forward packets. Such a router sets the Router Lifetime field in outgoing advertisements to zero.

A router MAY choose not to include some or all options when sending unsolicited Router Advertisements. For example, if prefix lifetimes are much longer than AdvDefaultLifetime, including them every few advertisements may be sufficient. However, when responding to a Router Solicitation or while sending the first few initial unsolicited advertisements, a router SHOULD include all options so that all information (e.g., prefixes) is propagated quickly during system initialization.

If including all options causes the size of an advertisement to exceed the link MTU, multiple advertisements can be sent, each containing a subset of the options.

6.2.4. Sending Unsolicited Router Advertisements

A host MUST NOT send Router Advertisement messages at any time.

Unsolicited Router Advertisements are not strictly periodic: the interval between subsequent transmissions is randomized to reduce the probability of synchronization with the advertisements from other routers on the same link [SYNC]. Each advertising interface has its own timer. Whenever a multicast advertisement is sent from an interface, the timer is reset to a uniformly-distributed random value between the interface's configured MinRtrAdvInterval and MaxRtrAdvInterval; expiration of the timer causes the next advertisement to be sent and a new random value to be chosen.

For the first few advertisements (up to MAX_INITIAL_RTR_ADVERTISEMENTS) sent from an interface when it becomes an advertising interface, if the randomly chosen interval is greater than MAX_INITIAL_RTR_ADVERT_INTERVAL, the timer SHOULD be set to MAX_INITIAL_RTR_ADVERT_INTERVAL instead. Using a smaller interval for the initial advertisements increases the likelihood of a router being discovered quickly when it first becomes available, in the presence of possible packet loss.

The information contained in Router Advertisements may change through actions of system management. For instance, the lifetime of advertised prefixes may change, new prefixes could be added, a router could cease to be a router (i.e., switch from being a router to being a host), etc. In such cases, the router MAY transmit up to MAX_INITIAL_RTR_ADVERTISEMENTS unsolicited advertisements, using the same rules as when an interface becomes an advertising interface.

6.2.5. Ceasing To Be An Advertising Interface

An interface may cease to be an advertising interface, through actions of system management such as:

- changing the AdvSendAdvertisements flag of an enabled interface from TRUE to FALSE, or
- administratively disabling the interface, or
- shutting down the system.

RFC 2461 46

In such cases the router SHOULD transmit one or more (but not more than MAX_FINAL_RTR_ADVERTISEMENTS) final multicast Router Advertisements on the interface with a Router Lifetime field of zero. In the case of a router becoming a host, the system SHOULD also depart from the all-routers IP multicast group on all interfaces on which the router supports IP multicast (whether or not they had been advertising interfaces). In addition, the host MUST insure that subsequent Neighbor Advertisement messages sent from the interface have the Router flag set to zero.

Note that system management may disable a router's IP forwarding capability (i.e., changing the system from being a router to being a host), a step that does not necessarily imply that the router's interfaces stop being advertising interfaces. In such cases, subsequent Router Advertisements MUST set the Router Lifetime field to zero.

6.2.6. Processing Router Solicitations

A host MUST silently discard any received Router Solicitation messages.

In addition to sending periodic, unsolicited advertisements, a router sends advertisements in response to valid solicitations received on an advertising interface. A router MAY choose to unicast the response directly to the soliciting host's address (if the solicitation's source address is not the unspecified address), but the usual case is to multicast the response to the all-nodes group. In the latter case, the interface's interval timer is reset to a new random value, as if an unsolicited advertisement had just been sent (see Section 6.2.4).

In all cases, Router Advertisements sent in response to a Router Solicitation MUST be delayed by a random time between 0 and MAX_RA_DELAY_TIME seconds. (If a single advertisement is sent in response to multiple solicitations, the delay is relative to the first solicitation.) In addition, consecutive Router Advertisements sent to the all-nodes multicast address MUST be rate limited to no more than one advertisement every MIN_DELAY_BETWEEN_RAS seconds.

A router might process Router Solicitations as follows:

- Upon receipt of a Router Solicitation, compute a random delay within the range 0 through MAX_RA_DELAY_TIME. If the computed value corresponds to a time later than the time the next multicast Router Advertisement is scheduled to be sent, ignore the random delay and send the advertisement at the already-scheduled time.

- If the router sent a multicast Router Advertisement (solicited or unsolicited) within the last MIN_DELAY_BETWEEN_RAS seconds, schedule the advertisement to be sent at a time corresponding to MIN_DELAY_BETWEEN_RAS plus the random value after the previous advertisement was sent. This ensures that the multicast Router Advertisements are rate limited.

- Otherwise, schedule the sending of a Router Advertisement at the time given by the random value.

Note that a router is permitted to send multicast Router Advertisements more frequently than indicated by the MinRtrAdvInterval configuration variable so long as the more frequent advertisements are responses to Router Solicitations. In all cases, however, unsolicited multicast advertisements MUST NOT be sent more frequently than indicated by MinRtrAdvInterval.

Router Solicitations in which the Source Address is the unspecified address MUST NOT update the router's Neighbor Cache; solicitations with a proper source address update the Neighbor Cache as follows. If the router already has a Neighbor Cache entry for the solicitation's sender, the solicitation contains a Source Link-Layer Address option, and the received link-layer address differs from that already in the cache, the link-layer address SHOULD be updated in the appropriate Neighbor Cache entry, and its reachability state MUST also be set to STALE. If there is no existing Neighbor Cache entry for the solicitation's sender, the router creates one, installs the link-layer address and sets its reachability state to STALE as specified in Section 7.3.3. Whether or not a Source Link-Layer Address option is provided, if a Neighbor Cache entry for the solicitation's sender exists (or is created) the entry's IsRouter flag MUST be set to FALSE.

6.2.7. Router Advertisement Consistency

Routers SHOULD inspect valid Router Advertisements sent by other routers and verify that the routers are advertising consistent information on a link. Detected inconsistencies indicate that one or more routers might be misconfigured and SHOULD be logged to system or network management. The minimum set of information to check includes:

- Cur Hop Limit values (except for the unspecified value of zero).

- Values of the M or O flags.

- Reachable Time values (except for the unspecified value of zero).

- Retrans Timer values (except for the unspecified value of zero).

- Values in the MTU options.

- Preferred and Valid Lifetimes for the same prefix. If AdvPreferredLifetime and/or AdvValidLifetime decrement in real time as specified in section 6.2.7 then the comparison of the lifetimes can not compare the content of the fields in the Router Advertisement but must instead compare the time at which the prefix will become deprecated and invalidated, respectively. Due to link propagation delays and potentially poorly synchronized clocks between the routers such comparison SHOULD allow some time skew.

Note that it is not an error for different routers to advertise different sets of prefixes. Also, some routers might leave some fields as unspecified, i.e., with the value zero, while other routers specify values. The logging of errors SHOULD be restricted to conflicting information that causes hosts to switch from one value to another with each received advertisement.

Any other action on reception of Router Advertisement messages by a router is beyond the scope of this document.

6.2.8. Link-local Address Change

The link-local address on a router SHOULD change rarely, if ever.

Nodes receiving Neighbor Discovery messages use the source address to identify the sender. If multiple packets from the same router contain different source addresses, nodes will assume they come from different routers, leading to undesirable behavior. For example, a node will ignore Redirect messages that are believed to have been sent by a router other than the current first-hop router. Thus the source address used in Router Advertisements sent by a particular router must be identical to the target address in a Redirect message when redirecting to that router.

Using the link-local address to uniquely identify routers on the link has the benefit that the address a router is known by should not change when a site renumbers.

If a router changes the link-local address for one of its interfaces, it SHOULD inform hosts of this change. The router SHOULD multicast a few Router Advertisements from the old link-local address with the Router Lifetime field set to zero and also multicast a few Router Advertisements from the new link-local address. The overall effect should be the same as if one interface ceases being an advertising interface, and a different one starts being an advertising interface.

6.3. Host Specification

6.3.1. Host Configuration Variables

None.

6.3.2. Host Variables

A host maintains certain Neighbor Discovery related variables in addition to the data structures defined in Section 5.1. The specific variable names are used for demonstration purposes only, and an implementation is not required to have them, so long as its external behavior is consistent with that described in this document.

These variables have default values that are overridden by information received in Router Advertisement messages. The default values are used when there is no router on the link or when all received Router Advertisements have left a particular value unspecified.

The default values in this specification may be overridden by specific documents that describe how IP operates over different link layers. This rule allows Neighbor Discovery to operate over links with widely varying performance characteristics.

For each interface:

LinkMTU
: The MTU of the link.
Default: The valued defined in the specific document that describes how IPv6 operates over the particular link layer (e.g., [IPv6-ETHER]).

CurHopLimit
: The default hop limit to be used when sending (unicast) IP packets.

Default: The value specified in the "Assigned Numbers" RFC [ASSIGNED] that was in effect at the time of implementation.

BaseReachableTime
: A base value used for computing the random ReachableTime value.

Default: REACHABLE_TIME milliseconds.

ReachableTime
: The time a neighbor is considered reachable after receiving a reachability confirmation.

This value should be a uniformly-distributed random value between MIN_RANDOM_FACTOR and MAX_RANDOM_FACTOR times BaseReachableTime milliseconds. A new random value should be calculated when BaseReachableTime changes (due to Router Advertisements) or at least every few hours even if no Router Advertisements are received.

RetransTimer — The time between retransmissions of Neighbor Solicitation messages to a neighbor when resolving the address or when probing the reachability of a neighbor.

Default: RETRANS_TIMER milliseconds

6.3.3. Interface Initialization

The host joins the all-nodes multicast address on all multicast-capable interfaces.

6.3.4. Processing Received Router Advertisements

When multiple routers are present, the information advertised collectively by all routers may be a superset of the information contained in a single Router Advertisement. Moreover, information may also be obtained through other dynamic means, such as stateful autoconfiguration. Hosts accept the union of all received information; the receipt of a Router Advertisement MUST NOT invalidate all information received in a previous advertisement or from another source. However, when received information for a specific parameter (e.g., Link MTU) or option (e.g., Lifetime on a specific Prefix) differs from information received earlier, and the parameter/option can only have one value, the most recently-received information is considered authoritative.

Some Router Advertisement fields (e.g., Cur Hop Limit, Reachable Time and Retrans Timer) may contain a value denoting unspecified. In such cases, the parameter should be ignored and the host should continue using whatever value it is already using. In particular, a host MUST NOT interpret the unspecified value as meaning change back to the default value that was in use before the first Router Advertisement was received. This rule prevents hosts from continually changing an internal variable when one router advertises a specific value, but other routers advertise the unspecified value.

On receipt of a valid Router Advertisement, a host extracts the source address of the packet and does the following:

- If the address is not already present in the host's Default Router List, and the advertisement's Router Lifetime is non-zero, create a new entry in the list, and initialize its invalidation timer value from the advertisement's Router Lifetime field.

- If the address is already present in the host's Default Router List as a result of a previously-received advertisement, reset its invalidation timer to the Router Lifetime value in the newly-received advertisement.

- If the address is already present in the host's Default Router List and the received Router Lifetime value is zero, immediately time-out the entry as specified in Section 6.3.5.

To limit the storage needed for the Default Router List, a host MAY choose not to store all of the router addresses discovered via advertisements. However, a host MUST retain at least two router addresses and SHOULD retain more. Default router selections are made whenever communication to a destination appears to be failing. Thus, the more routers on the list, the more likely an alternative working router can be found quickly (e.g., without having to wait for the next advertisement to arrive).

If the received Cur Hop Limit value is non-zero the host SHOULD set its CurHopLimit variable to the received value.

If the received Reachable Time value is non-zero the host SHOULD set its BaseReachableTime variable to the received value. If the new value differs from the previous value, the host SHOULD recompute a new random ReachableTime value. ReachableTime is computed as a uniformly-distributed random value between MIN_RANDOM_FACTOR and MAX_RANDOM_FACTOR times the BaseReachableTime. Using a random component eliminates the possibility Neighbor Unreachability Detection messages synchronize with each other.

In most cases, the advertised Reachable Time value will be the same in consecutive Router Advertisements and a host's BaseReachableTime rarely changes. In such cases, an implementation SHOULD insure that a new random value gets recomputed at least once every few hours.

The RetransTimer variable SHOULD be copied from the Retrans Timer field, if the received value is non-zero.

After extracting information from the fixed part of the Router Advertisement message, the advertisement is scanned for valid options. If the advertisement contains a Source Link-Layer Address option the link-layer address SHOULD be recorded in the Neighbor

Cache entry for the router (creating an entry if necessary) and the IsRouter flag in the Neighbor Cache entry MUST be set to TRUE. If no Source Link-Layer Address is included, but a corresponding Neighbor Cache entry exists, its IsRouter flag MUST be set to TRUE. The IsRouter flag is used by Neighbor Unreachability Detection to determine when a router changes to being a host (i.e., no longer capable of forwarding packets). If a Neighbor Cache entry is created for the router its reachability state MUST be set to STALE as specified in Section 7.3.3. If a cache entry already exists and is updated with a different link-layer address the reachability state MUST also be set to STALE,

If the MTU option is present, hosts SHOULD copy the option's value into LinkMTU so long as the value is greater than or equal to the minimum link MTU [IPv6] and does not exceed the default LinkMTU value specified in the link type specific document (e.g., [IPv6-ETHER]),

Prefix Information options that have the "on-link" (L) flag set indicate a prefix identifying a range of addresses that should be considered on-link. Note, however, that a Prefix Information option with the on-link flag set to zero conveys no information concerning on-link determination and MUST NOT be interpreted to mean that addresses covered by the prefix are off-link. The only way to cancel a previous on-link indication is to advertise that prefix with the L-bit set and the Lifetime set to zero. The default behavior (see Section 5.2) when sending a packet to an address for which no information is known about the on-link status of the address is to forward the packet to a default router; the reception of a Prefix Information option with the "on-link " (L) flag set to zero does not change this behavior. The reasons for an address being treated as on-link is specified in the definition of "on-link" in Section 2.1, Prefixes with the on-link flag set to zero would normally have the autonomous flag set and be used by [ADDRCONF],

For each Prefix Information option with the on-link flag set, a host does the following:

- If the prefix is the link-local prefix, silently ignore the Prefix Information option,

- If the prefix is not already present in the Prefix List, and the Prefix Information option's Valid Lifetime field is non-zero, create a new entry for the prefix and initialize its invalidation timer to the Valid Lifetime value in the Prefix Information option,

- If the prefix is already present in the host's Prefix List as the result of a previously-received advertisement, reset its invalidation timer to the Valid Lifetime value in the Prefix Information option. If the new Lifetime value is zero, time-out the prefix immediately (see Section 6.3.5).

- If the Prefix Information option's Valid Lifetime field is zero, and the prefix is not present in the host's Prefix List, silently ignore the option.

Stateless address autoconfiguration [ADDRCONF] may in some circumstances increase the Valid Lifetime of a prefix or ignore it completely in order to prevent a particular denial of service attack. However, since the effect of the same denial of service targeted at the on-link prefix list is not catastrophic (hosts would send packets to a default router and receive a redirect rather than sending packets directly to a neighbor) the Neighbor Discovery protocol does not impose such a check on the prefix lifetime values.

Note: Implementations can choose to process the on-link aspects of the prefixes separately from the address autoconfiguration aspects of the prefixes by, e.g., passing a copy of each valid Router Advertisement message to both an "on-link" and an "addrconf" function. Each function can then operate independently on the prefixes that have the appropriate flag set.

6.3.5. Timing out Prefixes and Default Routers

Whenever the invalidation timer expires for a Prefix List entry, that entry is discarded. No existing Destination Cache entries need be updated, however. Should a reachability problem arise with an existing Neighbor Cache entry, Neighbor Unreachability Detection will perform any needed recovery.

Whenever the Lifetime of an entry in the Default Router List expires, that entry is discarded. When removing a router from the Default Router list, the node MUST update the Destination Cache in such a way that all entries using the router perform next-hop determination again rather than continue sending traffic to the (deleted) router.

6.3.6. Default Router Selection

The algorithm for selecting a router depends in part on whether or not a router is known to be reachable. The exact details of how a node keeps track of a neighbor's reachability state are covered in Section 7.3. The algorithm for selecting a default router is invoked during next-hop determination when no Destination Cache entry exists for an off-link destination or when communication through an existing router appears to be failing. Under normal conditions, a router would be selected the first time traffic is sent to a destination, with subsequent traffic for that destination using the same router as indicated in the Destination Cache modulo any changes to the Destination Cache caused by Redirect messages.

The policy for selecting routers from the Default Router List is as follows:

1) Routers that are reachable or probably reachable (i.e., in any state other than INCOMPLETE) SHOULD be preferred over routers whose reachability is unknown or suspect (i.e., in the INCOMPLETE state, or for which no Neighbor Cache entry exists). An implementation may choose to always return the same router or cycle through the router list in a round-robin fashion as long as it always returns a reachable or a probably reachable router when one is available.

2) When no routers on the list are known to be reachable or probably reachable, routers SHOULD be selected in a round-robin fashion, so that subsequent requests for a default router do not return the same router until all other routers have been selected.

   Cycling through the router list in this case ensures that all available routers are actively probed by the Neighbor Unreachability Detection algorithm. A request for a default router is made in conjunction with the sending of a packet to a router, and the selected router will be probed for reachability as a side effect.

3) If the Default Router List is empty, assume that all destinations are on-link as specified in Section 5.2.

6.3.7. Sending Router Solicitations

When an interface becomes enabled, a host may be unwilling to wait for the next unsolicited Router Advertisement to locate default routers or learn prefixes. To obtain Router Advertisements quickly, a host SHOULD transmit up to MAX_RTR_SOLICITATIONS Router Solicitation messages each separated by at least RTR_SOLICITATION_INTERVAL seconds. Router Solicitations may be sent after any of the following events:

- The interface is initialized at system startup time.

- The interface is reinitialized after a temporary interface failure or after being temporarily disabled by system management.

- The system changes from being a router to being a host, by having its IP forwarding capability turned off by system management.

- The host attaches to a link for the first time.

- The host re-attaches to a link after being detached for some time.

A host sends Router Solicitations to the All-Routers multicast address. The IP source address is set to either one of the interface's unicast addresses or the unspecified address. The Source Link-Layer Address option SHOULD be set to the host's link-layer address, if the IP source address is not the unspecified address.

Before a host sends an initial solicitation, it SHOULD delay the transmission for a random amount of time between 0 and MAX_RTR_SOLICITATION_DELAY. This serves to alleviate congestion when many hosts start up on a link at the same time, such as might happen after recovery from a power failure. If a host has already performed a random delay since the interface became (re)enabled (e.g., as part of Duplicate Address Detection [ADDRCONF]) there is no need to delay again before sending the first Router Solicitation message.

Once the host sends a Router Solicitation, and receives a valid Router Advertisement with a non-zero Router Lifetime, the host MUST desist from sending additional solicitations on that interface, until the next time one of the above events occurs. Moreover, a host SHOULD send at least one solicitation in the case where an advertisement is received prior to having sent a solicitation. Unsolicited Router Advertisements may be incomplete (see Section 6.2.3); solicited advertisements are expected to contain complete information.

If a host sends MAX_RTR_SOLICITATIONS solicitations, and receives no Router Advertisements after having waited MAX_RTR_SOLICITATION_DELAY seconds after sending the last solicitation, the host concludes that there are no routers on the link for the purpose of [ADDRCONF]. However, the host continues to receive and process Router Advertisements messages in the event that routers appear on the link.

7. ADDRESS RESOLUTION AND NEIGHBOR UNREACHABILITY DETECTION

This section describes the functions related to Neighbor Solicitation and Neighbor Advertisement messages and includes descriptions of address resolution and the Neighbor Unreachability Detection algorithm.

Neighbor Solicitation and Advertisement messages are also used for Duplicate Address Detection as specified by [ADDRCONF]. In particular, Duplicate Address Detection sends Neighbor Solicitation messages with an unspecified source address targeting its own "tentative" address. Such messages trigger nodes already using the address to respond with a multicast Neighbor Advertisement indicating that the address is in use.

7.1. Message Validation

7.1.1. Validation of Neighbor Solicitations

A node MUST silently discard any received Neighbor Solicitation messages that do not satisfy all of the following validity checks:

- The IP Hop Limit field has a value of 255, i.e., the packet could not possibly have been forwarded by a router.

- If the message includes an IP Authentication Header, the message authenticates correctly.

- ICMP Checksum is valid.

- ICMP Code is 0.

- ICMP length (derived from the IP length) is 24 or more octets.

- Target Address is not a multicast address.

- All included options have a length that is greater than zero.

- If the IP source address is the unspecified address, the IP destination address is a solicited-node multicast address.

- If the IP source address is the unspecified address, there is no source link-layer address option in the message.

The contents of the Reserved field, and of any unrecognized options, MUST be ignored. Future, backward-compatible changes to the protocol may specify the contents of the Reserved field or add new options; backward-incompatible changes may use different Code values.

The contents of any defined options that are not specified to be used with Neighbor Solicitation messages MUST be ignored and the packet processed as normal. The only defined option that may appear is the Source Link-Layer Address option.

A Neighbor Solicitation that passes the validity checks is called a "valid solicitation".

7.1.2. Validation of Neighbor Advertisements

A node MUST silently discard any received Neighbor Advertisement messages that do not satisfy all of the following validity checks:

- The IP Hop Limit field has a value of 255, i.e., the packet could not possibly have been forwarded by a router.

- If the message includes an IP Authentication Header, the message authenticates correctly.

- ICMP Checksum is valid.

- ICMP Code is 0.

- ICMP length (derived from the IP length) is 24 or more octets.

- Target Address is not a multicast address.

- If the IP Destination Address is a multicast address the Solicited flag is zero.

- All included options have a length that is greater than zero.

The contents of the Reserved field, and of any unrecognized options, MUST be ignored. Future, backward-compatible changes to the protocol may specify the contents of the Reserved field or add new options; backward-incompatible changes may use different Code values.

The contents of any defined options that are not specified to be used with Neighbor Advertisement messages MUST be ignored and the packet processed as normal. The only defined option that may appear is the Target Link-Layer Address option.

A Neighbor Advertisements that passes the validity checks is called a "valid advertisement".

7.2. Address Resolution

Address resolution is the process through which a node determines the link-layer address of a neighbor given only its IP address. Address resolution is performed only on addresses that are determined to be on-link and for which the sender does not know the corresponding link-layer address. Address resolution is never performed on multicast addresses.

7.2.1. Interface Initialization

When a multicast-capable interface becomes enabled the node MUST join the all-nodes multicast address on that interface, as well as the solicited-node multicast address corresponding to each of the IP addresses assigned to the interface.

The set of addresses assigned to an interface may change over time. New addresses might be added and old addresses might be removed [ADDRCONF]. In such cases the node MUST join and leave the solicited-node multicast address corresponding to the new and old addresses, respectively. Note that multiple unicast addresses may map into the same solicited-node multicast address; a node MUST NOT leave the solicited-node multicast group until all assigned addresses corresponding to that multicast address have been removed.

7.2.2. Sending Neighbor Solicitations

When a node has a unicast packet to send to a neighbor, but does not know the neighbor's link-layer address, it performs address resolution. For multicast-capable interfaces this entails creating a Neighbor Cache entry in the INCOMPLETE state and transmitting a Neighbor Solicitation message targeted at the neighbor. The solicitation is sent to the solicited-node multicast address corresponding to the target address.

If the source address of the packet prompting the solicitation is the same as one of the addresses assigned to the outgoing interface, that address SHOULD be placed in the IP Source Address of the outgoing solicitation. Otherwise, any one of the addresses assigned to the interface should be used. Using the prompting packet's source address when possible insures that the recipient of the Neighbor Solicitation installs in its Neighbor Cache the IP address that is highly likely to be used in subsequent return traffic belonging to the prompting packet's "connection".

If the solicitation is being sent to a solicited-node multicast address, the sender MUST include its link-layer address (if it has one) as a Source Link-Layer Address option. Otherwise, the sender SHOULD include its link-layer address (if it has one) as a Source Link-Layer Address option. Including the source link-layer address in a multicast solicitation is required to give the target an address to which it can send the Neighbor Advertisement. On unicast solicitations, an implementation MAY omit the Source Link-Layer Address option. The assumption here is that if the sender has a peer's link-layer address in its cache, there is a high probability that the peer will also have an entry in its cache for the sender. Consequently, it need not be sent.

While waiting for address resolution to complete, the sender MUST, for each neighbor, retain a small queue of packets waiting for address resolution to complete. The queue MUST hold at least one packet, and MAY contain more. However, the number of queued packets per neighbor SHOULD be limited to some small value. When a queue overflows, the new arrival SHOULD replace the oldest entry. Once address resolution completes, the node transmits any queued packets.

While awaiting a response, the sender SHOULD retransmit Neighbor Solicitation messages approximately every RetransTimer milliseconds, even in the absence of additional traffic to the neighbor. Retransmissions MUST be rate-limited to at most one solicitation per neighbor every RetransTimer milliseconds.

If no Neighbor Advertisement is received after MAX_MULTICAST_SOLICIT solicitations, address resolution has failed. The sender MUST return ICMP destination unreachable indications with code 3 (Address Unreachable) for each packet queued awaiting address resolution.

7.2.3. Receipt of Neighbor Solicitations

A valid Neighbor Solicitation that does not meet any the following requirements MUST be silently discarded:

- The Target Address is a "valid" unicast or anycast address assigned to the receiving interface [ADDRCONF],

- The Target Address is a unicast address for which the node is offering proxy service, or

- The Target Address is a "tentative" address on which Duplicate Address Detection is being performed [ADDRCONF].

If the Target Address is tentative, the Neighbor Solicitation should be processed as described in [ADDRCONF]. Otherwise, the following description applies. If the Source Address is not the unspecified address and, on link layers that have addresses, the solicitation includes a Source Link-Layer Address option, then the recipient SHOULD create or update the Neighbor Cache entry for the IP Source Address of the solicitation. If an entry does not already exist, the node SHOULD create a new one and set its reachability state to STALE as specified in Section 7.3.3. If an entry already exists, and the cached link-layer address differs from the one in the received Source Link-Layer option, the cached address should be replaced by the received address and the entry's reachability state MUST be set to STALE.

If a Neighbor Cache entry is created the IsRouter flag SHOULD be set to FALSE. This will be the case even if the Neighbor Solicitation is sent by a router since the Neighbor Solicitation messages do not contain an indication of whether or not the sender is a router. In the event that the sender is a router, subsequent Neighbor Advertisement or Router Advertisement messages will set the correct IsRouter value. If a Neighbor Cache entry already exists its IsRouter flag MUST NOT be modified.

If the Source Address is the unspecified address the node MUST NOT create or update the Neighbor Cache entry.

After any updates to the Neighbor Cache, the node sends a Neighbor Advertisement response as described in the next section.

7.2.4. Sending Solicited Neighbor Advertisements

A node sends a Neighbor Advertisement in response to a valid Neighbor Solicitation targeting one of the node's assigned addresses. The Target Address of the advertisement is copied from the Target Address of the solicitation. If the solicitation's IP Destination Address is not a multicast address, the Target Link-Layer Address option MAY be omitted; the neighboring node's cached value must already be current in order for the solicitation to have been received. If the solicitation's IP Destination Address is a multicast address, the Target Link-Layer option MUST be included in the advertisement. Furthermore, if the node is a router, it MUST set the Router flag to one; otherwise it MUST set the flag to zero.

If the Target Address is either an anycast address or a unicast address for which the node is providing proxy service, or the Target Link-Layer Address option is not included, the Override flag SHOULD be set to zero. Otherwise, the Override flag SHOULD be set to one. Proper setting of the Override flag ensures that nodes give preference to non-proxy advertisements, even when received after proxy advertisements, and also ensures that the first advertisement for an anycast address "wins".

If the source of the solicitation is the unspecified address, the node MUST set the Solicited flag to zero and multicast the advertisement to the all-nodes address. Otherwise, the node MUST set the Solicited flag to one and unicast the advertisement to the Source Address of the solicitation.

If the Target Address is an anycast address the sender SHOULD delay sending a response for a random time between 0 and MAX_ANYCAST_DELAY_TIME seconds.

Because unicast Neighbor Solicitations are not required to include a Source Link-Layer Address, it is possible that a node sending a solicited Neighbor Advertisement does not have a corresponding link-layer address for its neighbor in its Neighbor Cache. In such situations, a node will first have to use Neighbor Discovery to determine the link-layer address of its neighbor (i.e, send out a multicast Neighbor Solicitation).

7.2.5. Receipt of Neighbor Advertisements

When a valid Neighbor Advertisement is received (either solicited or unsolicited), the Neighbor Cache is searched for the target's entry. If no entry exists, the advertisement SHOULD be silently discarded. There is no need to create an entry if none exists, since the recipient has apparently not initiated any communication with the target.

Once the appropriate Neighbor Cache entry has been located, the specific actions taken depend on the state of the Neighbor Cache entry, the flags in the advertisement and the actual link-layer address supplied.

If the target's Neighbor Cache entry is in the INCOMPLETE state when the advertisement is received, one of two things happens. If the link layer has addresses and no Target Link-Layer address option is included, the receiving node SHOULD silently discard the received advertisement. Otherwise, the receiving node performs the following steps:

- It records the link-layer address in the Neighbor Cache entry.

- If the advertisement's Solicited flag is set, the state of the entry is set to REACHABLE, otherwise it is set to STALE.

- It sets the IsRouter flag in the cache entry based on the Router flag in the received advertisement.

- It sends any packets queued for the neighbor awaiting address resolution.

Note that the Override flag is ignored if the entry is in the INCOMPLETE state.

If the target's Neighbor Cache entry is in any state other than INCOMPLETE when the advertisement is received, processing becomes quite a bit more complex. If the Override flag is clear and the supplied link-layer address differs from that in the cache, then one of two actions takes place: if the state of the entry is REACHABLE, set it to STALE, but do not update the entry in any other way; otherwise, the received advertisement should be ignored and MUST NOT update the cache. If the Override flag is set, both the Override flag is clear and the supplied link-layer address is the same as that in the cache, or no Target Link-layer address option was supplied, the received advertisement MUST update the Neighbor Cache entry as follows:

- The link-layer address in the Target Link-Layer Address option MUST be inserted in the cache (if one is supplied and is different than the already recorded address).

- If the Solicited flag is set, the state of the entry MUST be set to REACHABLE. If the Solicited flag is zero and the link-layer address was updated with a different address the state MUST be set to STALE. Otherwise, the entry's state remains unchanged.

  An advertisement's Solicited flag should only be set if the advertisement is a response to a Neighbor Solicitation. Because Neighbor Unreachability Detection Solicitations are sent to the cached link-layer address, receipt of a solicited advertisement indicates that the forward path is working. Receipt of an unsolicited advertisement, however, suggests that a neighbor has urgent information to announce (e.g., a changed link-layer address). If the urgent information indicates a change from what a node is currently using, the node should verify the reachability of the (new) path when it sends the next packet. There is no need to update the state for unsolicited advertisements that do not change the contents of the cache.

- The IsRouter flag in the cache entry MUST be set based on the Router flag in the received advertisement. In those cases where the IsRouter flag changes from TRUE to FALSE as a result of this update, the node MUST remove that router from the Default Router List and update the Destination Cache entries for all destinations using that neighbor as a router as specified in Section 7.3.3. This is needed to detect when a node that is used as a router stops forwarding packets due to being configured as a host.

The above rules ensure that the cache is updated either when the Neighbor Advertisement takes precedence (i.e., the Override flag is set) or when the Neighbor Advertisement refers to the same link-layer address that is currently recorded in the cache. If none of the above apply, the advertisement prompts future Neighbor Unreachability Detection (if it is not already in progress) by changing the state in the cache entry.

7.2.6. Sending Unsolicited Neighbor Advertisements

In some cases a node may be able to determine that its link-layer address has changed (e.g., hot-swap of an interface card) and may wish to inform its neighbors of the new link-layer address quickly. In such cases a node MAY send up to MAX_NEIGHBOR_ADVERTISEMENT unsolicited Neighbor Advertisement messages to the all-nodes multicast address. These advertisements MUST be separated by at least RetransTimer seconds.

The Target Address field in the unsolicited advertisement is set to an IP address of the interface, and the Target Link-Layer Address option is filled with the new link-layer address. The Solicited flag MUST be set to zero, in order to avoid confusing the Neighbor Unreachability Detection algorithm. If the node is a router, it MUST set the Router flag to one; otherwise it MUST set it to zero. The Override flag MAY be set to either zero or one. In either case, neighboring nodes will immediately change the state of their Neighbor Cache entries for the Target Address to STALE, prompting them to verify the path for reachability. If the Override flag is set to one, neighboring nodes will install the new link-layer address in their caches. Otherwise, they will ignore the new link-layer address, choosing instead to probe the cached address.

A node that has multiple IP addresses assigned to an interface MAY multicast a separate Neighbor Advertisement for each address. In such a case the node SHOULD introduce a small delay between the sending of each advertisement to reduce the probability of the advertisements being lost due to congestion.

A proxy MAY multicast Neighbor Advertisements when its link-layer address changes or when it is configured (by system management or other mechanisms) to proxy for an address. If there are multiple nodes that are providing proxy services for the same set of addresses the proxies SHOULD provide a mechanism that prevents multiple proxies from multicasting advertisements for any one address, in order to reduce the risk of excessive multicast traffic.

Also, a node belonging to an anycast address MAY multicast unsolicited Neighbor Advertisements for the anycast address when the node's link-layer address changes.

Note that because unsolicited Neighbor Advertisements do not reliably update caches in all nodes (the advertisements might not be received by all nodes), they should only be viewed as a performance optimization to quickly update the caches in most neighbors. The Neighbor Unreachability Detection algorithm ensures that all nodes obtain a reachable link-layer address, though the delay may be slightly longer.

7.2.7. Anycast Neighbor Advertisements

From the perspective of Neighbor Discovery, anycast addresses are treated just like unicast addresses in most cases. Because an anycast address is syntactically the same as a unicast address, nodes performing address resolution or Neighbor Unreachability Detection on an anycast address treat it as if it were a unicast address. No special processing takes place.

Nodes that have an anycast address assigned to an interface treat them exactly the same as if they were unicast addresses with two exceptions. First, Neighbor Advertisements sent in response to a Neighbor Solicitation SHOULD be delayed by a random time between 0 and MAX_ANYCAST_DELAY_TIME to reduce the probability of network congestion. Second, the Override flag in Neighbor Advertisements SHOULD be set to 0, so that when multiple advertisements are received, the first received advertisement is used rather than the most recently received advertisement.

As with unicast addresses, Neighbor Unreachability Detection ensures that a node quickly detects when the current binding for an anycast address becomes invalid.

7.2.8. Proxy Neighbor Advertisements

Under limited circumstances, a router MAY proxy for one or more other nodes, that is, through Neighbor Advertisements indicate that it is willing to accept packets not explicitly addressed to itself. For example, a router might accept packets on behalf of a mobile node that has moved off-link. The mechanisms used by proxy are identical to the mechanisms used with anycast addresses.

A proxy MUST join the solicited-node multicast address(es) that correspond to the IP address(es) assigned to the node for which it is proxying.

All solicited proxy Neighbor Advertisement messages MUST have the Override flag set to zero. This ensures that if the node itself is present on the link its Neighbor Advertisement (with the Override flag set to one) will take precedence of any advertisement received from a proxy. A proxy MAY send unsolicited advertisements with the Override flag set to one as specified in Section 7.2.6, but doing so may cause the proxy advertisement to override a valid entry created by the node itself.

Finally, when sending a proxy advertisement in response to a Neighbor Solicitation, the sender should delay its response by a random time between 0 and MAX_ANYCAST_DELAY_TIME seconds.

7.3. Neighbor Unreachability Detection

Communication to or through a neighbor may fail for numerous reasons at any time, including hardware failure, hot-swap of an interface card, etc. If the destination has failed, no recovery is possible and communication fails. On the other hand, if it is the path that has failed, recovery may be possible. Thus, a node actively tracks the reachability "state" for the neighbors to which it is sending packets.

Neighbor Unreachability Detection is used for all paths between hosts and neighboring nodes, including host-to-host, host-to-router, and router-to-host communication. Neighbor Unreachability Detection may also be used between routers, but is not required if an equivalent mechanism is available, for example, as part of the routing protocols.

When a path to a neighbor appears to be failing, the specific recovery procedure depends on how the neighbor is being used. If the neighbor is the ultimate destination, for example, address resolution should be performed again. If the neighbor is a router, however, attempting to switch to another router would be appropriate. The specific recovery that takes place is covered under next-hop determination; Neighbor Unreachability Detection signals the need for next-hop determination by deleting a Neighbor Cache entry.

Neighbor Unreachability Detection is performed only for neighbors to which unicast packets are sent; it is not used when sending to multicast addresses.

7.3.1. Reachability Confirmation

A neighbor is considered reachable if the node has recently received a confirmation that packets sent recently to the neighbor were received by its IP layer. Positive confirmation can be gathered in two ways: hints from upper layer protocols that indicate a connection is making "forward progress", or receipt of a Neighbor Advertisement message that is a response to a Neighbor Solicitation message.

A connection makes "forward progress" if the packets received from a remote peer can only be arriving if recent packets sent to that peer are actually reaching it. In TCP, for example, receipt of a (new) acknowledgement indicates that previously sent data reached the peer. Likewise, the arrival of new (non-duplicate) data indicates that earlier acknowledgements are being delivered to the remote peer. If packets are reaching the peer, they must also be reaching the sender's next-hop neighbor; thus "forward progress" is a confirmation that the next-hop neighbor is reachable. For off-link destinations, forward progress implies that the first-hop router is reachable. When available, this upper-layer information SHOULD be used.

In some cases (e.g., UDP-based protocols and routers forwarding packets to hosts) such reachability information may not be readily available from upper-layer protocols. When no hints are available and a node is sending packets to a neighbor, the node actively probes the neighbor using unicast Neighbor Solicitation messages to verify that the forward path is still working.

The receipt of a solicited Neighbor Advertisement serves as reachability confirmation, since advertisements with the Solicited flag set to one are sent only in response to a Neighbor Solicitation. Receipt of other Neighbor Discovery messages such as Router Advertisements and Neighbor Advertisement with the Solicited flag set to zero MUST NOT be treated as a reachability confirmation. Receipt of unsolicited messages only confirm the one-way path from the sender to the recipient node. In contrast, Neighbor Unreachability Detection requires that a node keep track of the reachability of the forward path to a neighbor from the its perspective, not the neighbor's perspective. Note that receipt of a solicited advertisement indicates that a path is working in both directions. The solicitation must have reached the neighbor, prompting it to generate an advertisement. Likewise, receipt of an advertisement indicates that the path from the sender to the recipient is working. However, the latter fact is known only to the recipient; the advertisement's sender has no direct way of knowing that the advertisement it sent actually reached a neighbor. From the perspective of Neighbor Unreachability Detection, only the reachability of the forward path is of interest.

7.3.2. Neighbor Cache Entry States

A Neighbor Cache entry can be in one of five states:

INCOMPLETE Address resolution is being performed on the entry. Specifically, a Neighbor Solicitation has been sent to the solicited-node multicast address of the target, but the corresponding Neighbor Advertisement has not yet been received.

REACHABLE Positive confirmation was received within the last ReachableTime milliseconds that the forward path to the neighbor was functioning properly. While

REACHABLE, no special action takes place as packets are sent.

STALE More than ReachableTime milliseconds have elapsed since the last positive confirmation was received that the forward path was functioning properly. While stale, no action takes place until a packet is sent.

The STALE state is entered upon receiving an unsolicited Neighbor Discovery message that updates the cached link-layer address. Receipt of such a message does not confirm reachability, and entering the STALE state insures reachability is verified quickly if the entry is actually being used. However, reachability is not actually verified until the entry is actually used.

DELAY More than ReachableTime milliseconds have elapsed since the last positive confirmation was received that the forward path was functioning properly, and a packet was sent within the last DELAY_FIRST_PROBE_TIME seconds. If no reachability confirmation is received within DELAY_FIRST_PROBE_TIME seconds of entering the DELAY state, send a Neighbor Solicitation and change the state to PROBE.

The DELAY state is an optimization that gives upper-layer protocols additional time to provide reachability confirmation in those cases where ReachableTime milliseconds have passed since the last confirmation due to lack of recent traffic. Without this optimization the opening of a TCP connection after a traffic lull would initiate probes even though the subsequent three-way handshake would provide a reachability confirmation almost immediately.

PROBE A reachability confirmation is actively sought by retransmitting Neighbor Solicitations every RetransTimer milliseconds until a reachability confirmation is received.

7.3.3. Node Behavior

Neighbor Unreachability Detection operates in parallel with the sending of packets to a neighbor. While reasserting a neighbor's reachability, a node continues sending packets to that neighbor using the cached link-layer address. If no traffic is sent to a neighbor, no probes are sent.

When a node needs to perform address resolution on a neighboring address, it creates an entry in the INCOMPLETE state and initiates address resolution as specified in Section 7.2. If address resolution fails, the entry SHOULD be deleted, so that subsequent traffic to that neighbor invokes the next-hop determination procedure again. Invoking next-hop determination at this point insures that alternate default routers are tried.

When a reachability confirmation is received (either through upper-layer advice or a solicited Neighbor Advertisement) an entry's state changes to REACHABLE. The one exception is that upper-layer advice has no effect on entries in the INCOMPLETE state (e.g., for which no link-layer address is cached).

When ReachableTime milliseconds have passed since receipt of the last reachability confirmation for a neighbor, the Neighbor Cache entry's state changes from REACHABLE to STALE.

Note: An implementation may actually defer changing the state from REACHABLE to STALE until a packet is sent to the neighbor, i.e., there need not be an explicit timeout event associated with the expiration of ReachableTime.

The first time a node sends a packet to a neighbor whose entry is STALE, the sender changes the state to DELAY and a sets a timer to expire in DELAY_FIRST_PROBE_TIME seconds. If the entry is still in the DELAY state when the timer expires, the entry's state changes to PROBE. If reachability confirmation is received, the entry's state changes to REACHABLE.

Upon entering the PROBE state, a node sends a unicast Neighbor Solicitation message to the neighbor using the cached link-layer address. While in the PROBE state, a node retransmits Neighbor Solicitation messages every RetransTimer milliseconds until reachability confirmation is obtained. Probes are retransmitted even if no additional packets are sent to the neighbor. If no response is received after waiting RetransTimer milliseconds after sending the MAX_UNICAST_SOLICIT solicitations, retransmissions cease and the entry SHOULD be deleted. Subsequent traffic to that neighbor will recreate the entry and performs address resolution again.

Note that all Neighbor Solicitations are rate-limited on a per-neighbor basis. A node MUST NOT send Neighbor Solicitations to the same neighbor more frequently than once every RetransTimer milliseconds.

A Neighbor Cache entry enters the STALE state when created as a result of receiving packets other than solicited Neighbor Advertisements (i.e., Router Solicitations, Router Advertisements, Redirects, and Neighbor Solicitations). These packets contain the link-layer address of either the sender or, in the case of Redirect, the redirection target. However, receipt of these link-layer addresses does not confirm reachability of the forward-direction path to that node. Placing a newly created Neighbor Cache entry for which the link-layer address is known in the STALE state provides assurance that path failures are detected quickly. In addition, should a cached link-layer address be modified due to receiving one of the above messages the state SHOULD also be set to STALE to provide prompt verification that the path to the new link-layer address is working.

To properly detect the case where a router switches from being a router to being a host (e.g., if its IP forwarding capability is turned off by system management), a node MUST compare the Router flag field in all received Neighbor Advertisement messages with the IsRouter flag recorded in the Neighbor Cache entry. When a node detects that a neighbor has changed from being a router to being a host, the node MUST remove that router from the Default Router List and update the Destination Cache as described in Section 6.3.5. Note that a router may not be listed in the Default Router List, even though a Destination Cache entry is using it (e.g., a host was redirected to it). In such cases, all Destination Cache entries that reference the (former) router must perform next-hop determination again before using the entry.

In some cases, link-specific information may indicate that a path to a neighbor has failed (e.g., the resetting of a virtual circuit). In such cases, link-specific information may be used to purge Neighbor Cache entries before the Neighbor Unreachability Detection would do so. However, link-specific information MUST NOT be used to confirm the reachability of a neighbor; such information does not provide end-to-end confirmation between neighboring IP layers.

8. REDIRECT FUNCTION

This section describes the functions related to the sending and processing of Redirect messages.

Redirect messages are sent by routers to redirect a host to a better first-hop router for a specific destination or to inform hosts that a destination is in fact a neighbor (i.e., on-link). The latter is accomplished by having the ICMP Target Address be equal to the ICMP Destination Address.

A router MUST be able to determine the link-local address for each of its neighboring routers in order to ensure that the target address in a Redirect message identifies the neighbor router by its link-local address. For static routing this requirement implies that the next-hop router's address should be specified using the link-local address of the router. For dynamic routing this requirement implies that all IPv6 routing protocols must somehow exchange the link-local addresses of neighboring routers.

8.1. Validation of Redirect Messages

A host MUST silently discard any received Redirect message that does not satisfy all of the following validity checks:

- IP Source Address is a link-local address. Routers must use their link-local address as the source for Router Advertisement and Redirect messages so that hosts can uniquely identify routers.

- The IP Hop Limit field has a value of 255, i.e., the packet could not possibly have been forwarded by a router.

- If the message includes an IP Authentication Header, the message authenticates correctly.

- ICMP Checksum is valid.

- ICMP Code is 0.

- ICMP length (derived from the IP length) is 40 or more octets.

- The IP source address of the Redirect is the same as the current first-hop router for the specified ICMP Destination Address.

- The ICMP Destination Address field in the redirect message does not contain a multicast address.

- The ICMP Target Address is either a link-local address (when redirected to a router) or the same as the ICMP Destination Address (when redirected to the on-link destination).

- All included options have a length that is greater than zero.

The contents of the Reserved field, and of any unrecognized options MUST be ignored. Future, backward-compatible changes to the protocol may specify the contents of the Reserved field or add new options; backward-incompatible changes may use different Code values.

The contents of any defined options that are not specified to be used with Redirect messages MUST be ignored and the packet processed as normal. The only defined options that may appear are the Target Link-Layer Address option and the Redirected Header option.

A host MUST NOT consider a redirect invalid just because the Target Address of the redirect is not covered under one of the link's prefixes. Part of the semantics of the Redirect message is that the Target Address is on-link.

A redirect that passes the validity checks is called a "valid redirect".

8.2. Router Specification

A router SHOULD send a redirect message, subject to rate limiting, whenever it forwards a packet that is not explicitly addressed to itself (i.e. a packet that is not source routed through the router) in which:

- the Source Address field of the packet identifies a neighbor, and

- the router determines that a better first-hop node resides on the same link as the sending node for the Destination Address of the packet being forwarded, and

- the Destination Address of the packet is not a multicast address, and

The transmitted redirect packet contains, consistent with the message format given in Section 4.5:

- In the Target Address field: the address to which subsequent packets for the destination SHOULD be sent. If the target is a router, that router's link-local address MUST be used. If the target is a host the target address field MUST be set to the same value as the Destination Address field.

- In the Destination Address field: the destination address of the invoking IP packet.

- In the options:

    - o Target Link-Layer Address option: link-layer address of the target, if known.

- o Redirected Header: as much of the forwarded packet as can fit without the redirect packet exceeding 1280 octets in size.

A router MUST limit the rate at which Redirect messages are sent, in order to limit the bandwidth and processing costs incurred by the Redirect messages when the source does not correctly respond to the Redirects, or the source chooses to ignore unauthenticated Redirect messages. More details on the rate-limiting of ICMP error messages can be found in [ICMPv6].

A router MUST NOT update its routing tables upon receipt of a Redirect.

8.3. Host Specification

A host receiving a valid redirect SHOULD update its Destination Cache accordingly so that subsequent traffic goes to the specified target. If no Destination Cache entry exists for the destination, an implementation SHOULD create such an entry.

If the redirect contains a Target Link-Layer Address option the host either creates or updates the Neighbor Cache entry for the target. In both cases the cached link-layer address is copied from the Target Link-Layer Address option. If a Neighbor Cache entry is created for the target its reachability state MUST be set to STALE as specified in Section 7.3.3. If a cache entry already existed and it is updated with a different link-layer address, its reachability state MUST also be set to STALE. If the link-layer address is the same as that already in the cache, the cache entry's state remains unchanged.

If the Target and Destination Addresses are the same, the host MUST treat the Target as on-link. If the Target Address is not the same as the Destination Address, the host MUST set IsRouter to TRUE for the target. If the Target and Destination Addresses are the same, however, one cannot reliably determine whether the Target Address is a router. Consequently, newly created Neighbor Cache entries should set the IsRouter flag to FALSE, while existing cache entries should leave the flag unchanged. If the Target is a router, subsequent Neighbor Advertisement or Router Advertisement messages will update IsRouter accordingly.

Redirect messages apply to all flows that are being sent to a given destination. That is, upon receipt of a Redirect for a Destination Address, all Destination Cache entries to that address should be updated to use the specified next-hop, regardless of the contents of the Flow Label field that appears in the Redirected Header option.

A host MAY have a configuration switch that can be set to make it ignore a Redirect message that does not have an IP Authentication header.

A host MUST NOT send Redirect messages.

9. EXTENSIBILITY - OPTION PROCESSING

Options provide a mechanism for encoding variable length fields, fields that may appear multiple times in the same packet, or information that may not appear in all packets. Options can also be used to add additional functionality to future versions of ND.

In order to ensure that future extensions properly coexist with current implementations, all nodes MUST silently ignore any options they do not recognize in received ND packets and continue processing the packet. All options specified in this document MUST be recognized. A node MUST NOT ignore valid options just because the ND message contains unrecognized ones.

The current set of options is defined in such a way that receivers can process multiple options in the same packet independently of each other. In order to maintain these properties future options SHOULD follow the simple rule:

> The option MUST NOT depend on the presence or absence of any other options. The semantics of an option should depend only on the information in the fixed part of the ND packet and on the information contained in the option itself.

Adhering to the above rule has the following benefits:

1) Receivers can process options independently of one another. For example, an implementation can choose to process the Prefix Information option contained in a Router Advertisement message in a user-space process while the link-layer address option in the same message is processed by routines in the kernel.

2) Should the number of options cause a packet to exceed a link's MTU, multiple packets can carry subsets of the options without any change in semantics.

3) Senders MAY send a subset of options in different packets. For instance, if a prefix's Valid and Preferred Lifetime are high enough, it might not be necessary to include the Prefix Information option in every Router Advertisement. In addition, different routers might send different sets of options. Thus, a receiver MUST NOT associate any action with the absence of an

option in a particular packet. This protocol specifies that receivers should only act on the expiration of timers and on the information that is received in the packets.

Options in Neighbor Discovery packets can appear in any order; receivers MUST be prepared to process them independently of their order. There can also be multiple instances of the same option in a message (e.g., Prefix Information options).

If the number of included options in a Router Advertisement causes the advertisement's size to exceed the link MTU, the router can send multiple separate advertisements each containing a subset of the options.

The amount of data to include in the Redirected Header option MUST be limited so that the entire redirect packet does not exceed 1280 octets.

All options are a multiple of 8 octets of length, ensuring appropriate alignment without any "pad" options. The fields in the options (as well as the fields in ND packets) are defined to align on their natural boundaries (e.g., a 16-bit field is aligned on a 16-bit boundary) with the exception of the 128-bit IP addresses/prefixes, which are aligned on a 64-bit boundary. The link-layer address field contains an uninterpreted octet string; it is aligned on an 8-bit boundary.

The size of an ND packet including the IP header is limited to the link MTU (which is at least 1280 octets). When adding options to an ND packet a node MUST NOT exceed the link MTU.

Future versions of this protocol may define new option types. Receivers MUST silently ignore any options they do not recognize and continue processing the message.

10. PROTOCOL CONSTANTS

Router constants:

MAX_INITIAL_RTR_ADVERT_INTERVAL	16 seconds
MAX_INITIAL_RTR_ADVERTISEMENTS	3 transmissions
MAX_FINAL_RTR_ADVERTISEMENTS	3 transmissions
MIN_DELAY_BETWEEN_RAS	3 seconds
MAX_RA_DELAY_TIME	.5 seconds

Host constants:

MAX_RTR_SOLICITATION_DELAY	1 second
RTR_SOLICITATION_INTERVAL	4 seconds
MAX_RTR_SOLICITATIONS	3 transmissions

Node constants:

MAX_MULTICAST_SOLICIT	3 transmissions
MAX_UNICAST_SOLICIT	3 transmissions
MAX_ANYCAST_DELAY_TIME	1 second
MAX_NEIGHBOR_ADVERTISEMENT	3 transmissions
REACHABLE_TIME	30,000 milliseconds
RETRANS_TIMER	1,000 milliseconds
DELAY_FIRST_PROBE_TIME	5 seconds
MIN_RANDOM_FACTOR	.5
MAX_RANDOM_FACTOR	1.5

Additional protocol constants are defined with the message formats in Section 4.

All protocol constants are subject to change in future revisions of the protocol.

The constants in this specification may be overridden by specific documents that describe how IPv6 operates over different link layers. This rule allows Neighbor Discovery to operate over links with widely varying performance characteristics.

11. SECURITY CONSIDERATIONS

Neighbor Discovery is subject to attacks that cause IP packets to flow to unexpected places. Such attacks can be used to cause denial of service but also allow nodes to intercept and optionally modify packets destined for other nodes.

The protocol reduces the exposure to such threats in the absence of authentication by ignoring ND packets received from off-link senders. The Hop Limit field of all received packets is verified to contain 255, the maximum legal value. Because routers decrement the Hop Limit on all packets they forward, received packets containing a Hop Limit of 255 must have originated from a neighbor.

An example of denial of service attacks is that a node on the link that can send packets with an arbitrary IP source address can both advertise itself as a default router and also send "forged" Router Advertisement messages that immediately time out all other default routers as well as all on-link prefixes. An intruder can achieve this by sending out multiple Router Advertisements, one for each legitimate router, with the source address set to the address of another router, the Router Lifetime field set to zero, and the Preferred and Valid lifetimes set to zero for all the prefixes. Such an attack would cause all packets, for both on-link and off-link destinations, to go to the rogue router. That router can then selectively examine, modify or drop all packets sent on the link. The Neighbor Unreachability Detection will not detect such a black hole as long as the rogue router politely answers the NUD probes with a Neighbor Advertisement with the R-bit set.

Many link layers are also subject to different denial of service attacks such as continuously occupying the link in CSMA/CD networks (e.g., by sending packets closely back-to-back or asserting the collision signal on the link), or originating packets with somebody else's source MAC address to confuse, e.g., Ethernet switches.

The trust model for redirects is the same as in IPv4. A redirect is accepted only if received from the same router that is currently being used for that destination. It is natural to trust the routers on the link. If a host has been redirected to another node (i.e., the destination is on-link) there is no way to prevent the target from issuing another redirect to some other destination. However, this exposure is no worse than it was; the target host, once subverted, could always act as a hidden router to forward traffic elsewhere.

The protocol contains no mechanism to determine which neighbors are authorized to send a particular type of message (e.g., Router Advertisements); any neighbor, presumably even in the presence of authentication, can send Router Advertisement messages thereby being able to cause denial of service. Furthermore, any neighbor can send proxy Neighbor Advertisements as well as unsolicited Neighbor Advertisements as a potential denial of service attack.

Neighbor Discovery protocol packet exchanges can be authenticated using the IP Authentication Header [IPv6-AUTH]. A node SHOULD include an Authentication Header when sending Neighbor Discovery packets if a security association for use with the IP Authentication Header exists for the destination address. The security associations may have been created through manual configuration or through the operation of some key management protocol.

Received Authentication Headers in Neighbor Discovery packets MUST be verified for correctness and packets with incorrect authentication MUST be ignored.

It SHOULD be possible for the system administrator to configure a node to ignore any Neighbor Discovery messages that are not authenticated using either the Authentication Header or Encapsulating Security Payload. The configuration technique for this MUST be documented. Such a switch SHOULD default to allowing unauthenticated messages.

Confidentiality issues are addressed by the IP Security Architecture and the IP Encapsulating Security Payload documents [IPv6-SA, IPv6-ESP].

12. RENUMBERING CONSIDERATIONS

The Neighbor Discovery protocol together with IPv6 Address Autoconfiguration [ADDRCONF] provides mechanisms to aid in renumbering - new prefixes and addresses can be introduced and old ones can be deprecated and removed.

The robustness of these mechanisms is based on all the nodes on the link receiving the Router Advertisement messages in a timely manner. However, a host might be turned off or be unreachable for an extended period of time (i.e., a machine is powered down for months after a project terminates). It is possible to preserve robust renumbering in such cases but it does place some constraints on how long prefixes must be advertised.

Consider the following example in which a prefix is initially advertised with a lifetime of 2 months, but on August 1st it is determined that the prefix needs to be deprecated and removed due to renumbering by September 1st. This can be done by reducing the advertised lifetime to 1 week starting on August 1st and as the cutoff gets closer the lifetimes can be made shorter until by September 1st the prefix is advertised with a zero lifetime. The point is that, if one or more nodes were unplugged from the link prior to September 1st they might still think that the prefix is valid since the last lifetime they received was 2 months. Thus if a node was unplugged on July 31st it thinks the prefix is valid until September 30th. If that node is plugged back in prior to September 30th it may continue to use the old prefix. The only way to force a node to stop using a prefix that was previously advertised with a long Lifetime is to have that node receive an advertisement for that prefix that changes the lifetime downward. The solution in this example is simple: continue advertising the prefix with a lifetime of 0 from September 1st until October 1st.

In general, in order to be robust against nodes that might be unplugged from the link it is important to track the furthest into the future a particular prefix can be viewed valid by any node on the link. The prefix must then be advertised with a 0 Lifetime until that point in future. This "furthest into the future" time is simply the maximum, over all Router Advertisements, of the time the advertisement was sent plus the prefix's Lifetime contained in the advertisement.

The above has an important implication on using infinite lifetimes. If a prefix is advertised with an infinite lifetime, and that prefix later needs to be renumbered, it is undesirable to continue advertising that prefix with a zero lifetime forever. Thus either infinite lifetimes should be avoided or there must be a limit on how long time a node can be unplugged from the link before it is plugged back in again. However, it is unclear how the network administrator can enforce a limit on how long time hosts such as laptops can be unplugged from the link.

Network administrators should give serious consideration to using relatively short lifetimes (i.e., no more than a few weeks). While it might appear that using long lifetimes would help insure robustness, in reality a host will be unable to communicate in the absence of properly functioning routers. Such routers will be sending Router Advertisements that contain appropriate (and current) prefixes. A host connected to a network that has no functioning routers is likely to have more serious problems than just a lack of a valid prefix and address.

The above discussion does not distinguish between the preferred and valid lifetimes. For all practical purposes it is probably sufficient to track the valid lifetime since the preferred lifetime will not exceed the valid lifetime.

REFERENCES

[ADDRCONF] Thomson, S. and T. Narten, "IPv6 Address Autoconfiguration", RFC 2462, December 1998.

[ADDR-ARCH] Hinden, R. and S. Deering, "IP Version 6 Addressing Architecture", RFC 2373, July 1998.

[ANYCST] Partridge, C., Mendez, T. and W. Milliken, "Host Anycasting Service", RFC 1546, November 1993.

[ARP] Plummer, D., "An Ethernet Address Resolution Protocol", STD 37, RFC 826, November 1982.

[HR-CL] Braden, R., Editor, "Requirements for Internet Hosts — Communication Layers", STD 3, RFC 1122, October 1989.

[ICMPv4] Postel, J., "Internet Control Message Protocol", STD 5, RFC 792, September 1981.

[ICMPv6] Conta, A. and S. Deering, "Internet Control Message Protocol (ICMPv6) for the Internet Protocol Version 6 (IPv6) Specification", RFC 2463, December 1998.

[IPv6] Deering, S. and R. Hinden, "Internet Protocol, Version 6 (IPv6) Specification", RFC 2460, December 1998.

[IPv6-ETHER] Crawford, M., "Transmission of IPv6 Packets over Ethernet Networks", RFC 2464, December 1998.

[IPv6-SA] Kent, S. and R. Atkinson, "Security Architecture for the Internet Protocol", RFC 2401, November 1998.

[IPv6-AUTH] Kent, S. and R. Atkinson, "IP Authentication Header", RFC 2402, November 1998.

[IPv6-ESP] Kent, S. and R. Atkinson, "IP Encapsulating Security Payload (ESP)", RFC 2406, November 1998.

[KEYWORDS] Bradner, S., "Key words for use in RFCs to Indicate Requirement Levels", BCP 14, RFC 2119, March 1997.

[RDISC] Deering, S., "ICMP Router Discovery Messages", RFC 1256, September 1991.

[SH-MEDIA] Braden, R., Postel, J. and Y. Rekhter, "Internet Architecture Extensions for Shared Media", RFC 1620, May 1994.

[ASSIGNED] Reynolds, J. and J. Postel, "ASSIGNED NUMBERS", STD 2, RFC 1700, October 1994. See also: http://www.iana.org/numbers.html

[SYNC] S. Floyd, V. Jacobson, "The Synchronization of Periodic Routing Messages", IEEE/ACM Transactions on Networking, April 1994. ftp://ftp.ee.lbl.gov/papers/sync_94.ps.Z

Authors' Addresses

Thomas Narten
IBM Corporation
P.O. Box 12195
Research Triangle Park, NC 27709-2195
USA

Phone: +1 919 254 7798
EMail: narten@raleigh.ibm.com

Erik Nordmark
Sun Microsystems, Inc.
901 San Antonio Road
Palo Alto, CA 94303
USA

Phone: +1 650 786 5166
Fax: +1 650 786 5896
EMail: nordmark@sun.com

William Allen Simpson
Daydreamer
Computer Systems Consulting Services
1384 Fontaine
Madison Heights, Michigan 48071
USA

EMail: Bill.Simpson@um.cc.umich.edu
bsimpson@MorningStar.com

APPENDIX A: MULTIHOMED HOSTS

There are a number of complicating issues that arise when Neighbor Discovery is used by hosts that have multiple interfaces. This section does not attempt to define the proper operation of multihomed hosts with regard to Neighbor Discovery. Rather, it identifies issues that require further study. Implementors are encouraged to experiment with various approaches to making Neighbor Discovery work on multihomed hosts and to report their experiences.

If a multihomed host receives Router Advertisements on all of its interfaces, it will (probably) have learned on-link prefixes for the addresses residing on each link. When a packet must be sent through a router, however, selecting the "wrong" router can result in a suboptimal or non-functioning path. There are number of issues to consider:

1) In order for a router to send a redirect, it must determine that the packet it is forwarding originates from a neighbor. The standard test for this case is to compare the source address of the packet to the list of on-link prefixes associated with the interface on which the packet was received. If the originating host is multihomed, however, the source address it uses may belong to an interface other than the interface from which it was sent. In such cases, a router will not send redirects, and suboptimal routing is likely. In order to be redirected, the sending host must always send packets out the interface corresponding to the outgoing packet's source address. Note that this issue never arises with non-multihomed hosts; they only have one interface.

2) If the selected first-hop router does not have a route at all for the destination, it will be unable to deliver the packet. However, the destination may be reachable through a router on one of the other interfaces. Neighbor Discovery does not address this scenario; it does not arise in the non-multihomed case.

3) Even if the first-hop router does have a route for a destination, there may be a better route via another interface. No mechanism exists for the multihomed host to detect this situation.

If a multihomed host fails to receive Router Advertisements on one or more of its interfaces, it will not know (in the absence of configured information) which destinations are on-link on the affected interface(s). This leads to a number of problems:

1) If no Router Advertisement is received on any interfaces, a multihomed host will have no way of knowing which interface to send packets out on, even for on-link destinations. Under similar conditions in the non-multihomed host case, a node treats all destinations as residing on-link, and communication proceeds. In the multihomed case, however, additional information is needed to select the proper outgoing interface. Alternatively, a node could attempt to perform address resolution on all interfaces, a step involving significant complexity that is not present in the non-multihomed host case.

2) If Router Advertisements are received on some, but not all interfaces, a multihomed host could choose to only send packets out on the interfaces on which it has received Router Advertisements. A key assumption made here, however, is that routers on those other interfaces will be able to route packets to the ultimate destination, even when those destinations reside on the subnet to which the sender connects, but has no on-link prefix information. Should the assumption be FALSE, communication would fail. Even if the assumption holds, packets will traverse a sub-optimal path.

APPENDIX B: FUTURE EXTENSIONS

Possible extensions for future study are:

- o Using dynamic timers to be able to adapt to links with widely varying delay. Measuring round trip times, however, requires acknowledgments and sequence numbers in order to match received Neighbor Advertisements with the actual Neighbor Solicitation that triggered the advertisement. Implementors wishing to experiment with such a facility could do so in a backwards-compatible way by defining a new option carrying the necessary information. Nodes not understanding the option would simply ignore it.

- o Adding capabilities to facilitate the operation over links that currently require hosts to register with an address resolution server. This could for instance enable routers to ask hosts to send them periodic unsolicited advertisements. Once again this can be added using a new option sent in the Router Advertisements.

- o Adding additional procedures for links where asymmetric and non-transitive reachability is part of normal operations. Such procedures might allow hosts and routers to find usable paths on, e.g., radio links.

APPENDIX C: STATE MACHINE FOR THE REACHABILITY STATE

This appendix contains a summary of the rules specified in Sections 7.2 and 7.3. This document does not mandate that implementations adhere to this model as long as their external behavior is consistent with that described in this document.

When performing address resolution and Neighbor Unreachability Detection the following state transitions apply using the conceptual model:

State	Event	Action	New state
-	Packet to send.	Create entry. Send multicast NS. Start retransmit timer	INCOMPLETE
INCOMPLETE	Retransmit timeout, less than N retransmissions.	Retransmit NS Start retransmit timer	INCOMPLETE
INCOMPLETE	Retransmit timeout, N or more retransmissions.	Discard entry Send ICMP error	-
INCOMPLETE	NA, Solicited=0, Override=any	Record link-layer address. Send queued packets.	STALE
INCOMPLETE	NA, Solicited=1, Override=any	Record link-layer address. Send queued packets.	REACHABLE
!INCOMPLETE	NA, Solicited=1, Override=0 Same link-layer address as cached.	-	REACHABLE
REACHABLE	NA, Solicited=1, Override=0 Different link-layer address than cached.	-	STALE
STALE or PROBE	NA, Solicited=1, Override=0 Different link-layer address than cached.	-	unchanged

!INCOMPLETE	NA, Solicited=1, Override=1	Record link-layer address (if different).	REACHABLE
!INCOMPLETE	NA, Solicited=0, Override=0	-	unchanged
!INCOMPLETE	NA, Solicited=0, Override=1 Same link-layer address as cached.	-	unchanged
!INCOMPLETE	NA, Solicited=0, Override=1 Different link-layer address than cached.	Record link-layer address.	STALE
!INCOMPLETE	upper-layer reachability confirmation	-	REACHABLE
REACHABLE	timeout, more than N seconds since reachability confirm.	-	STALE
STALE	Sending packet	Start delay timer	DELAY
DELAY	Delay timeout	Send unicast NS probe Start retransmit timer	PROBE
PROBE	Retransmit timeout, less than N retransmissions.	Retransmit NS	PROBE
PROBE	Retransmit timeout, N or more retransmissions.	Discard entry	-

The state transitions for receiving unsolicited information other than Neighbor Advertisement messages apply to either the source of the packet (for Neighbor Solicitation, Router Solicitation, and Router Advertisement messages) or the target address (for Redirect messages) as follows:

State	Event	Action	New state
-	NS, RS, RA, Redirect	Create entry.	STALE
INCOMPLETE	NS, RS, RA, Redirect	Record link-layer address. Send queued packets.	STALE
!INCOMPLETE	NS, RS, RA, Redirect Different link-layer address than cached.	Update link-layer address	STALE
!INCOMPLETE	NS, RS, RA, Redirect Same link-layer address as cached.	-	unchanged

APPENDIX D: SUMMARY OF ISROUTER RULES

This appendix presents a summary of the rules for maintaining the IsRouter flag as specified in this document.

The background for these rules is that the ND messages contain, either implicitly or explicitly, information that indicates whether or not the sender (or Target Address) is a host or a router. The following assumptions are used:

- The sender of a Router Solicitation is implicitly assumed to be a host since there is no need for routers to send such messages.

- The sender of a Router Advertisement is implicitly assumed to be a router.

- Neighbor Solicitation messages do not contain either an implicit or explicit indication about the sender. Both hosts and routers send such messages.

- Neighbor Advertisement messages contain an explicit "IsRouter flag", the R-bit.

- The target of the redirect, when the target differs from the destination address in the packet being redirected, is implicitly assumed to be a router. This is a natural assumption since that node is expected to be able to forward the packets towards the destination.

- The target of the redirect, when the target is the same as the destination, does not carry any host vs. router information. All that is known is that the destination (i.e. target) is on-link but it could be either a host or a router.

The rules for setting the IsRouter flag are based on the information content above. If an ND message contains explicit or implicit information the receipt of the message will cause the IsRouter flag to be updated. But when there is no host vs. router information in the ND message the receipt of the message MUST NOT cause a change to the IsRouter state. When the receipt of such a message causes a Neighbor Cache entry to be created this document specifies that the IsRouter flag be set to FALSE. There is greater potential for mischief when a node incorrectly thinks a host is a router, than the other way around. In these cases a subsequent Neighbor Advertisement or Router Advertisement message will set the correct IsRouter value.

APPENDIX E: IMPLEMENTATION ISSUES

Appendix E.1: Reachability confirmations

Neighbor Unreachability Detection requires explicit confirmation that a forward-path is functioning properly. To avoid the need for Neighbor Solicitation probe messages, upper layer protocols should provide such an indication when the cost of doing so is small. Reliable connection-oriented protocols such as TCP are generally aware when the forward-path is working. When TCP sends (or receives) data, for instance, it updates its window sequence numbers, sets and cancels retransmit timers, etc. Specific scenarios that usually indicate a properly functioning forward-path include:

- Receipt of an acknowledgement that covers a sequence number (e.g., data) not previously acknowledged indicates that the forward path was working at the time the data was sent.

- Completion of the initial three-way handshake is a special case of the previous rule; although no data is sent during the handshake, the SYN flags are counted as data from the sequence number perspective. This applies to both the SYN+ACK for the active open the ACK of that packet on the passively opening peer.

- Receipt of new data (i.e., data not previously received) indicates that the forward-path was working at the time an acknowledgement was sent that advanced the peer's send window that allowed the new data to be sent.

To minimize the cost of communicating reachability information between the TCP and IP layers, an implementation may wish to rate-limit the reachability confirmations its sends IP. One possibility is to process reachability only every few packets. For example, one might update reachability information once per round trip time, if an implementation only has one round trip timer per connection. For those implementations that cache Destination Cache entries within control blocks, it may be possible to update the Neighbor Cache entry directly (i.e., without an expensive lookup) once the TCP packet has been demultiplexed to its corresponding control block. For other implementation it may be possible to piggyback the reachability confirmation on the next packet submitted to IP assuming that the implementation guards against the piggybacked confirmation becoming stale when no packets are sent to IP for an extended period of time.

TCP must also guard against thinking "stale" information indicates current reachability. For example, new data received 30 minutes after a window has opened up does not constitute a confirmation that the path is currently working. In merely indicates that 30 minutes ago the window update reached the peer i.e. the path was working at that point in time. An implementation must also take into account TCP zero-window probes that are sent even if the path is broken and the window update did not reach the peer.

For UDP based applications (RPC, DNS) it is relatively simple to make the client send reachability confirmations when the response packet is received. It is more difficult and in some cases impossible for the server to generate such confirmations since there is no flow control, i.e., the server can not determine whether a received request indicates that a previous response reached the client.

Note that an implementation can not use negative upper-layer advise as a replacement for the Neighbor Unreachability Detection algorithm. Negative advise (e.g. from TCP when there are excessive retransmissions) could serve as a hint that the forward path from the sender of the data might not be working. But it would fail to detect when the path from the receiver of the data is not functioning causing, none of the acknowledgement packets to reach the sender.

APPENDIX F: CHANGES SINCE RFC 1970

- o Removed all references to the IPv6 priority field.

- o Replaced definition of solicited node multicast address with a reference to the [ADDR-ARCH] specification. That specification says that "the solicited-node multicast address is formed by taking the low-order 24 bits of the address (unicast or anycast) and appending those bits to the prefix FF02:0:0:0:0:1:FF00::/104".

- o Updated the references section to list (new) RFC numbers.

- o Updated the text in section 7.2.5 and the tables in appendix C to have the receipt of an NS message update the state of an existing neighbor cache entry only if the link-layer address is different than the recorded link-layer address.

- o Added an explicit check in section 7.1.1 so that received NS messages from an unsolicited address must be sent the solicited-node multicast address; if sent to unicast destination, silently discard.

- o Added a requirement in section 6.2.1 that Lifetimes be configurable in either of two ways: as a fixed value that doesn't change over time, or one that decrements in real time.

- o Added text in section 6.2.7 to relax the consistency checks on prefix lifetimes when the lifetimes are configured to decrement in real time. This is needed to avoid false alarms due to link propagation delay and lack of synchronized clocks.

- o Added text to section 6.3.4 to point out that [ADDRCONF] might ignore short lifetimes but that Neighbor Discovery does not ignore short prefix lifetimes.

- o Clarified the rules for RS and NS packets with an unspecified source address. Such packets MUST NOT include source link-layer address option; verified by receivers.

- o Clarified in section 7.2.3 that addresses for which the node proxies are acceptable in NS messages. Previously the text only mentioned unicast and anycast addresses assigned to the interface (i.e., wasn't clear that proxy addresses were allowed).

- o Tightened up ambiguities an inconsistencies regarding when to set the IsRouter flag in Neighbor Cache entries. Added an appendix to summarize these rules.

o Added a section on renumbering considerations to clarify how long prefixes have to be advertised when the lifetime(s) are reduced.

o Added additional text to the rules in section 7 for the NS/NA packets used for NUD probes so that the Link-Layer Address options can be omitted from these packets in certain cases without causing an infinite NS "recursion". Specifically, added text that permits the Link-Layer address to be omitted in unicast solicitations (i.e., MAY language).

o Changed the default AdvValidLifetime from infinity to 30 days.

o Changed the constant "576" to "1280" in places where its context was that of the minimum sized IP packet that all links must be able to carry.

Full Copyright Statement

Network Working Group
Request for Comments: 2462
Obsoletes: 1971
Category: Standards Track

S. Thomson
Bellcore
T. Narten
IBM

December 1998

IPv6 Stateless Address Autoconfiguration

Status of this Memo

This document specifies an Internet standards track protocol for the Internet community, and requests discussion and suggestions for improvements. Please refer to the current edition of the "Internet Official Protocol Standards" (STD 1) for the standardization state and status of this protocol. Distribution of this memo is unlimited.

Copyright Notice

Abstract

This document specifies the steps a host takes in deciding how to autoconfigure its interfaces in IP version 6. The autoconfiguration process includes creating a link-local address and verifying its uniqueness on a link, determining what information should be autoconfigured (addresses, other information, or both), and in the case of addresses, whether they should be obtained through the stateless mechanism, the stateful mechanism, or both. This document defines the process for generating a link-local address, the process for generating site-local and global addresses via stateless address autoconfiguration, and the Duplicate Address Detection procedure. The details of autoconfiguration using the stateful protocol are specified elsewhere.

Table of Contents

1. INTRODUCTION

This document specifies the steps a host takes in deciding how to autoconfigure its interfaces in IP version 6. The autoconfiguration process includes creating a link-local address and verifying its uniqueness on a link, determining what information should be autoconfigured (addresses, other information, or both), and in the case of addresses, whether they should be obtained through the stateless mechanism, the stateful mechanism, or both. This document defines the process for generating a link-local address, the process for generating site-local and global addresses via stateless address autoconfiguration, and the Duplicate Address Detection procedure. The details of autoconfiguration using the stateful protocol are specified elsewhere.

IPv6 defines both a stateful and stateless address autoconfiguration mechanism. Stateless autoconfiguration requires no manual configuration of hosts, minimal (if any) configuration of routers, and no additional servers. The stateless mechanism allows a host to generate its own addresses using a combination of locally available information and information advertised by routers. Routers advertise prefixes that identify the subnet(s) associated with a link, while hosts generate an "interface identifier" that uniquely identifies an interface on a subnet. An address is formed by combining the two. In the absence of routers, a host can only generate link-local addresses. However, link-local addresses are sufficient for allowing communication among nodes attached to the same link.

In the stateful autoconfiguration model, hosts obtain interface addresses and/or configuration information and parameters from a server. Servers maintain a database that keeps track of which addresses have been assigned to which hosts. The stateful autoconfiguration protocol allows hosts to obtain addresses, other configuration information or both from a server. Stateless and stateful autoconfiguration complement each other. For example, a host can use stateless autoconfiguration to configure its own addresses, but use stateful autoconfiguration to obtain other information. Stateful autoconfiguration for IPv6 is the subject of future work [DHCPv6].

The stateless approach is used when a site is not particularly concerned with the exact addresses hosts use, so long as they are unique and properly routable. The stateful approach is used when a site requires tighter control over exact address assignments. Both stateful and stateless address autoconfiguration may be used simultaneously. The site administrator specifies which type of autoconfiguration to use through the setting of appropriate fields in Router Advertisement messages [DISCOVERY].

IPv6 addresses are leased to an interface for a fixed (possibly infinite) length of time. Each address has an associated lifetime that indicates how long the address is bound to an interface. When a lifetime expires, the binding (and address) become invalid and the address may be reassigned to another interface elsewhere in the Internet. To handle the expiration of address bindings gracefully, an address goes through two distinct phases while assigned to an interface. Initially, an address is "preferred", meaning that its use in arbitrary communication is unrestricted. Later, an address becomes "deprecated" in anticipation that its current interface binding will become invalid. While in a deprecated state, the use of an address is discouraged, but not strictly forbidden. New communication (e.g., the opening of a new TCP connection) should use a preferred address when possible. A deprecated address should be used only by applications that have been using it and would have difficulty switching to another address without a service disruption.

To insure that all configured addresses are likely to be unique on a given link, nodes run a "duplicate address detection" algorithm on addresses before assigning them to an interface. The Duplicate Address Detection algorithm is performed on all addresses, independent of whether they are obtained via stateless or stateful autoconfiguration. This document defines the Duplicate Address Detection algorithm.

The autoconfiguration process specified in this document applies only to hosts and not routers. Since host autoconfiguration uses information advertised by routers, routers will need to be configured by some other means. However, it is expected that routers will generate link-local addresses using the mechanism described in this document. In addition, routers are expected to successfully pass the Duplicate Address Detection procedure described in this document on all addresses prior to assigning them to an interface.

Section 2 provides definitions for terminology used throughout this document. Section 3 describes the design goals that lead to the current autoconfiguration procedure. Section 4 provides an overview of the protocol, while Section 5 describes the protocol in detail.

2. TERMINOLOGY

IP - Internet Protocol Version 6. The terms IPv4 and are used only in contexts where necessary to avoid ambiguity.

node - a device that implements IP.

router - a node that forwards IP packets not explicitly addressed to itself.

host - any node that is not a router.

upper layer - a protocol layer immediately above IP. Examples are transport protocols such as TCP and UDP, control protocols such as ICMP, routing protocols such as OSPF, and internet or lower-layer protocols being "tunneled" over (i.e., encapsulated in) IP such as IPX, AppleTalk, or IP itself.

link - a communication facility or medium over which nodes can communicate at the link layer, i.e., the layer immediately below IP. Examples are Ethernets (simple or bridged); PPP links; X.25, Frame Relay, or ATM networks; and internet (or higher) layer "tunnels", such as tunnels over IPv4 or IPv6 itself.

interface - a node's attachment to a link.

packet - an IP header plus payload.

address - an IP-layer identifier for an interface or a set of interfaces.

unicast address - an identifier for a single interface. A packet sent to a unicast address is delivered to the interface identified by that address.

multicast address - an identifier for a set of interfaces (typically belonging to different nodes). A packet sent to a multicast address is delivered to all interfaces identified by that address.

anycast address - an identifier for a set of interfaces (typically belonging to different nodes). A packet sent to an anycast address is delivered to one of the interfaces identified by that address (the "nearest" one, according to the routing protocol's measure of distance). See [ADDR-ARCH].

solicited-node multicast address - a multicast address to which Neighbor Solicitation messages are sent. The algorithm for computing the address is given in [DISCOVERY].

link-layer address - a link-layer identifier for an interface. Examples include IEEE 802 addresses for Ethernet links and E.164 addresses for ISDN links.

link-local address - an address having link-only scope that can be used to reach neighboring nodes attached to the same link. All interfaces have a link-local unicast address.

site-local address - an address having scope that is limited to the local site.

global address - an address with unlimited scope.

communication - any packet exchange among nodes that requires that the address of each node used in the exchange remain the same for the duration of the packet exchange. Examples are a TCP connection or a UDP request- response.

tentative address - an address whose uniqueness on a link is being verified, prior to its assignment to an interface. A tentative address is not considered assigned to an interface in the usual sense. An interface discards received packets addressed to a tentative address, but accepts Neighbor Discovery packets related to Duplicate Address Detection for the tentative address.

preferred address - an address assigned to an interface whose use by upper layer protocols is unrestricted. Preferred addresses may be used as the source (or destination) address of packets sent from (or to) the interface.

deprecated address - An address assigned to an interface whose use is discouraged, but not forbidden. A deprecated address should no longer be used as a source address in new communications, but packets sent from or to deprecated addresses are delivered as expected. A deprecated address may continue to be used as a source address in communications where switching to a preferred address causes hardship to a specific upper-layer activity (e.g., an existing TCP connection).

valid address - a preferred or deprecated address. A valid address may appear as the source or destination address of a packet, and the internet routing system is expected to deliver packets sent to a valid address to their intended recipients.

invalid address - an address that is not assigned to any interface. A valid address becomes invalid when its valid lifetime expires. Invalid addresses should not appear as the destination or source address of a packet. In the former case, the internet routing system will be unable to deliver the packet, in the later case the recipient of the packet will be unable to respond to it.

preferred lifetime - the length of time that a valid address is preferred (i.e., the time until deprecation). When the preferred lifetime expires, the address becomes deprecated.

valid lifetime - the length of time an address remains in the valid state (i.e., the time until invalidation). The valid lifetime must be greater then or equal to the preferred lifetime. When the valid lifetime expires, the address becomes invalid.

interface identifier - a link-dependent identifier for an interface that is (at least) unique per link [ADDR-ARCH]. Stateless address autoconfiguration combines an interface identifier with a prefix to form an address. From address autoconfiguration's perspective, an interface identifier is a bit string of known length. The exact length of an interface identifier and the way it is created is defined in a separate link-type specific document that covers issues related to the transmission of IP over a particular link type (e.g., [IPv6-ETHER]). In many cases, the identifier will be the same as the interface's link-layer address.

2.1. Requirements

The keywords MUST, MUST NOT, REQUIRED, SHALL, SHALL NOT, SHOULD, SHOULD NOT, RECOMMENDED, MAY, and OPTIONAL, when they appear in this document, are to be interpreted as described in [KEYWORDS].

3. DESIGN GOALS

Stateless autoconfiguration is designed with the following goals in mind:

- o Manual configuration of individual machines before connecting them to the network should not be required. Consequently, a mechanism is needed that allows a host to obtain or create unique addresses for each of its interfaces. Address autoconfiguration assumes that each interface can provide a unique identifier for that interface (i.e., an "interface identifier"). In the simplest case, an interface identifier consists of the interface's link-layer address. An interface identifier can be combined with a prefix to form an address.

- o Small sites consisting of a set of machines attached to a single link should not require the presence of a stateful server or router as a prerequisite for communicating. Plug-and-play communication is achieved through the use of link-local addresses. Link-local addresses have a well-known prefix that identifies the (single) shared link to which a set of nodes attach. A host forms a link-local address by appending its interface identifier to the link-local prefix.

- o A large site with multiple networks and routers should not require the presence of a stateful address configuration server. In order to generate site-local or global addresses, hosts must determine the prefixes that identify the subnets to which they attach. Routers generate periodic Router Advertisements that include options listing the set of active prefixes on a link.

- o Address configuration should facilitate the graceful renumbering of a site's machines. For example, a site may wish to renumber all of its nodes when it switches to a new network service provider. Renumbering is achieved through the leasing of addresses to interfaces and the assignment of multiple addresses to the same interface. Lease lifetimes provide the mechanism through which a site phases out old prefixes. The assignment of multiple addresses to an interface provides for a transition period during which both a new address and the one being phased out work simultaneously.

- o System administrators need the ability to specify whether stateless autoconfiguration, stateful autoconfiguration, or both should be used. Router Advertisements include flags specifying which mechanisms a host should use.

4. PROTOCOL OVERVIEW

This section provides an overview of the typical steps that take place when an interface autoconfigures itself. Autoconfiguration is performed only on multicast-capable links and begins when a multicast-capable interface is enabled, e.g., during system startup. Nodes (both hosts and routers) begin the autoconfiguration process by generating a link-local address for the interface. A link-local address is formed by appending the interface's identifier to the well-known link-local prefix.

Before the link-local address can be assigned to an interface and used, however, a node must attempt to verify that this "tentative" address is not already in use by another node on the link. Specifically, it sends a Neighbor Solicitation message containing the tentative address as the target. If another node is already using that address, it will return a Neighbor Advertisement saying so. If another node is also attempting to use the same address, it will send a Neighbor Solicitation for the target as well. The exact number of times the Neighbor Solicitation is (re)transmitted and the delay time between consecutive solicitations is link-specific and may be set by system management.

If a node determines that its tentative link-local address is not unique, autoconfiguration stops and manual configuration of the interface is required. To simplify recovery in this case, it should be possible for an administrator to supply an alternate interface identifier that overrides the default identifier in such a way that the autoconfiguration mechanism can then be applied using the new (presumably unique) interface identifier. Alternatively, link-local and other addresses will need to be configured manually.

Once a node ascertains that its tentative link-local address is unique, it assigns it to the interface. At this point, the node has IP-level connectivity with neighboring nodes. The remaining autoconfiguration steps are performed only by hosts; the (auto)configuration of routers is beyond the scope of this document.

The next phase of autoconfiguration involves obtaining a Router Advertisement or determining that no routers are present. If routers are present, they will send Router Advertisements that specify what sort of autoconfiguration a host should do. If no routers are present, stateful autoconfiguration should be invoked.

Routers send Router Advertisements periodically, but the delay between successive advertisements will generally be longer than a host performing autoconfiguration will want to wait [DISCOVERY]. To obtain an advertisement quickly, a host sends one or more Router

Solicitations to the all-routers multicast group. Router Advertisements contain two flags indicating what type of stateful autoconfiguration (if any) should be performed. A "managed address configuration" flag indicates whether hosts should use stateful autoconfiguration to obtain addresses. An "other stateful configuration" flag indicates whether hosts should use stateful autoconfiguration to obtain additional information (excluding addresses).

Router Advertisements also contain zero or more Prefix Information options that contain information used by stateless address autoconfiguration to generate site-local and global addresses. It should be noted that the stateless and stateful address autoconfiguration fields in Router Advertisements are processed independently of one another, and a host may use both stateful and stateless address autoconfiguration simultaneously. One Prefix Information option field, the "autonomous address-configuration flag", indicates whether or not the option even applies to stateless autoconfiguration. If it does, additional option fields contain a subnet prefix together with lifetime values indicating how long addresses created from the prefix remain preferred and valid.

Because routers generate Router Advertisements periodically, hosts will continually receive new advertisements. Hosts process the information contained in each advertisement as described above, adding to and refreshing information received in previous advertisements.

For safety, all addresses must be tested for uniqueness prior to their assignment to an interface. In the case of addresses created through stateless autoconfig, however, the uniqueness of an address is determined primarily by the portion of the address formed from an interface identifier. Thus, if a node has already verified the uniqueness of a link-local address, additional addresses created from the same interface identifier need not be tested individually. In contrast, all addresses obtained manually or via stateful address autoconfiguration should be tested for uniqueness individually. To accommodate sites that believe the overhead of performing Duplicate Address Detection outweighs its benefits, the use of Duplicate Address Detection can be disabled through the administrative setting of a per-interface configuration flag.

To speed the autoconfiguration process, a host may generate its link-local address (and verify its uniqueness) in parallel with waiting for a Router Advertisement. Because a router may delay responding to a Router Solicitation for a few seconds, the total time needed to complete autoconfiguration can be significantly longer if the two steps are done serially.

4.1. Site Renumbering

Address leasing facilitates site renumbering by providing a mechanism to time-out addresses assigned to interfaces in hosts. At present, upper layer protocols such as TCP provide no support for changing end-point addresses while a connection is open. If an end-point address becomes invalid, existing connections break and all communication to the invalid address fails. Even when applications use UDP as a transport protocol, addresses must generally remain the same during a packet exchange.

Dividing valid addresses into preferred and deprecated categories provides a way of indicating to upper layers that a valid address may become invalid shortly and that future communication using the address will fail, should the address's valid lifetime expire before communication ends. To avoid this scenario, higher layers should use a preferred address (assuming one of sufficient scope exists) to increase the likelihood that an address will remain valid for the duration of the communication. It is up to system administrators to set appropriate prefix lifetimes in order to minimize the impact of failed communication when renumbering takes place. The deprecation period should be long enough that most, if not all, communications are using the new address at the time an address becomes invalid.

The IP layer is expected to provide a means for upper layers (including applications) to select the most appropriate source address given a particular destination and possibly other constraints. An application may choose to select the source address itself before starting a new communication or may leave the address unspecified, in which case the upper networking layers will use the mechanism provided by the IP layer to choose a suitable address on the application's behalf.

Detailed address selection rules are beyond the scope of this document.

5. PROTOCOL SPECIFICATION

Autoconfiguration is performed on a per-interface basis on multicast-capable interfaces. For multihomed hosts, autoconfiguration is performed independently on each interface. Autoconfiguration applies primarily to hosts, with two exceptions. Routers are expected to generate a link-local address using the procedure outlined below. In addition, routers perform Duplicate Address Detection on all addresses prior to assigning them to an interface.

5.1. Node Configuration Variables

A node MUST allow the following autoconfiguration-related variable to be configured by system management for each multicast interface:

DupAddrDetectTransmits

The number of consecutive Neighbor Solicitation messages sent while performing Duplicate Address Detection on a tentative address. A value of zero indicates that Duplicate Address Detection is not performed on tentative addresses. A value of one indicates a single transmission with no follow up retransmissions.

Default: 1, but may be overridden by a link-type specific value in the document that covers issues related to the transmission of IP over a particular link type (e.g., [IPv6-ETHER]).

Autoconfiguration also assumes the presence of the variable RetransTimer as defined in [DISCOVERY]. For autoconfiguration purposes, RetransTimer specifies the delay between consecutive Neighbor Solicitation transmissions performed during Duplicate Address Detection (if DupAddrDetectTransmits is greater than 1), as well as the time a node waits after sending the last Neighbor Solicitation before ending the Duplicate Address Detection process.

5.2. Autoconfiguration-Related Variables

A host maintains a number of data structures and flags related to autoconfiguration. In the following, we present conceptual variables and show how they are used to perform autoconfiguration. The specific variables are used for demonstration purposes only, and an implementation is not required to have them, so long as its external behavior is consistent with that described in this document.

Beyond the formation of a link-local address and using Duplicate Address Detection, how routers (auto)configure their interfaces is beyond the scope of this document.

Hosts maintain the following variables on a per-interface basis:

ManagedFlag Copied from the M flag field (i.e., the "managed address configuration" flag) of the most recently received Router Advertisement message. The flag indicates whether or not addresses are to be configured using the stateful autoconfiguration mechanism. It starts out in a FALSE state.

OtherConfigFlag Copied from the O flag field (i.e., the "other stateful configuration" flag) of the most recently received Router Advertisement message. The flag indicates whether or not information other than addresses is to be obtained using the stateful autoconfiguration mechanism. It starts out in a FALSE state.

In addition, when the value of the ManagedFlag is TRUE, the value of OtherConfigFlag is implicitely TRUE as well. It is not a valid configuration for a host to use stateful address autoconfiguration to request addresses only, without also accepting other configuration information.

A host also maintains a list of addresses together with their corresponding lifetimes. The address list contains both autoconfigured addresses and those configured manually.

5.3. Creation of Link-Local Addresses

A node forms a link-local address whenever an interface becomes enabled. An interface may become enabled after any of the following events:

- The interface is initialized at system startup time.

- The interface is reinitialized after a temporary interface failure or after being temporarily disabled by system management.

- The interface attaches to a link for the first time.

- The interface becomes enabled by system management after having been administratively disabled.

A link-local address is formed by prepending the well-known link-local prefix FE80::0 [ADDR-ARCH] (of appropriate length) to the interface identifier. If the interface identifier has a length of N bits, the interface identifier replaces the right-most N zero bits of the link-local prefix. If the interface identifier is more than 118 bits in length, autoconfiguration fails and manual configuration is required. Note that interface identifiers will typically be 64-bits long and based on EUI-64 identifiers as described in [ADDR-ARCH].

A link-local address has an infinite preferred and valid lifetime; it is never timed
out.

5.4. Duplicate Address Detection

Duplicate Address Detection is performed on unicast addresses prior to assigning them to an interface whose DupAddrDetectTransmits variable is greater than zero. Duplicate Address Detection MUST take place on all unicast addresses, regardless of whether they are obtained through stateful, stateless or manual configuration, with the exception of the following cases:

- Duplicate Address Detection MUST NOT be performed on anycast addresses.

- Each individual unicast address SHOULD be tested for uniqueness. However, when stateless address autoconfiguration is used, address uniqueness is determined solely by the interface identifier, assuming that subnet prefixes are assigned correctly (i.e., if all of an interface's addresses are generated from the same identifier, either all addresses or none of them will be duplicates). Thus, for a set of addresses formed from the same interface identifier, it is sufficient to check that the link-local address generated from the identifier is unique on the link. In such cases, the link-local address MUST be tested for uniqueness, and if no duplicate address is detected, an implementation MAY choose to skip Duplicate Address Detection for additional addresses derived from the same interface identifier.

The procedure for detecting duplicate addresses uses Neighbor Solicitation and Advertisement messages as described below. If a duplicate address is discovered during the procedure, the address cannot be assigned to the interface. If the address is derived from an interface identifier, a new identifier will need to be assigned to the interface, or all IP addresses for the interface will need to be manually configured. Note that the method for detecting duplicates is not completely reliable, and it is possible that duplicate addresses will still exist (e.g., if the link was partitioned while Duplicate Address Detection was performed).

An address on which the duplicate Address Detection Procedure is applied is said to be tentative until the procedure has completed successfully. A tentative address is not considered "assigned to an interface" in the traditional sense. That is, the interface must accept Neighbor Solicitation and Advertisement messages containing the tentative address in the Target Address field, but processes such packets differently from those whose Target Address matches an address assigned to the interface. Other packets addressed to the tentative address should be silently discarded.

It should also be noted that Duplicate Address Detection must be performed prior to assigning an address to an interface in order to prevent multiple nodes from using the same address simultaneously. If a node begins using an address in parallel with Duplicate Address Detection, and another node is already using the address, the node performing Duplicate Address Detection will erroneously process traffic intended for the other node, resulting in such possible negative consequences as the resetting of open TCP connections.

The following subsections describe specific tests a node performs to verify an address's uniqueness. An address is considered unique if none of the tests indicate the presence of a duplicate address within RetransTimer milliseconds after having sent DupAddrDetectTransmits Neighbor Solicitations. Once an address is determined to be unique, it may be assigned to an interface.

5.4.1. Message Validation

A node MUST silently discard any Neighbor Solicitation or Advertisement message that does not pass the validity checks specified in [DISCOVERY]. A solicitation that passes these validity checks is called a valid solicitation or valid advertisement.

5.4.2. Sending Neighbor Solicitation Messages

Before sending a Neighbor Solicitation, an interface MUST join the all-nodes multicast address and the solicited-node multicast address of the tentative address. The former insures that the node receives Neighbor Advertisements from other nodes already using the address; the latter insures that two nodes attempting to use the same address simultaneously detect each other's presence.

To check an address, a node sends DupAddrDetectTransmits Neighbor Solicitations, each separated by RetransTimer milliseconds. The solicitation's Target Address is set to the address being checked, the IP source is set to the unspecified address and the IP destination is set to the solicited-node multicast address of the target address.

If the Neighbor Solicitation is the first message to be sent from an interface after interface (re)initialization, the node should delay sending the message by a random delay between 0 and MAX_RTR_SOLICITATION_DELAY as specified in [DISCOVERY]. This serves to alleviate congestion when many nodes start up on the link at the same time, such as after a power failure, and may help to avoid race conditions when more than one node is trying to solicit for the same address at the same time. In order to improve the robustness of the Duplicate Address Detection algorithm, an interface MUST receive and process datagrams sent to the all-nodes multicast address or solicited-node multicast address of the tentative address while delaying transmission of the initial Neighbor Solicitation.

5.4.3. Receiving Neighbor Solicitation Messages

On receipt of a valid Neighbor Solicitation message on an interface, node behavior depends on whether the target address is tentative or not. If the target address is not tentative (i.e., it is assigned to the receiving interface), the solicitation is processed as described in [DISCOVERY]. If the target address is tentative, and the source address is a unicast address, the solicitation's sender is performing address resolution on the target; the solicitation should be silently ignored. Otherwise, processing takes place as described below. In all cases, a node MUST NOT respond to a Neighbor Solicitation for a tentative address.

If the source address of the Neighbor Solicitation is the unspecified address, the solicitation is from a node performing Duplicate Address Detection. If the solicitation is from another node, the tentative address is a duplicate and should not be used (by either node). If the solicitation is from the node itself (because the node loops back multicast packets), the solicitation does not indicate the presence of a duplicate address.

Implementor's Note: many interfaces provide a way for upper layers to selectively enable and disable the looping back of multicast packets. The details of how such a facility is implemented may prevent Duplicate Address Detection from working correctly. See the Appendix for further discussion.

The following tests identify conditions under which a tentative address is not unique:

- If a Neighbor Solicitation for a tentative address is received prior to having sent one, the tentative address is a duplicate. This condition occurs when two nodes run Duplicate Address Detection simultaneously, but transmit initial solicitations at different times (e.g., by selecting different random delay values before transmitting an initial solicitation).

- If the actual number of Neighbor Solicitations received exceeds the number expected based on the loopback semantics (e.g., the interface does not loopback packet, yet one or more solicitations was received), the tentative address is a duplicate. This condition occurs when two nodes run Duplicate Address Detection simultaneously and transmit solicitations at roughly the same time.

5.4.4. Receiving Neighbor Advertisement Messages

On receipt of a valid Neighbor Advertisement message on an interface, node behavior depends on whether the target address is tentative or matches a unicast or anycast address assigned to the interface. If the target address is assigned to the receiving interface, the solicitation is processed as described in [DISCOVERY]. If the target address is tentative, the tentative address is not unique.

5.4.5. When Duplicate Address Detection Fails

A tentative address that is determined to be a duplicate as described above, MUST NOT be assigned to an interface and the node SHOULD log a system management error. If the address is a link-local address formed from an interface identifier, the interface SHOULD be disabled.

5.5. Creation of Global and Site-Local Addresses

Global and site-local addresses are formed by appending an interface identifier to a prefix of appropriate length. Prefixes are obtained from Prefix Information options contained in Router Advertisements. Creation of global and site-local addresses and configuration of other parameters as described in this section SHOULD be locally configurable. However, the processing described below MUST be enabled by default.

5.5.1. Soliciting Router Advertisements

Router Advertisements are sent periodically to the all-nodes multicast address. To obtain an advertisement quickly, a host sends out Router Solicitations as described in [DISCOVERY].

5.5.2. Absence of Router Advertisements

If a link has no routers, a host MUST attempt to use stateful autoconfiguration to obtain addresses and other configuration information. An implementation MAY provide a way to disable the invocation of stateful autoconfiguration in this case, but the default SHOULD be enabled. From the perspective of autoconfiguration, a link has no routers if no Router Advertisements are received after having sent a small number of Router Solicitations as described in [DISCOVERY].

5.5.3. Router Advertisement Processing

On receipt of a valid Router Advertisement (as defined in [DISCOVERY]), a host copies the value of the advertisement's M bit into ManagedFlag. If the value of ManagedFlag changes from FALSE to TRUE, and the host is not already running the stateful address autoconfiguration protocol, the host should invoke the stateful address autoconfiguration protocol, requesting both address information and other information. If the value of the ManagedFlag changes from TRUE to FALSE, the host should continue running the stateful address autoconfiguration, i.e., the change in the value of the ManagedFlag has no effect. If the value of the flag stays unchanged, no special action takes place. In particular, a host MUST NOT reinvoke stateful address configuration if it is already participating in the stateful protocol as a result of an earlier advertisement.

An advertisement's O flag field is processed in an analogous manner. A host copies the value of the O flag into OtherConfigFlag. If the value of OtherConfigFlag changes from FALSE to TRUE, the host should invoke the stateful autoconfiguration protocol, requesting information (excluding addresses if ManagedFlag is set to FALSE). If the value of the OtherConfigFlag changes from TRUE to FALSE, the host should continue running the stateful address autoconfiguration protocol, i.e., the change in the value of OtherConfigFlag has no effect. If the value of the flag stays unchanged, no special action takes place. In particular, a host MUST NOT reinvoke stateful configuration if it is already participating in the stateful protocol as a result of an earlier advertisement.

For each Prefix-Information option in the Router Advertisement:

a) If the Autonomous flag is not set, silently ignore the Prefix Information option.

b) If the prefix is the link-local prefix, silently ignore the Prefix Information option.

c) If the preferred lifetime is greater than the valid lifetime, silently ignore the Prefix Information option. A node MAY wish to log a system management error in this case.

d) If the prefix advertised does not match the prefix of an address already in the list, and the Valid Lifetime is not 0, form an address (and add it to the list) by combining the advertised prefix with the link's interface identifier as follows:

```
|            128 - N bits               |       N bits          |
+---------------------------------------+------------------------+
|            link prefix                |  interface identifier  |
+---------------------------------------+------------------------+
```

If the sum of the prefix length and interface identifier length does not equal 128 bits, the Prefix Information option MUST be ignored. An implementation MAY wish to log a system management error in this case. It is the responsibility of the system administrator to insure that the lengths of prefixes contained in Router Advertisements are consistent with the length of interface identifiers for that link type. Note that interface identifiers will typically be 64-bits long and based on EUI-64 identifiers as described in [ADDR-ARCH].

If an address is formed successfully, the host adds it to the list of addresses assigned to the interface, initializing its preferred and valid lifetime values from the Prefix Information option.

e) If the advertised prefix matches the prefix of an autoconfigured address (i.e., one obtained via stateless or stateful address autoconfiguration) in the list of addresses associated with the interface, the specific action to perform depends on the Valid Lifetime in the received advertisement and the Lifetime associated with the previously autoconfigured address (which we call StoredLifetime in the discussion that follows):

1) If the received Lifetime is greater than 2 hours or greater than StoredLifetime, update the stored Lifetime of the corresponding address.

2) If the StoredLifetime is less than or equal to 2 hours and the received Lifetime is less than or equal to StoredLifetime, ignore the prefix, unless the Router Advertisement from which

this Prefix Information option was obtained has been authenticated (e.g., via IPSec [RFC2402]). If the Router Advertisment was authenticated, the StoredLifetime should be set to the Lifetime in the received option.

3) Otherwise, reset the stored Lifetime in the corresponding address to two hours.

The above rules address a specific denial of service attack in which a bogus advertisement could contain prefixes with very small Valid Lifetimes. Without the above rules, a single unauthenticated advertisement containing bogus Prefix Information options with short Lifetimes could cause all of a node's addresses to expire prematurely. The above rules insure that legitimate advertisements (which are sent periodically) will "cancel" the short lifetimes before they actually take effect.

5.5.4. Address Lifetime Expiry

A preferred address becomes deprecated when its preferred lifetime expires. A deprecated address SHOULD continue to be used as a source address in existing communications, but SHOULD NOT be used in new communications if an alternate (non-deprecated) address is available and has sufficient scope. IP and higher layers (e.g., TCP, UDP) MUST continue to accept datagrams destined to a deprecated address since a deprecated address is still a valid address for the interface. An implementation MAY prevent any new communication from using a deprecated address, but system management MUST have the ability to disable such a facility, and the facility MUST be disabled by default.

An address (and its association with an interface) becomes invalid when its valid lifetime expires. An invalid address MUST NOT be used as a source address in outgoing communications and MUST NOT be recognized as a destination on a receiving interface.

5.6. Configuration Consistency

It is possible for hosts to obtain address information using both stateless and stateful protocols since both may be enabled at the same time. It is also possible that the values of other configuration parameters such as MTU size and hop limit will be learned from both Router Advertisements and the stateful autoconfiguration protocol. If the same configuration information is provided by multiple sources, the value of this information should be consistent. However, it is not considered a fatal error if information received from multiple sources is inconsistent. Hosts accept the union of all information received via the stateless and stateful protocols. If inconsistent information is learned different sources, the most recently obtained values always have precedence over information learned earlier.

6. SECURITY CONSIDERATIONS

Stateless address autoconfiguration allows a host to connect to a network, configure an address and start communicating with other nodes without ever registering or authenticating itself with the local site. Although this allows unauthorized users to connect to and use a network, the threat is inherently present in the Internet architecture. Any node with a physical attachment to a network can generate an address (using a variety of ad hoc techniques) that provides connectivity.

The use of Duplicate Address Detection opens up the possibility of denial of service attacks. Any node can respond to Neighbor Solicitations for a tentative address, causing the other node to reject the address as a duplicate. This attack is similar to other attacks involving the spoofing of Neighbor Discovery messages and can be addressed by requiring that Neighbor Discovery packets be authenticated [RFC2402].

7. References

[RFC2402] Kent, S. and R. Atkinson, "IP Authentication Header", RFC 2402, November 1998.

[IPv6-ETHER] Crawford, M., "A Method for the Transmission of IPv6 Packets over Ethernet Networks", RFC 2464, December 1998.

[KEYWORDS] Bradner, S., "Key words for use in RFCs to Indicate Requirement Levels", BCP 14, RFC 2119, March 1997.

[RFC1112] Deering, S., "Host Extensions for IP Multicasting", STD 5, RFC 1112, August 1989.

[ADDR-ARCH] Hinden, R. and S. Deering, "Internet Protocol Version (IPv6) Addressing Architecture", RFC 2373, July 1998

[DHCPv6] Bound, J. and C. Perkins, "Dynamic Host Configuration Protocol for IPv6 (DHCPv6)", Work in Progress.

[DISCOVERY] Narten, T., Nordmark, E. and W. Simpson, "Neighbor Discovery for IP Version 6 (IPv6)", RFC 2461, December 1998.

8. Acknowledgements

The authors would like to thank the members of both the IPNG and ADDRCONF working groups for their input. In particular, thanks to Jim Bound, Steve Deering, Richard Draves, and Erik Nordmark. Thanks also goes to John Gilmore for alerting the WG of the "0 Lifetime Prefix Advertisement" denial of service attack vulnerability; this document incorporates changes that address this vulnerability.

AUTHORS' ADDRESSES

Susan Thomson
Bellcore
445 South Street
Morristown, NJ 07960
USA

Phone: +1 201-829-4514
EMail: set@thumper.bellcore.com

Thomas Narten
IBM Corporation
P.O. Box 12195
Research Triangle Park, NC 27709-2195
USA

Phone: +1 919 254 7798
EMail: narten@raleigh.ibm.com

9. APPENDIX A: LOOPBACK SUPPRESSION & DUPLICATE ADDRESS DETECTION

Determining whether a received multicast solicitation was looped back to the sender or actually came from another node is implementation-dependent. A problematic case occurs when two interfaces attached to the same link happen to have the same identifier and link-layer address, and they both send out packets with identical contents at roughly the same time (e.g., Neighbor Solicitations for a tentative address as part of Duplicate Address Detection messages). Although a receiver will receive both packets, it cannot determine which packet was looped back and which packet came from the other node by simply comparing packet contents (i.e., the contents are identical). In this particular case, it is not necessary to know precisely which packet was looped back and which was sent by another node; if one receives more solicitations than were sent, the tentative address is a duplicate. However, the situation may not always be this straightforward.

The IPv4 multicast specification [RFC1112] recommends that the service interface provide a way for an upper-layer protocol to inhibit local delivery of packets sent to a multicast group that the sending host is a member of. Some applications know that there will be no other group members on the same host, and suppressing loopback prevents them from having to receive (and discard) the packets they themselves send out. A straightforward way to implement this facility is to disable loopback at the hardware level (if supported by the hardware), with packets looped back (if requested) by software. On interfaces in which the hardware itself suppresses loopbacks, a node running Duplicate Address Detection simply counts the number of Neighbor Solicitations received for a tentative address and compares them with the number expected. If there is a mismatch, the tentative address is a duplicate.

In those cases where the hardware cannot suppress loopbacks, however, one possible software heuristic to filter out unwanted loopbacks is to discard any received packet whose link-layer source address is the same as the receiving interface's. Unfortunately, use of that criteria also results in the discarding of all packets sent by another node using the same link-layer address. Duplicate Address Detection will fail on interfaces that filter received packets in this manner:

- o If a node performing Duplicate Address Detection discards received packets having the same source link-layer address as the receiving interface, it will also discard packets from other nodes also using the same link-layer address, including Neighbor Advertisement and Neighbor Solicitation messages required to make Duplicate Address Detection work correctly. This particular problem can be avoided by temporarily disabling the software suppression of loopbacks while a node performs Duplicate Address Detection.

- If a node that is already using a particular IP address discards received packets having the same link-layer source address as the interface, it will also discard Duplicate Address Detection-related Neighbor Solicitation messages sent by another node also using the same link-layer address. Consequently, Duplicate Address Detection will fail, and the other node will configure a non-unique address. Since it is generally impossible to know when another node is performing Duplicate Address Detection, this scenario can be avoided only if software suppression of loopback is permanently disabled.

Thus, to perform Duplicate Address Detection correctly in the case where two interfaces are using the same link-layer address, an implementation must have a good understanding of the interface's multicast loopback semantics, and the interface cannot discard received packets simply because the source link-layer address is the same as the interfaces.

10. APPENDIX B: CHANGES SINCE RFC 1971

- o Changed document to use term "interface identifier" rather than "interface token" for consistency with other IPv6 documents.
- o Clarified definition of deprecated address to make clear it is OK to continue sending to or from deprecated addresses.
- o Reworded section 5.4 for clarity (no substantive change).
- o Added rules to Section 5.5.3 Router Advertisement processing to address potential denial-of-service attack when prefixes are advertised with very short Lifetimes.
- o Clarified wording in Section 5.5.4 to make clear that all upper layer protocols must process (i.e., send and receive) packets sent to deprecated addresses.

11. Full Copyright Statement

Network Working Group
Request for Comments: 2463
Obsoletes: 1885
Category: Standards Track

A. Conta
Lucent
S. Deering
Cisco Systems
December 1998

Internet Control Message Protocol (ICMPv6) for the Internet Protocol Version 6 (IPv6) Specification

Status of this Memo

Copyright Notice

Abstract

This document specifies a set of Internet Control Message Protocol (ICMP) messages for use with version 6 of the Internet Protocol (IPv6).

Table of Contents

1. Introduction

The Internet Protocol, version 6 (IPv6) is a new version of IP. IPv6 uses the Internet Control Message Protocol (ICMP) as defined for IPv4 [RFC-792], with a number of changes. The resulting protocol is called ICMPv6, and has an IPv6 Next Header value of 58.

This document describes the format of a set of control messages used in ICMPv6. It does not describe the procedures for using these messages to achieve functions like Path MTU discovery; such procedures are described in other documents (e.g., [PMTU]). Other documents may also introduce additional ICMPv6 message types, such as Neighbor Discovery messages [IPv6-DISC], subject to the general rules for ICMPv6 messages given in section 2 of this document.

Terminology defined in the IPv6 specification [IPv6] and the IPv6 Routing and Addressing specification [IPv6-ADDR] applies to this document as well.

The key words "MUST", "MUST NOT", "REQUIRED", "SHALL", "SHALL NOT", "SHOULD", "SHOULD NOT", "RECOMMENDED", "MAY", and "OPTIONAL" in this document are to be interpreted as described in [RFC-2119].

2. ICMPv6 (ICMP for IPv6)

ICMPv6 is used by IPv6 nodes to report errors encountered in processing packets, and to perform other internet-layer functions, such as diagnostics (ICMPv6 "ping"). ICMPv6 is an integral part of IPv6 and MUST be fully implemented by every IPv6 node.

2.1 Message General Format

ICMPv6 messages are grouped into two classes: error messages and informational messages. Error messages are identified as such by having a zero in the high-order bit of their message Type field values. Thus, error messages have message Types from 0 to 127; informational messages have message Types from 128 to 255.

This document defines the message formats for the following ICMPv6 messages:

ICMPv6 error messages:

```
     1    Destination Unreachable      (see section 3.1)
     2    Packet Too Big               (see section 3.2)
     3    Time Exceeded                (see section 3.3)
     4    Parameter Problem            (see section 3.4)
```

ICMPv6 informational messages:

```
     128  Echo Request                 (see section 4.1)
     129  Echo Reply                   (see section 4.2)
```

Every ICMPv6 message is preceded by an IPv6 header and zero or more IPv6 extension headers. The ICMPv6 header is identified by a Next Header value of 58 in the immediately preceding header. (NOTE: this is different than the value used to identify ICMP for IPv4.)

The ICMPv6 messages have the following general format:

```
 0                   1                   2                   3
 0 1 2 3 4 5 6 7 8 9 0 1 2 3 4 5 6 7 8 9 0 1 2 3 4 5 6 7 8 9 0 1
+-+-+-+-+-+-+-+-+-+-+-+-+-+-+-+-+-+-+-+-+-+-+-+-+-+-+-+-+-+-+-+-+
|     Type      |     Code      |          Checksum             |
+-+-+-+-+-+-+-+-+-+-+-+-+-+-+-+-+-+-+-+-+-+-+-+-+-+-+-+-+-+-+-+-+
|                                                               |
+                         Message Body                          +
|                                                               |
```

The type field indicates the type of the message. Its value determines the format of the remaining data.

The code field depends on the message type. It is used to create an additional level of message granularity.

The checksum field is used to detect data corruption in the ICMPv6 message and parts of the IPv6 header.

2.2 Message Source Address Determination

A node that sends an ICMPv6 message has to determine both the Source and Destination IPv6 Addresses in the IPv6 header before calculating the checksum. If the node has more than one unicast address, it must choose the Source Address of the message as follows:

(a) If the message is a response to a message sent to one of the node's unicast addresses, the Source Address of the reply must be that same address.

(b) If the message is a response to a message sent to a multicast or anycast group in which the node is a member, the Source Address of the reply must be a unicast address belonging to the interface on which the multicast or anycast packet was received.

(c) If the message is a response to a message sent to an address that does not belong to the node, the Source Address should be that unicast address belonging to the node that will be most helpful in diagnosing the error. For example, if the message is a response to a packet forwarding action that cannot complete successfully, the Source Address should be a unicast address belonging to the interface on which the packet forwarding failed.

(d) Otherwise, the node's routing table must be examined to determine which interface will be used to transmit the message to its destination, and a unicast address belonging to that interface must be used as the Source Address of the message.

2.3 Message Checksum Calculation

The checksum is the 16-bit one's complement of the one's complement sum of the entire ICMPv6 message starting with the ICMPv6 message type field, prepended with a "pseudo-header" of IPv6 header fields, as specified in [IPv6, section 8.1]. The Next Header value used in the pseudo-header is 58. (NOTE: the inclusion of a pseudo-header in the ICMPv6 checksum is a change from IPv4; see [IPv6] for the rationale for this change.)

For computing the checksum, the checksum field is set to zero.

2.4 Message Processing Rules

Implementations MUST observe the following rules when processing ICMPv6 messages (from [RFC-1122]):

(a) If an ICMPv6 error message of unknown type is received, it MUST be passed to the upper layer.

(b) If an ICMPv6 informational message of unknown type is received, it MUST be silently discarded.

(c) Every ICMPv6 error message (type < 128) includes as much of the IPv6 offending (invoking) packet (the packet that caused the error) as will fit without making the error message packet exceed the minimum IPv6 MTU [IPv6].

(d) In those cases where the internet-layer protocol is required to pass an ICMPv6 error message to the upper-layer process, the upper-layer protocol type is extracted from the original packet (contained in the body of the ICMPv6 error message) and used to select the appropriate upper-layer process to handle the error.

If the original packet had an unusually large amount of extension headers, it is possible that the upper-layer protocol type may not be present in the ICMPv6 message, due to truncation of the original packet to meet the minimum IPv6 MTU [IPv6] limit. In that case, the error message is silently dropped after any IPv6-layer processing.

(e) An ICMPv6 error message MUST NOT be sent as a result of receiving:

(e.1) an ICMPv6 error message, or

(e.2) a packet destined to an IPv6 multicast address (there are two exceptions to this rule: (1) the Packet Too Big Message - Section 3.2 - to allow Path MTU discovery to work for IPv6 multicast, and (2) the Parameter Problem Message, Code 2 - Section 3.4 - reporting an unrecognized IPv6 option that has the Option Type highest-order two bits set to 10), or

(e.3) a packet sent as a link-layer multicast, (the exception from e.2 applies to this case too), or

(e.4) a packet sent as a link-layer broadcast, (the exception from e.2 applies to this case too), or

(e.5) a packet whose source address does not uniquely identify a single node — e.g., the IPv6 Unspecified Address, an IPv6 multicast address, or an address known by the ICMP message sender to be an IPv6 anycast address.

(f) Finally, in order to limit the bandwidth and forwarding costs incurred sending ICMPv6 error messages, an IPv6 node MUST limit the rate of ICMPv6 error messages it sends. This situation may occur when a source sending a stream of erroneous packets fails to heed the resulting ICMPv6 error messages. There are a variety of ways of implementing the rate-limiting function, for example:

(f.1) Timer-based - for example, limiting the rate of transmission of error messages to a given source, or to any source, to at most once every T milliseconds.

(f.2) Bandwidth-based - for example, limiting the rate at which error messages are sent from a particular interface to some fraction F of the attached link's bandwidth.

The limit parameters (e.g., T or F in the above examples) MUST be configurable for the node, with a conservative default value (e.g., T = 1 second, NOT 0 seconds, or F = 2 percent, NOT 100 percent).

The following sections describe the message formats for the above ICMPv6 messages.

3. ICMPv6 Error Messages

3.1 Destination Unreachable Message

```
 0                   1                   2                   3
 0 1 2 3 4 5 6 7 8 9 0 1 2 3 4 5 6 7 8 9 0 1 2 3 4 5 6 7 8 9 0 1
+-+-+-+-+-+-+-+-+-+-+-+-+-+-+-+-+-+-+-+-+-+-+-+-+-+-+-+-+-+-+-+-+
|     Type      |     Code      |          Checksum             |
+-+-+-+-+-+-+-+-+-+-+-+-+-+-+-+-+-+-+-+-+-+-+-+-+-+-+-+-+-+-+-+-+
|                             Unused                            |
+-+-+-+-+-+-+-+-+-+-+-+-+-+-+-+-+-+-+-+-+-+-+-+-+-+-+-+-+-+-+-+-+
|                    As much of invoking packet                 |
+                as will fit without the ICMPv6 packet          +
|                exceeding the minimum IPv6 MTU [IPv6]          |
```

IPv6 Fields:

Destination Address

Copied from the Source Address field of the invoking packet.

ICMPv6 Fields:

Type 1

Code 0 - no route to destination
1 - communication with destination
administratively prohibited
2 - (not assigned)
3 - address unreachable
4 - port unreachable

Unused This field is unused for all code values. It must be initialized to zero by the sender and ignored by the receiver.

Description

A Destination Unreachable message SHOULD be generated by a router, or by the IPv6 layer in the originating node, in response to a packet that cannot be delivered to its destination address for reasons other than congestion. (An ICMPv6 message MUST NOT be generated if a packet is dropped due to congestion.)

If the reason for the failure to deliver is lack of a matching entry in the forwarding node's routing table, the Code field is set to 0 (NOTE: this error can occur only in nodes that do not hold a "default route" in their routing tables).

If the reason for the failure to deliver is administrative prohibition, e.g., a "firewall filter", the Code field is set to 1.

If there is any other reason for the failure to deliver, e.g., inability to resolve the IPv6 destination address into a corresponding link address, or a link-specific problem of some sort, then the Code field is set to 3.

A destination node SHOULD send a Destination Unreachable message with Code 4 in response to a packet for which the transport protocol (e.g., UDP) has no listener, if that transport protocol has no alternative means to inform the sender.

Upper layer notification

A node receiving the ICMPv6 Destination Unreachable message MUST notify the upper-layer process.

3.2 Packet Too Big Message

```
 0                   1                   2                   3
 0 1 2 3 4 5 6 7 8 9 0 1 2 3 4 5 6 7 8 9 0 1 2 3 4 5 6 7 8 9 0 1
+-+-+-+-+-+-+-+-+-+-+-+-+-+-+-+-+-+-+-+-+-+-+-+-+-+-+-+-+-+-+-+-+
|     Type      |     Code      |          Checksum             |
+-+-+-+-+-+-+-+-+-+-+-+-+-+-+-+-+-+-+-+-+-+-+-+-+-+-+-+-+-+-+-+-+
|                             MTU                               |
+-+-+-+-+-+-+-+-+-+-+-+-+-+-+-+-+-+-+-+-+-+-+-+-+-+-+-+-+-+-+-+-+
|                    As much of invoking packet                 |
+               as will fit without the ICMPv6 packet           +
|               exceeding the minimum IPv6 MTU [IPv6]           |
```

IPv6 Fields:

Destination Address

Copied from the Source Address field of the invoking packet.

ICMPv6 Fields:

Type	2
Code	Set to 0 (zero) by the sender and ignored by the receiver
MTU	The Maximum Transmission Unit of the next-hop link.

Description

A Packet Too Big MUST be sent by a router in response to a packet that it cannot forward because the packet is larger than the MTU of the outgoing link. The information in this message is used as part of the Path MTU Discovery process [PMTU].

Sending a Packet Too Big Message makes an exception to one of the rules of when to send an ICMPv6 error message, in that unlike other messages, it is sent in response to a packet received with an IPv6 multicast destination address, or a link-layer multicast or link-layer broadcast address.

Upper layer notification

An incoming Packet Too Big message MUST be passed to the upper-layer process.

3.3 Time Exceeded Message

```
 0                   1                   2                   3
 0 1 2 3 4 5 6 7 8 9 0 1 2 3 4 5 6 7 8 9 0 1 2 3 4 5 6 7 8 9 0 1
+-+-+-+-+-+-+-+-+-+-+-+-+-+-+-+-+-+-+-+-+-+-+-+-+-+-+-+-+-+-+-+-+
|     Type      |     Code      |          Checksum             |
+-+-+-+-+-+-+-+-+-+-+-+-+-+-+-+-+-+-+-+-+-+-+-+-+-+-+-+-+-+-+-+-+
|                             Unused                            |
+-+-+-+-+-+-+-+-+-+-+-+-+-+-+-+-+-+-+-+-+-+-+-+-+-+-+-+-+-+-+-+-+
|                    As much of invoking packet                 |
+               as will fit without the ICMPv6 packet           +
|               exceeding the minimum IPv6 MTU [IPv6]           |
```

IPv6 Fields:

Destination Address

Copied from the Source Address field of the invoking packet.

ICMPv6 Fields:

Type 3

Code 0 - hop limit exceeded in transit

1 - fragment reassembly time exceeded

Unused This field is unused for all code values. It must be initialized to zero by the sender and ignored by the receiver.

Description

If a router receives a packet with a Hop Limit of zero, or a router decrements a packet's Hop Limit to zero, it MUST discard the packet and send an ICMPv6 Time Exceeded message with Code 0 to the source of the packet. This indicates either a routing loop or too small an initial Hop Limit value.

The rules for selecting the Source Address of this message are defined in section 2.2.

Upper layer notification

An incoming Time Exceeded message MUST be passed to the upper-layer process.

3.4 Parameter Problem Message

```
    0                   1                   2                   3
    0 1 2 3 4 5 6 7 8 9 0 1 2 3 4 5 6 7 8 9 0 1 2 3 4 5 6 7 8 9 0 1
   +-+-+-+-+-+-+-+-+-+-+-+-+-+-+-+-+-+-+-+-+-+-+-+-+-+-+-+-+-+-+-+-+
   |     Type      |     Code      |          Checksum             |
   +-+-+-+-+-+-+-+-+-+-+-+-+-+-+-+-+-+-+-+-+-+-+-+-+-+-+-+-+-+-+-+-+
   |                            Pointer                            |
   +-+-+-+-+-+-+-+-+-+-+-+-+-+-+-+-+-+-+-+-+-+-+-+-+-+-+-+-+-+-+-+-+
   |                    As much of invoking packet                 |
   +               as will fit without the ICMPv6 packet           +
   |               exceeding the minimum IPv6 MTU [IPv6]           |
```

IPv6 Fields:

Destination Address

Copied from the Source Address field of the invoking packet.

ICMPv6 Fields:

Type 4

Code 0 - erroneous header field encountered

1 - unrecognized Next Header type encountered

2 - unrecognized IPv6 option encountered

Pointer Identifies the octet offset within the invoking packet where the error was detected.

The pointer will point beyond the end of the ICMPv6 packet if the field in error is beyond what can fit in the maximum size of an ICMPv6 error message.

Description

If an IPv6 node processing a packet finds a problem with a field in the IPv6 header or extension headers such that it cannot complete processing the packet, it MUST discard the packet and SHOULD send an ICMPv6 Parameter Problem message to the packet's source, indicating the type and location of the problem.

The pointer identifies the octet of the original packet's header where the error was detected. For example, an ICMPv6 message with Type field = 4, Code field = 1, and Pointer field = 40 would indicate that the IPv6 extension header following the IPv6 header of the original packet holds an unrecognized Next Header field value.

Upper layer notification

A node receiving this ICMPv6 message MUST notify the upper-layer process.

4. ICMPv6 Informational Messages

4.1 Echo Request Message

```
 0                   1                   2                   3
 0 1 2 3 4 5 6 7 8 9 0 1 2 3 4 5 6 7 8 9 0 1 2 3 4 5 6 7 8 9 0 1
+-+-+-+-+-+-+-+-+-+-+-+-+-+-+-+-+-+-+-+-+-+-+-+-+-+-+-+-+-+-+-+-+
|     Type      |     Code      |          Checksum             |
+-+-+-+-+-+-+-+-+-+-+-+-+-+-+-+-+-+-+-+-+-+-+-+-+-+-+-+-+-+-+-+-+
|           Identifier          |        Sequence Number        |
+-+-+-+-+-+-+-+-+-+-+-+-+-+-+-+-+-+-+-+-+-+-+-+-+-+-+-+-+-+-+-+-+
|     Data ...
+-+-+-+-+-
```

IPv6 Fields:

Destination Address

Any legal IPv6 address.

ICMPv6 Fields:

Type 128

Code 0

Identifier An identifier to aid in matching Echo Replies to this Echo Request. May be zero.

Sequence Number

A sequence number to aid in matching Echo Replies to this Echo Request. May be zero.

Data Zero or more octets of arbitrary data.

Description

Every node MUST implement an ICMPv6 Echo responder function that receives Echo Requests and sends corresponding Echo Replies. A node SHOULD also implement an application-layer interface for sending Echo Requests and receiving Echo Replies, for diagnostic purposes.

Upper layer notification

Echo Request messages MAY be passed to processes receiving ICMP messages.

4.2 Echo Reply Message

```
 0                   1                   2                   3
 0 1 2 3 4 5 6 7 8 9 0 1 2 3 4 5 6 7 8 9 0 1 2 3 4 5 6 7 8 9 0 1
+-+-+-+-+-+-+-+-+-+-+-+-+-+-+-+-+-+-+-+-+-+-+-+-+-+-+-+-+-+-+-+-+
|     Type      |     Code      |          Checksum             |
+-+-+-+-+-+-+-+-+-+-+-+-+-+-+-+-+-+-+-+-+-+-+-+-+-+-+-+-+-+-+-+-+
|           Identifier          |        Sequence Number        |
+-+-+-+-+-+-+-+-+-+-+-+-+-+-+-+-+-+-+-+-+-+-+-+-+-+-+-+-+-+-+-+-+
|     Data ...
+-+-+-+-+-
```

IPv6 Fields:

Destination Address

Copied from the Source Address field of the invoking Echo Request packet.

ICMPv6 Fields:

Type 129

Code 0

Identifier The identifier from the invoking Echo Request message.

Sequence Number The sequence number from the invoking Echo Request message.

Data The data from the invoking Echo Request message.

RFC 2463 12

Description

Every node MUST implement an ICMPv6 Echo responder function that receives Echo Requests and sends corresponding Echo Replies. A node SHOULD also implement an application-layer interface for sending Echo Requests and receiving Echo Replies, for diagnostic purposes.

The source address of an Echo Reply sent in response to a unicast Echo Request message MUST be the same as the destination address of that Echo Request message.

An Echo Reply SHOULD be sent in response to an Echo Request message sent to an IPv6 multicast address. The source address of the reply MUST be a unicast address belonging to the interface on which the multicast Echo Request message was received.

The data received in the ICMPv6 Echo Request message MUST be returned entirely and unmodified in the ICMPv6 Echo Reply message.

Upper layer notification

Echo Reply messages MUST be passed to the process that originated an Echo Request message. It may be passed to processes that did not originate the Echo Request message.

5. Security Considerations

5.1 Authentication and Encryption of ICMP messages

ICMP protocol packet exchanges can be authenticated using the IP Authentication Header [IPv6-AUTH]. A node SHOULD include an Authentication Header when sending ICMP messages if a security association for use with the IP Authentication Header exists for the destination address. The security associations may have been created through manual configuration or through the operation of some key management protocol.

Received Authentication Headers in ICMP packets MUST be verified for correctness and packets with incorrect authentication MUST be ignored and discarded.

It SHOULD be possible for the system administrator to configure a node to ignore any ICMP messages that are not authenticated using either the Authentication Header or Encapsulating Security Payload. Such a switch SHOULD default to allowing unauthenticated messages.

Confidentiality issues are addressed by the IP Security Architecture and the IP Encapsulating Security Payload documents [IPv6-SA, IPv6-ESP].

5.2 ICMP Attacks

ICMP messages may be subject to various attacks. A complete discussion can be found in the IP Security Architecture [IPv6-SA]. A brief discussion of such attacks and their prevention is as follows:

1. ICMP messages may be subject to actions intended to cause the receiver believe the message came from a different source than the message originator. The protection against this attack can be achieved by applying the IPv6 Authentication mechanism [IPv6-Auth] to the ICMP message.

2. ICMP messages may be subject to actions intended to cause the message or the reply to it go to a destination different than the message originator's intention. The ICMP checksum calculation provides a protection mechanism against changes by a malicious interceptor in the destination and source address of the IP packet carrying that message, provided the ICMP checksum field is protected against change by authentication [IPv6-Auth] or encryption [IPv6-ESP] of the ICMP message.

3. ICMP messages may be subject to changes in the message fields, or payload. The authentication [IPv6-Auth] or encryption [IPv6-ESP] of the ICMP message is a protection against such actions.

4. ICMP messages may be used as attempts to perform denial of service attacks by sending back to back erroneous IP packets. An implementation that correctly followed section 2.4, paragraph (f) of this specifications, would be protected by the ICMP error rate limiting mechanism.

6. References

[IPv6] Deering, S. and R. Hinden, "Internet Protocol, Version 6, (IPv6) Specification", RFC 2460, December 1998.

[IPv6-ADDR] Hinden, R. and S. Deering, "IP Version 6 Addressing Architecture", RFC 2373, July 1998.

[IPv6-DISC] Narten, T., Nordmark, E. and W. Simpson, "Neighbor Discovery for IP Version 6 (IPv6)", RFC 2461, December 1998.

[RFC-792] Postel, J., "Internet Control Message Protocol", STD 5, RFC 792, September 1981.

[RFC-1122] Braden, R., "Requirements for Internet Hosts - Communication Layers", STD 5, RFC 1122, August 1989.

[PMTU] McCann, J., Deering, S. and J. Mogul, "Path MTU Discovery for IP version 6", RFC 1981, August 1996.

[RFC-2119] Bradner, S., "Key words for use in RFCs to Indicate Requirement Levels", BCP 14, RFC 2119, March 1997.

[IPv6-SA] Kent, S. and R. Atkinson, "Security Architecture for the Internet Protocol", RFC 2401, November 1998.

[IPv6-Auth] Kent, S. and R. Atkinson, "IP Authentication Header", RFC 2402, November 1998.

[IPv6-ESP] Kent, S. and R. Atkinson, "IP Encapsulating Security Protocol (ESP)", RFC 2406, November 1998.

7. Acknowledgments

The document is derived from previous ICMP drafts of the SIPP and IPng working group.

The IPng working group and particularly Robert Elz, Jim Bound, Bill Simpson, Thomas Narten, Charlie Lynn, Bill Fink, Scott Bradner, Dimitri Haskin, and Bob Hinden (in chronological order) provided extensive review information and feedback.

8. Authors' Addresses

Alex Conta
Lucent Technologies Inc.
300 Baker Ave, Suite 100
Concord, MA 01742
USA

Phone: +1 978 287-2842
EMail: aconta@lucent.com

Stephen Deering
Cisco Systems, Inc.
170 West Tasman Drive
San Jose, CA 95134-1706
USA

Phone: +1 408 527-8213
EMail: deering@cisco.com

Appendix A - Changes from RFC 1885

Version 2-02

- Excluded mentioning informational replies from paragraph (f.2) of section 2.4.
- In "Upper layer notification" sections changed "upper-layer protocol" and "User Interface" to "process".
- Changed section 5.2, item 2 and 3 to also refer to AH authentication.
- Removed item 5. from section 5.2 on denial of service attacks.
- Updated phone numbers and Email addresses in the "Authors' Addresses" section.

Version 2-01

- Replaced all references to "576 octets" as the maximum for an ICMP message size with "minimum IPv6 MTU" as defined by the base IPv6 specification.
- Removed rate control from informational messages.
- Added requirement that receivers ignore Code value in Packet Too Big message.
- Removed "Not a Neighbor" (code 2) from destination unreachable message.
- Fixed typos and update references.

Version 2-00

- Applied rate control to informational messages
- Removed section 2.4 on Group Management ICMP messages
- Removed references to IGMP in Abstract and Section 1.
- Updated references to other IPv6 documents
- Removed references to RFC-1112 in Abstract, and Section 1, and to RFC-1191 in section 1, and section 3.2
- Added security section
- Added Appendix A - changes

Full Copyright Statement

Network Working Group
Request for Comments: 2464
Obsoletes: 1972
Category: Standards Track

M. Crawford
Fermilab
December 1998

Transmission of IPv6 Packets over Ethernet Networks

Status of this Memo

This document specifies an Internet standards track protocol for the Internet community, and requests discussion and suggestions for improvements. Please refer to the current edition of the "Internet Official Protocol Standards" (STD 1) for the standardization state and status of this protocol. Distribution of this memo is unlimited.

Copyright Notice

1. Introduction

This document specifies the frame format for transmission of IPv6 packets and the method of forming IPv6 link-local addresses and statelessly autoconfigured addresses on Ethernet networks. It also specifies the content of the Source/Target Link-layer Address option used in Router Solicitation, Router Advertisement, Neighbor Solicitation, Neighbor Advertisement and Redirect messages when those messages are transmitted on an Ethernet.

This document replaces RFC 1972, "A Method for the Transmission of IPv6 Packets over Ethernet Networks", which will become historic.

The key words "MUST", "MUST NOT", "REQUIRED", "SHALL", "SHALL NOT", "SHOULD", "SHOULD NOT", "RECOMMENDED", "MAY", and "OPTIONAL" in this document are to be interpreted as described in [RFC 2119].

2. Maximum Transmission Unit

The default MTU size for IPv6 [IPV6] packets on an Ethernet is 1500 octets. This size may be reduced by a Router Advertisement [DISC] containing an MTU option which specifies a smaller MTU, or by manual configuration of each node. If a Router Advertisement received on an Ethernet interface has an MTU option specifying an MTU larger than 1500, or larger than a manually configured value, that MTU option may be logged to system management but must be otherwise ignored.

For purposes of this document, information received from DHCP is considered "manually configured" and the term Ethernet includes CSMA/CD and full-duplex subnetworks based on ISO/IEC 8802-3, with various data rates.

3. Frame Format

IPv6 packets are transmitted in standard Ethernet frames. The Ethernet header contains the Destination and Source Ethernet addresses and the Ethernet type code, which must contain the value 86DD hexadecimal. The data field contains the IPv6 header followed immediately by the payload, and possibly padding octets to meet the minimum frame size for the Ethernet link.

```
 0                   1
 0 1 2 3 4 5 6 7 8 9 0 1 2 3 4 5
+-+-+-+-+-+-+-+-+-+-+-+-+-+-+-+-+
|          Destination          |
+-                             -+
|            Ethernet           |
+-                             -+
|            Address            |
+-+-+-+-+-+-+-+-+-+-+-+-+-+-+-+-+
|             Source            |
+-                             -+
|            Ethernet           |
+-                             -+
|            Address            |
+-+-+-+-+-+-+-+-+-+-+-+-+-+-+-+-+
|1 0 0 0 0 1 1 0 1 1 0 1 1 1 0 1|
+-+-+-+-+-+-+-+-+-+-+-+-+-+-+-+-+
|             IPv6              |
+-                             -+
|            header             |
+-                             -+
|             and               |
+-                             -+
/            payload ...        /
+-+-+-+-+-+-+-+-+-+-+-+-+-+-+-+-+
```

(Each tic mark represents one bit.)

4. Stateless Autoconfiguration

The Interface Identifier [AARCH] for an Ethernet interface is based on the EUI-64 identifier [EUI64] derived from the interface's built-in 48-bit IEEE 802 address. The EUI-64 is formed as follows. (Canonical bit order is assumed throughout.)

The OUI of the Ethernet address (the first three octets) becomes the company_id of the EUI-64 (the first three octets). The fourth and fifth octets of the EUI are set to the fixed value FFFE hexadecimal. The last three octets of the Ethernet address become the last three octets of the EUI-64.

The Interface Identifier is then formed from the EUI-64 by complementing the "Universal/Local" (U/L) bit, which is the next-to-lowest order bit of the first octet of the EUI-64. Complementing this bit will generally change a 0 value to a 1, since an interface's built-in address is expected to be from a universally administered address space and hence have a globally unique value. A universally administered IEEE 802 address or an EUI-64 is signified by a 0 in the U/L bit position, while a globally unique IPv6 Interface Identifier is signified by a 1 in the corresponding position. For further discussion on this point, see [AARCH].

For example, the Interface Identifier for an Ethernet interface whose built-in address is, in hexadecimal,

34-56-78-9A-BC-DE

would be

36-56-78-FF-FE-9A-BC-DE.

A different MAC address set manually or by software should not be used to derive the Interface Identifier. If such a MAC address must be used, its global uniqueness property should be reflected in the value of the U/L bit.

An IPv6 address prefix used for stateless autoconfiguration [ACONF] of an Ethernet interface must have a length of 64 bits.

5. Link-Local Addresses

The IPv6 link-local address [AARCH] for an Ethernet interface is formed by appending the Interface Identifier, as defined above, to the prefix FE80::/64.

```
  10 bits            54 bits                  64 bits
+----------+-----------------------+----------------------------+
|1111111010|         (zeros)       |    Interface Identifier    |
+----------+-----------------------+----------------------------+
```

6. Address Mapping -- Unicast

The procedure for mapping IPv6 unicast addresses into Ethernet link-layer addresses is described in [DISC]. The Source/Target Link-layer Address option has the following form when the link layer is Ethernet.

```
 0                   1
 0 1 2 3 4 5 6 7 8 9 0 1 2 3 4 5
+-+-+-+-+-+-+-+-+-+-+-+-+-+-+-+-+
|     Type      |    Length     |
+-+-+-+-+-+-+-+-+-+-+-+-+-+-+-+-+
|                               |
+-           Ethernet          -+
|                               |
+-           Address           -+
|                               |
+-+-+-+-+-+-+-+-+-+-+-+-+-+-+-+-+
```

Option fields:

Type   1 for Source Link-layer address.
            2 for Target Link-layer address.

Length   1 (in units of 8 octets).

Ethernet Address
            The 48 bit Ethernet IEEE 802 address, in canonical bit order. This is the address the interface currently responds to, and may be different from the built-in address used to derive the Interface Identifier.

7. Address Mapping – Multicast

An IPv6 packet with a multicast destination address DST, consisting of the sixteen octets DST[1] through DST[16], is transmitted to the Ethernet multicast address whose first two octets are the value 3333 hexadecimal and whose last four octets are the last four octets of DST.

```
+-+-+-+-+-+-+-+-+-+-+-+-+-+-+-+-+
|0 0 1 1 0 0 1 1|0 0 1 1 0 0 1 1|
+-+-+-+-+-+-+-+-+-+-+-+-+-+-+-+-+
|   DST[13]     |   DST[14]     |
+-+-+-+-+-+-+-+-+-+-+-+-+-+-+-+-+
|   DST[15]     |   DST[16]     |
+-+-+-+-+-+-+-+-+-+-+-+-+-+-+-+-+
```

8. Differences From RFC 1972

The following are the functional differences between this specification and RFC 1972.

The Address Token, which was a node's 48-bit MAC address, is replaced with the Interface Identifier, which is 64 bits in length and based on the EUI-64 format [EUI64]. An IEEE-defined mapping exists from 48-bit MAC addresses to EUI-64 form.

A prefix used for stateless autoconfiguration must now be 64 bits long rather than 80. The link-local prefix is also shortened to 64 bits.9. Security Considerations

The method of derivation of Interface Identifiers from MAC addresses is intended to preserve global uniqueness when possible. However, there is no protection from duplication through accident or forgery.

10. References

[AARCH] Hinden, R. and S. Deering "IP Version 6 Addressing Architecture", RFC 2373, July 1998.

[ACONF] Thomson, S. and T. Narten, "IPv6 Stateless Address Autoconfiguration", RFC 2462, December 1998.

[DISC] Narten, T., Nordmark, E. and W. Simpson, "Neighbor Discovery for IP Version 6 (IPv6)", RFC 2461, December 1998.

[EUI64] "Guidelines For 64-bit Global Identifier (EUI-64)", http://standards.ieee.org/db/oui/tutorials/EUI64.html

[IPV6] Deering, S. and R. Hinden, "Internet Protocol, Version 6 (IPv6) Specification", RFC 2460, December 1998.

[RFC 2119] Bradner, S., "Key words for use in RFCs to Indicate Requirement Levels", BCP 14, RFC 2119, March 1997.

11. Author's Address

Matt Crawford
Fermilab MS 368
PO Box 500
Batavia, IL 60510
USA

Phone: +1 630 840-3461
EMail: crawdad@fnal.gov

12. Full Copyright Statement

M. Crawford
Fermilab
December 1998

Transmission of IPv6 Packets over FDDI Networks

Status of this Memo

This document specifies an Internet standards track protocol for the Internet community, and requests discussion and suggestions for improvements. Please refer to the current edition of the "Internet Official Protocol Standards" (STD 1) for the standardization state and status of this protocol. Distribution of this memo is unlimited.

Copyright Notice

1. Introduction

This document specifies the frame format for transmission of IPv6 packets and the method of forming IPv6 link-local addresses and statelessly autoconfigured addresses on FDDI networks. It also specifies the content of the Source/Target Link-layer Address option used in Router Solicitation, Router Advertisement, Neighbor Solicitation, Neighbor Advertisement and Redirect messages when those messages are transmitted on an FDDI network.

This document replaces RFC 2019, "Transmission of IPv6 Packets Over FDDI", which will become historic.

The key words "MUST", "MUST NOT", "REQUIRED", "SHALL", "SHALL NOT", "SHOULD", "SHOULD NOT", "RECOMMENDED", "MAY", and "OPTIONAL" in this document are to be interpreted as described in [RFC 2119].

2. Maximum Transmission Unit

FDDI permits a frame length of 4500 octets (9000 symbols), including at least 22 octets (44 symbols) of Data Link encapsulation when long-format addresses are used. Subtracting 8 octets of LLC/SNAP header, this would, in principle, allow the IPv6 [IPV6] packet in the Information field to be up to 4470 octets. However, it is desirable to allow for the variable sizes and possible future extensions of the MAC header and frame status fields. The default MTU size for IPv6 packets on an FDDI network is therefore 4352 octets. This size may be reduced by a Router Advertisement [DISC] containing an MTU option which specifies a smaller MTU, or by manual configuration of each node. If a Router Advertisement received on an FDDI interface has an MTU option specifying an MTU larger than 4352, or larger than a manually configured value, that MTU option may be logged to system management but must be otherwise ignored.

For purposes of this document, information received from DHCP is considered "manually configured" and the term FDDI includes CDDI.

3. Frame Format

FDDI provides both synchronous and asynchronous transmission, with the latter class further subdivided by the use of restricted and unrestricted tokens. Only asynchronous transmission with unrestricted tokens is required for FDDI interoperability. Accordingly, IPv6 packets shall be sent in asynchronous frames using unrestricted tokens. The robustness principle dictates that nodes should be able to receive synchronous frames and asynchronous frames sent using restricted tokens.

IPv6 packets are transmitted in LLC/SNAP frames, using long-format (48 bit) addresses. The data field contains the IPv6 header and payload and is followed by the FDDI Frame Check Sequence, Ending Delimiter, and Frame Status symbols.

```
                  0                   1
                  0 1 2 3 4 5 6 7 8 9 0 1 2 3 4 5
                                  +-+-+-+-+-+-+-+-+
                                  |      FC       |
                  +-+-+-+-+-+-+-+-+-+-+-+-+-+-+-+-+
                  |           Destination         |
                  +-                             -+
                  |              FDDI             |
                  +-                             -+
                  |            Address            |
                  +-+-+-+-+-+-+-+-+-+-+-+-+-+-+-+-+
                  |             Source            |
                  +-                             -+
                  |              FDDI             |
                  +-                             -+
                  |            Address            |
                  +-+-+-+-+-+-+-+-+-+-+-+-+-+-+-+-+
                  |     DSAP      |     SSAP      |
                  +-+-+-+-+-+-+-+-+-+-+-+-+-+-+-+-+
                  |      CTL      |     OUI ...   |
                  +-+-+-+-+-+-+-+-+               +
                  |            ... OUI            |
                  +-+-+-+-+-+-+-+-+-+-+-+-+-+-+-+-+
                  |           Ethertype           |
                  +-+-+-+-+-+-+-+-+-+-+-+-+-+-+-+-+
                  |              IPv6             |
                  +-                             -+
                  |             header            |
                  +-                             -+
                  |              and              |
                  +-                             -+
                  /            payload ...        /
                  +-+-+-+-+-+-+-+-+-+-+-+-+-+-+-+-+

                (Each tic mark represents one bit.)
```

FDDI Header Fields:

FC   The Frame Code must be in the range 50 to 57 hexadecimal, inclusive, with the three low order bits indicating the frame priority.

DSAP, SSAP   Both the DSAP and SSAP fields shall contain the value AA hexadecimal, indicating SNAP encapsulation.

CTL   The Control field shall be set to 03 hexadecimal, indicating Unnumbered Information.

OUI The Organizationally Unique Identifier shall be set to 000000 hexadecimal.

Ethertype The Ethernet protocol type ("ethertype") shall be set to the value 86DD hexadecimal.

4. Interaction with Bridges

802.1d MAC bridges which connect different media, for example Ethernet and FDDI, have become very widespread. Some of them do IPv4 packet fragmentation and/or support IPv4 Path MTU discovery [RFC 1981], many others do not, or do so incorrectly. Use of IPv6 in a bridged mixed-media environment must not depend on support from MAC bridges, unless those bridges are known to correctly implement IPv6 Path MTU Discovery [RFC 1981, ICMPV6].

For correct operation when mixed media are bridged together by bridges which do not support IPv6 Path MTU Discovery, the smallest MTU of all the media must be advertised by routers in an MTU option. If there are no routers present, this MTU must be manually configured in each node which is connected to a medium with a default MTU larger than the smallest MTU.

5. Stateless Autoconfiguration

The Interface Identifier [AARCH] for an FDDI interface is based on the EUI-64 identifier [EUI64] derived from the interface's built-in 48-bit IEEE 802 address. The EUI-64 is formed as follows. (Canonical bit order is assumed throughout. See [CANON] for a caution on bit-order effects in LAN interfaces.)

The OUI of the FDDI MAC address (the first three octets) becomes the company_id of the EUI-64 (the first three octets). The fourth and fifth octets of the EUI are set to the fixed value FFFE hexadecimal. The last three octets of the FDDI MAC address become the last three octets of the EUI-64.

The Interface Identifier is then formed from the EUI-64 by complementing the "Universal/Local" (U/L) bit, which is the next-to-lowest order bit of the first octet of the EUI-64. For further discussion on this point, see [ETHER] and [AARCH].

For example, the Interface Identifier for an FDDI interface whose built-in address is, in hexadecimal,

34-56-78-9A-BC-DE

would be

36-56-78-FF-FE-9A-BC-DE.

A different MAC address set manually or by software should not be used to derive the Interface Identifier. If such a MAC address must be used, its global uniqueness property should be reflected in the value of the U/L bit.

An IPv6 address prefix used for stateless autoconfiguration [ACONF] of an FDDI interface must have a length of 64 bits.

6. Link-Local Addresses

The IPv6 link-local address [AARCH] for an FDDI interface is formed by appending the Interface Identifier, as defined above, to the prefix FE80::/64.

```
  10 bits            54 bits                  64 bits
+----------+-----------------------+----------------------------+
|1111111010|        (zeros)        |    Interface Identifier    |
+----------+-----------------------+----------------------------+
```

7. Address Mapping — Unicast

The procedure for mapping IPv6 unicast addresses into FDDI link-layer addresses is described in [DISC]. The Source/Target Link-layer Address option has the following form when the link layer is FDDI.

```
 0                   1
 0 1 2 3 4 5 6 7 8 9 0 1 2 3 4 5
+-+-+-+-+-+-+-+-+-+-+-+-+-+-+-+-+
|     Type      |    Length     |
+-+-+-+-+-+-+-+-+-+-+-+-+-+-+-+-+
|                               |
+-            FDDI             -+
|                               |
+-           Address           -+
|                               |
+-+-+-+-+-+-+-+-+-+-+-+-+-+-+-+-+
```

Option fields:

```
Type         1 for Source Link-layer address.
             2 for Target Link-layer address.

Length       1 (in units of 8 octets).

FDDI Address
             The 48 bit FDDI IEEE 802 address, in canonical bit order.
             This is the address the interface currently responds to,
             and may be different from the built-in address used to
             derive the Interface Identifier.
```


8. Address Mapping — Multicast

An IPv6 packet with a multicast destination address DST, consisting of the sixteen octets DST[1] through DST[16], is transmitted to the FDDI multicast address whose first two octets are the value 3333 hexadecimal and whose last four octets are the last four octets of DST.

```
+-+-+-+-+-+-+-+-+-+-+-+-+-+-+-+-+
|0 0 1 1 0 0 1 1|0 0 1 1 0 0 1 1|
+-+-+-+-+-+-+-+-+-+-+-+-+-+-+-+-+
|   DST[13]     |   DST[14]     |
+-+-+-+-+-+-+-+-+-+-+-+-+-+-+-+-+
|   DST[15]     |   DST[16]     |
+-+-+-+-+-+-+-+-+-+-+-+-+-+-+-+-+
```

9. Differences From RFC 2019

The following are the functional differences between this specification and RFC 2019.

"FDDI adjacency detection" has been removed, due to recent work in IEEE 802.1p.

The Address Token, which was a node's 48-bit MAC address, is replaced with the Interface Identifier, which is 64 bits in length and based on the EUI-64 format [EUI64]. An IEEE-defined mapping exists from 48-bit MAC addresses to EUI-64 form.

A prefix used for stateless autoconfiguration must now be 64 bits long rather than 80. The link-local prefix is also shortened to 64 bits.

10. Security Considerations

The method of derivation of Interface Identifiers from MAC addresses is intended to preserve global uniqueness when possible. However, there is no protection from duplication through accident or forgery.

11. References

[AARCH] Hinden, R. and S. Deering "IP Version 6 Addressing Architecture", RFC 2373, July 1998.

[ACONF] Thomson, S. and T. Narten, "IPv6 Stateless Address Autoconfiguration", RFC 2462, December 1998.

[CANON] Narten, T. and C. Burton, "A Caution On The Canonical Ordering Of Link-Layer Addresses", RFC 2469, December 1998.

[DISC] Narten, T., Nordmark, E. and W. Simpson, "Neighbor Discovery for IP Version 6 (IPv6)", RFC 2461, December 1998.

[ETHER] Crawford, M., "Transmission of IPv6 Packets over Ethernet Networks", RFC 2464, December 1998.

[EUI64] "Guidelines For 64-bit Global Identifier (EUI-64)", http://standards.ieee.org/db/oui/tutorials/EUI64.html.

[ICMPV6] Conta, A. and S. Deering, "Internet Control Message Protocol (ICMPv6) for the Internet Protocol Version 6 (IPv6) Specification", RFC 2463, December 1998.

[IPV6] Deering, S. and R. Hinden, "Internet Protocol, Version 6 (IPv6) Specification", RFC 2460, December 1998.

[RFC 1981] McCann, J., Deering, S. and J. Mogul, "Path MTU Discovery for IP version 6", RFC 1981, August 1996.

[RFC 2119] Bradner, S., "Key words for use in RFCs to Indicate Requirement Levels", BCP 14, RFC 2119, March 1997.

12. Author's Address

Matt Crawford
Fermilab MS 368
PO Box 500
Batavia, IL 60510
USA

Phone: +1 630 840-3461
EMail: crawdad@fnal.gov

13. Full Copyright Statement

Network Working Group
Request for Comments: 2471
Obsoletes: 1897
Category: Experimental

R. Hinden
Nokia
R. Fink
LBNL
J. Postel
ISI

December 1998

IPv6 Testing Address Allocation

Status of this Memo

This memo defines an Experimental Protocol for the Internet community. It does not specify an Internet standard of any kind. Discussion and suggestions for improvement are requested. Distribution of this memo is unlimited.

Copyright Notice

1.0 Introduction

This document describes an allocation plan for IPv6 addresses to be used in testing IPv6 prototype software. These addresses are temporary and will be reclaimed in the future. Any IPv6 system using these addresses will have to renumber at some time in the future. These addresses will not to be routable in the Internet other than for IPv6 testing.

The address format for the IPv6 test address is consistent with the "Aggregatable Global Unicast Address Allocation" [AGGR] and "TLA and NLA Assignment Rules" [TLAASN].

This document is intended to replace RFC 1897 "IPv6 Testing Address Allocation", January 1996. RFC 1897 will become historic.

The addresses described in this document are consistent with the IPv6 Addressing Architecture [ARCH]. They may be assigned to nodes manually, with IPv6 Auto Address Allocation [AUTO], or with DHCP for IPv6 [DHCPv6].

The key words "MUST", "MUST NOT", "REQUIRED", "SHALL", "SHALL NOT", "SHOULD", "SHOULD NOT", "RECOMMENDED", "MAY", and "OPTIONAL" in this document are to be interpreted as described in [RFC2119].

2.0 Address Format

The Aggregatable Global Unicast Address Allocation format defined in [AGGR] is as follows:

```
| 3 |  13 |    32     |   16   |          64 bits               |
+---+-----+-----------+--------+--------------------------------+
|FP | TLA | NLA ID    | SLA ID |         Interface ID           |
|   | ID  |           |        |                                |
+---+-----+-----------+--------+--------------------------------+
```

where:

FP = 001 = Format Prefix

This is the Format Prefix used to identify aggregatable global unicast addresses.

TLA = 0x1FFE = Top-Level Aggregation Identifier

This is a TLA ID assigned by the IANA for 6bone testing under the auspices of the IETF IPng Transition Working Group 6bone testbed activity. It is to be administered by the chair of the 6bone activity (currently Bob Fink <rlfink@lbl.gov>).

The use of this TLA ID is temporary. All users of these addresses in this TLA ID will be required to renumber at some time in the future.

NLA ID = Next-Level Aggregation Identifier

The NLA ID space will be assigned, by the TLA ID administrator, in an addressing hierarchy sufficient to identify transit networks and end user sites consistent with the architecture and topology of the 6bone. This will provide a multi-level transit service consistent with the 6bone goals of fully testing IPv6 technology in real use environments.

SLA ID = Site-Level Aggregation Identifier

The SLA ID field is used by an individual organization to create its own local addressing hierarchy and to identify subnets. Assignment of the SLA ID field is the responsibility of each individual organization.

Interface ID

This is the interface identifier of the interface on the link as defined in the appropriate IPv6 over <link> document, such as [ETHER], [FDDI], etc.

4.0 References

[ARCH] Hinden, R., "IP Version 6 Addressing Architecture", RFC 2373, July 1998.

[AGGR] Hinden, R., Deering, S., O'Dell, M., "An Aggregatable Global Unicast Address Format", RFC 2374, July 1998.

[AUTO] Thompson, S. and T. Narten, "IPv6 Stateless Address Autoconfiguration", RFC 1971, August 1996.

[DHCP6] Bound, J., "Host Configuration Protocol for IPv6", Work in Progress.

[ETHER] Crawford, M., "Transmission of IPv6 Packets over Ethernet Networks", RFC 2464, December 1998.

[FDDI] Crawford, M., "Transmission of IPv6 Packets over FDDI Networks", RFC 2467, December 1998.

[RFC2119] Bradner, S., "Key words for use in RFCs to Indicate Requirement Levels", BCP 14, RFC 2119, March 1997.

[TLAASN] Hinden, R., "TLA and NLA Assignment Rules", Work in Progress.

5.0 Security Considerations

This document defines a test approach for creating aggregatable address consistent with [AGGR]. It does not have any direct impact on Internet infrastructure security. Authentication of IPv6 packets is defined in [AUTH].

6.0 Authors' Addresses

Robert M. Hinden
Nokia
232 Java Drive
Sunnyvale, CA 94089
USA

Phone: +1 408 990-2004
EMail: hinden@iprg.nokia.com

Robert Fink
Lawrence Berkeley National Laboratory
MS 50A-3111
Berkeley, CA 94720
USA

Phone: +1 510 486-5692
EMail: rlfink@lbl.gov

Jon Postel (Deceased)
Information Sciences Institute
4676 Admiralty Way
Marina del Rey, CA 90292-6695
USA

7.0 Full Copyright Statement

Network Working Group
Request for Comments: 2472
Obsoletes: 2023
Category: Standards Track

D. Haskin
E. Allen
Bay Networks, Inc.

December 1998

IP Version 6 over PPP

Status of this Memo

This document specifies an Internet standards track protocol for the Internet community, and requests discussion and suggestions for improvements. Please refer to the current edition of the "Internet Official Protocol Standards" (STD 1) for the standardization state and status of this protocol. Distribution of this memo is unlimited.

Copyright Notice

Abstract

The Point-to-Point Protocol (PPP) [1] provides a standard method of encapsulating Network Layer protocol information over point-to-point links. PPP also defines an extensible Link Control Protocol, and proposes a family of Network Control Protocols (NCPs) for establishing and configuring different network-layer protocols.

This document defines the method for transmission of IP Version 6 [2] packets over PPP links as well as the Network Control Protocol (NCP) for establishing and configuring the IPv6 over PPP. It also specifies the method of forming IPv6 link-local addresses on PPP links.

Table of Contents

1. Introduction

PPP has three main components:

1) A method for encapsulating datagrams over serial links.

2) A Link Control Protocol (LCP) for establishing, configuring, and testing the data-link connection.

3) A family of Network Control Protocols (NCPs) for establishing and configuring different network-layer protocols.

In order to establish communications over a point-to-point link, each end of the PPP link must first send LCP packets to configure and test the data link. After the link has been established and optional facilities have been negotiated as needed by the LCP, PPP must send NCP packets to choose and configure one or more network-layer protocols. Once each of the chosen network-layer protocols has been configured, datagrams from each network-layer protocol can be sent over the link.

In this document, the NCP for establishing and configuring the IPv6 over PPP is referred as the IPv6 Control Protocol (IPV6CP).

The link will remain configured for communications until explicit LCP or NCP packets close the link down, or until some external event occurs (power failure at the other end, carrier drop, etc.).

1.1. Specification of Requirements

In this document, several words are used to signify the requirements of the specification.

The key words "MUST", "MUST NOT", "REQUIRED", "SHALL", "SHALL NOT", "SHOULD", "SHOULD NOT", "RECOMMENDED", "MAY", and "OPTIONAL" in this document are to be interpreted as described in [7].

2. Sending IPv6 Datagrams

Before any IPv6 packets may be communicated, PPP MUST reach the Network-Layer Protocol phase, and the IPv6 Control Protocol MUST reach the Opened state.

Exactly one IPv6 packet is encapsulated in the Information field of PPP Data Link Layer frames where the Protocol field indicates type hex 0057 (Internet Protocol Version 6).

The maximum length of an IPv6 packet transmitted over a PPP link is the same as the maximum length of the Information field of a PPP data link layer frame. PPP links supporting IPv6 MUST allow the information field at least as large as the minimum link MTU size required for IPv6 [2].

3. A PPP Network Control Protocol for IPv6

The IPv6 Control Protocol (IPV6CP) is responsible for configuring, enabling, and disabling the IPv6 protocol modules on both ends of the point-to-point link. IPV6CP uses the same packet exchange mechanism as the Link Control Protocol (LCP). IPV6CP packets may not be exchanged until PPP has reached the Network-Layer Protocol phase. IPV6CP packets received before this phase is reached should be silently discarded.

The IPv6 Control Protocol is exactly the same as the Link Control Protocol [1] with the following exceptions:

Data Link Layer Protocol Field

Exactly one IPV6CP packet is encapsulated in the Information field of PPP Data Link Layer frames where the Protocol field indicates type hex 8057 (IPv6 Control Protocol).

Code field

Only Codes 1 through 7 (Configure-Request, Configure-Ack, Configure-Nak, Configure-Reject, Terminate-Request, Terminate-Ack and Code-Reject) are used. Other Codes should be treated as unrecognized and should result in Code-Rejects.

Timeouts

IPV6CP packets may not be exchanged until PPP has reached the Network-Layer Protocol phase. An implementation should be prepared to wait for Authentication and Link Quality Determination to finish before timing out waiting for a Configure-Ack or other response. It is suggested that an implementation give up only after user intervention or a configurable amount of time.

Configuration Option Types

IPV6CP has a distinct set of Configuration Options.

4. IPV6CP Configuration Options

IPV6CP Configuration Options allow negotiation of desirable IPv6 parameters. IPV6CP uses the same Configuration Option format defined for LCP [1], with a separate set of Options. If a Configuration Option is not included in a Configure-Request packet, the default value for that Configuration Option is assumed.

Up-to-date values of the IPV6CP Option Type field are specified in the most recent "Assigned Numbers" RFC [4]. Current values are assigned as follows:

1 Interface-Identifier
2 IPv6-Compression-Protocol

The only IPV6CP options defined in this document are Interface-Identifier and IPv6-Compression-Protocol. Any other IPV6CP configuration options that can be defined over time are to be defined in separate documents.

4.1. Interface-Identifier

Description

This Configuration Option provides a way to negotiate a unique 64-bit interface identifier to be used for the address autoconfiguration [3] at the local end of the link (see section 5). A Configure-Request MUST contain exactly one instance of the Interface-Identifier option [1]. The interface identifier MUST be unique within the PPP link; i.e. upon completion of the negotiation different Interface-Identifier values are to be selected for the ends of the PPP link. The interface identifier MAY also be unique over a broader scope.

Before this Configuration Option is requested, an implementation chooses its tentative Interface-Identifier. The non-zero value of the tentative Interface-Identifier SHOULD be chosen such that the value is both unique to the link and, if possible, consistently reproducible across initializations of the IPV6CP finite state machine (administrative Close and reOpen, reboots, etc). The rationale for preferring a consistently reproducible unique interface identifier to a completely random interface identifier is to provide stability to global scope addresses that can be formed from the interface identifier.

Assuming that interface identifier bits are numbered from 0 to 63 in canonical bit order where the most significant bit is the bit number 0, the bit number 6 is the "u" bit (universal/local bit in IEEE EUI-64 [5] terminology) which indicates whether or not the interface identifier is based on a globally unique IEEE identifier (EUI-48 or EUI-64 [5]) (see the case 1 below). It is set to one (1) if a globally unique IEEE identifier is used to derive the interface identifier, and it is set to zero (0) otherwise.

The following are methods for choosing the tentative Interface Identifier in the preference order:

1) If an IEEE global identifier (EUI-48 or EUI-64) is available anywhere on the node, it should be used to construct the tentative Interface-Identifier due to its uniqueness properties. When extracting an IEEE global identifier from another device on the node, care should be taken to that the extracted identifier is presented in canonical ordering [8].

   The only transformation from an EUI-64 identifier is to invert the "u" bit (universal/local bit in IEEE EUI-64 terminology). For example, for a globally unique EUI-64 identifier of the form:

```
most-significant                                     least-significant
bit                                                                bit
|0              1|1              3|3              4|4              6|
|0              5|6              1|2              7|8              3|
+----------------+----------------+----------------+----------------+
|cccccc0gcccccccc|cccccccceeeeeeee|eeeeeeeeeeeeeeee|eeeeeeeeeeeeeeee|
+----------------+----------------+----------------+----------------+
```

   where "c" are the bits of the assigned company_id, "0" is the value of the universal/local bit to indicate global scope, "g" is group/individual bit, and "e" are the bits of the extension identifier,

   the IPv6 interface identifier would be of the form:

```
most-significant                                     least-significant
bit                                                                bit
|0              1|1              3|3              4|4              6|
|0              5|6              1|2              7|8              3|
+----------------+----------------+----------------+----------------+
|cccccc1gcccccccc|cccccccceeeeeeee|eeeeeeeeeeeeeeee|eeeeeeeeeeeeeeee|
+----------------+----------------+----------------+----------------+
```

   The only change is inverting the value of the universal/local bit.

In the case of a EUI-48 identifier, it is first converted to the EUI-64 format by inserting two bytes, with hexadecimal values of 0xFF and 0xFE, in the middle of the 48 bit MAC (between the company_id and extension-identifier portions of the EUI-48 value). For example, for a globally unique 48 bit EUI-48 identifier of the form:

```
most-significant                    least-significant
bit                                               bit
|0              1|1              3|3              4|
|0              5|6              1|2              7|
+----------------+----------------+----------------+
|cccccc0gcccccccc|cccccccceeeeeeee|eeeeeeeeeeeeeeee|
+----------------+----------------+----------------+
```

where "c" are the bits of the assigned company_id, "0" is the value of the universal/local bit to indicate global scope, "g" is group/individual bit, and "e" are the bits of the extension identifier, the IPv6 interface identifier would be of the form:

```
most-significant                                     least-significant
bit                                                                bit
|0              1|1              3|3              4|4              6|
|0              5|6              1|2              7|8              3|
+----------------+----------------+----------------+----------------+
|cccccc1gcccccccc|cccccccc11111111|11111110eeeeeeee|eeeeeeeeeeeeeeee|
+----------------+----------------+----------------+----------------+
```

2) If an IEEE global identifier is not available a different source of uniqueness should be used. Suggested sources of uniqueness include link-layer addresses, machine serial numbers, et cetera.

   In this case the "u" bit of the interface identifier MUST be set to zero (0).

3) If a good source of uniqueness cannot be found, it is recommended that a random number be generated. In this case the "u" bit of the interface identifier MUST be set to zero (0).

Good sources [1] of uniqueness or randomness are required for the Interface-Identifier negotiation to succeed. If neither a unique number or a random number can be generated it is recommended that a zero value be used for the Interface-Identifier transmitted in the Configure-Request. In this case the PPP peer may provide a valid non-zero Interface-Identifier in its response as described below. Note that if at least one of the PPP peers is able to generate separate non-zero numbers for itself and its peer, the identifier negotiation will succeed.

When a Configure-Request is received with the Interface-Identifier Configuration Option and the receiving peer implements this option, the received Interface-Identifier is compared with the Interface-Identifier of the last Configure-Request sent to the peer. Depending on the result of the comparison an implementation MUST respond in one of the following ways:

If the two Interface-Identifiers are different but the received Interface-Identifier is zero, a Configure-Nak is sent with a non-zero Interface-Identifier value suggested for use by the remote peer. Such a suggested Interface-Identifier MUST be different from the Interface-Identifier of the last Configure-Request sent to the peer. It is recommended that the value suggested be consistently reproducible across initializations of the IPV6CP finite state machine (administrative Close and reOpen, reboots, etc). The "u" universal/local) bit of the suggested identifier MUST be set to zero (0) regardless of its source unless the globally unique EUI-48/EUI-64 derived identifier is provided for the exclusive use by the remote peer.

If the two Interface-Identifiers are different and the received Interface-Identifier is not zero, the Interface-Identifier MUST be acknowledged, i.e. a Configure-Ack is sent with the requested Interface-Identifier, meaning that the responding peer agrees with the Interface-Identifier requested.

If the two Interface-Identifiers are equal and are not zero, a Configure-Nak MUST be sent specifying a different non-zero Interface-Identifier value suggested for use by the remote peer. It is recommended that the value suggested be consistently reproducible across initializations of the IPV6CP finite state machine (administrative Close and reOpen, reboots, etc). The "u" universal/local) bit of the suggested identifier MUST be set to zero (0) regardless of its source unless the globally unique EUI-48/EUI-64 derived identifier is provided for the exclusive use by the remote peer.

If the two Interface-Identifiers are equal to zero, the Interface-Identifiers negotiation MUST be terminated by transmitting the Configure-Reject with the Interface-Identifier value set to zero. In this case a unique Interface-Identifier can not be negotiated.

If a Configure-Request is received with the Interface-Identifier Configuration Option and the receiving peer does not implement this option, Configure-Rej is sent.

A new Configure-Request SHOULD NOT be sent to the peer until normal processing would cause it to be sent (that is, until a Configure-Nak is received or the Restart timer runs out).

A new Configure-Request MUST NOT contain the Interface-Identifier option if a valid Interface-Identifier Configure-Reject is received.

Reception of a Configure-Nak with a suggested Interface-Identifier different from that of the last Configure-Nak sent to the peer indicates a unique Interface-Identifier. In this case a new Configure-Request MUST be sent with the identifier value suggested in the last Configure-Nak from the peer. But if the received Interface-Identifier is equal to the one sent in the last Configure-Nak, a new Interface-Identifier MUST be chosen. In this case, a new Configure-Request SHOULD be sent with the new tentative Interface-Identifier. This sequence (transmit Configure-Request, receive Configure-Request, transmit Configure-Nak, receive Configure-Nak) might occur a few times, but it is extremely unlikely to occur repeatedly. More likely, the Interface-Identifiers chosen at either end will quickly diverge, terminating the sequence.

If negotiation of the Interface-Identifier is required, and the peer did not provide the option in its Configure-Request, the option SHOULD be appended to a Configure-Nak. The tentative value of the Interface-Identifier given must be acceptable as the remote Interface-Identifier; i.e. it should be different from the identifier value selected for the local end of the PPP link. The next Configure-Request from the peer may include this option. If the next Configure-Request does not include this option the peer MUST NOT send another Configure-Nak with this option included. It should assume that the peer's implementation does not support this option.

By default, an implementation SHOULD attempt to negotiate the Interface-Identifier for its end of the PPP connection.

A summary of the Interface-Identifier Configuration Option format is shown below. The fields are transmitted from left to right.

```
 0                   1                   2                   3
 0 1 2 3 4 5 6 7 8 9 0 1 2 3 4 5 6 7 8 9 0 1 2 3 4 5 6 7 8 9 0 1
+-+-+-+-+-+-+-+-+-+-+-+-+-+-+-+-+-+-+-+-+-+-+-+-+-+-+-+-+-+-+-+-+
|     Type      |    Length     | Interface-Identifier (MS Bytes)
+-+-+-+-+-+-+-+-+-+-+-+-+-+-+-+-+-+-+-+-+-+-+-+-+-+-+-+-+-+-+-+-+
                     Interface-Identifier (cont)
+-+-+-+-+-+-+-+-+-+-+-+-+-+-+-+-+-+-+-+-+-+-+-+-+-+-+-+-+-+-+-+-+
Interface-Identifier (LS Bytes) |
+-+-+-+-+-+-+-+-+-+-+-+-+-+-+-+-+
```

Type

1

Length

10

Interface-Identifier

The 64-bit Interface-Identifier which is very likely to be unique on the link or zero if a good source of uniqueness can not be found.

Default

If no valid interface identifier can be successfully negotiated, no default Interface-Identifier value should be assumed. The procedures for recovering from such a case are unspecified. One approach is to manually configure the interface identifier of the interface.

4.2. IPv6-Compression-Protocol

Description

This Configuration Option provides a way to negotiate the use of a specific IPv6 packet compression protocol. The IPv6-Compression-Protocol Configuration Option is used to indicate the ability to receive compressed packets. Each end of the link must separately request this option if bi-directional compression is desired. By default, compression is not enabled.

IPv6 compression negotiated with this option is specific to IPv6 datagrams and is not to be confused with compression resulting from negotiations via Compression Control Protocol (CCP), which potentially effect all datagrams.

A summary of the IPv6-Compression-Protocol Configuration Option format is shown below. The fields are transmitted from left to right.

```
 0                   1                   2                   3
 0 1 2 3 4 5 6 7 8 9 0 1 2 3 4 5 6 7 8 9 0 1 2 3 4 5 6 7 8 9 0 1
+-+-+-+-+-+-+-+-+-+-+-+-+-+-+-+-+-+-+-+-+-+-+-+-+-+-+-+-+-+-+-+-+
|     Type      |    Length     |   IPv6-Compression-Protocol   |
+-+-+-+-+-+-+-+-+-+-+-+-+-+-+-+-+-+-+-+-+-+-+-+-+-+-+-+-+-+-+-+-+
|    Data ...
+-+-+-+-+
```

Type

2

Length

>= 4

IPv6-Compression-Protocol

The IPv6-Compression-Protocol field is two octets and indicates the compression protocol desired. Values for this field are always the same as the PPP Data Link Layer Protocol field values for that same compression protocol.

No IPv6-Compression-Protocol field values are currently assigned. Specific assignments will be made in documents that define specific compression algorithms.

Data

The Data field is zero or more octets and contains additional data as determined by the particular compression protocol.

Default

No IPv6 compression protocol enabled.

5. Stateless Autoconfiguration and Link-Local Addresses

The Interface Identifier of IPv6 unicast addresses [6] of a PPP interface, SHOULD be negotiated in the IPV6CP phase of the PPP connection setup (see section 4.1). If no valid Interface Identifier has been successfully negotiated, procedures for recovering from such a case are unspecified. One approach is to manually configure the Interface Identifier of the interface.

As long as the Interface Identifier is negotiated in the IPV6CP phase of the PPP connection setup, it is redundant to perform duplicate address detection as a part of the IPv6 Stateless Autoconfiguration protocol [3]. Therefore it is recommended that for PPP links with the IPV6CP Interface-Identifier option enabled the default value of the DupAddrDetectTransmits autoconfiguration variable [3] be zero.

Link-local addresses of PPP interfaces have the following format:

```
| 10 bits  |        54 bits          |        64 bits            |
+----------+-------------------------+
|1111111010|           0             |   Interface Identifier    |
+----------+-------------------------+
```

The most significant 10 bits of the address is the Link-Local prefix FE80::. 54 zero bits pad out the address between the Link-Local prefix and the Interface Identifier fields.

6. Security Considerations

The IPv6 Control Protocol extension to PPP can be used with all defined PPP authentication and encryption mechanisms.

7. Acknowledgments

This document borrows from the Magic-Number LCP option and as such is partially based on previous work done by the PPP working group.

8. Changes from RFC-2023

The following changes were made from RFC-2023 "IP Version 6 over PPP":

- Changed to use "Interface Identifier" instead of the "Interface Token" term according to the terminology adopted in [6].

- Increased the size of Interface Identifier to 64 bits according to the newly adopted IPv6 addressing architecture [6].

- Added methods for selection of an interface identifier that is consistently reproducible across initializations of the IPV6CP finite state machine.

- Added the interface identifier selection methods for generating globally unique interface identifier from an unique an IEEE global identifier when it is available anywhere on the node.

- Changed to send a Configure-Nak instead a Configure-Ack in response to receiving a Configure-Request with a zero Interface-Identifier value.

- Replaced the value assignment of the IPv6-Compression-Protocol field of the IPv6-Compression-Protocol Configuration option with the text stating that no IPv6-Compression-Protocol field values are currently assigned and that specific assignments will be made in documents that define specific compression algorithms.

- Added new and updated references.

- Minor text clarifications and improvements.

9. References

[1] Simpson, W., "The Point-to-Point Protocol", STD 51, RFC 1661, July 1994.

[2] Deering, S., and R. Hinden, Editors, "Internet Protocol, Version 6 (IPv6) Specification", RFC 2460, December 1998.

[3] Thomson, S., and T. Narten, "IPv6 Stateless Address Autoconfiguration", RFC 2462, December 1998.

[4] Reynolds, J., and J. Postel, "Assigned Numbers", STD 2, RFC 1700, October 1994. See also: http://www.iana.org/numbers.html

[5] IEEE, "Guidelines for 64-bit Global Identifier (EUI-64) Registration Authority", http://standards.ieee.org/db/oui/tutorials/EUI64.html, March 1997.

[6] Hinden, R., and S. Deering, "IP Version 6 Addressing Architecture", RFC 2373, July 1998.

[7] Bradner, S., "Key words for use in RFCs to Indicate Requirement Levels," BCP 14, RFC 2119, March 1997.

[8] Narten T., and C. Burton, "A Caution On The Canonical Ordering Of Link-Layer Addresses", RFC 2469, December 1998.

10. Authors' Addresses

Dimitry Haskin
Bay Networks, Inc.
600 Technology Park
Billerica, MA 01821

EMail: dhaskin@baynetworks.com

Ed Allen
Bay Networks, Inc.
600 Technology Park
Billerica, MA 01821

EMail: eallen@baynetworks.com

11. Full Copyright Statement

Network Working Group
Request for Comments: 2473
Category: Standards Track

A. Conta
Lucent Technologies Inc.
S. Deering
Cisco Systems
December 1998

Generic Packet Tunneling in IPv6 Specification

Status of this Memo

This document specifies an Internet standards track protocol for the Internet community, and requests discussion and suggestions for improvements. Please refer to the current edition of the "Internet Official Protocol Standards" (STD 1) for the standardization state and status of this protocol. Distribution of this memo is unlimited.

Copyright Notice

Abstract

This document defines the model and generic mechanisms for IPv6 encapsulation of Internet packets, such as IPv6 and IPv4. The model and mechanisms can be applied to other protocol packets as well, such as AppleTalk, IPX, CLNP, or others.

Table of Contents

1. Introduction

This document specifies a method and generic mechanisms by which a packet is encapsulated and carried as payload within an IPv6 packet. The resulting packet is called an IPv6 tunnel packet. The forwarding path between the source and destination of the tunnel packet is called an IPv6 tunnel. The technique is called IPv6 tunneling.

A typical scenario for IPv6 tunneling is the case in which an intermediate node exerts explicit routing control by specifying particular forwarding paths for selected packets. This control is achieved by prepending IPv6 headers to each of the selected original packets. These prepended headers identify the forwarding paths.

In addition to the description of generic IPv6 tunneling mechanisms, which is the focus of this document, specific mechanisms for tunneling IPv6 and IPv4 packets are also described herein.

The keywords MUST, MUST NOT, MAY, OPTIONAL, REQUIRED, RECOMMENDED, SHALL, SHALL NOT, SHOULD, SHOULD NOT are to be interpreted as defined in RFC 2119.

2. Terminology

original packet
    a packet that undergoes encapsulation.

original header

the header of an original packet.

tunnel

a forwarding path between two nodes on which the payloads of packets are original packets.

tunnel end-node

a node where a tunnel begins or ends.

tunnel header

the header prepended to the original packet during encapsulation. It specifies the tunnel end-points as source and destination.

tunnel packet

a packet that encapsulates an original packet.

tunnel entry-point

the tunnel end-node where an original packet is encapsulated.

tunnel exit-point

the tunnel end-node where a tunnel packet is decapsulated.

IPv6 tunnel

a tunnel configured as a virtual link between two IPv6 nodes, on which the encapsulating protocol is IPv6.

tunnel MTU

the maximum size of a tunnel packet payload without requiring fragmentation, that is, the Path MTU between the tunnel entry-point and the tunnel exit-point nodes minus the size of the tunnel header.

tunnel hop limit

the maximum number of hops that a tunnel packet can travel from the tunnel entry-point to the tunnel exit-point.

inner tunnel

a tunnel that is a hop (virtual link) of another tunnel.

outer tunnel

a tunnel containing one or more inner tunnels.

nested tunnel packet

a tunnel packet that has as payload a tunnel packet.

nested tunnel header

the tunnel header of a nested tunnel packet.

nested encapsulation

encapsulation of an encapsulated packet.

recursive encapsulation

encapsulation of a packet that reenters a tunnel before exiting it.

tunnel encapsulation limit

the maximum number of nested encapsulations of a packet.

3. IPv6 Tunneling

IPv6 tunneling is a technique for establishing a "virtual link" between two IPv6 nodes for transmitting data packets as payloads of IPv6 packets (see Fig.1). From the point of view of the two nodes, this "virtual link", called an IPv6 tunnel, appears as a point to point link on which IPv6 acts like a link-layer protocol. The two IPv6 nodes play specific roles. One node encapsulates original packets received from other nodes or from itself and forwards the resulting tunnel packets through the tunnel. The other node decapsulates the received tunnel packets and forwards the resulting original packets towards their destinations, possibly itself. The encapsulator node is called the tunnel entry-point node, and it is the source of the tunnel packets. The decapsulator node is called the tunnel exit-point, and it is the destination of the tunnel packets.

Note:
This document refers in particular to tunnels between two nodes identified by unicast addresses - such tunnels look like "virtual point to point links". The mechanisms described herein apply also to tunnels in which the exit-point nodes are identified by other types of addresses, such as anycast or multicast. These tunnels may look like "virtual point to multipoint links". At the time of writing this document, IPv6 anycast addresses are a subject of ongoing specification and experimental work.

```
                    Tunnel from node B to node C
                     <---------------------->
                  Tunnel                     Tunnel
                  Entry-Point                Exit-Point
                  Node                       Node
   +-+            +-+                        +-+             +-+
   |A|-->--//-->--|B|=====>=====//=====>=====|C|-->--//-->--|D|
   +-+            +-+                        +-+             +-+
   Original                                                  Original
   Packet                                                    Packet
   Source                                                    Destination
   Node                                                      Node
                          Fig.1 Tunnel
```

An IPv6 tunnel is a unidirectional mechanism - tunnel packet flow takes place in one direction between the IPv6 tunnel entry-point and exit-point nodes (see Fig.1).

```
                    Tunnel from Node B to Node C
                     <---------------------->
                  Tunnel                      Tunnel
   Original       Entry-Point                 Exit-Point     Original
   Packet         Node                        Node           Packet
   Source                                                    Destination
   Node                                                      Node
   +-+            +-+                         +-+            +-+
   | |-->--//-->--| |=====>=====//=====>======| |-->--//-->--| |
   |A|            |B|                         |C|            |D|
   | |--<--//--<--| |=====<=====//=====<======| |--<--//--<--| |
   +-+            +-+                         +-+            +-+
   Original                                                  Original
   Packet                                                    Packet
   Destination    Tunnel                      Tunnel         Source
   Node           Exit-Point                  Entry-Point    Node
                  Node                        Node
                   <---------------------->
                   Tunnel from Node C to Node B
              Fig.2 Bi-directional Tunneling Mechanism
```

Bi-directional tunneling is achieved by merging two unidirectional mechanisms, that is, configuring two tunnels, each in opposite direction to the other - the entry-point node of one tunnel is the exit-point node of the other tunnel (see Fig.2).

3.1 IPv6 Encapsulation

IPv6 encapsulation consists of prepending to the original packet an IPv6 header and, optionally, a set of IPv6 extension headers (see Fig.3), which are collectively called tunnel IPv6 headers. The encapsulation takes place in an IPv6 tunnel entry-point node, as the result of an original packet being forwarded onto the virtual link represented by the tunnel. The original packet is processed during forwarding according to the forwarding rules of the protocol of that packet. For instance if the original packet is an:

(a) IPv6 packet, the IPv6 original header hop limit is decremented by one.

(b) IPv4 packet, the IPv4 original header time to live field (TTL) is decremented by one.

At encapsulation, the source field of the tunnel IPv6 header is filled with an IPv6 address of the tunnel entry-point node, and the destination field with an IPv6 address of the tunnel exit-point. Subsequently, the tunnel packet resulting from encapsulation is sent towards the tunnel exit-point node.

```
                                +----------------------------------//-----+
                                | Original |                              |
                                |          |   Original Packet Payload    |
                                | Header   |                              |
                                +----------------------------------//-----+
                                 <           Original Packet              >
                                                  |
                                                  v
    <Tunnel IPv6 Headers> <         Original Packet                       >
   +---------+ - - - - - +-------------------------//--------------+
   | IPv6    | IPv6      |                                          |
   |         | Extension |         Original Packet                  |
   | Header  | Headers   |                                          |
   +---------+ - - - - - +-------------------------//--------------+
    <                         Tunnel IPv6 Packet                   >
```

Fig.3 Encapsulating a Packet

Tunnel extension headers should appear in the order recommended by the specifications that define the extension headers, such as [IPv6-Spec].

A source of original packets and a tunnel entry-point that encapsulates those packets can be the same node.

3.2 Packet Processing in Tunnels

The intermediate nodes in the tunnel process the IPv6 tunnel packets according to the IPv6 protocol. For example, a tunnel Hop by Hop Options extension header is processed by each receiving node in the tunnel; a tunnel Routing extension header identifies the intermediate processing nodes, and controls at a finer granularity the forwarding path of the tunnel packet through the tunnel; a tunnel Destination Options extension header is processed at the tunnel exit-point node.

3.3 IPv6 Decapsulation

Decapsulation is graphically shown in Fig.4:

```
+---------+- - - - - -+----------------------------------//-----+
| IPv6    | IPv6      |                                         |
|         | Extension |         Original Packet                 |
| Header  | Headers   |                                         |
+---------+- - - - - -+----------------------------------//-----+
 <                      Tunnel IPv6 Packet                       >
                                |
                                v
                      +----------------------------------//-----+
                      | Original |                              |
                      |          |   Original Packet Payload    |
                      | Headers  |                              |
                      +----------------------------------//-----+
                       <            Original Packet              >
```

Fig.4 Decapsulating a Packet

Upon receiving an IPv6 packet destined to an IPv6 address of a tunnel exit-point node, its IPv6 protocol layer processes the tunnel headers. The strict left-to-right processing rules for extension headers is applied. When processing is complete, control is handed to the next protocol engine, which is identified by the Next Header field value in the last header processed. If this is set to a tunnel protocol value, the tunnel protocol engine discards the tunnel headers and passes the resulting original packet to the Internet or lower layer protocol identified by that value for further processing.

For example, in the case the Next Header field has the IPv6 Tunnel Protocol value, the resulting original packet is passed to the IPv6 protocol layer.

The tunnel exit-point node, which decapsulates the tunnel packets, and the destination node, which receives the resulting original packets can be the same node.

3.4 IPv6 Tunnel Protocol Engine

Packet flow (paths #1-7) through the IPv6 Tunnel Protocol Engine on a node is graphically shown in Fig.5:

Note:

In Fig.5, the Upper-Layer Protocols box represents transport protocols such as TCP, UDP, control protocols such as ICMP, routing protocols such as OSPF, and internet or lower-layer protocol being "tunneled" over IPv6, such as IPv4, IPX, etc. The Link-Layer Protocols box represents Ethernet, Token Ring, FDDI, PPP, X.25, Frame Relay, ATM, etc..., as well as internet layer "tunnels" such as IPv4 tunnels.

The IPv6 tunnel protocol engine acts as both an "upper-layer" and a "link-layer", each with a specific input and output as follows:

(u.i) "tunnel upper-layer input" - consists of tunnel IPv6 packets that are going to be decapsulated. The tunnel packets are incoming through the IPv6 layer from:

(u.i.1) a link-layer - (path #1, Fig.5)

These are tunnel packets destined to this node and will undergo decapsulation.

(u.i.2) a tunnel link-layer - (path #7, Fig.5)

These are tunnel packets that underwent one or more decapsulations on this node, that is, the packets had one or more nested tunnel headers and one nested tunnel header was just discarded. This node is the exit-point of both an outer tunnel and one or more of its inner tunnels.

For both above cases the resulting original packets are passed back to the IPv6 layer as "tunnel link-layer" output for further processing (see b.2).

```
+-----------------------+   +-----------------------------------+
| Upper-Layer Protocols |   | IPv6 Tunnel Upper-Layer           |
|                       |   |                                   |
|                       |   | ---<-------------------<-------   |
|                       |   | | ---->---|------>---------   |   |
|                       |   | | |       | |             |   |   |
+-----------------------+   +-----------------------+   |   |   |
   | |             | |        | |       | |         |   v   ^   |
   v ^             v ^        v ^       v ^  Tunnel |   |   |   |
   | |             | |        | |       | |  Packets|   |   |   |
+---------------------------------------------+     |   |   |   |
|  | |             | |       / /        | |   |     |   D   E   |
|  v ^    IPv6     | --<-3--/-/--<----  | |   |     |   E   N   |
|  | |    Layer    ---->-4-/-/--->-- |  | |   |     |   C   C   |
|  v ^                    / /      | |  | |   |     |   A   A   |
|  | |                   2 1       | |  | |   |     |   P   P   |
|  v ^     -----<---5---/-/-<----  v ^  v ^   |     |   S   S   |
|  | |     | -->---6---/-/-->-- |  | |  | |   |     |   U   U   |
|  v ^     | |        / /     6 5  4 3  8 7   |     |   L   L   |
|  | |     | |       / /      | |  | |  | |   |     |   A   A   |
|  v ^     v ^      / /       v ^  | |  | |   |     |   T   T   |
+---------------------------------------------+     |   E   E   |
   | |     | |     | |        | |  | |  | |         |   |   |   |
   v ^     v ^     v ^        v ^  v ^  v ^ Original|   |   |   |
   | |     | |     | |        | |  | |  | | Packets |   v   ^   |
+-----------------------+   +-----------------------+   |   |   |
|                       |   | | |  | |  | |             |   |   |
|                       |   | | ---|----|-------<--------   |   |
|                       |   | --->--------------->------>----   |
|                       |   |                                   |
| Link-Layer Protocols  |   | IPv6 Tunnel Link-Layer            |
+-----------------------+   +-----------------------------------+
```

Fig.5 Packet Flow in the IPv6 Tunneling Protocol Engine on a Node

(u.o) "tunnel upper-layer output" - consists of tunnel IPv6 packets that are passed through the IPv6 layer down to:

(u.o.1) a link-layer - (path #2, Fig.5)
These packets underwent encapsulation and are sent towards the tunnel exit-point

(u.o.2) a tunnel link-layer - (path #8, Fig.5)
These tunnel packets undergo nested encapsulation. This node is the entry-point node of both an outer tunnel and one or more of its inner tunnel.

Implementation Note:

The tunnel upper-layer input and output can be implemented similar to the input and output of the other upper-layer protocols. The tunnel link-layer input and output are as follows:

(l.i) "tunnel link-layer input" - consists of original IPv6 packets that are going to be encapsulated.

The original packets are incoming through the IPv6 layer from:

(l.i.1) an upper-layer - (path #4, Fig.5)

These are original packets originating on this node that undergo encapsulation. The original packet source and tunnel entry-point are the same node.

(l.i.2) a link-layer - (path #6, Fig.5)

These are original packets incoming from a different node that undergo encapsulation on this tunnel entry-point node.

(l.i.3) a tunnel upper-layer - (path #8, Fig.5)

These packets are tunnel packets that undergo nested encapsulation. This node is the entry-point node of both an outer tunnel and one or more of its inner tunnels.

The resulting tunnel packets are passed as tunnel upper-layer output packets through the IPv6 layer (see u.o) down to:

(l.o) "tunnel link-layer output" - consists of original IPv6 packets resulting from decapsulation. These packets are passed through the IPv6 layer to:

(l.o.1) an upper-layer - (path #3, Fig.5)

These original packets are destined to this node.

(l.o.2) a link-layer - (path #5, Fig.5)

These original packets are destined to another node; they are transmitted on a link towards their destination.

(1.o.3) a tunnel upper-layer - (path #7, Fig.5)

These packets undergo another decapsulation; they were nested tunnel packets. This node is both the exit-point node of an outer tunnel and one or more inner tunnels.

Implementation Note:

The tunnel link-layer input and output can be implemented similar to the input and output of other link-layer protocols, for instance, associating an interface or pseudo-interface with the IPv6 tunnel.

The selection of the "IPv6 tunnel link" over other links results from the packet forwarding decision taken based on the content of the node's routing table.

4. Nested Encapsulation

Nested IPv6 encapsulation is the encapsulation of a tunnel packet. It takes place when a hop of an IPv6 tunnel is a tunnel. The tunnel containing a tunnel is called an outer tunnel. The tunnel contained in the outer tunnel is called an inner tunnel - see Fig.6. Inner tunnels and their outer tunnels are nested tunnels.

The entry-point node of an "inner IPv6 tunnel" receives tunnel IPv6 packets encapsulated by the "outer IPv6 tunnel" entry-point node. The "inner tunnel entry-point node" treats the receiving tunnel packets as original packets and performs encapsulation. The resulting packets are "tunnel packets" for the "inner IPv6 tunnel", and "nested tunnel packets" for the "outer IPv6 tunnel".

```
                    Outer Tunnel
                    <------------------------------------->
                    <--links--><-virtual link-><--links--->
                                 Inner Tunnel

                Outer Tunnel                        Outer Tunnel
                Entry-Point                         Exit-Point
                Node                                Node
    +-+         +-+         +-+            +-+         +-+         +-+
    | |         | |         | |            | |         | |         | |
    | |->-//->-| |=>=//=>=| |**>**//**>**| |=>=//=>==| |->-//->-| |
    | |         | |         | |            | |         | |         | |
    +-+         +-+         +-+            +-+         +-+         +-+
 Original                Inner Tunnel   Inner Tunnel          Original
 Packet                  Entry-Point    Exit-Point            Packet
 Source                  Node           Node                  Destination
 Node                                                         Node
```

Fig.6. Nested Encapsulation

4.1 Limiting Nested Encapsulation

A tunnel IPv6 packet is limited to the maximum IPv6 packet size [IPv6-Spec]. Each encapsulation adds to the size of an encapsulated packet the size of the tunnel IPv6 headers. Consequently, the number of tunnel headers, and therefore, the number of nested encapsulations is limited by the maximum packet size. However this limit is so large (more than 1600 encapsulations for an original packet of minimum size) that it is not an effective limit in most cases.

The increase in the size of a tunnel IPv6 packet due to nested encapsulations may require fragmentation [IPv6-Spec] at a tunnel entry point - see section 7. Furthermore, each fragmentation, due to nested encapsulation, of an already fragmented tunnel packet results in a doubling of the number of fragments. Moreover, it is probable that once this fragmentation begins, each new nested encapsulation results in yet additional fragmentation. Therefore limiting nested encapsulation is recommended.

The proposed mechanism for limiting excessive nested encapsulation is a "Tunnel Encapsulation Limit" option, which is carried in an IPv6 Destination Options extension header accompanying an encapsulating IPv6 header.

4.1.1 Tunnel Encapsulation Limit Option

A tunnel entry-point node may be configured to include a Tunnel Encapsulation Limit option as part of the information prepended to all packets entering a tunnel at that node. The Tunnel Encapsulaton Limit option is carried in a Destination Options extension header [IPv6-Spec] placed between the encapsulating IPv6 header and the IPv6 header of the original packet. (Other IPv6 extension headers may also be present preceding or following the Destination Options extension header, depending on configuration information at the tunnel entry-point node.)

The Tunnel Encapsulation Limit option specifies how many additional levels of encapsulation are permitted to be prepended to the packet – or, in other words, how many further levels of nesting the packet is permitted to undergo – not counting the encapsulation in which the option itself is contained. For example, a Tunnel Encapsulation Limit option containing a limit value of zero means that a packet carrying that option may not enter another tunnel before exiting the current tunnel.

The Tunnel Encapsulation Limit option has the following format:

```
   Option Type     Opt Data Len   Opt Data Len
 0 1 2 3 4 5 6 7
+-+-+-+-+-+-+-+-+-+-+-+-+-+-+-+-+-+-+-+-+-+-+-+-+
|0 0 0 0 0 1 0 0|       1       | Tun Encap Lim |
+-+-+-+-+-+-+-+-+-+-+-+-+-+-+-+-+-+-+-+-+-+-+-+-+
```

Option Type decimal value 4

- the highest-order two bits - set to 00 - indicate "skip over this option if the option is not recognized".

- the third-highest-order bit - set to 0 - indicates that the option data in this option does not change en route to the packet's destination [IPv6-Spec].

Opt Data Len value 1 - the data portion of the Option is one octet long.

Opt Data Value the Tunnel Encapsulation Limit value - 8-bit unsigned integer specifying how many further levels of encapsulation are permitted for the

Tunnel Encapsulation Limit options are of interest only to tunnel entry points. A tunnel entry-point node is required to execute the following procedure for every packet entering a tunnel at that node:

(a) Examine the packet to see if a Tunnel Encapsulation Limit option is present following its IPv6 header. The headers following the IPv6 header must be examined in strict "left-to-right" order, with the examination stopping as soon as any one of the following headers is encountered: (i) a Destination Options extension header containing a Tunnel Encapsulation Limit, (ii) another IPv6 header, (iii) a non-extension header, such as TCP, UDP, or ICMP, or (iv) a header that cannot be parsed because it is encrypted or its type is unknown. (Note that this requirment is an exception to the general IPv6 rule that a Destination Options extension header need only be examined by a packet's destination node. An alternative and "cleaner" approach would have been to use a Hop-by-Hop extension header for this purpose, but that would have imposed an undesirable extra processing burden, and possible consequent extra delay, at every IPv6 node along the path of a tunnel.)

(b) If a Tunnel Encapsulation Limit option is found in the packet entering the tunnel and its limit value is zero, the packet is discarded and an ICMP Parameter Problem message [ICMP-Spec] is sent to the source of the packet, which is the previous tunnel entry-point node. The Code field of the Parameter Problem message is set to zero ("erroneous header field encountered") and the Pointer field is set to point to the third octet of the Tunnel Encapsulation Limit option (i.e., the octet containing the limit value of zero).

(c) If a Tunnel Encapsulation Limit option is found in the packet entering the tunnel and its limit value is non-zero, an additional Tunnel Encapsulation Limit option must be included as part of the encapsulating headers being added at this entry point. The limit value in the encapsulating option is set to one less than the limit value found in the packet being encapsulated.

(d) If a Tunnel Encapsulation Limit option is not found in the packet entering the tunnel and if an encapsulation limit has been configured for this tunnel, a Tunnel Encapsulation Limit option must be included as part of the encapsulating headers being added at this entry point. The limit value in the option is set to the configured limit.

(e) If a Tunnel Encapsulation Limit option is not found in the packet entering the tunnel and if no encapsulation limit has been configured for this tunnel, then no Tunnel Encapsulation Limit option is included as part of the encapsulating headers being added at this entry point.

A Tunnel Encapsulation Limit option added at a tunnel entry-point node is removed as part of the decapsulation process at that tunnel's exit-point node.

Two cases of encapsulation that should be avoided are described below:

4.1.2 Loopback Encapsulation

A particular case of encapsulation which must be avoided is the loopback encapsulation. Loopback encapsulation takes place when a tunnel IPv6 entry-point node encapsulates tunnel IPv6 packets originated from itself, and destined to itself. This can generate an infinite processing loop in the entry-point node.

To avoid such a case, it is recommended that an implementation have a mechanism that checks and rejects the configuration of a tunnel in which both the entry-point and exit-point node addresses belong to the same node. It is also recommended that the encapsulating engine check for and reject the encapsulation of a packet that has the pair of tunnel entry-point and exit-point addresses identical with the pair of original packet source and final destination addresses.

4.1.3 Routing-Loop Nested Encapsulation

In the case of a forwarding path with multiple-level nested tunnels, a routing-loop from an inner tunnel to an outer tunnel is particularly dangerous when packets from the inner tunnels reenter an outer tunnel from which they have not yet exited. In such a case, the nested encapsulation becomes a recursive encapsulation with the negative effects described in 4.1. Because each nested encapsulation adds a tunnel header with a new hop limit value, the IPv6 hop limit mechanism cannot control the number of times the packet reaches the outer tunnel entry-point node, and thus cannot control the number of recursive encapsulations.

When the path of a packet from source to final destination includes tunnels, the maximum number of hops that the packet can traverse should be controlled by two mechanisms used together to avoid the negative effects of recursive encapsulation in routing loops:

(a) the original packet hop limit.
It is decremented at each forwarding operation performed on an original packet. This includes each encapsulation of the original packet. It does not include nested encapsulations of the original packet

(b) the tunnel IPv6 packet encapsulation limit.

It is decremented at each nested encapsulation of the packet.

For a discussion of the excessive encapsulation risk factors in nested encapsulation see Appendix A.

5. Tunnel IPv6 Header

The tunnel entry-point node fills out a tunnel IPv6 main header [IPv6-Spec] as follows:

Version:

value 6

Traffic Class:

Depending on the entry-point node tunnel configuration, the traffic class can be set to that of either the original packet or a pre-configured value - see section 6.4.

Flow Label:

Depending on the entry-point node tunnel configuration, the flow label can be set to a pre-configured value. The typical value is zero - see section 6.5.

Payload Length:

The original packet length, plus the length of the encapsulating (prepended) IPv6 extension headers, if any.

Next Header:

The next header value according to [IPv6-Spec] from the Assigned Numbers RFC [RFC-1700 or its successors].

For example, if the original packet is an IPv6 packet, this is set to:

- decimal value 41 (Assigned Next Header number for IPv6) - if there are no tunnel extension headers.

- value 0 (Assigned Next Header number for IPv6 Hop by Hop Options extension header) - if a hop by hop options extension header immediately follows the tunnel IPv6 header.

- decimal value 60 (Assigned Next Header number for IPv6 Destination Options extension header) - if a destination options extension header immediately follows the tunnel IPv6 header.

Hop Limit:

The tunnel IPv6 header hop limit is set to a pre-configured value - see section 6.3.

The default value for hosts is the Neighbor Discovery advertised hop limit [ND-Spec]. The default value for routers is the default IPv6 Hop Limit value from the Assigned Numbers RFC (64 at the time of writing this document).

Source Address:

An IPv6 address of the outgoing interface of the tunnel entry-point node. This address is configured as the tunnel entry-point node address - see section 6.1.

Destination Address:

An IPv6 address of the tunnel exit-point node. This address is configured as the tunnel exit-point node address - see section 6.2.

5.1 Tunnel IPv6 Extension Headers

Depending on IPv6 node configuration parameters, a tunnel entry-point node may append to the tunnel IPv6 main header one or more IPv6 extension headers, such as a Hop-by-Hop Options header, a Routing header, or others.

To limit the number of nested encapsulations of a packet, if it was configured to do so - see section 6.6 - a tunnel entry-point includes a Destination Options extension header containing a Tunnel Encapsulation Limit option. If that option is the only option present in the Destination Options header, the header has the following format:

```
+-+-+-+-+-+-+-+-+-+-+-+-+-+-+-+-+-+-+-+-+-+-+-+-+-+-+-+-+-+-+-+-+
|  Next Header   |Hdr Ext Len = 0| Opt Type = 4  |Opt Data Len=1 |
+-+-+-+-+-+-+-+-+-+-+-+-+-+-+-+-+-+-+-+-+-+-+-+-+-+-+-+-+-+-+-+-+
| Tun Encap Lim  |PadN Opt Type=1|Opt Data Len=1 |       0       |
+-+-+-+-+-+-+-+-+-+-+-+-+-+-+-+-+-+-+-+-+-+-+-+-+-+-+-+-+-+-+-+-+
```

Next Header:

Identifies the type of the original packet header. For example, if the original packet is an IPv6 packet, the next header protocol value is set to decimal value 41 (Assigned payload type number for IPv6).

Hdr Ext Len:

Length of the Destination Options extension header in 8-octet units, not including the first 8 octets. Set to value 0, if no other options are present in this destination options header.

Option Type:

value 4 - see section 4.1.1.

Opt Data Len:

value 1 - see section 4.1.1.

Tun Encap Lim:

8 bit unsigned integer - see section 4.1.1.

Option Type:

value 1 - PadN option, to align the header following this header.

Opt Data Len:

value 1 - one octet of option data.

Option Data:

value 0 - one zero-valued octet.

6. IPv6 Tunnel State Variables

The IPv6 tunnel state variables, some of which are or may be configured on the tunnel entry-point node, are:

6.1 IPv6 Tunnel Entry-Point Node Address

The tunnel entry-point node address is one of the valid IPv6 unicast addresses of the entry-point node - the validation of the address at tunnel configuration time is recommended.

The tunnel entry-point node address is copied to the source address field in the tunnel IPv6 header during packet encapsulation.

6.2 IPv6 Tunnel Exit-Point Node Address

The tunnel exit-point node address is used as IPv6 destination address for the tunnel IPv6 header. A tunnel acts like a virtual point to point link between the entry-point node and exit-point node.

The tunnel exit-point node address is copied to the destination address field in the tunnel IPv6 header during packet encapsulation.

The configuration of the tunnel entry-point and exit-point addresses is not subject to IPv6 Autoconfiguration or IPv6 Neighbor Discovery.

6.3 IPv6 Tunnel Hop Limit

An IPv6 tunnel is modeled as a "single-hop virtual link" tunnel, in which the passing of the original packet through the tunnel is like the passing of the original packet over a one hop link, regardless of the number of hops in the IPv6 tunnel.

The "single-hop" mechanism should be implemented by having the tunnel entry point node set a tunnel IPv6 header hop limit independently of the hop limit of the original header.

The "single-hop" mechanism hides from the original IPv6 packets the number of IPv6 hops of the tunnel.

It is recommended that the tunnel hop limit be configured with a value that ensures:

(a) that tunnel IPv6 packets can reach the tunnel exit-point node

(b) a quick expiration of the tunnel packet if a routing loop occurs within the IPv6 tunnel.

The tunnel hop limit default value for hosts is the IPv6 Neighbor Discovery advertised hop limit [ND-Spec]. The tunnel hop limit default value for routers is the default IPv6 Hop Limit value from the Assigned Numbers RFC (64 at the time of writing this document).

The tunnel hop limit is copied into the hop limit field of the tunnel IPv6 header of each packet encapsulated by the tunnel entry-point node.

6.4 IPv6 Tunnel Packet Traffic Class

The IPv6 Tunnel Packet Traffic Class indicates the value that a tunnel entry-point node sets in the Traffic Class field of a tunnel header. The default value is zero. The configured Packet Traffic Class can also indicate whether the value of the Traffic Class field in the tunnel header is copied from the original header, or it is set to the pre-configured value.

6.5 IPv6 Tunnel Flow Label

The IPv6 Tunnel Flow Label indicates the value that a tunnel entry-point node sets in the flow label of a tunnel header. The default value is zero.

6.6 IPv6 Tunnel Encapsulation Limit

The Tunnel Encapsulation Limit value can indicate whether the entry-point node is configured to limit the number of encapsulations of tunnel packets originating on that node. The IPv6 Tunnel Encapsulation Limit is the maximum number of additional encapsulations permitted for packets undergoing encapsulation at that entry-point node. Recommended default value is 4. An entry-point node configured to limit the number of nested encapsulations prepends a Destination Options extension header containing a Tunnel Encapsulation Limit option to an original packet undergoing encapsulation - see sections 4.1 and 4.1.1.

6.7 IPv6 Tunnel MTU

The tunnel MTU is set dynamically to the Path MTU between the tunnel entry-point and the tunnel exit-point nodes, minus the size of the tunnel headers: the maximum size of a tunnel packet payload that can be sent through the tunnel without fragmentation [IPv6-Spec]. The tunnel entry-point node performs Path MTU discovery on the path between the tunnel entry-point and exit-point nodes [PMTU-Spec], [ICMP-Spec]. The tunnel MTU of a nested tunnel is the tunnel MTU of the outer tunnel minus the size of the nested tunnel headers.

7. IPv6 Tunnel Packet Size Issues

Prepending a tunnel header increases the size of a packet, therefore a tunnel packet resulting from the encapsulation of an IPv6 original packet may require fragmentation.

A tunnel IPv6 packet resulting from the encapsulation of an original packet is considered an IPv6 packet originating from the tunnel entry-point node. Therefore, like any source of an IPv6 packet, a tunnel entry-point node must support fragmentation of tunnel IPv6 packets.

A tunnel intermediate node that forwards a tunnel packet to another node in the tunnel follows the general IPv6 rule that it must not fragment a packet undergoing forwarding.

A tunnel exit-point node receiving tunnel packets at the end of the tunnel for decapsulation applies the strict left-to-right processing rules for extension headers. In the case of a fragmented tunnel packet, the fragments are reassembled into a complete tunnel packet before determining that an embedded packet is present.

Note:

A particular problem arises when the destination of a fragmented tunnel packet is an exit-point node identified by an anycast address. The problem, which is similar to that of original fragmented IPv6 packets destined to nodes identified by an anycast address, is that all the fragments of a packet must arrive at the same destination node for that node to be able to perform a successful reassembly, a requirement that is not necessarily satisfied by packets sent to an anycast address.

7.1 IPv6 Tunnel Packet Fragmentation

When an IPv6 original packet enters a tunnel, if the original packet size exceeds the tunnel MTU (i.e., the Path MTU between the tunnel entry-point and the tunnel exit-point, minus the size of the tunnel header(s)), it is handled as follows:

(a) if the original IPv6 packet size is larger than the IPv6 minimum link MTU [IPv6-Spec], the entry-point node discards the packet and sends an ICMPv6 "Packet Too Big" message to the source address of the original packet with the recommended MTU size field set to the tunnel MTU or the IPv6 minimum link MTU, whichever is larger, i.e. max (tunnel MTU, IPv6 minimum link MTU). Also see sections 6.7 and 8.2.

(b) if the original IPv6 packet is equal or smaller than the IPv6 minimum link MTU, the tunnel entry-point node encapsulates the original packet, and subsequently fragments the resulting IPv6 tunnel packet into IPv6 fragments that do not exceed the Path MTU to the tunnel exit-point.

7.2 IPv4 Tunnel Packet Fragmentation

When an IPv4 original packet enters a tunnel, if the original packet size exceeds the tunnel MTU (i.e., the Path MTU between the tunnel entry-point and the tunnel exit-point, minus the size of the tunnel header(s)), it is handled as follows:

(a) if in the original IPv4 packet header the Don't Fragment - DF - bit flag is SET, the entry-point node discards the packet and returns an ICMP message. The ICMP message has the type = "unreachable", the code = "packet too big", and the recommended MTU size field set to the size of the tunnel MTU - see sections 6.7 and 8.3.

(b) if in the original packet header the Don't Fragment - DF - bit flag is CLEAR, the tunnel entry-point node encapsulates the original packet, and subsequently fragments the resulting IPv6 tunnel packet into IPv6 fragments that do not exceed the Path MTU to the tunnel exit-point.

8. IPv6 Tunnel Error Processing and Reporting

IPv6 Tunneling follows the general rule that an error detected during the processing of an IPv6 packet is reported through an ICMP message to the source of the packet.

On a forwarding path that includes IPv6 tunnels, an error detected by a node that is not in any tunnel is directly reported to the source of the original IPv6 packet.

An error detected by a node inside a tunnel is reported to the source of the tunnel packet, that is, the tunnel entry-point node. The ICMP message sent to the tunnel entry-point node has as ICMP payload the tunnel IPv6 packet that has the original packet as its payload.

The cause of a packet error encountered inside a tunnel can be a problem with:

(a) the tunnel header, or

(b) the tunnel packet.

Both tunnel header and tunnel packet problems are reported to the tunnel entry-point node.

If a tunnel packet problem is a consequence of a problem with the original packet, which is the payload of the tunnel packet, then the problem is also reported to the source of the original packet.

To report a problem detected inside the tunnel to the source of an original packet, the tunnel entry point node must relay the ICMP message received from inside the tunnel to the source of that original IPv6 packet.

An example of the processing that can take place in the error reporting mechanism of a node is illustrated in Fig.7, and Fig.8:

Fig.7 path #0 and Fig.8 (a) - The IPv6 tunnel entry-point receives an ICMP packet from inside the tunnel, marked Tunnel ICMPv6 Message in Fig.7. The tunnel entry-point node IPv6 layer passes the received ICMP message to the ICMPv6 Input. The ICMPv6 Input, based on the ICMP type and code [ICMP-Spec] generates an internal "error code".

Fig.7 path #1 - The internal error code, is passed with the "ICMPv6 message payload" to the upper-layer protocol - in this case the IPv6 tunnel upper-layer error input.

```
 +-------+   +-------+   +-----------------------+
 | Upper |   | Upper |   | Upper                 |
 | Layer |   | Layer |   | Layer                 |
 | Proto.|   | Proto |   | IPv6 Tunnel           |
 | Error |   | Error |   | Error                 |
 | Input |   | Input |   | Input                 |
 |       |   |       |   |       Decapsulate     |
 |       |   |       |   |  -->--ICMPv6--#2->--  |
 |       |   |       |   |  |    Payload      |  |
 +-------+   +-------+   +--|-----------------|--+
     |           |          |                 |
     ^           ^          ^                 v
     |           |          |                 |
     --------------------#1--    ------Orig.Packet?-- - - - - - - -
           #1            #3  Int.Error Code, #5              |
Int.Error Code,^          v  Source Address, v               v
ICMPv6 Payload |     IPv6 |  Orig. Packet    | IPv4          |
      +-------------+   +-----------+   +-----------+    + - - +
      |             |   |           |   |           |
      | ICMP v6     |   | ICMP v6   |   | ICMP v4   |    |     |
      | Input       |   | Err Report|   | Err Report|
      |  - - - -  +----+  - - - -  |   +  - - - -  +    + - - +
      |                             |   |           |
      |          IPv6 Layer         |   | IPv4 Layer|    |     |
      |                             |   |           |
      +-----------------------------+   +-----------+    + - - +
             |                |                |
             ^                V                V
             #0               #4               #6
             |                |                |
        Tunnel ICMPv6       ICMPv6           ICMPv4
          Message           Message          Message
             |                |                |
```

Fig.7 Error Reporting Flow in a Node (IPv6 Tunneling Protocol Engine)

Fig.7 path #2 and Fig.8 (b) - The IPv6 tunnel error input decapsulates the tunnel IPv6 packet, which is the ICMPv6 message payload, obtaining the original packet, and thus the original headers and dispatches the "internal error code", the source address from the original packet header, and the original packet, down to the error report block of the protocol identified by the Next Header field in the tunnel header immediately preceding the original packet in the ICMP message payload.

From here the processing depends on the protocol of the original packet:

(a) - for an IPv6 original packet

Fig.7 path #3 and Fig.8 (c.1)- for an IPv6 original packet, the ICMPv6 error report builds an ICMP message of a type and code according to the "internal error code", containing the "original packet" as ICMP payload.

Fig.7 path #4 and Fig.8 (d.1)- The ICMP message has the tunnel entry-point node address as source address, and the original packet source node address as destination address. The tunnel entry-point node sends the ICMP message to the source node of the original packet.

(b) - for an IPv4 original packet

Fig.7 path #5 and Fig.8 (c.2) - for an IPv4 original packet, the ICMPv4 error report builds an ICMP message of a type and code derived from the the "internal error code", containing the "original packet" as ICMP payload.

Fig.7 path #6 and Fig.8 (d.2) - The ICMP message has the tunnel entry-point node IPv4 address as source address, and the original packet IPv4 source node address as destination address. The tunnel entry-point node sends the ICMP message to the source node of the original packet.

A graphical description of the header processing taking place is the following:

```
    <                     Tunnel Packet                                >
   +--------+- - - - - -+--------+------------------------------//------+
   | IPv6   | IPv6      | ICMP   |             Tunnel                   |
(a)|        | Extension |        |             IPv6                     |
   | Header | Headers   | Header |             Packet in error          |
   +--------+- - - - - -+--------+------------------------------//------+
    < Tunnel Headers   > <       Tunnel ICMP Message                   >
                                  <         ICMPv6 Message Payload     >
                                 |
                                 v
        <                    Tunnel ICMP Message                   >
                        <       Tunnel IPv6 Packet in Error        >
       +--------+      +---------+      +----------+--------//------+
       | ICMP   |      | Tunnel  |      | Original | Original       |
(b)    |        |  +   | IPv6    |  +   |          | Packet         |
       | Header |      | Headers |      | Headers  | Payload        |
       +--------+      +---------+      +----------+--------//------+
           |                             <Original Packet in Error >
           -----------------              |
                           |              |
             --------------|---------------
             |             |
             V             V
       +---------+      +--------+      +-------------------//------+
       | New     |      | ICMP   |      |                           |
(c.1)  | IPv6    |  +   |        |  +   | Orig. Packet in Error     |
       | Headers |      | Header |      |                           |
       +---------+      +--------+      +-------------------//------+
                             |
                             v
                 +---------+--------+-------------------//------+
                 | New     | ICMP   |  Original                 |
(d.1)            | IPv6    |        |                           |
                 | Headers | Header |  Packet in Error          |
                 +---------+--------+-------------------//------+
                  <             New ICMP Message               >
```

```
                or for an IPv4 original packet

         +---------+      +--------+      +------------------//------+
         | New     |      | ICMP   |      |                          |
(c.2)    | IPv4    |  +   |        |  +   | Orig. Packet in Error    |
         | Header  |      | Header |      |                          |
         +---------+      +--------+      +------------------//------+
                              |
                              v
                 +---------+--------+------------------//------+
                 | New     | ICMP   |  Original                |
(d.2)            | IPv4    |        |                          |
                 | Header  | Header |  Packet in Error         |
                 +---------+--------+------------------//------+
                  <             New ICMP Message              >

               Fig.8 ICMP Error Reporting and Processing
```

8.1 Tunnel ICMP Messages

The tunnel ICMP messages that are reported to the source of the original packet are:

hop limit exceeded

The tunnel has a misconfigured hop limit, or contains a routing loop, and packets do not reach the tunnel exit-point node. This problem is reported to the tunnel entry-point node, where the tunnel hop limit can be reconfigured to a higher value. The problem is further reported to the source of the original packet as described in section 8.2, or 8.3.

unreachable node

One of the nodes in the tunnel is not or is no longer reachable. This problem is reported to the tunnel entry-point node, which should be reconfigured with a valid and active path between the entry and exit-point of the tunnel.

The problem is further reported to the source of the original packet as described in section 8.2, or 8.3.

parameter problem

A Parameter Problem ICMP message pointing to a valid Tunnel Encapsulation Limit Destination header with a Tun Encap Lim field value set to one is an indication that the tunnel packet exceeded the maximum number of encapsulations allowed. The problem is further reported to the source of the original packet as described in section 8.2, or 8.3.

The above three problems detected inside the tunnel, which are a tunnel configuration and a tunnel topology problem, are reported to the source of the original IPv6 packet, as a tunnel generic "unreachable" problem caused by a "link problem" - see section 8.2 and 8.3.

packet too big

The tunnel packet exceeds the tunnel Path MTU.

The information carried by this type of ICMP message is used as follows:

- by a receiving tunnel entry-point node to set or adjust the tunnel MTU

- by a sending tunnel entry-point node to indicate to the source of an original packet the MTU size that should be used in sending IPv6 packets towards the tunnel entry-point node.

8.2 ICMP Messages for IPv6 Original Packets

The tunnel entry-point node builds the ICMP and IPv6 headers of the ICMP message that is sent to the source of the original packet as follows:

IPv6 Fields:

Source Address

A valid unicast IPv6 address of the outgoing interface.

Destination Address

Copied from the Source Address field of the Original IPv6 header.

ICMP Fields:

For any of the following tunnel ICMP error messages:

"hop limit exceeded"

"unreachable node"

"parameter problem" - pointing to a valid Tunnel Encapsulation Limit destination header with the Tun Encap Lim field set to a value zero:

Type 1 - unreachable node

Code 3 - address unreachable

For tunnel ICMP error message "packet too big":

Type 2 - packet too big

Code 0

MTU The MTU field from the tunnel ICMP message minus the length of the tunnel headers.

According to the general rules described in 7.1, an ICMP "packet too big" message is sent to the source of the original packet only if the original packet size is larger than the minimum link MTU size required for IPv6 [IPv6-Spec].

8.3 ICMP Messages for IPv4 Original Packets

The tunnel entry-point node builds the ICMP and IPv4 header of the ICMP message that is sent to the source of the original packet as follows:

IPv4 Fields:

Source Address

A valid unicast IPv4 address of the outgoing interface.

Destination Address

Copied from the Source Address field of the Original IPv4 header.

ICMP Fields:

For any of the following tunnel ICMP error messages:

"hop limit exceeded"

"unreachable node"

"parameter problem" - pointing to a valid Tunnel Enacpsulation Limit destination header with the Tun Encap Lim field set to a value zero:

Type 3 - destination unreachable

Code 1 - host unreachable

For a tunnel ICMP error message "packet too big":

Type 3 - destination unreachable

Code 4 - packet too big

MTU The MTU field from the tunnel ICMP message minus the length of the tunnel headers.

According to the general rules described in section 7.2, an ICMP "packet too big" message is sent to the original IPv4 packet source node if the the original IPv4 header has the DF - don't fragment - bit flag SET.

8.4 ICMP Messages for Nested Tunnel Packets

In case of an error uncovered with a nested tunnel packet, the inner tunnel entry-point, which receives the ICMP error message from the inner tunnel reporting node, relays the ICMP message to the outer tunnel entry-point following the mechanisms described in sections 8.,8.1, 8.2, and 8.3. Further, the outer tunnel entry-point relays the ICMP message to the source of the original packet, following the same mechanisms.

9. Security Considerations

An IPv6 tunnel can be secured by securing the IPv6 path between the tunnel entry-point and exit-point node. The security architecture, mechanisms, and services are described in [RFC2401], [RFC2402], and [RFC2406]. A secure IPv6 tunnel may act as a gateway-to-gateway secure path as described in [RFC2401].

For a secure IPv6 tunnel, in addition to the mechanisms described earlier in this document, the entry-point node of the tunnel performs security algorithms on the packet and prepends as part of the tunnel headers one or more security headers in conformance with [IPv6-Spec], [RFC2401], and [RFC2402], or [RFC2406].

The exit-point node of a secure IPv6 tunnel performs security algorithms and processes the tunnel security header[s] as part of the tunnel headers processing described earlier, and in conformance with [RFC2401], and [RFC2402], or [RFC2406]. The exit-point node discards the tunnel security header[s] with the rest of the tunnel headers after tunnel headers processing completion.

The degree of integrity, authentication, and confidentiality and the security processing performed on a tunnel packet at the entry-point and exit-point node of a secure IPv6 tunnel depend on the type of security header - authentication (AH) or encryption (ESP) - and parameters configured in the Security Association for the tunnel. There is no dependency or interaction between the security level and mechanisms applied to the tunnel packets and the security applied to the original packets which are the payloads of the tunnel packets. In case of nested tunnels, each inner tunnel may have its own set of security services, independently from those of the outer tunnels, or of those between the source and destination of the original packet.

10. Acknowledgments

This document is partially derived from several discussions about IPv6 tunneling on the IPng Working Group Mailing List and from feedback from the IPng Working Group to an IPv6 presentation that focused on IPv6 tunneling at the 33rd IETF, in Stockholm, in July 1995.

Additionally, the following documents that focused on tunneling or encapsulation were helpful references: RFC 1933 (R. Gilligan, E. Nordmark), RFC 1241 (R. Woodburn, D. Mills), RFC 1326 (P. Tsuchiya), RFC 1701, RFC 1702 (S. Hanks, D. Farinacci, P. Traina), RFC 1853 (W. Simpson), as well as RFC 2003 (C. Perkins).

Brian Carpenter, Richard Draves, Bob Hinden, Thomas Narten, Erik Nordmark (in alphabetical order) gave valuable reviewing comments and suggestions for the improvement of this document. Scott Bradner, Ross Callon, Dimitry Haskin, Paul Traina, and James Watt (in alphabetical order) shared their view or experience on matters of concern in this document. Judith Grossman provided a sample of her many years of editorial and writing experience as well as a good amount of probing technical questions.

11. References

[IPv6-Spec] Deering, S. and R. Hinden, "Internet Protocol Version 6 (IPv6) Specification", RFC 2460, December 1998.

[ICMP-Spec] Conta, A. and S. Deering "Internet Control Message Protocol for the Internet Protocol Version 6 (IPv6)", RFC 2463, December 1998.

[ND-Spec] Narten, T., Nordmark, E., and W. Simpson "Neighbor Discovery for IP Version 6 (IPv6)", RFC 2461, December 1998.

[PMTU-Spec] McCann, J., Deering, S. and J. Mogul, "Path MTU Discovery for IP Version 6 (IPv6)", RFC 1981, August 1996.

[RFC2401] Atkinson, R., "Security Architecture for the Internet Protocol", RFC 2401, November 1998.

[RFC2402] Atkinson, R., "IP Authentication Header", RFC 2402, November 1998.

[RFC2406] Atkinson, R., "IP Encapsulation Security Payload (ESP)", RFC 2406, November 1998.

[RFC-1853] Simpson, W., "IP in IP Tunneling", RFC 1853, October 1995.

[Assign-Nr] Reynolds, J. and J. Postel, "Assigned Numbers", STD 2, RFC 1700, October 1994. See also: http://www.iana.org/numbers.html

[RFC2119] Bradner, S., "Key words for use in RFCs to indicate Requirement Levels", BCP 14, RFC 2119, March 1997.

Authors' Addresses

Alex Conta
Lucent Technologies Inc.
300 Baker Ave
Concord, MA 01742-2168
+1-978-287-2842

EMail: aconta@lucent.com

Stephen Deering
Cisco Systems
170 West Tasman Dr
San Jose, CA 95132-1706

Phone: +1-408-527-8213
EMail: deering@cisco.com

Appendix A

A.1

Risk Factors in Nested Encapsulation

Nested encapsulations of a packet become a recursive encapsulation if the packet reenters an outer tunnel before exiting it. The cases which present a high risk of recursive encapsulation are those in which a tunnel entry-point node cannot determine whether a packet that undergoes encapsulation reenters the tunnel before exiting it. Routing loops that cause tunnel packets to reenter a tunnel before exiting it are certainly the major cause of the problem. But since routing loops exist, and happen, it is important to understand and describe, the cases in which the risk for recursive encapsulation is higher.

There are two significant elements that determine the risk factor of routing loop recursive encapsulation:

(a) the type of tunnel,

(b) the type of route to the tunnel exit-point, which determines the packet forwarding through the tunnel, that is, over the tunnel virtual-link.

A.1.1 Risk Factor in Nested Encapsulation - type of tunnel.

The type of tunnels which were identified as a high risk factor for recursive encapsulation in routing loops are:

"inner tunnels with identical exit-points".

Since the source and destination of an original packet is the main information used to decide whether to forward a packet through a tunnel or not, a recursive encapsulation can be avoided in case of a single tunnel (non-inner), by checking that the packet to be encapsulated is not originated on the entry-point node. This mechanism is suggested in [RFC-1853].

However, this type of protection does not seem to work well in case of inner tunnels with different entry-points, and identical exit-points.

Inner tunnels with different entry-points and identical exit-points introduce ambiguity in deciding whether to encapsulate a packet, when a packet encapsulated in an inner tunnel reaches the entry-point node of an outer tunnel by means of a routing loop. Because the source of the tunnel packet is the inner tunnel entry-point node which is different than the entry-point node of the outer tunnel, the source address checking (mentioned above) fails to detect an invalid encapsulation, and as a consequence the tunnel packet gets encapsulated at the outer tunnel each time it reaches it through the routing loop.

A.1.2 Risk Factor in Nested Encapsulation - type of route.

The type of route to a tunnel exit-point node has been also identified as a high risk factor of recursive encapsulation in routing loops.

One type of route to a tunnel exit-point node is a route to a specified destination node, that is, the destination is a valid specified IPv6 address (route to node). Such a route can be selected based on the longest match of an original packet destination address with the destination address stored in the tunnel entry-point node routing table entry for that route. The packet forwarded on such a route is first encapsulated and then forwarded towards the tunnel exit-point node.

Another type of route to a tunnel exit-point node is a route to a specified prefix-net, that is, the destination is a valid specified IPv6 prefix (route to net). Such a route can be selected based on the longest path match of an original packet destination address with the prefix destination stored in the tunnel entry-point node routing table entry for that route. The packet forwarded on such a route is first encapsulated and then forwarded towards the tunnel exit-point node.

And finally another type of route to a tunnel exit-point is a default route, or a route to an unspecified destination. This route is selected when no-other match for the destination of the original packet has been found in the routing table. A tunnel that is the first hop of a default route is a "default tunnel".

If the route to a tunnel exit-point is a route to node, the risk factor for recursive encapsulation is minimum.

If the route to a tunnel exit-point is a route to net, the risk factor for recursive encapsulation is medium. There is a range of destination addresses that will match the prefix the route is associated with. If one or more inner tunnels with different tunnel entry-points have exit-point node addresses that match the route to net of an outer tunnel exit-point, then a recursive encapsulation may occur if a tunnel packet gets diverted from inside such an inner tunnel to the entry-point of the outer tunnel that has a route to its exit-point that matches the exit-point of an inner tunnel.

If the route to a tunnel exit-point is a default route, the risk factor for recursive encapsulation is maximum. Packets are forwarded through a default tunnel for lack of a better route. In many situations, forwarding through a default tunnel can happen for a wide range of destination addresses which at the maximum extent is the entire Internet minus the node's link. As consequence, it is likely that in a routing loop case, if a tunnel packet gets diverted from an inner tunnel to an outer tunnel entry-point in which the tunnel is a default tunnel, the packet will be once more encapsulated, because the default routing mechanism will not be able to discern differently, based on the destination.

Network Working Group
Request for Comments: 2474
Obsoletes: 1455, 1349
Category: Standards Track

K. Nichols
Cisco Systems
S. Blake
Torrent Networking Technologies
F. Baker
Cisco Systems
D. Black
EMC Corporation
December 1998

Definition of the Differentiated Services Field (DS Field) in the IPv4 and IPv6 Headers

Status of this Memo

Copyright Notice

Abstract

Differentiated services enhancements to the Internet protocol are intended to enable scalable service discrimination in the Internet without the need for per-flow state and signaling at every hop. A variety of services may be built from a small, well-defined set of building blocks which are deployed in network nodes. The services may be either end-to-end or intra-domain; they include both those that can satisfy quantitative performance requirements (e.g., peak bandwidth) and those based on relative performance (e.g., "class" differentiation). Services can be constructed by a combination of:

- setting bits in an IP header field at network boundaries (autonomous system boundaries, internal administrative boundaries, or hosts),
- using those bits to determine how packets are forwarded by the nodes inside the network, and
- conditioning the marked packets at network boundaries in accordance with the requirements or rules of each service.

The requirements or rules of each service must be set through administrative policy mechanisms which are outside the scope of this document. A differentiated services-compliant network node includes a classifier that selects packets based on the value of the DS field, along with buffer management and packet scheduling mechanisms capable of delivering the specific packet forwarding treatment indicated by the DS field value. Setting of the DS field and conditioning of the temporal behavior of marked packets need only be performed at network boundaries and may vary in complexity.

This document defines the IP header field, called the DS (for differentiated services) field. In IPv4, it defines the layout of the TOS octet; in IPv6, the Traffic Class octet. In addition, a base set of packet forwarding treatments, or per-hop behaviors, is defined.

For a more complete understanding of differentiated services, see also the differentiated services architecture [ARCH].

Table of Contents

1. Introduction

Differentiated services are intended to provide a framework and building blocks to enable deployment of scalable service discrimination in the Internet. The differentiated services approach aims to speed deployment by separating the architecture into two major components, one of which is fairly well-understood and the other of which is just beginning to be understood. In this, we are guided by the original design of the Internet where the decision was made to separate the forwarding and routing components. Packet forwarding is the relatively simple task that needs to be performed on a per-packet basis as quickly as possible. Forwarding uses the packet header to find an entry in a routing table that determines the packet's output interface. Routing sets the entries in that table and may need to reflect a range of transit and other policies as well as to keep track of route failures. Routing tables are maintained as a background process to the forwarding task. Further, routing is the more complex task and it has continued to evolve over the past 20 years.

Analogously, the differentiated services architecture contains two main components. One is the fairly well-understood behavior in the forwarding path and the other is the more complex and still emerging background policy and allocation component that configures parameters used in the forwarding path. The forwarding path behaviors include the differential treatment an individual packet receives, as implemented by queue service disciplines and/or queue management disciplines. These per-hop behaviors are useful and required in network nodes to deliver differentiated treatment of packets no matter how we construct end-to-end or intra-domain services. Our focus is on the general semantics of the behaviors rather than the specific mechanisms used to implement them since these behaviors will evolve less rapidly than the mechanisms.

Per-hop behaviors and mechanisms to select them on a per-packet basis can be deployed in network nodes today and it is this aspect of the differentiated services architecture that is being addressed first. In addition, the forwarding path may require that some monitoring, policing, and shaping be done on the network traffic designated for "special" treatment in order to enforce requirements associated with the delivery of the special treatment. Mechanisms for this kind of traffic conditioning are also fairly well-understood. The wide deployment of such traffic conditioners is also important to enable the construction of services, though their actual use in constructing services may evolve over time.

The configuration of network elements with respect to which packets get special treatment and what kinds of rules are to be applied to the use of resources is much less well-understood. Nevertheless, it is possible to deploy useful differentiated services in networks by using simple policies and static configurations. As described in [ARCH], there are a number of ways to compose per-hop behaviors and traffic conditioners to create services. In the process, additional experience is gained that will guide more complex policies and allocations. The basic behaviors in the forwarding path can remain the same while this component of the architecture evolves. Experiences with the construction of such services will continue for some time, thus we avoid standardizing this construction as it is premature. Further, much of the details of service construction are covered by legal agreements between different business entities and we avoid this as it is very much outside the scope of the IETF.

This document concentrates on the forwarding path component. In the packet forwarding path, differentiated services are realized by mapping the codepoint contained in a field in the IP packet header to a particular forwarding treatment, or per-hop behavior (PHB), at each network node along its path. The codepoints may be chosen from a set of mandatory values defined later in this document, from a set of recommended values to be defined in future documents, or may have purely local meaning. PHBs are expected to be implemented by employing a range of queue service and/or queue management disciplines on a network node's output interface queue: for example weighted round-robin (WRR) queue servicing or drop-preference queue management.

Marking is performed by traffic conditioners at network boundaries, including the edges of the network (first-hop router or source host) and administrative boundaries. Traffic conditioners may include the primitives of marking, metering, policing and shaping (these mechanisms are described in [ARCH]). Services are realized by the use of particular packet classification and traffic conditioning mechanisms at boundaries coupled with the concatenation of per-hop behaviors along the transit path of the traffic. A goal of the differentiated services architecture is to specify these building blocks for future extensibility, both of the number and type of the building blocks and of the services built from them.

Terminology used in this memo is defined in Sec. 2. The differentiated services field definition (DS field) is given in Sec. 3. In Sec. 4, we discuss the desire for partial backwards compatibility with current use of the IPv4 Precedence field. As a solution, we introduce Class Selector Codepoints and Class Selector

Compliant PHBs. Sec. 5 presents guidelines for per-hop behavior standardization. Sec. 6 discusses guidelines for allocation of codepoints. Sec. 7 covers security considerations.

This document is a concise description of the DS field and its uses. It is intended to be read along with the differentiated services architecture [ARCH].

The key words "MUST", "MUST NOT", "REQUIRED", "SHALL", "SHALL NOT", "SHOULD", "SHOULD NOT", "RECOMMENDED", "MAY", and "OPTIONAL" in this document are to be interpreted as described in [RFC2119].

2. Terminology Used in This Document

Behavior Aggregate: a collection of packets with the same codepoint crossing a link in a particular direction. The terms "aggregate" and "behavior aggregate" are used interchangeably in this document.

Classifier: an entity which selects packets based on the content of packet headers according to defined rules.

Class Selector Codepoint: any of the eight codepoints in the range ' xxx000' (where 'x' may equal '0' or '1'). Class Selector Codepoints are discussed in Sec. 4.2.2.

Class Selector Compliant PHB: a per-hop behavior satisfying the Class Selector PHB Requirements specified in Sec. 4.2.2.2.

Codepoint: a specific value of the DSCP portion of the DS field. Recommended codepoints SHOULD map to specific, standardized PHBs. Multiple codepoints MAY map to the same PHB.

Differentiated Services Boundary: the edge of a DS domain, where classifiers and traffic conditioners are likely to be deployed. A differentiated services boundary can be further sub-divided into ingress and egress nodes, where the ingress/egress nodes are the downstream/upstream nodes of a boundary link in a given traffic direction. A differentiated services boundary typically is found at the ingress to the first-hop differentiated services-compliant router (or network node) that a host's packets traverse, or at the egress of the last-hop differentiated services-compliant router or network node that packets traverse before arriving at a host. This is sometimes referred to as the boundary at a leaf router. A differentiated services boundary may be co-located with a host, subject to local policy. Also DS boundary.

Differentiated Services-Compliant: in compliance with the requirements specified in this document. Also DS-compliant.

Differentiated Services Domain: a contiguous portion of the Internet over which a consistent set of differentiated services policies are administered in a coordinated fashion. A differentiated services domain can represent different administrative domains or autonomous systems, different trust regions, different network technologies (e.g., cell/frame), hosts and routers, etc. Also DS domain.

Differentiated Services Field: the IPv4 header TOS octet or the IPv6 Traffic Class octet when interpreted in conformance with the definition given in this document. Also DS field.

Mechanism: The implementation of one or more per-hop behaviors according to a particular algorithm.

Microflow: a single instance of an application-to-application flow of packets which is identified by source address, destination address, protocol id, and source port, destination port (where applicable).

Per-hop Behavior (PHB): a description of the externally observable forwarding treatment applied at a differentiated services-compliant node to a behavior aggregate. The description of a PHB SHOULD be sufficiently detailed to allow the construction of predictable services, as documented in [ARCH].

Per-hop Behavior Group: a set of one or more PHBs that can only be meaningfully specified and implemented simultaneously, due to a common constraint applying to all PHBs in the set such as a queue servicing or queue management policy. Also PHB Group.

Traffic Conditioning: control functions that can be applied to a behavior aggregate, application flow, or other operationally useful subset of traffic, e.g., routing updates. These MAY include metering, policing, shaping, and packet marking. Traffic conditioning is used to enforce agreements between domains and to condition traffic to receive a differentiated service within a domain by marking packets with the appropriate codepoint in the DS field and by monitoring and altering the temporal characteristics of the aggregate where necessary. See [ARCH].

Traffic Conditioner: an entity that performs traffic conditioning functions and which MAY contain meters, policers, shapers, and markers. Traffic conditioners are typically deployed in DS boundary nodes (i.e., not in interior nodes of a DS domain).

Service: a description of the overall treatment of (a subset of) a customer's traffic across a particular domain, across a set of interconnected DS domains, or end-to-end. Service descriptions are covered by administrative policy and services are constructed by applying traffic conditioning to create behavior aggregates which experience a known PHB at each node within the DS domain. Multiple services can be supported by a single per-hop behavior used in concert with a range of traffic conditioners.

To summarize, classifiers and traffic conditioners are used to select which packets are to be added to behavior aggregates. Aggregates receive differentiated treatment in a DS domain and traffic conditioners MAY alter the temporal characteristics of the aggregate to conform to some requirements. A packet's DS field is used to designate the packet's behavior aggregate and is subsequently used to determine which forwarding treatment the packet receives. A behavior aggregate classifier which can select a PHB, for example a differential output queue servicing discipline, based on the codepoint in the DS field SHOULD be included in all network nodes in a DS domain. The classifiers and traffic conditioners at DS boundaries are configured in accordance with some service specification, a matter of administrative policy outside the scope of this document.

Additional differentiated services definitions are given in [ARCH].

3. Differentiated Services Field Definition

A replacement header field, called the DS field, is defined, which is intended to supersede the existing definitions of the IPv4 TOS octet [RFC791] and the IPv6 Traffic Class octet [IPv6].

Six bits of the DS field are used as a codepoint (DSCP) to select the PHB a packet experiences at each node. A two-bit currently unused (CU) field is reserved and its definition and interpretation are outside the scope of this document. The value of the CU bits are ignored by differentiated services-compliant nodes when determining the per-hop behavior to apply to a received packet.

The DS field structure is presented below:

```
  0   1   2   3   4   5   6   7
+---+---+---+---+---+---+---+---+
|         DSCP          |  CU   |
+---+---+---+---+---+---+---+---+

  DSCP: differentiated services codepoint
  CU:   currently unused
```

In a DSCP value notation 'xxxxxx' (where 'x' may equal '0' or '1') used in this document, the left-most bit signifies bit 0 of the DS field (as shown above), and the right-most bit signifies bit 5.

Implementors should note that the DSCP field is six bits wide. DS-compliant nodes MUST select PHBs by matching against the entire 6-bit DSCP field, e.g., by treating the value of the field as a table index which is used to select a particular packet handling mechanism which has been implemented in that device. The value of the CU field MUST be ignored by PHB selection. The DSCP field is defined as an unstructured field to facilitate the definition of future per-hop behaviors.

With some exceptions noted below, the mapping of codepoints to PHBs MUST be configurable. A DS-compliant node MUST support the logical equivalent of a configurable mapping table from codepoints to PHBs. PHB specifications MUST include a recommended default codepoint, which MUST be unique for codepoints in the standard space (see Sec. 6). Implementations should support the recommended codepoint-to-PHB mappings in their default configuration. Operators may choose to use different codepoints for a PHB, either in addition to or in place of the recommended default. Note that if operators do so choose, re-marking of DS fields may be necessary at administrative boundaries even if the same PHBs are implemented on both sides of the boundary.

See [ARCH] for further discussion of re-marking.

The exceptions to general configurability are for codepoints 'xxx000' and are noted in Secs. 4.2.2 and 4.3.

Packets received with an unrecognized codepoint SHOULD be forwarded as if they were marked for the Default behavior (see Sec. 4), and their codepoints should not be changed. Such packets MUST NOT cause the network node to malfunction.

The structure of the DS field shown above is incompatible with the existing definition of the IPv4 TOS octet in [RFC791]. The presumption is that DS domains protect themselves by deploying re-marking boundary nodes, as should networks using the RFC 791 Precedence designations. Correct operational procedure SHOULD follow [RFC791], which states: "If the actual use of these precedence designations is of concern to a particular network, it is the responsibility of that network to control the access to, and use of, those precedence designations." Validating the value of the DS field at DS boundaries is sensible in any case since an upstream node can easily set it to any arbitrary value. DS domains that are not isolated by suitably configured boundary nodes may deliver unpredictable service.

Nodes MAY rewrite the DS field as needed to provide a desired local or end-to-end service. Specifications of DS field translations at DS boundaries are the subject of service level agreements between providers and users, and are outside the scope of this document. Standardized PHBs allow providers to build their services from a well-known set of packet forwarding treatments that can be expected to be present in the equipment of many vendors.

4. Historical Codepoint Definitions and PHB Requirements

The DS field will have a limited backwards compatibility with current practice, as described in this section. Backwards compatibility is addressed in two ways. First, there are per-hop behaviors that are already in widespread use (e.g., those satisfying the IPv4 Precedence queueing requirements specified in [RFC1812]), and we wish to permit their continued use in DS-compliant nodes. In addition, there are some codepoints that correspond to historical use of the IP Precedence field and we reserve these codepoints to map to PHBs that meet the general requirements specified in Sec. 4.2.2.2, though the specific differentiated services PHBs mapped to by those codepoints MAY have additional specifications.

No attempt is made to maintain backwards compatibility with the "DTR" or TOS bits of the IPv4 TOS octet, as defined in [RFC791].

4.1 A Default PHB

A "default" PHB MUST be available in a DS-compliant node. This is the common, best-effort forwarding behavior available in existing routers as standardized in [RFC1812]. When no other agreements are in place, it is assumed that packets belong to this aggregate. Such packets MAY be sent into a network without adhering to any particular rules and the network will deliver as many of these packets as possible and as soon as possible, subject to other resource policy constraints. A reasonable implementation of this PHB would be a queueing discipline that sends packets of this aggregate whenever the output link is not required to satisfy another PHB. A reasonable policy for constructing services would ensure that the aggregate was not "starved". This could be enforced by a mechanism in each node that reserves some minimal resources (e.g, buffers, bandwidth) for Default behavior aggregates. This permits senders that are not differentiated services-aware to continue to use the network in the same manner as today. The impact of the introduction of differentiated services into a domain on the service expectations of its customers and peers is a complex matter involving policy decisions by the domain and is outside the scope of this document. The RECOMMENDED codepoint for the Default PHB is the bit pattern ' 000000'; the value '000000' MUST map to a PHB that meets these specifications. The codepoint chosen for Default behavior is compatible with existing practice [RFC791]. Where a codepoint is not mapped to a standardized or local use PHB, it SHOULD be mapped to the Default PHB.

A packet initially marked for the Default behavior MAY be re-marked with another codepoint as it passes a boundary into a DS domain so that it will be forwarded using a different PHB within that domain, possibly subject to some negotiated agreement between the peering domains.

4.2 Once and Future IP Precedence Field Use

We wish to maintain some form of backward compatibility with present uses of the IP Precedence Field: bits 0-2 of the IPv4 TOS octet. Routers exist that use the IP Precedence field to select different per-hop forwarding treatments in a similar way to the use proposed here for the DSCP field. Thus, a simple prototype differentiated services architecture can be quickly deployed by appropriately configuring these routers. Further, IP systems today understand the location of the IP Precedence field, and thus if these bits are used in a similar manner as DS-compliant equipment is deployed, significant failures are not likely during early deployment. In other words, strict DS-compliance need not be ubiquitous even within a single service provider's network if bits 0-2 of the DSCP field are employed in a manner similar to, or subsuming, the deployed uses of the IP Precedence field.

4.2.1 IP Precedence History and Evolution in Brief

The IP Precedence field is something of a forerunner of the DS field. IP Precedence, and the IP Precedence Field, were first defined in [RFC791]. The values that the three-bit IP Precedence Field might take were assigned to various uses, including network control traffic, routing traffic, and various levels of privilege. The least level of privilege was deemed "routine traffic". In [RFC791], the notion of Precedence was defined broadly as "An independent measure of the importance of this datagram." Not all values of the IP Precedence field were assumed to have meaning across boundaries, for instance "The Network Control precedence designation is intended to be used within a network only. The actual use and control of that designation is up to each network." [RFC791]

Although early BBN IMPs implemented the Precedence feature, early commercial routers and UNIX IP forwarding code generally did not. As networks became more complex and customer requirements grew, commercial router vendors developed ways to implement various kinds of queueing services including priority queueing, which were generally based on policies encoded in filters in the routers, which examined IP addresses, IP protocol numbers, TCP or UDP ports, and other header fields. IP Precedence was and is among the options such filters can examine.

In short, IP Precedence is widely deployed and widely used, if not in exactly the manner intended in [RFC791]. This was recognized in [RFC1122], which states that while the use of the IP Precedence field is valid, the specific assignment of the priorities in [RFC791] were merely historical.

4.2.2 Subsuming IP Precedence into Class Selector Codepoints

A specification of the packet forwarding treatments selected by the IP Precedence field today would have to be quite general; probably not specific enough to build predictable services from in the differentiated services framework. To preserve partial backwards compatibility with known current uses of the IP Precedence field without sacrificing future flexibility, we have taken the approach of describing minimum requirements on a set of PHBs that are compatible with most of the deployed forwarding treatments selected by the IP Precedence field. In addition, we give a set of codepoints that MUST map to PHBs meeting these minimum requirements. The PHBs mapped to by these codepoints MAY have a more detailed list of specifications in addition to the required ones stated here. Other codepoints MAY map to these same PHBs. We refer to this set of codepoints as the Class Selector Codepoints, and the minimum requirements for PHBs that these codepoints may map to are called the Class Selector PHB Requirements.

4.2.2.1 The Class Selector Codepoints

A specification of the packet forwarding treatments selected by the The DS field values of 'xxx000|xx', or DSCP = 'xxx000' and CU subfield unspecified, are reserved as a set of Class Selector Codepoints. PHBs which are mapped to by these codepoints MUST satisfy the Class Selector PHB requirements in addition to preserving the Default PHB requirement on codepoint '000000' (Sec. 4.1).

4.2.2.2 The Class Selector PHB Requirements

We refer to a Class Selector Codepoint with a larger numerical value than another Class Selector Codepoint as having a higher relative order while a Class Selector Codepoint with a smaller numerical value than another Class Selector Codepoint is said to have a lower relative order. The set of PHBs mapped to by the eight Class Selector Codepoints MUST yield at least two independently forwarded classes of traffic, and PHBs selected by a Class Selector Codepoint

SHOULD give packets a probability of timely forwarding that is not lower than that given to packets marked with a Class Selector codepoint of lower relative order, under reasonable operating conditions and traffic loads. A discarded packet is considered to be an extreme case of untimely forwarding. In addition, PHBs selected by codepoints '11x000' MUST give packets a preferential forwarding treatment by comparison to the PHB selected by codepoint '000000' to preserve the common usage of IP Precedence values '110' and '111' for routing traffic.

Further, PHBs selected by distinct Class Selector Codepoints SHOULD be independently forwarded; that is, packets marked with different Class Selector Codepoints MAY be re-ordered. A network node MAY enforce limits on the amount of the node's resources that can be utilized by each of these PHBs.

PHB groups whose specification satisfy these requirements are referred to as Class Selector Compliant PHBs.

The Class Selector PHB Requirements on codepoint '000000' are compatible with those listed for the Default PHB in Sec. 4.1.

4.2.2.3 Using the Class Selector PHB Requirements for IP Precedence Compatibility

A DS-compliant network node can be deployed with a set of one or more Class Selector Compliant PHB groups. This document states that the set of codepoints 'xxx000' MUST map to such a set of PHBs. As it is also possible to map multiple codepoints to the same PHB, the vendor or the network administrator MAY configure the network node to map codepoints to PHBs irrespective of bits 3-5 of the DSCP field to yield a network that is compatible with historical IP Precedence use. Thus, for example, codepoint '011010' would map to the same PHB as codepoint '011000'.

4.2.2.4 Example Mechanisms for Implementing Class Selector Compliant PHB Groups

Class Selector Compliant PHBs can be realized by a variety of mechanisms, including strict priority queueing, weighted fair queueing (WFQ), WRR, or variants [RPS, HPFQA, DRR], or Class-Based Queuing [CBQ]. The distinction between PHBs and mechanisms is described in more detail in Sec. 5.

It is important to note that these mechanisms might be available through other PHBs (standardized or not) that are available in a particular vendor's equipment. For example, future documents may standardize a Strict Priority Queueing PHB group for a set of recommended codepoints. A network administrator might configure those routers to select the Strict Priority Queueing PHBs with codepoints 'xxx000' in conformance with the requirements of this document.

As a further example, another vendor might employ a CBQ mechanism in its routers. The CBQ mechanism could be used to implement the Strict Priority Queueing PHBs as well as a set of Class Selector Compliant PHBs with a wider range of features than would be available in a set of PHBs that did no more than meet the minimum Class Selector PHB requirements.

4.3 Summary

This document defines codepoints 'xxx000' as the Class Selector codepoints, where PHBs selected by these codepoints MUST meet the Class Selector PHB Requirements described in Sec. 4.2.2.2. This is done to preserve a useful level of backward compatibility with current uses of the IP Precedence field in the Internet without unduly limiting future flexibility. In addition, codepoint '000000' is used as the Default PHB value for the Internet and, as such, is not configurable. The remaining seven non-zero Class Selector codepoints are configurable only to the extent that they map to PHBs that meet the requirements in Sec. 4.2.2.2.

5. Per-Hop Behavior Standardization Guidelines

The behavioral characteristics of a PHB are to be standardized, and not the particular algorithms or the mechanisms used to implement them. A node may have a (possibly large) set of parameters that can be used to control how packets are scheduled onto an output interface (e.g., N separate queues with settable priorities, queue lengths, round-robin weights, drop algorithm, drop preference weights and thresholds, etc). To illustrate the distinction between a PHB and a mechanism, we point out that Class Selector Compliant PHBs might be implemented by several mechanisms, including: strict priority queueing, WFQ, WRR, or variants [HPFQA, RPS, DRR], or CBQ [CBQ], in isolation or in combination.

PHBs may be specified individually, or as a group (a single PHB is a special case of a PHB group). A PHB group usually consists of a set of two or more PHBs that can only be meaningfully specified and implemented simultaneously, due to a common constraint applying to each PHB within the group, such as a queue servicing or queue management policy. A PHB group specification SHOULD describe conditions under which a packet might be re-marked to select another PHB within the group. It is RECOMMENDED that PHB implementations do not introduce any packet re-ordering within a microflow. PHB group specifications MUST identify any possible packet re-ordering implications which may occur for each individual PHB, and which may occur if different packets within a microflow are marked for different PHBs within the group.

Only those per-hop behaviors that are not described by an existing PHB standard, and have been implemented, deployed, and shown to be useful, SHOULD be standardized. Since current experience with differentiated services is quite limited, it is premature to hypothesize the exact specification of these per-hop behaviors.

Each standardized PHB MUST have an associated RECOMMENDED codepoint, allocated out of a space of 32 codepoints (see Sec. 6). This specification has left room in the codepoint space to allow for evolution, thus the defined space ('xxx000') is intentionally sparse.

Network equipment vendors are free to offer whatever parameters and capabilities are deemed useful or marketable. When a particular, standardized PHB is implemented in a node, a vendor MAY use any algorithm that satisfies the definition of the PHB according to the standard. The node's capabilities and its particular configuration determine the different ways that packets can be treated.

Service providers are not required to use the same node mechanisms or configurations to enable service differentiation within their networks, and are free to configure the node parameters in whatever way that is appropriate for their service offerings and traffic engineering objectives. Over time certain common per-hop behaviors are likely to evolve (i.e., ones that are particularly useful for implementing end-to-end services) and these MAY be associated with particular EXP/LU PHB codepoints in the DS field, allowing use across domain boundaries (see Sec. 6). These PHBs are candidates for future standardization.

It is RECOMMENDED that standardized PHBs be specified in accordance with the guidelines set out in [ARCH].

6. IANA Considerations

The DSCP field within the DS field is capable of conveying 64 distinct codepoints. The codepoint space is divided into three pools for the purpose of codepoint assignment and management: a pool of 32 RECOMMENDED codepoints (Pool 1) to be assigned by Standards Action as defined in [CONS], a pool of 16 codepoints (Pool 2) to be reserved for experimental or Local Use (EXP/LU) as defined in [CONS], and a pool of 16 codepoints (Pool 3) which are initially available for experimental or local use, but which should be preferentially utilized for standardized assignments if Pool 1 is ever exhausted. The pools are defined in the following table (where 'x' refers to either '0' or '1'):

Pool	Codepoint space	Assignment Policy
1	xxxxx0	Standards Action
2	xxxx11	EXP/LU
3	xxxx01	EXP/LU (*)

(*) may be utilized for future Standards Action allocations as necessary

This document assigns eight RECOMMENDED codepoints ('xxx000') which are drawn from Pool 1 above. These codepoints MUST be mapped, not to specific PHBs, but to PHBs that meet "at least" the requirements set forth in Sec. 4.2.2.2 to provide a minimal level of backwards compatibility with IP Precedence as defined in [RFC791] and as deployed in some current equipment.

7. Security Considerations

This section considers security issues raised by the introduction of differentiated services, primarily the potential for denial-of-service attacks, and the related potential for theft of service by unauthorized traffic (Section 7.1). Section 7.2 addresses the operation of differentiated services in the presence of IPsec including its interaction with IPsec tunnel mode and other tunnelling protocols. See [ARCH] for more extensive treatment of the security concerns raised by the overall differentiated services architecture.

7.1 Theft and Denial of Service

The primary goal of differentiated services is to allow different levels of service to be provided for traffic streams on a common network infrastructure. A variety of techniques may be used to achieve this, but the end result will be that some packets receive different (e.g., better) service than others. The mapping of network traffic to the specific behaviors that result in different (e.g., better or worse) service is indicated primarily by the DS codepoint, and hence an adversary may be able to obtain better service by modifying the codepoint to values indicating behaviors used for enhanced services or by injecting packets with such codepoint values. Taken to its limits, such theft-of-service becomes a denial-of-service attack when the modified or injected traffic depletes the resources available to forward it and other traffic streams.

The defense against this class of theft- and denial-of-service attacks consists of the combination of traffic conditioning at DS domain boundaries with security and integrity of the network infrastructure within a DS domain. DS domain boundary nodes MUST ensure that all traffic entering the domain is marked with codepoint values appropriate to the traffic and the domain, remarking the traffic with new codepoint values if necessary. These DS boundary nodes are the primary line of defense against theft- and denial-of-service attacks based on modified codepoints, as success of any such attack indicates that the codepoints used by the attacking traffic were inappropriate. An important instance of a boundary node is that any traffic-originating node within a DS domain is the initial boundary node for that traffic. Interior nodes in a DS domain rely on DS codepoints to associate traffic with the forwarding PHBs, and are NOT REQUIRED to check codepoint values before using them. As a result, the interior nodes depend on the correct operation of the DS domain boundary nodes to prevent the arrival of traffic with inappropriate codepoints or in excess of provisioned levels that would disrupt operation of the domain.

7.2 IPsec and Tunnelling Interactions

The IPsec protocol, as defined in [ESP, AH], does not include the IP header's DS field in any of its cryptographic calculations (in the case of tunnel mode, it is the outer IP header's DS field that is not included). Hence modification of the DS field by a network node has no effect on IPsec's end-to-end security, because it cannot cause any IPsec integrity check to fail. As a consequence, IPsec does not provide any defense against an adversary's modification of the DS field (i.e., a man-in-the-middle attack), as the adversary's modification will also have no effect on IPsec's end-to-end security.

IPsec's tunnel mode provides security for the encapsulated IP header's DS field. A tunnel mode IPsec packet contains two IP headers: an outer header supplied by the tunnel ingress node and an encapsulated inner header supplied by the original source of the packet. When an IPsec tunnel is hosted (in whole or in part) on a differentiated services network, the intermediate network nodes operate on the DS field in the outer header. At the tunnel egress node, IPsec processing includes removing the outer header and forwarding the packet (if required) using the inner header. The IPsec protocol REQUIRES that the inner header's DS field not be changed by this decapsulation processing to ensure that modifications to the DS field cannot be used to launch theft- or denial-of-service attacks across an IPsec tunnel endpoint. This document makes no change to that requirement. If the inner IP header has not been processed by a DS boundary node for the tunnel egress node's DS domain, the tunnel egress node is the boundary node for traffic exiting the tunnel, and hence MUST ensure that the resulting traffic has appropriate DS codepoints.

When IPsec tunnel egress decapsulation processing includes a sufficiently strong cryptographic integrity check of the encapsulated packet (where sufficiency is determined by local security policy), the tunnel egress node can safely assume that the DS field in the inner header has the same value as it had at the tunnel ingress node. An important consequence is that otherwise insecure links within a DS domain can be secured by a sufficiently strong IPsec tunnel. This analysis and its implications apply to any tunnelling protocol that performs integrity checks, but the level of assurance of the inner header's DS field depends on the strength of the integrity check performed by the tunnelling protocol. In the absence of sufficient assurance for a tunnel that may transit nodes outside the current DS domain (or is otherwise vulnerable), the encapsulated packet MUST be treated as if it had arrived at a boundary from outside the DS domain.

8. Acknowledgements

The authors would like to acknowledge the Differentiated Services Working Group for discussions which helped shape this document.

9. References

[AH] Kent, S. and R. Atkinson, "IP Authentication Header", RFC 2402, November 1998.

[ARCH] Blake, S., Black, D., Carlson, M., Davies, E., Wang, Z.

and W. Weiss, "An Architecture for Differentiated Services", RFC 2475, December 1998.

[CBQ] S. Floyd and V. Jacobson, "Link-sharing and Resource Management Models for Packet Networks", IEEE/ACM Transactions on Networking, Vol. 3 no. 4, pp. 365-386, August 1995.

[CONS] Narten, T. and H. Alvestrand, "Guidelines for Writing an IANA Considerations Section in RFCs", RFC 2434, October 1998.

[DRR] M. Shreedhar and G. Varghese, Efficient Fair Queueing using Deficit Round Robin", Proc. ACM SIGCOMM 95, 1995.

[ESP] Kent, S. and R. Atkinson, "IP Encapsulating Security Payload (ESP)", RFC 2406, November 1998.

[HPFQA] J. Bennett and Hui Zhang, "Hierarchical Packet Fair Queueing Algorithms", Proc. ACM SIGCOMM 96, August 1996.

[IPv6] Deering, S. and R. Hinden, "Internet Protocol, Version 6 (IPv6) Specification", RFC 2460, December 1998.

[RFC791] Postel, J., Editor, "Internet Protocol", STD 5, RFC 791, September 1981.

[RFC1122] Braden, R., "Requirements for Internet hosts - communication layers", STD 3, RFC 1122, October 1989.

[RFC1812] Baker, F., Editor, "Requirements for IP Version 4 Routers", RFC 1812, June 1995.

[RFC2119] Bradner, S., "Key words for use in RFCs to Indicate Requirement Levels", BCP 14, RFC 2119, March 1997.

[RPS] D. Stiliadis and A. Varma, "Rate-Proportional Servers: A Design Methodology for Fair Queueing Algorithms", IEEE/ ACM Trans. on Networking, April 1998.

Authors' Addresses

Kathleen Nichols
Cisco Systems
170 West Tasman Drive
San Jose, CA 95134-1706

Phone: +1-408-525-4857
EMail: kmn@cisco.com

Steven Blake
Torrent Networking Technologies
3000 Aerial Center, Suite 140
Morrisville, NC 27560

Phone: +1-919-468-8466 x232
EMail: slblake@torrentnet.com

Fred Baker
Cisco Systems
519 Lado Drive
Santa Barbara, CA 93111

Phone: +1-408-526-4257
EMail: fred@cisco.com

David L. Black
EMC Corporation
35 Parkwood Drive
Hopkinton, MA 01748

Phone: +1-508-435-1000 x76140
EMail: black_david@emc.com

Full Copyright Statement

Network Working Group
Request for Comments: 2491
Category: Standards Track

G. Armitage
Lucent Technologies
P. Schulter
Bright Tiger Technologies
M. Jork
Digital Equipment GmbH
G. Harter
Compaq

January 1999

IPv6 over Non-Broadcast Multiple Access (NBMA) networks

Status of this Memo

This document specifies an Internet standards track protocol for the Internet community, and requests discussion and suggestions for improvements. Please refer to the current edition of the "Internet Official Protocol Standards" (STD 1) for the standardization state and status of this protocol. Distribution of this memo is unlimited.

Copyright Notice

Abstract

This document describes a general architecture for IPv6 over NBMA networks. It forms the basis for subsidiary companion documents that describe details for various specific NBMA technologies (such as ATM or Frame Relay). The IPv6 over NBMA architecture allows conventional host-side operation of the IPv6 Neighbor Discovery protocol, while also supporting the establishment of 'shortcut' NBMA forwarding paths when dynamically signaled NBMA links are available. Operations over administratively configured Point to Point NBMA links are also described.

Dynamic NBMA shortcuts are achieved through the use of IPv6 Neighbor Discovery protocol operation within Logical Links, and inter-router NHRP for the discovery of off-Link NBMA destinations. Both flow-triggered and explicitly source-triggered shortcuts are supported.

1. Introduction.

Non Broadcast Multiple Access (NBMA) networks may be utilized in a variety of ways. At one extreme, they can be used to simply provide administratively configurable point to point service, sufficient to interconnect IPv6 routers (and even IPv6 hosts, in certain situations). At the other extreme, NBMA networks that support dynamic establishment and teardown of Virtual Circuits (or functional equivalents) may be used to emulate the service provided to the IPv6 layer by conventional broadcast media such as Ethernet. Typically this emulation requires complex convergence protocols, particularly to support IPv6 multicast.

This document describes a general architecture for IPv6 over NBMA networks. It forms the basis for companion documents that provide details specific to various NBMA technologies (for example, ATM [17] or Frame Relay). The IPv6 over NBMA architecture allows conventional host-side operation of the IPv6 Neighbor Discovery protocol, while also supporting the establishment of 'shortcut' NBMA forwarding paths (when dynamically signaled NBMA links are available).

The majority of this document focuses on the use of dynamically managed point to point and point to multipoint calls between interfaces on an NBMA network. These will be generically referred to as "SVCs" in the rest of the document. The use of administratively configured point to point calls will also be discussed. Such calls will be generically referred to as "PVCs". Depending on context, either may be shortened to "VC".

Certain NBMA networks may provide a form of connectionless service (e.g. SMDS). In these cases, a "call" or "VC" shall be considered to implicitly exist if the sender has an NBMA destination address to which it can transmit packets whenever it desires.

1.1 Neighbor Discovery.

A key difference between this architecture and previous IP over NBMA protocols is its mechanism for supporting IPv6 Neighbor Discovery.

The IPv4 world evolved an approach to address resolution that depended on the operation of an auxiliary protocol operating at the 'link layer' - starting with Ethernet ARP (RFC 826 [14]). In the world of NBMA (Non Broadcast, Multiple Access) networks ARP has been applied to IPv4 over SMDS (RFC 1209 [13]) and IPv4 over ATM (RFC 1577 [3]). More recently the ION working group has developed NHRP (Next Hop Resolution Protocol [8]), a general protocol for performing intra-subnet and inter-subnet address resolution applicable to a range of NBMA network technologies.

IPv6 developers opted to migrate away from a link layer specific approach, chosing to combine a number of tasks into a protocol known as Neighbor Discovery [7], intended to be non-specific across a number of link layer technologies. A key assumption made by Neighbor Discovery's actual protocol is that the link technology underlying a given IP interface is capable of native multicasting. This is not particularly true of most NBMA network services, and usually requires convergence protocols to emulate the desired service. (The MARS protocol, RFC 2022 [5], is an example of such a convergence protocol.) This document augments and optimizes the MARS protocol for use in support of IPv6 Neighbor Discovery, generalizing the applicability of RFC 2022 beyond ATM networks.

1.2 NBMA Shortcuts.

A shortcut is an NBMA level call (VC) directly connecting two IP endpoints that are logically separated by one or more routers at the IP level. IPv6 packets traversing this VC are said to 'shortcut' the routers that are in the logical IPv6 path between the VC's endpoints.

NBMA shortcuts are a mechanism for minimizing the consumption of resources within an IP over NBMA cloud (e.g. router hops and NBMA VCs).

It is important that NBMA shortcuts are supported whenever IP is deployed across NBMA networks capable of supporting dynamic establishment of calls (SVCs or functional equivalent). For IPv6 over NBMA, shortcut discovery and management is achieved through a mixture of Neighbor Discovery and NHRP.

1.3 Key components of the IPv6 over NBMA architecture.

1.3.1 NBMA networks providing PVC support.

When the NBMA network is used in PVC mode, each PVC will connect exactly two nodes and the use of Neighbor Discovery and other IPv6 features is limited. IPv6/NBMA interfaces have only one neighbor on each Link. The MARS and NHRP protocols are NOT necessary, since multicast and broadcast operations collapse down to an NBMA level unicast operation. Dynamically discovered shortcuts are not supported.

The actual details of encapsulations and link token generation SHALL be covered by companion documents covering specific NBMA technology. They SHALL conform to the following guidelines:

Both unicast and multicast IPv6 packets SHALL be transmitted over PVC links using the encapsulation described in section 4.4.1.

Interface tokens for PVC links SHALL be constructed as described in section 5. Interface tokens need only be unique between the two nodes on the PVC link.

This use of PVC links does not mandate, nor does it prohibit the use of extensions to the Neighbor Discovery protocol which may be developed for either general use of for use in PVC connections (for example, Inverse Neighbor Discovery).

NBMA-specific companion documents MAY additionally specify the concatenation of IPv6 over PPP and PPP over NBMA mechanisms as an OPTIONAL approach to point to point IPv6.

Except where noted above, the remainder of this document focuses on the SVC case.

1.3.2 NBMA networks providing SVC support.

When the NBMA network is used in SVC mode, the key components are:

- The IPv6 Neighbor model, where neighbors are discovered through the use of messages multicast to members of an IPv6 interface's local IPv6 Link.
- The MARS model, allowing emulation of general multicast using multipoint calls provided by the underlying NBMA network.
- The NHRP service for seeking out the NBMA identities of IP interfaces who are logically distant in an IP topological sense.
- The modeling of IP traffic as 'flows', and optionally using the existence of a flow as the basis for attempting to set up a shortcut link level connection.

In summary:

The IPv6 "Link" is generalized to "Logical Link" (LL) in NBMA environments (analogous to the generalization of IPv4 IP Subnet to Logical IP Subnet in RFC 1209 and subsequently RFC 1577).

IPv6/NBMA interfaces utilize RFC 2022 (MARS) for general intra-Logical Link multicasting. The MARS itself is used to optimally distribute discovery messages within the Logical Link.

For destinations not currently considered to be Neighbors, a host sends the packets to one of its default routers.

When appropriately configured, the egress router from a Logical Link is responsible for detecting the existence of an IP packet flow through it that might benefit from a shortcut connection.

While continuing to conventionally forward the flow's packets, the router initiates an NHRP query for the flow's destination IP address.

The last router/NHS before the target of the NHRP query ascertains the target interface's preferred NBMA address.

The originally querying router then issues a Redirect to the IP source, identifying the flow's destination as a transient Neighbor.

Host-initiated triggering of shortcut discovery, regardless of the existence of a packet flow, is also supported through specific Neighbor Solicitations sent to a source host's default router.

A number of key advantages are claimed for this approach. These are:

The IPv6 stacks on hosts do not implement separate ND protocols for each link layer technology.

When the destination of a flow is solicited as a transient neighbor, the returned NBMA address will be the one chosen by the destination when the flow was originally established through hop-by-hop processing. This supports the existing ND ability for IPv6 destinations to perform their own dynamic interface load sharing.

1.4 Terminology.

The bit-pattern or numeric value used to identify a particular NBMA interface at the NBMA level will be referred to as an "NBMA address". (An example would be an ATM End System Address, AESA, when applying this architecture to ATM networks, or an E.164 number when applying this architecture to SMDS networks.)

The call that, once established, is used to transfer IP packets from one NBMA interface to another will be referred to as an SVC or PVC depending on whether the call is dynamically established through some signaling mechanism, or administratively established. The specific signaling mechanisms used to establish or tear down an SVC will be defined in the NBMA-specific companion specifications. Certain NBMA networks may provide a form of connectionless service (e.g. SMDS). In these cases, a "call" or "SVC" shall be considered to implicitly exist if the sender has an NBMA destination address to which it can transmit packets whenever it desires.

The key words "MUST", "MUST NOT", "REQUIRED", "SHALL", "SHALL NOT", "SHOULD", "SHOULD NOT", "RECOMMENDED", "MAY", and "OPTIONAL" in this document are to be interpreted as described in RFC 2119 [16].

1.5 Document Structure.

The remainder of this document is structured as follows: Section 2 explains the generalization of IPv6 Link to "Logical Link" when used over NBMA networks, and introduces the notion of the Transient Neighbor. Section 3 describes the modifications to the MARS protocol for efficient distribution of ND messages within a Logical Link, and the rules and mechanisms for discovering Transient Neighbors. Section 4 covers the basic rules governing IPv6/NBMA interface initialization, packet and control message encapsulations, and rules for SVC management. Section 5 describes the general rules for constructing Interface Tokens, the Link Layer Address Option, and Link Local addresses. Section 6 concludes the normative sections of the document. Appendix A provides some non-normative descriptive text regarding the operation of Ipv6 Neighbor Discovery. Appendix B describes some sub-optimal solutions for emulating the multicasting of Neighbor Discovery messages around a Logical Link. Appendix C discusses shortcut suppression and briefly reviews the future relationships between flow detection and mapping of flows onto SVCs of differing qualities of service.

2. Logical Links, and Transient Neighbors.

IPv6 contains a concept of on-link and off-link. Neighbors are those nodes that are considered on-link and whose link-layer addresses may therefore be located using Neighbor Discovery. Borrowing from the terminology definitions in the ND text:

on-link - an address that is assigned to a neighbor's interface on a shared link. A host considers an address to be on-link if:
  - it is covered by one of the link's prefixes, or
  - a neighboring router specifies the address as the target of a Redirect message, or
  - a Neighbor Advertisement message is received for the target address, or
  - a Neighbor Discovery message is received from the address.

off-link - the opposite of "on-link"; an address that is not assigned to any interfaces attached to a shared link.

Off-link nodes are considered to only be accessible through one of the routers directly attached to the link.

The NBMA environment complicates the sense of the word 'link' in much the same way as it complicated the sense of 'subnet' in the IPv4 case. For IPv4 this required the definition of the Logical IP Subnet (LIS) - an administratively constructed set of hosts that would share the same routing prefixes (network and subnetwork masks).

This document considers the IPv6 analog to be a Logical Link (LL).

> An LL consists of nodes administratively configured to be 'on link' with respect to each other.
>
> The members of an LL are an IPv6 interface's initial set of neighbors, and each interface's Link Local address only needs to be unique amongst this set.

It should be noted that whilst members of an LL are IPv6 Neighbors, it is possible for Neighbors to exist that are not, administratively, members of the same LL.

Neighbor Discovery events can result in the expansion of an IPv6 interface's set of Neighbors. However, this does not change the set of interfaces that make up its LL. This leads to three possible relationships between any two IPv6 interfaces:

- On LL, Neighbor.
- Off LL, Neighbor.
- Off LL, not Neighbor.

Off LL Neighbors represent the 'shortcut' connections, where it has been ascertained that direct connectivity at the NBMA level is possible to a target that is not a member of the source's LL.

Neighbors discovered through the operation of unsolicited messages, such as Redirects, are termed 'Transient Neighbors'.

3. Intra-LL and Inter-LL Discovery.

This document makes a distinction between the discovery of neighbors within a Logical Link (intra-LL) and neighbors beyond the LL (inter-LL). The goal is to allow both inter- and intra-LL neighbor discovery to involve no changes to the host-side IPv6 stack for NBMA interfaces.

Note that section 1.3.1 applies when the NBMA network is being used to provide only configured point to point (PVC) service.

3.1 Intra-LL - ND over emulated multicast.

The basic model of ND assumes that a link layer interface will do something meaningful with an ICMPv6 packet sent to a multicast IP destination address. (IPv6 assumes that multicasting is an integral part of the Internet service.) This document assumes multicast support will be provided using the RFC 2022 (MARS) [5] service (generalized for use over other NBMA technologies in addition to ATM). An IPv6 LL maps directly onto an IPv6 MARS Cluster in the same way an IPv4 LIS maps directly onto an IPv4 MARS Cluster.

The goal of intra-LL operation is that the IPv6 layer must be able to simply pass multicast ICMPv6 packets down to the IPv6/NBMA driver without any special, NBMA specific processing. The underlying mechanism for distributing Neighbor Discovery and Router Discovery messages then works as expected.

Sections 3.1.1 describes the additional functionality that SHALL be required of any MARS used in conformance with this document. Background discussion of these additions is provided in Appendix B.

3.1.1 Mandatory augmented MARS and MARS Client behavior.

IPv6/NBMA interfaces SHALL register as MARS Cluster members as described in section 4.1, and SHALL send certain classes of outgoing IPv6 packets directly to their local MARS as described in section 4.4.2.

The MARS itself SHALL then re-transmit these packets according to the following rules:

- When the MARS receives an IPv6 packet, it scans the group membership database to find the NBMA addresses of the IPv6 destination group's members.

- The MARS then checks to see if every group member currently has its pt-pt control VC open to the MARS. If so, the MARS sends a copy of the data packet directly to each group member over the existing pt-pt VCs.

- If one or more of the discovered group members do not have an open pt-pt VC to the MARS, or if there are no group members listed, the packet is sent out ClusterControlVC instead. No copies of the packet are sent over the existing (if any) pt-pt VCs.

3.2 Inter-LL - Redirects, and their generation.

Shortcut connections are justified on the grounds that demanding flows of IP packets may exist between source/destination pairs that are separated by IP routing boundaries. Shortcuts are created between Transient Neighbors.

The key to creating transient neighbors is the Redirect message (section 8 [7]). IPv6 allows a router to inform the members of an LL that there is a better 'first hop' to a given destination (section 8.2 [7]). The advertisement itself is achieved through a Router Redirect message, which may carry the link layer address of this better hop.

A transmitting host only listens to Router Redirects from the router that is currently acting as the default router for the IP destination that the Redirect refers to. If a Redirect arrives that indicates a better first hop for a given destination, and supplies a link layer (NBMA) address to use as the better first hop, the associated Neighbor Cache entry in the source host is updated and its reachability set to STALE. Updating the cache in this context involves building a new VC to the new NBMA address. If this is successful, the old VC is torn down only if it no longer required (since the old VC was to the router, it may still be required by other packets from the host that are heading to the router).

Two mechanisms are provided for triggering the discovery of a better first hop:

Router-based flow identification/detection.

Host-initiated shortcut request.

Section 3.2.1 discusses flow-based triggers, section 3.2.2 discusses the host initiated trigger, and section 3.2.3 discusses the use of NHRP to discover mappings for IPv6 targets in remote LLs.

3.2.1 Flow Triggered Redirection.

The modification of forwarding paths based on the dynamic detection of IP packet flows is at the core of models such as the Cell Switch Router [11] and the IP Switch [12]. Responsibility for detecting flows is placed into the routers, where packets cross the edges of IP routing boundaries.

For the purpose of conformance with this document, a router MAY choose to initiate the discovery of a better first-hop when it determines that an identifiable flow of IP packets are passing through it.

Such a router:

SHALL only track flows that originate from a directly attached host (a host that is within the LL-local scope of one of the router's interfaces).

SHALL NOT use IP packets arriving from another router to trigger the generation of a Router Redirect.

SHALL only consider IPv6 packets with FlowID of zero for the purposes of flow detection as defined in this section.

SHALL utilize NHRP as described in section 3.2.3 to ascertain a better first-hop when a suitable flow is detected, and advertise the information in a Router Redirect.

IPv6 routers that support the OPTIONAL flow detection behavior described above SHALL support administrative mechanisms to switch off flow-detection. They MAY provide mechanisms for adding additional constraints to the categories of IPv6 packets that constitute a 'flow'.

The actual algorithm(s) for determining what sequence of IPv6 packets constitute a 'flow' are outside the scope of this document. Appendix C discusses the rationale behind the use of non-zero FlowID to suppress flow detection.

3.2.2 Host Triggered Redirection

A source host MAY also trigger a redirection to a transient neighbor. To support host-triggered redirects, routers conforming to this document SHALL recognize specific Neighbor Solicitation messages sent by hosts as requests for the resolution of off-link addresses.

To perform a host-triggered redirect, a source host SHALL:

Create a Neighbor Solicitation message referring to the off-LL destination (target) for which a shortcut is desired

Address the NS message to the router that would be the next hop for traffic sent towards the off-LL target (rather than the target's solicited node multicast address).

Use the standard ND hop limit of 255 to ensure the NS won't be discarded by the router.

Include the shortcut limit option defined in appendix D. The value of this option should be equal to the hop limit of the data flow for which this trigger is being sent. This ensures that the router is able to restrict the shortcut attempt to not exceed the reach of the data flow.

Forward the NS packet to the router that would be the next hop for traffic sent towards the off-LL target.

Routers SHALL consider a unicast NS with shortcut limit option as a request for a host-triggered redirect. However, actual shortcut discovery is OPTIONAL for IPv6 routers.

When shortcut discovery is not supported, the router SHALL construct a Redirect message identifying the router itself as the best 'shortcut', and return it to the soliciting host.

If shortcut discovery is to be supported, the router's response SHALL be:

A suitable NHRP Request is constructed and sent as described in section 3.2.3. The original NS message SHOULD be discarded.

Once the NHRP Reply is received by the originating router, the router SHALL construct a Redirect message containing the IPv6 address of the transient neighbor, and the NBMA link layer address returned by the NHRP resolution process.

The resulting Redirect message SHALL then be transmitted back to the source host. When the Redirect message is received, the source host SHALL update its Neighbor and Destination caches.

The off-LL target is now considered a Transient Neighbor. The next packet sent to the Transient Neighbor will result in the creation of the direct, shortcut VC (to the off-LL target itself, or to the best egress router towards that neighbor as determined by NHRP).

If a NHRP NAK or error indication is received for a host-triggered shortcut attempt, the requesting router SHALL construct a Redirect message identifying the router itself as the best 'shortcut', and return it to the soliciting host.

3.2.3 Use of NHRP between routers.

Once flow detection has occurred, or a host trigger has been detected, routers SHALL use NHRP in an NHS to NHS mode to establish the IPv6 to link level address mapping of a better first hop.

IPv6/NBMA routers supporting shortcut discovery will need to perform some or all of the following functions:

- Construct NHRP Requests and Replies.
- Parse incoming NHRP Requests and Replies from other NHSes (routers).
- Forward NHRP Requests towards an NHS that is topologically closer to the IPv6 target.
- Forward NHRP Replies towards an NHS that is topologically closer to the requester.
- Perform syntax translation between Neighbor Solicitations and outbound NHRP Requests.
- Perform syntax translation between inbound NHRP Replies and Redirects.

The destination of the flow that caused the trigger (or the target of the host initiated trigger) is used as the target for resolution in a NHRP Request. The router then forwards this NHRP Request to the next closest NHS. The process continues (as it would for normal NHRP) until the Request reaches an NHS that believes the IP target is within link-local scope of one of its interfaces. (This may potentially occur within a single router.)

As NHRP resolution requests always follow the routed path for a given target protocol address, the scope of a shortcut request will be automatically bounded to the scope of the IPv6 target address. (e.g. resolution requests for site-local addresses will not be forwarded across site boundaries.)

The last hop router SHALL resolve the NHRP Request from mapping information contained in its neighbor cache for the interface on which the specified target is reachable. If there is no appropriate entry in the Neighbor cache, or the destination is currently considered unreachable, the last hop router SHALL perform Neighbor Discovery on the local interface, and build the NHRP Reply from the resulting answer. (Note, in the case where the NHRP Request originated due to flow detection, there must already be a hop-by-hop flow of packets going through the last hop router towards the target. In this typical case the Neighbor cache will already have the desired information.)

The NHRP Reply is propagated back to the source of the NHRP Request, using a hop-by-hop path as it would for normal NHRP.

If the discovery process was triggered through flow detection at the originating router, the return of the NHRP Reply results in the following events:

A Redirect is constructed using the IPv6/NBMA mapping carried in the NHRP Reply.

The Redirect is unicast to the IP packet flow's source (using the VC on which the flow is arriving at the router, if it is a bi-directional pt-pt VC).

Any Redirect message sent by a router MUST conform to all the rules described in [7] so that the packet is properly validated by the receiving host. Specifically, if the target of the resulting short-cut is the destination host then the ICMP Target Address MUST be the same as the ICMP Destination Address in the original message. If the target of the short-cut is an egress router then the ICMP Target Address MUST be a Link Local address of the egress router that is unique to the NBMA cloud to which the router's NBMA interface is attached.

Also note that egress routers may subsequently redirect the source host. To do so, the Link Local ICMP Source Address of the Redirect message MUST be the same as the Link Local ICMP Target Address of the original Redirect message.

Note that the router constructing the NHRP Reply does so using the NBMA address returned by the target host when the target host first accepted the flow of IP traffic. This retains a useful feature of Neighbor Discovery - destination interface load sharing.

Upon receipt of a NHRP NAK reply or error indication for a flow-triggered shortcut attempt, no indication is sent to the source of the flow.

3.2.3.1 NHRP/ND packet translation rules.

The following translation rules are meant to augment the packet format specification in section 5 of the NHRP specification [8], covering those packet fields specifically utilized by the IPv6/NBMA architecture.

NHRP messages are constructed and sent according to the rules in [8]. The value of the NBMA technology specific fields such as arafn, arpro.type, ar$pro.snap and link layer address format are defined in NBMA-specific companion documents. Source, destination or client protocol addresses in the common header or CIE of a NHRP message are always IPv6 addresses of length 16.

When constructing an host-triggered NHRP resolution request in response to a Neighbor Solicitation:

The ar$hopcnt field MUST be smaller than the shortcut limit value specified in the shortcut limit option included in the triggering NS message. This ensures that hosts have control over the reach of their shortcut request. Note that the shortcut limit given in the option is relative to the requesting host, thus the requirement of ar$hopcnt being smaller than the given shortcut limit.

The Flags field in the common header of the NHRP resolution request SHOULD have the Q and S bits set.

The U bit SHOULD be set. NBMA and protocol source addresses are those of the router constructing the request.

The target address from the NS message is used as the NHRP destination protocol address. A CIE SHALL NOT be specified.

When constructing a NHRP resolution request as a result of flow detection, the choice of values is configuration dependent.

A NHRP resolution reply is build according to the rules in [8].

For each CIE returned, the holding time is 10 minutes.

The MTU may be 0 or a value specified in the NBMA-specific companion document.

A successful NHRP resolution reply for a host-triggered shortcut attempt is translated into an IPv6 Redirect message as follows:

```
IP Fields:
   Source Address
         The link-local address assigned to the router's interface
         from which this message is sent.
   Destination Address
         IPv6 Source Address of the triggering NS
   Hop Limit
         255
```

ICMP Fields:
  Target Address
      NHRP Client Protocol Address
  Destination Address
      Target of triggering NS (this is equivalent to the NHRP Destination Protocol Address)
  Target link-layer address
      NHRP Client NBMA Address

All NHRP extensions currently defined in [8] have no effect on NHRP/ND translation and MAY be used in NHRP messages for IPv6.

3.2.3.2 NHRP Purge rules.

Purges are generated by NHRP when changes are detected that invalidate a previously issued NHRP Reply (this may include topology changes, or a target host going down or changing identity). Any IPv6 shortcut previously established on the basis of newly purged information SHOULD be torn down.

Routers SHALL keep track of NHRP cache entries for which they have issued Neighbor Advertisements or Router Redirects. If a NHRP Purge is received that invalidates information previously issued to local host, the router SHALL issue a Router Redirect specifying the router itself as the new best next-hop for the affected IPv6 target.

Routers SHALL keep track of Neighbor cache entries that have previously been used to generate an NHRP Reply. The expiry of any such Neighbor cache entry SHALL result in a NHRP Purge being sent towards the router that originally requested the NHRP Reply.

3.3. Neighbor Unreachability Detection.

Neighbor Solicitations sent for the purposes of Neighbor Unreachability Detection (NUD) are unicast to the Neighbor in question, using the VC that is already open to that Neighbor. This suggests that as far as NUD is concerned, the Transient Neighbor is indistinguishable from an On-LL Neighbor.

3.4. Duplicate Address Detection.

Duplicate Address Detection is only required within the link-local scope, which in this case is the LL-local scope. Transient Neighbors are outside the scope of the LL. No particular interaction is required between the mechanism for establishing shortcuts and the mechanism for detection of duplicate link local addresses.

4 Node Operation Concepts.

This section describes node operations for performing basic functions (such as sending and receiving data) on a Logical Link. The application of these basic functions to the operation of the various IPv6 protocols such as Neighbor Discovery is described in Appendix A.

The majority of this section applies only to NBMA networks when used to provide point to point and point to multipoint SVCs. Section 7 discusses the case where the NBMA network is being used to supply only point to point PVCs.

4.1.Connecting to a Logical Link.

Before a node can send or receive IPv6 datagrams its underlying IPv6/NBMA interface(s) must first join a Logical Link.

An IPv6/NBMA driver SHALL establish a pt-pt VC to the MARS associated with its Logical Link, and register as a Cluster Member [5]. The node's IPv6/NBMA interface will then be a member of the LL, have a Cluster Member ID (CMI) assigned, and can begin supporting IPv6 and IPv6 ND operations.

If the node is a host or router starting up it SHALL issue a single group MARS_JOIN for the following groups:

- Its derived Solicited-node address(es) with link-local scope.
- The All-nodes address with link-local scope.
- Other configured multicast groups with at least link-local scope.

If the node is a router it SHALL additionally issue:

- A single group MARS_JOIN for the All-routers address with link-local scope.
- A block MARS_JOIN for the range(s) of IPv6 multicast addresses (with greater than link-local scope) for which promiscuous reception is required.

The encapsulation mechanism for, and key field values of, MARS control messages SHALL be defined in companion documents specific to particular NBMA network technologies.

4.2 Joining a Multicast Group.

This section describes the node's behavior when it gets a JoinLocalGroup request from the IPv6 Layer. The details of how this behavior is achieved are going to be implementation specific.

If a JoinLocalGroup for a node-local address is received, the IPv6/NBMA driver SHALL return success indication to the caller and take no additional action. (Packets sent to node-local addresses never reach the IPv6/NBMA driver.)

If a JoinLocalGroup is received for an address with greater than node-local scope, the IPv6/NBMA driver SHALL send an appropriate single group MARS_JOIN request to register this address with the MARS.

4.3. Leaving a Multicast Group.

This section describes the node's behavior when it gets a LeaveLocalGroup request from the IPv6 Layer. The details of how this behavior is achieved are going to be implementation specific.

If a LeaveLocalGroup for a node-local address is received, the IPv6/NBMA driver SHALL return success indication to the caller and take no additional action. (Packets sent to node-local addresses never reach the IPv6/NBMA driver.)

If a LeaveLocalGroup is received for an address with greater than node-local scope, the IPv6/NBMA driver SHALL send an appropriate single group MARS_LEAVE request to deregister this address with the MARS.

4.4. Sending Data.

Separate processing and encapsulation rules apply for outbound unicast and multicast packets.

4.4.1. Sending Unicast Data.

The IP level 'next hop' for each outbound unicast IPv6 packet is used to identify a pt-pt VC on which to forward the packet.

For NBMA networks where LLC/SNAP encapsulation is typically used (e.g. ATM or SMDS), the IPv6 packet SHALL be encapsulated with the following LLC/SNAP header and sent over the VC.

```
[0xAA-AA-03][0x00-00-00][0x86-DD][IPv6 packet]
    (LLC)        (OUI)      (PID)
```

For NBMA networks that do not use LLC/SNAP encapsulation, an alternative rule SHALL be specified in the NBMA-specific companion document.

If no pt-pt VC exists for the next hop address for the packet, the node SHALL place a call to set up a VC to the next hop destination. Any time the IPv6/NBMA driver receives a unicast packet for transmission the IPv6 layer will already have determined the link-layer (NBMA) address of the next hop. Thus, the information needed to place the NBMA call to the next hop will be available.

The sending node SHOULD queue the packet that triggered the call request, and send it when the call is established.

If the call to the next hop destination node fails the sending node SHALL discard the packet that triggered the call setup. Persistent failure to create a VC to the next hop destination will be detected and handled at the IPv6 Network Layer through NUD.

At this time no rules are specified for mapping outbound packets to VCs using anything more than the packet's destination address.

4.4.2. Sending Multicast Data.

The IP level 'next hop' for each outbound multicast IPv6 packet is used to identify a pt-pt or pt-mpt VC on which to forward the packet.

For NBMA networks where LLC/SNAP encapsulation is typically used (e.g. ATM or SMDS), multicast packets SHALL be encapsulated in the following manner:

```
[0xAA-AA-03][0x00-00-5E][0x00-01][pkt$cmi][0x86DD][IPv6
packet]
    (LLC)        (OUI)      (PID)     (mars encaps)
```

The IPv6/NBMA driver's Cluster Member ID SHALL be copied into the 2 octet pkt$cmi field prior to transmission.

For NBMA networks that do not use LLC/SNAP encapsulation, an alternative rule SHALL be specified in the NBMA-specific companion document. Some mechanism for carrying the IPv6/NBMA driver's Cluster Member ID SHALL be provided.

If the packet's destination is one of the following multicast addresses, it SHALL be sent over the IPv6/NBMA driver's direct pt-pt VC to the MARS:

- A Solicited-node address with link-local scope.
- The All-nodes address with link-local scope.
- The All-routers address with link-local scope.
- A DHCP-v6 relay or server multicast address.

The MARS SHALL then redistribute the IPv6 packet as described in section 3.1.1. (If the VC to the MARS has been idle timed out for some reason, it MUST be re-established before forwarding the packet to the MARS.)

If packet's destination is any other address, then the usual MARS client mechanisms are used by the IPv6/NBMA driver to select and/or establish a pt-mpt VC on which the packet is to be sent.

At this time no rules are specified for mapping outbound packets to VCs using anything more than the packet's destination address.

4.5. Receiving Data.

Packets received using the encapsulation shown in section 4.4.1 SHALL be de-encapsulated and passed up to the IPv6 layer. The IPv6 layer then determines how the incoming packet is to be handled.

Packets received using the encapsulation specified in section 4.4.2 SHALL have their pkt$cmi field compared to the local IPv6/NBMA driver's own CMI. If the pkt$cmi in the header matches the local CMI the packet SHALL be silently dropped. Otherwise, the packet SHALL be de-encapsulated and passed to the IPv6 layer. The IPv6 layer then determines how the incoming packet is to be handled.

For NBMA networks that do not use LLC/SNAP encapsulation, alternative rules SHALL be specified in the NBMA-specific companion document.

The IPv6/NBMA driver SHALL NOT attempt to filter out multicast IPv6 packets arriving with encapsulation defined for unicast packets, nor attempt to filter out unicast IPv6 packets arriving with encapsulation defined for multicast packets.

4.6. VC Setup and release for unicast data.

Unicast VCs are maintained separately from multicast VCs. The setup and maintenance of multicast VCs are handled by the MARS client in each IPv6/NBMA driver [5]. Only the setup and maintenance of pt-pt VCs for unicast IPv6 traffic will be described here. Only best effort unicast VCs are considered. The creation of VCs for other classes of service is outside the scope of this document.

Before sending a packet to a new destination within the same LL a node will first perform a Neighbor Discovery on the intra-LL target. This is done to resolve the IPv6 destination address into a link-layer address which the sender can then use to send unicast packets.

Appendix A.1.1 contains non-normative, descriptive text covering the Neighbor Solicitation/Advertisement exchange and eventual establishment of a new SVC.

A Redirect message (either a redirect to a node on the same LL, or a shortcut redirect to a node outside the LL) results in the sending (redirected) node creating a new pt-pt VC to a new receiving node. the Redirect message SHALL contain the link layer (NBMA) address of the new receiving IPv6/NBMA interface. The redirected node does not concern itself where the new receiving node is located on the NBMA network. The redirected node will set up a pt-pt VC to the new node if one does not previously exist. The redirected node will then use the new VC to send data rather than whatever VC it had previously been using.

Redirects are unidirectional. Even after the source has reacted to a redirect, the destination will continue to send IPv6 packets back to the redirected node on the old path. This happens because the destination node has no way of determining the IPv6 address of the other end of a new VC in the absence of Neighbor Discovery. Thus, redirects will not result in both ends of a connection using the new VC. IPv6 redirects are not intended to provide symmetrical redirection. If the non-redirected node eventually receives a redirect it MAY discover the existing VC to the target node and use that rather than creating a new VC.

It is desirable that VCs are released when no longer needed.

> An IPv6/NBMA driver SHALL release any VC that has been idle for 20 minutes.

This time limit MAY be reduced through configuration or as specified in companion documents for specific NBMA networks.

If a Neighbor or Destination cache entry is purged then any VCs associated with the purged entry SHOULD be released.

If the state of an entry in the Neighbor cache is set to STALE, then any VCs associated with the stale entry SHOULD be released.

4.7 NBMA SVC Signaling Support and MTU issues.

Mechanisms for signaling the establishment and teardown of pt-pt and pt-mpt SVCs for different NBMA networks SHALL be specified in companion documents.

Since any given IPv6/NBMA driver will not know if the remote end of a VC is in the same LL, drivers SHALL implement NBMA-specific mechanisms to negotiate acceptable MTUs at the VC level. These mechanisms SHALL be specified in companion documents.

However, IPv6/NBMA drivers can assume that they will always be talking to another driver attached to the same type of NBMA network. (For example, an IPv6/NBMA driver does not need to consider the possibility of establishing a shortcut VC directly to an IPv6/FR driver.)

5. Interface Tokens, Link Layer Address Options, Link-Local Addresses

5.1 Interface Tokens

Each IPv6 interface must have an interface token from which to form IPv6 autoconfigured addresses. This interface token must be unique within a Logical Link to prevent the creation of duplicate addresses when stateless address configuration is used.

In cases where two nodes on the same LL produce the same interface token then one interface MUST choose another host-token. All implementations MUST support manual configuration of interface tokens to allow operators to manually change a interface token on a per-LL basis. Operators may choose to manually set interface tokens for reasons other than eliminating duplicate addresses.

All interface tokens MUST be 64 bits in length and formatted as described in the following sections. The hosts tokens will be based on the format of an EUI-64 identifier [10]. Refer to [19 - Appendix A] for a description of creating IPv6 EUI-64 based interface identifiers.

5.1.1 Single Logical Links on a Single NBMA Interface

Physical NBMA interfaces will generally have some local identifier that may be used to generate a unique IPv6/NBMA interface token. The exact mechanism for generating interface tokens SHALL be specified in companion documents specific to each NBMA network.

5.1.2 Multiple Logical Links on a Single NBMA Interface

Physical NBMA interfaces MAY be used to provide multiple logical NBMA interfaces. Since each logical NBMA interface MAY support an independent IPv6 interface, two separate scenarios are possible:

- A single host with separate IPv6/NBMA interfaces onto a number of independent Logical Links.

- A set of 2 or more 'virtual hosts' (vhosts) sharing a common NBMA driver. Each vhost is free to establish IPv6/NBMA interfaces associated with different or common LLs. However, vhosts are bound by the same requirement as normal hosts - no two interfaces to the same LL can share the same interface token.

In the first scenario, since each IPv6/NBMA interface is associated with a different LL, each interface's external identity can be differentiated by the LL's routing prefix. Thus, the host can re-use a single unique interface token across all its IPv6/NBMA interfaces. (Internally the host will tag received packets in some locally specific manner to identify what IPv6/NBMA interface they arrived on. However, this is an issue generic to IPv6, and does not required clarification in this document.)

The second scenario is more complex, but likely to be rarer.

When supporting multiple logical NBMA interfaces over a single physical NBMA interface, independent and unique identifiers SHALL be generated for each virtual NBMA interface to enable the construction of unique IPv6/NBMA interface tokens. The exact mechanism for generating interface tokens SHALL be specified in companion documents specific to each NBMA network.

5.2 Link Layer Address Options

Neighbor Discovery defines two option fields for carrying link-layer specific source and target addresses.

Between IPv6/NBMA interfaces, the format for these two options is adapted from the MARS [5] and NHRP [8] specs. It SHALL be:

```
[Type][Length][NTL][STL][..NBMA Number..][..NBMA
Subaddress..]
|   Fixed    ||             Link layer address
|
```

[Type] is a one octet field.

1 for Source link-layer address.
2 for Target link-layer address.

[Length] is a one octet field.

The total length of the option in multiples of 8 octets. Zeroed bytes are added to the end of the option to ensure its length is a multiple of 8 octets.

[NTL] is a one octet 'Number Type & Length' field.

[STL] is a one octet 'SubAddress Type & Length' field.

[NBMA Number] is a variable length field. It is always present. This contains the primary NBMA address.

[NBMA Subaddress] is a variable length field. It may or may not be present. This contains any NBMA subaddress that may be required.

If the [NBMA Subaddress] is not present, the option ends after the [NBMA Number] (and any additional padding for 8 byte alignment).

The contents and interpretation of the [NTL], [STL], [NBMA Number], and [NBMA Subaddress] fields are specific to each NBMA network, and SHALL be specified in companion documents.

5.3 Link-Local Addresses

The IPv6 link-local address is formed by appending the interface token, as defined above, to the prefix FE80::/64.

```
   10 bits            54 bits                  64 bits
 +----------+-----------------------+----------------------------+
 |1111111010|         (zeros)       |     Interface Token        |
 +----------+-----------------------+----------------------------+
```

6. Conclusion and Open Issues

This document describes a general architecture for IPv6 over NBMA networks. It forms the basis for subsidiary companion documents that provide details for various specific NBMA technologies (such as ATM or Frame Relay). The IPv6 over NBMA architecture allows conventional host-side operation of the IPv6 Neighbor Discovery protocol, while also supporting the establishment of 'shortcut' NBMA forwarding paths (when dynamically signaled NBMA links are available).

The IPv6 "Link" is generalized to "Logical Link" in an analagous manner to the IPv4 "Logical IP Subnet". The MARS protocol is augmented and used to provide relatively efficient intra Logical Link multicasting of IPv6 packets, and distribution of Discovery messages. Shortcut NBMA level paths are supported either through router based flow detection, or host originated explicit requests. Neighbor Discovery is used without modification for all intra-LL control (including the initiation of NBMA shortcut discovery). Router to router NHRP is used to obtain the IPv6/NBMA address mappings for shortcut targets outside a source's Logical Link.

7. Security Considerations

This architecture introduces no new protocols, but depends on existing protocols (NHRP, IPv6, ND, MARS) and is therefore subject to all the security threats inherent in these protocols. This architecture should not be used in a domain where any of the base protocols are considered unacceptably insecure. However, this protocol itself does not introduce additional security threats.

While this proposal does not introduce any new security mechanisms all current IPv6 security mechanisms will work without modification for NBMA. This includes both authentication and encryption for both Neighbor Discovery protocols as well as the exchange of IPv6 data packets. The MARS protocol is modified in a manner that does not affect or augment the security offered by RFC 2022.

Acknowledgments

Eric Nordmark confirmed the usefulness of ND Redirect messages in private email during the March 1996 IETF. The discussions with various ION WG members during the June and December 1996 IETF helped solidify the architecture described here. Grenville Armitage's original work on IPv6/NBMA occurred while employed at Bellcore. Elements of section 5 were borrowed from Matt Crawford's memo on IPv6 over Ethernet.

Authors' Addresses

Grenville Armitage
Bell Laboratories, Lucent Technologies
101 Crawfords Corner Road
Holmdel, NJ 07733
USA

EMail: gja@lucent.com

Peter Schulter
Bright Tiger Technologies
125 Nagog Park
Acton, MA 01720

EMail: paschulter@acm.org

Markus Jork
European Applied Research Center
Digital Equipment GmbH
CEC Karlsruhe
Vincenz-Priessnitz-Str. 1
D-76131 Karlsruhe
Germany

EMail: jork@kar.dec.com

Geraldine Harter
Digital UNIX Networking
Compaq Computer Corporation
110 Spit Brook Road
Nashua, NH 03062

EMail: harter@zk3.dec.com

References

[1] Deering, S. and R. Hinden, "Internet Protocol, Version 6 (IPv6) Specification", RFC 2460, December 1998.

[2] ATM Forum, "ATM User Network Interface (UNI) Specification Version 3.1", ISBN 0-13-393828-X, Prentice Hall, Englewood Cliffs, NJ, June 1995.

[3] Crawford, M., "A Method for the Transmission of IPv6 Packets over Ethernet Networks", RFC 1972, August 1996.

[4] Heinanen, J., "Multiprotocol Encapsulation over ATM Adaptation Layer 5", RFC 1483, July 1993.

[5] Armitage, G., "Support for Multicast over UNI 3.1 based ATM Networks", RFC 2022, November 1996.

[6] Hinden, R. and S. Deering, "IP Version 6 Addressing Architecture", RFC 2373, July 1998.

[7] Narten, T., Nordmark, E. and W. Simpson, "Neighbor Discovery for IP Version 6 (IPv6)", RFC 2461, December 1998.

[8] Luciani, J., Katz, D., Piscitello, D. Cole B and N. Doraswamy, "NBMA Next Hop Resolution Protocol (NHRP)", RFC 2332, April 1998.

[9] Thomson, S. and T. Narten, "IPv6 Stateless Address Autoconfiguration", RFC 2462, December 1998.

[10] "64-Bit Global Identifier Format Tutorial", http://standards.ieee.org/db/oui/tutorials/EUI64.html.

[11] Katsube, Y., Nagami, K. and H. Esaki, "Toshiba's Router Architecture Extensions for ATM : Overview", RFC 2098, February 1997.

[12] P. Newman, T. Lyon, G. Minshall, "Flow Labeled IP: ATM under IP", Proceedings of INFOCOM'96, San Francisco, March 1996, pp.1251-1260

[13] Piscitello, D. and J. Lawrence, "The Transmission of IP Datagrams over the SMDS Service", RFC 1209, March 1991.

[14] Plummer, D., "An Ethernet Address Resolution Protocol - or - Converting Network Protocol Addresses to 48.bit Ethernet Address for Transmission on Ethernet Hardware", STD 37, RFC 826, November 1982.

[15] McCann, J., Deering, S. and J. Mogul, "Path MTU Discovery for IP version 6", RFC 1981, August 1996.

[16] Bradner, S., "Key words for use in RFCs to Indicate Requirement Levels", BCP 14, RFC 2119, March 1997.

[17] Armitage, G., Schulter, P. and M. Jork, "IPv6 over ATM Networks", RFC 2492, January 1999.

[18] C. Perkins, J. Bound, "Dynamic Host Configuration Protocol for IPv6 (DHCPv6)", Work in Progress.

[19] Hinden, R. and S. Deering, "IP Version 6 Addressing Architecture", RFC 2373, July 1998.

Appendix A. IPv6 Protocol Operation Description

The IPv6 over NBMA model described in this document maintains the complete semantics of the IPv6 protocols. No changes need to be made to the IPv6 Network Layer. Since the concept of the security association is not being changed for NBMA, this framework maintains complete IPv6 security semantics and features. This allows IPv6 nodes to choose their responses to solicitations based on security information as is done with other datalinks, thereby maintaining the semantics of Neighbor Discovery since it is always the solicited node that chooses what (and even if) to reply to the solicitation. Thus, NBMA will be transparent to the network layer except in cases where extra services (such as QoS VCs) are offered.

The remainder of this Appendix describes how the core IPv6 protocols will operate within the model described here.

A.1 Neighbor Discovery Operations

Before performing any sort of Neighbor discover operation, each node must first join the all-node multicast group, and it's solicited node multicast address (the use of this address in relation to DAD is described in A.1.4). The IPv6 network layer will join these multicast groups as described in 4.2.

A.1.1 Performing Address Resolution

An IPv6 host performs address resolution by sending a Neighbor Solicitation to the solicited-node multicast address of the target host, as described in [7]. The Neighbor Solicitation message will contain a Source Link-Layer Address Option set to the soliciting node's NBMA address on the LL.

When the local node's IPv6/NBMA driver is passed the Neighbor Solicitation message from the IPv6 network layer, it follows the steps described in section 4.4.2 Sending Multicast Data.

One or more nodes will receive the Neighbor Solicitation message. The nodes will process the data as described in section 4.5 and pass the de-encapsulated packets to the IPv6 network layer.

If the receiving node is the target of the Neighbor Solicitation it will update its Neighbor cache with the soliciting node's NBMA address, contained in the Neighbor Solicitation message's Source Link-Layer Address Option as described in [7].

The solicited IPv6 host will respond to the Neighbor Solicitation with a Neighbor Advertisement message sent to the IPv6 unicast address of the soliciting node. The Neighbor Advertisement message will contain a Target Link-Layer Address Option set to the solicited node's NBMA address on the LL.

The solicited node's IPv6/NBMA driver will be passed the Neighbor Advertisement and the soliciting node's link-layer address from the IPv6 network layer. It will then follow the steps described in section section 4.4.1 to send the NA message to the soliciting node. This will create a pt-pt VC between the solicited node and soliciting node if one did not already exist.

The soliciting node will then receive the Neighbor Advertisement message over the new PtP VC, de-encapsulate the message, and pass it to the IPv6 Network layer for processing as described in section 4.5. The soliciting node will then make the appropriate entries in it's Neighbor cache, including caching the NBMA link-layer address of the solicited node as described in [7].

At this point each system has a complete Neighbor cache entry for the other system. They can exchange data over the pt-pt VC newly created by the solicited node when it returned the Neighbor Advertisement, or create a new VC.

An IPv6 host can also send an Unsolicited Neighbor Advertisemnent to the all-nodes multicast address. When the local node IPv6/NBMA driver is passed the Neighbor Advertisement from the IPv6 network layer, it follows the steps described in section 4.4.2 to send the NA message to the all-nodes multicast address. Each node will process the incoming packet as described in section 4.5 and then pass the packet to the IPv6 network layer where it will be processed as described in [7].

A.1.2 Performing Router Discovery

Router Discovery is described in [7]. To support Router Discovery an IPv6 router will join the IPv6 all-routers multicast group address. When the IPv6/NBMA driver gets the JoinLocalGroup request from the IPv6 Network Layer, it follows the process described in section 4.2.

IPv6 routers periodically send unsolicited Router Advertisements announcing their availability on the LL. When an IPv6 router sends an unsolicited Router Advertisement, it sends a data packet addressed to the IPv6 all-nodes multicast address. When the local node IPv6/NBMA driver gets the Router Advertisement message from the IPv6 network layer, it transmits the message by following steps described in section 4.4.2. The MARS will transmit the packet on the LL's

ClusterControlVC, which sends the packets to all nodes on the LL. Each node on the LL will then process the incoming packet as described in section 4.5 and pass the received packet to the IPv6 Network layer for processing as appropriate.

To perform Router Discovery, an IPv6 host sends a Router Solicitation message to the all-routers multicast address. When the local node IPv6/NBMA driver gets the request from the IPv6 Network Layer to send the packet, it follows the steps described in section 4.4.2. The RS message will be sent to either those nodes which have joined the all-routers multicast group or to all nodes. The nodes which receive the RA message will process the message as described in section 4.5 and pass the RA message up to the IPv6 layer for processing. Only those nodes which are routers will process the message and respond to it.

An IPv6 router responds to a Router Solicitation by sending a Router Advertisement addressed to the IPv6 all-nodes multicast address if the source address of the Router Solicitation was the unspecified address. If the source address in the Router Solicitation is not the unspecified address, the the router will unicast the Router Advertisement to the soliciting node. If the router sends the Router Advertisement to the all-nodes multicast address then it follows the steps described above for unsolicited Router Advertisements.

If the Router Advertisement is to be unicast to the soliciting node, the IPv6 network layer will give the node's IPv6/NBMA driver the Router Advertisement and link-layer address of the soliciting node (obtained through Address Resolution if necessary) which will send the packet according to the steps described in section 4.4.1 This will result in a new pt-pt VC being created between the router and the soliciting node if one did not already exist.

The soliciting node will receive and process the Router Advertisement as described in section 4.5 and will pass the RA message to the IPv6 network layer. The IPv6 network layer may, depending on the state of the Neighbor cache entry, update the Neighbor cache with the router's NBMA address, contained in the Router Advertisement message's Source Link-Layer Address Option.

If a pt-pt VC is set up during Router Discovery, subsequent IPv6 best effort unicast data between the soliciting node and the router will be transmitted over the new PtP VC.

A.1.3 Performing Neighbor Unreachability Detection (NUD)

Neighbor Unreachability Detection (NUD) is the process by which an IPv6 host determines that a neighbor is no longer reachable, as described in [7]. Each Neighbor cache entry contains information used by the NUD algorithm to detect reachability failures. Confirmation of a neighbor's reachability comes either from upper-layer protocol indications that data recently sent to the neighbor was received, or from the receipt of a Neighbor Advertisement message in response to a Neighbor Solicitation probe.

Connectivity failures at the node's IPv6/NBMA driver, such as released VCs (see section 4.6) and the inability to create a VC to a neighbor (see section 4.4.1), are detected and handled at the IPv6 network layer, through Neighbor Unreachability Detection. The node's IPv6/NBMA driver does not attempt to detect or recover from these conditions.

A persistent failure to create a VC from the IPv6 host to one of its IPv6 neighbors will be detected and handled through NUD. On each attempt to send data from the IPv6 host to its neighbor, the node's IPv6/NBMA driver will attempt to set up a VC to the neighbor, and failing to do so, will drop the packet. IPv6 reachability confirmation timers will eventually expire, and the neighbor's Neighbor cache entry will enter the PROBE state. The PROBE state will cause the IPv6 host to unicast Neighbor Solicitations to the neighbor, which will be dropped by the local node's IPv6/NBMA driver after again failing to setup the VC. The IPv6 host will therefore never receive the solicited Neighbor Advertisements needed for reachability confirmation, causing the neighbor's entry to be deleted from the Neighbor cache. The next time the IPv6 host tries to send data to that neighbor, address resolution will be performed. Depending on the reason for the previous failure, connectivity to the neighbor could be re-established (for example, if the previous VC setup failure was caused by an obsolete link-layer address in the Neighbor cache).

In the event that a VC from an IPv6 neighbor is released, the next time a packet is sent from the IPv6 host to the neighbor, the node's IPv6/NBMA driver will recognize that it no longer has a VC to that neighbor and attempt to setup a new VC to the neighbor. If, on the first and on subsequent transmissions, the node is unable to create a VC to the neighbor, NUD will detect and handle the failure as described earlier (handling the persistent failure to create a VC from the IPv6 host to one of its IPv6 neighbors). Depending on the reason for the previous failure, connectivity to the neighbor may or may not be re-established.

A.1.4 Performing Duplicate Address Detection (DAD)

An IPv6 host performs Duplicate Address Detection (DAD) to determine that the address it wishes to use on the LL (i.e. a tentative address) is not already in use, as described in [9] and [7]. Duplicate Address Detection is performed on all addresses the host wishes to use, regardless of the configuration mechanism used to obtain the address.

Prior to performing Duplicate Address Detection, a host will join the all-nodes multicast address and the solicited-node multicast address corresponding to the host's tentative address (see 4.2. Joining a Multicast Group). The IPv6 host initiates Duplicate Address Detection by sending a Neighbor Solicitation to solicited-node multicast address corresponding to the host's tentative address, with the tentative address as the target. When the local node's IPv6/NBMA driver gets the Neighbor Solicitation message from the IPv6 network layer, it follows the steps outlined in section 4.4.2. The NS message will be sent to those nodes which joined the target solicited-node multicast group or to all nodes. The DAD NS message will be received by one or more nodes on the LL and processed by each as described in section 4.5. Note that the MARS client of the sending node will filter out the message so that the sending node's IPv6 network layer will not see the message. The IPv6 network layer of any node which is not a member of the target solicited-node multicast group will discard the Neighbor Solicitation message.

If no other hosts have joined the solicited-node multicast address corresponding to the tentative address, then the host will not receive a Neighbor Advertisement containing its tentative address as the target. The host will perform the retransmission logic described in [9], terminate Duplicate Address Detection, and assign the tentative address to the NBMA interface.

Otherwise, other hosts on the LL that have joined the solicited-node multicast address corresponding to the tentative address will process the Neighbor Solicitation. The processing will depend on whether or not receiving IPv6 host considers the target address to be tentative.

If the receiving IPv6 host's address is not tentative, the host will respond with a Neighbor Advertisement containing the target address. Because the source of the Neighbor Solicitation is the unspecified address, the host sends the Neighbor Advertisement to the all-nodes multicast address following the steps outlined in section 4.4.2. The DAD NA message will be received and processed by the MARS clients on all nodes in the LL as described in section 4.5. Note that the sending node will filter the incoming message since the CMI in the message header will match that of the receiving node. All other nodes will de-encapsulate the message and pass it to the IPv6 network layer. The host performing DAD will detect that its tentative address is the target of the Neighbor Advertisement, and determine that the tentative address is not unique and cannot be assigned to its NBMA interface.

If the receiving IPv6 host's address is tentative, then both hosts are performing DAD using the same tentative address. The receiving host will determine that the tentative address is not unique and cannot be assigned to its NBMA interface.

A.1.5 Processing Redirects

An IPv6 router uses a Redirect Message to inform an IPv6 host of a better first-hop for reaching a particular destination, as described in [7]. This can be used to direct hosts to a better first hop router, another host on the same LL, or to a transient neighbor on another LL. The IPv6 router will unicast the Redirect to the IPv6 source address that triggered the Redirect. The router's IPv6/NBMA driver will transmit the Redirect message using the procedure described in section 4.4.1. This will create a VC between the router and the redirected host if one did not previously exist.

The IPv6/NBMA driver of the IPv6 host that triggered the Redirect will receive the encapsulated Redirect over one of it's pt-pt VCs. It will the de-encapsulate the packet, and pass the Redirect message to the IPv6 Network Layer, as described section 4.5.

Subsequent data sent from the IPv6 host to the destination will be sent to the next-hop address specified in the Redirect Message. For NBMA networks, the Redirect Message should contain the link-layer address option as described in [7] and section 5.2, thus the redirected node will not have to perform a Neighbor Solicitation to learn the link-layer address of the node to which it has been redirected. Thus, the redirect can be to any node on the NBMA network, regardless of the LL membership of the new target node. This allows NBMA hosts to be redirected off their LL to achieve shortcut by using standard IPv6 protocols.

Once redirected, the IPv6 network layer will give the node's IPv6/NBMA driver the IPv6 packet and the link-layer address of the next-hop node when it sends data to the redirected destination. The node's IPv6/NBMA driver will determine if a VC to the next-hop destination exists. If a pt-pt VC does not exist, then the IPv6/NBMA driver will queue the data packet and initiate a setup of a VC to the destination. When the VC is created, or if one already exists, then the node will encapsulate the outgoing data packet and send it on the VC.

Note that Redirects are unidirectional. The redirected host will create a VC to the next-hop destination as specified in the Redirect message, but the next-hop will not be redirected to the source host. Because no Neighbor Discovery takes place, the next-hop destination has no way of determining the identity of the caller when it receives the new VC. Also, since ND does not take place on redirects, the next-hop receives no event that would cause it to update it's neighbor or destination caches. However, it will continue to transmit data back to the redirected host on the former path to the redirected host. The next-hop node should be able to use the new VC from the redirected destination if it too receives a redirect redirecting it to the redirected node. This behavior is consistent with [7].

A.2 Address Configuration

IPv6 addresses are auto-configured using the stateless or stateful address auto-configuration mechanisms, as described in [9] and [18]. The IPv6 auto-configuration process involves creating and verifying the uniqueness of a link-local address on an LL, determining whether to use stateless and/or stateful configurationmechanisms to obtain addresses, and determining if other (non- address) information is to be autoconfigured. IPv6 addresses can also be manually configured, if for example, auto-configuration fails because the autoconfigured link-local address is not unique. An LL administrator specifies the type of autoconfiguration to use; the hosts on an LL receive this autoconfiguration information through Router Advertisement messages.

The following sections describe how stateless, stateful and manual address configuration will work in an IPv6/NBMA environment.

A.2.1 Stateless Address Configuration

IPv6 stateless address configuration is the process by which an IPv6 host autoconfigures its interfaces, as described in [IPV6-ADDRCONF].

When an IPv6 host first starts up, it generates a link-local address for the interface attached to the Logical Link. It then verifies the uniqueness of the link-local address using Duplicate Address Detection (DAD). If the IPv6 host detects that the link-local address is not unique, the autoconfiguration process terminates. The IPv6 host must then be manually configured.

After the IPv6 host determines that the link-local address is unique and has assigned it to the interface on the Logical Link, the IPv6 host will perform Router Discovery to obtain auto-configuration information. The IPv6 host will send out a Router Solicitation and will receive a Router Advertisement, or it will wait for an unsolicited Router Advertisement. The IPv6 host will process the M and O bits of the Router Advertisement, as described in [9] and as a result may invoke stateful address auto- configuration.

If there are no routers on the Logical Link, the IPv6 host will be able to communicate with other IPv6 hosts on the Logical Link using link-local addresses. The IPv6 host will obtain a neighbor's link-layer address using Address Resolution. The IPv6 host will also attempt to invoke stateful auto-configuration, unless it has been explicitly configured not to do so.

A.2.2 Stateful Address Configuration (DHCP)

IPv6 hosts use the Dynamic Host Configuration Protocol (DHCPv6) to perform stateful address auto-configuration, as described in [18].

A DHCPv6 server or relay agent is present on a Logical Link that has been configured with manual or stateful auto-configuration. The DHCPv6 server or relay agent will join the IPv6 DHCPv6 Server/Relay-Agent multicast group on the Logical Link. When the node's IPv6/NBMA driver gets the JoinLocalGroup request from the IPv6 network layer, it follows the process described in section 4.2.

An IPv6 host will invoke stateful auto-configuration if M and O bits of Router Advertisements indicate it should do so, and may invoke stateful auto-configuration if it detects that no routers are present on the Logical Link. An IPv6 host that is obtaining configuration information through the stateful mechanism will hereafter be referred to as a DHCPv6 client.

A DHCPv6 client will send a DHCPv6 Solicit message to the DHCPv6 Server/Relay-Agent multicast address to locate a DHCPv6 Agent. When the soliciting node's IPv6/NBMA driver gets the request from the IPv6 Network Layer to send the packet, it follows the steps described in section 4.4.2. This will result in one or more nodes on the LL receiving the message. Each node that receives the solicitation packet will process it as described in section section 4.5. Only the IPv6 network layer of the DHCPv6 server/relay-agent will accept the packet and process it.

A DHCPv6 Server or Relay Agent on the Logical Link will unicast a DHCPv6 Advertisement to the DHCPv6 client. The IPv6 network layer will give the node's IPv6/NBMA driver the packet and link-layer address of the DHCPv6 client (obtained through Neighbor Discovery if necessary). The node IPv6/NBMA driver will then transmit the packet as described in section 4.4.1. This will result in a new pt-pt VC being created between the server and the client if one did not previously exist.

The DHCP client's IPv6/NBMA driver will receive the encapsulated packet from the DHCP Server or Relay Agent, as described in section 4.5. The node will de-encapsulate the multicast packet and then pass it up to the IPv6 Network Layer for processing. The IPv6 network layer will deliver the DHCPv6 Advertise message to the DHCPv6 client.

Other DHCPv6 messages (Request, Reply, Release and Reconfigure) are unicast between the DHCPv6 client and the DHCPv6 Server. Depending on the reachability of the DHCPv6 client's address, messages exchanged between a DHCPv6 client and a DHCPv6 Server on another LL are sent either via a router or DHCPv6 Relay-Agent. Prior to sending the DHCPv6 message, the IPv6 network layer will perform Neighbor Discovery (if necessary) to obtain the link-layer address corresponding to the packet's next-hop. A pt-pt VC will be set up between the sender and the next hop, and the encapsulated packet transmitted over it, as described in 4.4. Sending Data.

A.2.3 Manual Address Configuration

An IPv6 host will be manually configured if it discovers through DAD that its link-local address is not unique. Once the IPv6 host is configured with a unique interface token, the auto-configuration mechanisms can then be invoked.

A.3 Internet Group Management Protocol (IGMP)

IPv6 multicast routers will use the IGMPv6 protocol to periodically determine group memberships of local hosts. In the framework described here, the IGMPv6 protocols can be used without any special modifications for NBMA. While these protocols might not be the most efficient in this environment, they will still work as described below. However, IPv6 multicast routers connected to an NBMA LL could optionally optimize the IGMP functions by sending MARS_GROUPLIST_REQUEST messages to the MARS serving the LL and determining group memberships by the MARS_GROUPLIST_REPLY messages. Querying the MARS for multicast group membership is an optional enchancement and is not required for routers to determine IPv6 multicast group membership on a LL.

There are three ICMPv6 message types that carry multicast group membership information: the Group Membership Query, Group Membership Report and Group Membership Reduction messages. IGMPv6 will continue to work unmodified over the IPv6/NBMA architecture described in this document.

An IPv6 multicast router receives all IPv6 multicast packets on the LL by joining all multicast groups in promiscuous mode [5]. The MARS server will then cause the multicast router to be added to all existing and future multicast VCs. The IPv6 multicast router will thereafter be the recipient of all IPv6 multicast packets sent within the Logical Link.

An IPv6 multicast router discovers which multicast groups have members in the Logical Link by periodically sending Group Membership Query messages to the IPv6 all-nodes multicast address. When the local node's IPv6/NBMA driver gets the request from the IPv6 network layer to send the Group Membership Query packet, it follows the steps described in 4.4.2. The node determines that the destination address of the packet is the all-nodes multicast address and passes the packet to the node's MARS client where the packet is encapsulated and directly transmitted to the MARS. The MARS then relays the packet to all nodes in the LL. Each node's IPv6/NBMA drivers will receive the packet, de-encapsulate it, and passed it up to the IPv6 Network layer. If the originating node receives the encapsulated packet, the packet will be filtered out by the MARS client since the Cluster Member ID of the receiving node will match the CMI in the packet's MARS encapsulation header.

IPv6 hosts in the Logical Link will respond to a Group Membership Query with a Group Membership Report for each IPv6 multicast group joined by the host. IPv6 hosts can also transmit a Group Membership Report when the host joins a new IPv6 multicast group. The Group Membership Report is sent to the multicast group whose address is being reported. When the local node IPv6/NBMA driver gets the request from the IPv6 network layer to send the packet, it follows the steps described in 4.4.2. The node determines that the packet is being sent to a multicast address so forwards it to the node's MARS client for sending on the appropriate VC.

The Group Membership Report packets will arrive at every node which is a member of the group being reported through one of the VC attached to each node's MARS client. The MARS client will de-encapsulate the incoming packet and the packet will be passed to the IPv6 network layer for processing. The MARS client of the sending node will filter out the packet when it receives it.

An IPv6 host sends a Group Membership Reduction message when the host leaves an IPv6 multicast group. The Group Membership Reduction is sent to the multicast group the IPv6 host is leaving. The transmission and receipt of Group Membership Reduction messages are handled in the same manner as Group Membership Reports.

Appendix B. Alternative models of MARS support for Intra-LL ND

B.1 Simplistic approach - Use MARS 'as is'.

The IPv6/NBMA driver utilizes the standard MARS protocol to establish a VC forwarding path out of the interface on which it can transmit all multicast IPv6 packets, including ICMPv6 packets. The IPv6 packets are then transmitted, and received by the intended destination set, using separate pt-mpt VCs per destination group.

In this approach all the protocol elements in [5] are used 'as is'. However, SVC resource consumption must be taken into consideration. Unfortunately, ND assumes that link level multicast resources are best conserved by generating a sparsely distributed set of Solicited Node multicast addresses (to which discovery queries are initially sent). The original goal was to minimize the number of innocent nodes that simultaneously received discovery messages really intended for someone else.

However, in connection oriented NBMA environments it becomes equally (or more) important to minimize the number of independent VCs that a given NBMA interface is required to originate or terminate. If we treat the MARS service as a 'black box' the sparse Solicited Node address space can lead to a large number of short-use, but longer lived, pt-mpt VCs (generated whenever the node is transmitting Neighbor Solicitations). Even more annoying, these VCs are only useful for additional packets being sent to their associated Solicited Node multicast address. A new pt-pt VC is required to actually carry the unicast IPv6 traffic that prompted the Neighbor Solicitation.

The axis of inefficiency brought about by the sparse Solicited Nodes address space is orthogonal to the VC mesh vs Multicast Server tradeoff. Typically a multicast server aggregates traffic flow to a common multicast group onto a single VC. To reduce the VC consumption for ND, we need to aggregate across the Solicited Node address space - performing aggregation on the basis of a packet's function rather than its explicit IPv6 destination. The trade-off here is that the aggregation removes the original value of scattering nodes sparsely across the Solicited Nodes space. This is a price of the mismatch between ND and connection oriented networks.

B.2 MARS as a Link (Multicast) Server.

One possible aggregation mechanism is for every node's IPv6/NBMA driver to trap multicast ICMPv6 packets carrying multicast ND or RD messages, and logically remap their destinations to the All Nodes group (link local scope). By ensuring that the All Nodes group is supported by an MCS, the resultant VC load within the LL will be significantly reduced.

A further optimization is for every node's IPv6/NBMA driver to trap multicast ICMPv6 packets carrying multicast ND or RD messages, and send them to the MARS itself for retransmission on ClusterControlVC (involving a trivial extension to the MARS itself.) This approach recognizes that in any LL where IPv6 multicasting is supported:

- Nodes already have a pt-pt VC to their MARS.

- The MARS has a pt-mpt VC (ClusterControlVC) out to all Cluster members (LL members registered for multicast support).

Because the VCs between a MARS and its MARS clients carry LLC/SNAP encapsulated packets, ICMP packets can be multiplexed along with normal MARS control messages. In essence the MARS behaves as a multicast server for non-MARS packets that it receives from around the LL.

As there is no requirement that a MARS client accepts only MARS control messages on ClusterControlVC, ICMP packets received in this fashion may be passed to every node's IP layer without further comment. Within the IP layer, filtering will occur based on the packet's actual destination IP address, and only the targeted node will end up responding.

Regrettably this approach does result in the entire Cluster's membership having to receive a variety of ICMPv6 messages that they will always throw away.

Appendix C. Flow detection

The relationship between IPv6 packet flows, Quality of Service guarantees, and optimal use of underlying IP and NBMA network resources are still subjects of ongoing research in the IETF (specifically the ISSLL, RSVP, IPNG, and ION working groups). This document currently only describes the use of flow detection as a means to optimize the use of NBMA network resources through the establishment of inter-LL shortcuts.

C.1. The use of non-zero FlowID to suppress flow detection

For the purposes of this IPv6/NBMA architecture, a flow is:

> A related sequence of IPv6 packets that the first hop router is allowed to perform flow-detection on for the purposes of triggering shortcut discovery.

How these packets are considered to be related to each other (e.g. through common header fields such as IPv6 destination addresses) is a local configuration issue.

The flow-detection rule specifies that only packets with a zero FlowID can be considered as flows for which shortcut discovery may be triggered. The rationale behind this decision is:

> NBMA shortcuts are for the benefit of 'the network' optimizing its forwarding of IPv6 packets in the absence of any other guidance from the host.
>
> It is desirable for an IPv6/NBMA host to have some mechanism for overriding attempts by 'the network' to optimize its internal forwarding path.
>
> A zero FlowID has IPv6 semantics of "the source allows the network to utilize its own discretion in providing best-effort forwarding service for packets with zero FlowID"
>
> The IPv6 semantics of zero FlowID are consistent with the flow-detection rule in this document of "if the FlowID is zero, we are free to optimize the forwarding path using shortcuts"
>
> A non-zero FlowID has IPv6 semantics of "the source has previously established some preferred, end to end hop by hop forwarding behaviour for packets with this FlowID"

The IPv6 semantics of non-zero FlowID are consistent with the flow-detection rule in this document of "if the FlowID is non-zero, do not attempt to impose a shortcut".

A non-zero FlowID might be assigned by the source host after negotiating a preferred forwarding mechanism with 'the network' (e.g. through dynamic means such as RSVP, or administrative means). Alternatively it can simply be assigned randomly by the source host, and the network will provide default best effort forwarding (an IPv6 router defaults to providing best-effort forwarding for packets whose FlowID/source-address pair is not recognized).

Thus, the modes of operation supported by this document becomes:

Zero FlowID
Best effort forwarding, with optional shortcut discovery triggered through flow-detection.

Non-zero FlowID
Best effort forwarding if the routers along the path have not been otherwise configured with alternative processing rules for this FlowID/source-address pair. Flow detection relating to shortcut discovery is suspended.

If the routers along the path have been configured with particular processing rules for this FlowID/source-address pair, the flow is handled according to those rules. Flow detection relating to shortcut discovery is suspended.

Mechanisms for establishing particular per-hop processing rules for packets with non-zero FlowID are neither constrained by, nor implied by, this document.

C.2. Future directions for Flow Detection

In the future, accurate mapping of IPv6 flows onto NBMA VCs may require more information to be exchanged during the Neighbor Discovery process than is currently available in Neighbor Discovery packets. In these cases, the IPv6 Neighbor Discover protocols can be extended to include new TLV options (see section 4.6 of RFC 1970 [7]). However, if new options are required, the specification of these options must be co-ordinated with the IPNG working group. Since RFC 1970 specifies that nodes must silently ignore options they do not understand, new options can be added at any time without breaking backward compatibility with existing implementations.

NHRP also provides mechanisms for adding optional TLVs to NHRP Requests and NHRP Replies. Future developments of this document's architecture will require consistent QoS extensions to both ND and NHRP in order to ensure they are semantically equivalent (syntactic differences are undesirable, but can be tolerated).

Support for QoS on IPv6 unicast flows will not require further extensions to the existing MARS protocol. However, future support for QoS on IPv6 multicast flows may require extensions. MARS control messages share the same TLV extension mechanism as NHRP, allowing QoS extensions to be developed as needed.

Appendix D. Shortcut Limit Option

For NS messages sent as a shortcut trigger, a new type of ND option is needed to pass on the information about the data flow hop limit from the host to the router. The use of this ND option is defined in section 3.2.2 of this specification. Its binary representation follows the rules of section 4.6 of RFC 1970:

```
 0                   1                   2                   3
 0 1 2 3 4 5 6 7 8 9 0 1 2 3 4 5 6 7 8 9 0 1 2 3 4 5 6 7 8 9 0 1
+-+-+-+-+-+-+-+-+-+-+-+-+-+-+-+-+-+-+-+-+-+-+-+-+-+-+-+-+-+-+-+-+
|     Type      |    Length     | Shortcut Limit|   Reserved1   |
+-+-+-+-+-+-+-+-+-+-+-+-+-+-+-+-+-+-+-+-+-+-+-+-+-+-+-+-+-+-+-+-+
|                           Reserved2                           |
+-+-+-+-+-+-+-+-+-+-+-+-+-+-+-+-+-+-+-+-+-+-+-+-+-+-+-+-+-+-+-+-+
```

Fields:

Type	6
Length	1
Shortcut Limit	8-bit unsigned integer. Hop limit for shortcut attempt.
Reserved1	This field is unused. It MUST be initialized to zero by the sender and MUST be ignored by the receiver.
Reserved2	This field is unused. It MUST be initialized to zero by the sender and MUST be ignored by the receiver.

Description

The shortcut limit option is used by a host in a Neighbor Solicitation message sent as a shortcut trigger to a default router. It restricts the router's shortcut query to targets reachable via the specified number of hops. The shortcut limit is given relative to the host requesting the shortcut. NS messages with shortcut limit values of 0 or 1 MUST be silently ignored.

Full Copyright Statement

Network Working Group
Request for Comments: 2492
Category: Standards Track

G. Armitage
Lucent Technologies
P. Schulter
BrightTiger Technologies
M. Jork
Digital Equipment GmbH
January 1999

IPv6 over ATM Networks

Status of this Memo

This document specifies an Internet standards track protocol for the Internet community, and requests discussion and suggestions for improvements. Please refer to the current edition of the "Internet Official Protocol Standards" (STD 1) for the standardization state and status of this protocol. Distribution of this memo is unlimited.

Copyright Notice

Abstract

This document is a companion to the ION working group's architecture document, "IPv6 over Non Broadcast Multiple Access (NBMA) networks". It provides specific details on how to apply the IPv6 over NBMA architecture to ATM networks. This architecture allows conventional host-side operation of the IPv6 Neighbor Discovery protocol, while also supporting the establishment of 'shortcut' ATM forwarding paths (when using SVCs). Operation over administratively configured Point to Point PVCs is also supported.

1. Introduction.

This document is an ATM-specific companion document to the ION working group's, "IPv6 over Non Broadcast Multiple Access (NBMA) networks" specification [1]. Terminology and architectural descriptions will not be repeated here.

The use of ATM to provide point to point PVC service, or flexible point to point and point to multipoint SVC service, is covered by this document.

A minimally conforming IPv6/ATM driver SHALL support the PVC mode of operation. An IPv6/ATM driver that supports the full SVC mode SHALL also support PVC mode of operation.

2. Specification Terminology

The key words "MUST", "MUST NOT", "REQUIRED", "SHALL", "SHALL NOT", "SHOULD", "SHOULD NOT", "RECOMMENDED", "MAY", and "OPTIONAL" in this document are to be interpreted as described in RFC 2119 [16].

3. PVC Environments

When the ATM network is used in PVC mode, each PVC will connect exactly two nodes and the use of Neighbor Discovery and other IPv6 features is limited. IPv6/ATM interfaces have only one neighbor on each Link. The MARS and NHRP protocols are NOT necessary, since multicast and broadcast operations collapse down to an ATM level unicast operation. Dynamically discovered shortcuts are not supported.

The actual details of encapsulations, MTU, and link token generation are provided in the following sections.

This use of PVC links does not mandate, nor does it prohibit the use of extensions to the Neighbor Discovery protocol which may be developed for either general use of for use in PVC connections (for example, Inverse Neighbor Discovery).

Since ATM PVC links do not use link-layer addresses, the link-layer address options SHOULD not be included in any ND message [11]. If a link-layer address option is present in an ND message, then the option SHOULD be ignored.

A minimally conforming IPv6/ATM driver SHALL support the PVC mode of operation. PVC only implementations are not required to support any SVC mode of operation.

3.1 Default Packet Encapsulation

Following the model in RFC 1483 [2], AAL5 SHALL be the default Adaptation Layer service, and (LLC/SNAP) encapsulation SHALL be default encapsulation used by unicast and multicast packets across pt-pt PVC links. As defined in [1], the default IPv6 packet encapsulation SHALL be:

```
[0xAA-AA-03][0x00-00-00][0x86-DD][IPv6 packet]
    (LLC)       (OUI)      (PID)
```

3.2 Optional null encapsulation

IPv6/ATM drivers MAY also support null encapsulation as a configurable option. When null encapsulation is enabled, the IPv6 packet is passed directly to the AAL5 layer. Both ends of the PVC MUST be configured to use null encapsulation. The PVC will not be available for use by protocols other than IPv6.

3.3 PPP encapsulation

The concatentation of IPv6 over PPP with PPP over AAL5 PVCs is not covered by this specification.

3.4 MTU For PVC Environments

The default IP MTU size for PVC links is 9180 bytes as specified in [7]. Other IP MTU values MAY be used.

3.5 Interface Token Formats in PVC Environments

When the ATM network is used in PVC mode interface tokens SHALL be generated using one of the methods described in section 5. Interface tokens need only be unique between the two nodes on the PVC link.

4 SVC environments

4.1 SVC Specific Code Points

4.1.1 ATM Adaptation Layer encapsulation for SVC environments

Following the model in RFC 1483 [2], AAL5 SHALL be the default Adaptation Layer service, and (LLC/SNAP) encapsulation SHALL be the default encapsulation used by unicast and multicast packets across SVC links.

4.1.2 Unicast Packet Encapsulation

As defined in [1], the default IPv6 unicast packet encapsulation SHALL be:

```
[0xAA-AA-03][0x00-00-00][0x86-DD][IPv6 packet]
    (LLC)       (OUI)      (PID)
```

4.1.3 Multicast packet encapsulation

As defined in [1], the default IPv6 multicast packet encapsulation SHALL be:

```
[0xAA-AA-03][0x00-00-5E][0x00-01][pkt$cmi][0x86DD][IPv6
packet]             (LLC)        (OUI)      (PID)     (mars encaps)
```

The IPv6/ATM driver's Cluster Member ID SHALL be copied into the 2 octet pkt$cmi field prior to transmission.

4.1.4 Optional null encapsulation

IPv6/ATM drivers MAY also support null encapsulation as a configurable option. Null encapsulation SHALL only be used for passing IPv6 packets from one IPv6/ATM driver to another. Null encapsulation SHALL NOT be used on the pt-pt SVC between the IPv6/ATM driver and its local MARS.

If null encapsulation is enabled, the IPv6 packet is passed directly to the AAL5 layer. Both ends of the SVC MUST agree to use null encapsulation during the call SETUP phase. The SVC will not be available for use by protocols other than IPv6.

If null encapsulation is enabled on data SVCs between routers, inter-router NHRP traffic SHALL utilize a separate, parallel SVC.

Use of null encapsulation is not encouraged when IPv6/ATM is used with MARS/NHRP/ND as described in [1].

4.1.5 MARS control messages

The encapsulation of MARS control messages (between MARS and MARS Clients) remains the same as shown in RFC 2022 [3]:

```
[0xAA-AA-03][0x00-00-5E][0x00-03][MARS control message]
   (LLC)        (OUI)      (PID)
```

The key control field values are:

The mar$afn field remains 0x0F (ATM addresses)

The mar$pro field SHALL be 0x86DD (IPv6)

The mar$op.version field remains 0x00 (MARS)

The mar$spln and mar$tpln fields (where relevant) are either 0 (for null or non-existent information) or 16 (for the full IPv6 protocol address)

The way in which ATM addresses are stored remains the same as shown in RFC 2022 [3]

4.1.6 NHRP control messages

The encapsulation of NHRP control messages remains the same as shown in RFC 2332 [4]:

```
[0xAA-AA-03][0x00-00-5E][0x00-03][NHRP control message]
   (LLC)        (OUI)      (PID)
```

The key control field values are:

The ar$afn field remains 0x0F (ATM addresses)

The ar$pro field SHALL be 0x86DD (IPv6)

The ar$op.version field remains 0x01 (NHRP)

The ar$spln and ar$tpln fields (where relevant) are either 0 (for null or non-existent information) or 16 (for the full IPv6 protocol address)

The way in which ATM addresses are stored remains the same as shown in RFC 2022 [3]

4.1.7 Neigbor Discovery control messages

Section 5.2 of [1] describes the ND Link-layer address option. For IPv6/ATM drivers, the subfields SHALL be encoded in the following manner:

[NTL] defines the type and length of the ATM number immediately following the [STL] field. The format is as follows:

```
 7 6 5 4 3 2 1 0
+-+-+-+-+-+-+-+-+
|0|x|  length   |
+-+-+-+-+-+-+-+-+
```

The most significant bit is reserved and MUST be set to zero. The second most significant bit (x) is a flag indicating whether the ATM number is in:

ATM Forum AESA format (x = 0).
Native E.164 format (x = 1).

The bottom 6 bits represent an unsigned integer value indicating the length of the associated ATM address field in octets.

The [STL] format is the same as the [NTL] field. Defines the length of the subaddress field, if it exists. If it does not exist this entire octet field MUST be zero. If the subaddress exists it will be in AESA format, so flag x SHALL be zero.

[NBMA Number] is a variable length field containing the ATM address of the Link layer target. It is always present.

[NBMA Subaddress] is a variable length field containing the ATM subaddress of the Link layer target. It may or may not be present. When it is not, the option ends after the [NBMA Number] (or any additional padding for 8 byte alignment).

The octet ordering of the [NBMA Number] and [NBMA Subaddress] fields SHALL be the same as that used in MARS and NHRP control messages.

4.2 UNI 3.0/3.1 signaling issues (SVC mode).

When an IPv6 node places a call to another IPv6 node, it SHOULD follow the procedures in [6] and [7] for signalling UNI 3.0/3.1 SVCs [9] and negotiating MTU. The default IP MTU size on a LL is 9180 bytes as specified in [7].

Note that while the procedures in [7] still apply to IPv6 over ATM, IPv6 Path MTU Discovery [8] is used by nodes and routers rather than IPv4 MTU discovery. Additionally, while IPv6 nodes are not required to implement Path MTU Discovery, IPv6/ATM nodes SHOULD implement it. Also, since IPv6 nodes will negotiate an appropriate MTU for each VC, Path MTU should never be triggered since neither node should ever receive a Packet Too Big message to trigger Path MTU Discovery. When nodes are communicating via one or more routers Path MTU Discovery will be used just as it is for legacy networks.

5 Interface Tokens

For both PVC and SVC modes of operation, one of the following methods SHALL be used to generate Interface Tokens as required by section 5.1 of [1].

5.1 Interface Tokens Based on ESI values

When the underlying ATM interface is identified by an ATM End System Address (AESA, formerly known as an NSAPA), the interface token MAY be formed from the ESI and SEL values in the AESA as follows:

[0x00][ESI][SEL]

[0x00] is a one octet field which is always set to 0.
Note that the bit corresponding to the EUI-64 Global/Local bit [5] is always reset indicating that this address is not a globally unique IPv6 interface token.

[ESI] is a six octet field.
This field always contains the six octet ESI value for the AESA used to address the specific instance of the IPv6/ATM interface.

[SEL] is a one octet field.
This field always contains the SEL value from the AESA used to address the specific instance of the IPv6/ATM interface.

5.2 Interface Tokens Based on 48 Bit MAC Values

Where the underlying ATM NIC driver has access to a set of one or more 48 bit MAC values unique to the ATM NIC (e.g. MAC addresses configured into the NIC's ROM), the IPv6/ATM interface MAY use one of these values to create a unique interface token as described in [10].

5.3 Interface Tokens Based on EUI-64 Values

Where the underlying ATM NIC driver has access to a set of one or more 64 bit EUI-64 values unique to the ATM NIC (e.g. EUI-64 addresses configured into the NIC's ROM), the IPv6/ATM interface SHOULD use one of these values to create a unique interface token. after inverting the Global/Local identifier bit [10]. (Any relationship between these values and the ESI(s) registered with the local ATM switch by the ATM driver are outside the scope of this document.)

When EUI-64 values are used for IPv6 interface tokens the only modification allowed to the octet string read from the NIC is inversion of the Global/Local identifier bit.

5.4 Interface Tokens Based on Native E.164 Addresses

When an interface uses Native E.164 addresses then the E.164 values MAY be used to generate an interface token as follows:

[D14][D13D12][D11D10][D9D8][D9D6][D5D4][D3D2][D1D0]

[D14] A single octet containing the semi-octet representing the most significant E.164 digit shifted left four bits to the most significant four bits of the octet. The lower four bits MUST be set to 0. Note that the EUI-64 Global/Local indicator is set to 0 indicating that this is not a globally unique IPv6 interface token.

[D13D12] A single octet containing the semi-octet representing the second most significant E.164 digit [D13] shifted left four places to the most significant bits of the octet, and the third most significant semi-octet in the four least significant bits of the octet.

[D11D10] - [D1D0] Octets each containing two E.164 digits, one in the most significant four bits, and one in the least significant four bits as indicated.

5.5 Nodes Without Unique Identifiers

If no MAC, EUI-64, AESA, or E.164 value is available for generating an interface token, then the interface token SHALL be generated as described in Appendix A of [10].

5.6 Multiple Logical Links on a Single Interface

A logical ATM interface might be associated with a different SEL field of a common AESA prefix, or a set of entirely separate ESIs might have been registered with the local ATM switch to create a range of unique AESAs.

The minimum information required to uniquely identify each logical ATM interface is (within the context of the local switch port) their ESI+SEL combination.

For the vhost case described in section 5.1.2 of [1], vhost SHALL select a different interface token from the range of 64 bit values available to the ATM NIC (as described in 4.1). Each vhost SHALL implement IPv6/ATM interfaces in such a way that no two or more vhosts end up advertising the same interface token onto the same LL. (Conformance with this requirement may be achieved by choosing different SEL values, ESI values, or both.)

6. Conclusion and Open Issues.

This document is an ATM-specific companion document to the ION working group's, "IPv6 over Non Broadcast Multiple Access (NBMA) networks" specification [1]. It specifies codepoints for the administratively configured PVC, and dynamically established SVC, modes of operation.

There are no major open issues. Comments to the ION mailing list are solicited (ion@nexen.com).

7. Security Considerations

While this proposal does not introduce any new security mechanisms all current IPv6 security mechanisms will work without modification for ATM. This includes both authentication and encryption for both Neighbor Discovery protocols as well as the exchange of IPv6 data packets.

Acknowledgments

The original IPv6/ATM work by G. Armitage occurred while employed at Bellcore. Elements of section 4 were borrowed from Matt Crawford's memo on IPv6 over Ethernet.

The authors would like to thank Kazuhiko Yamamoto, Kenjiro Cho, Yoshinobu Inoue, Hiroshi Esaki, Yoshifumi Atarashi, and Atsushi Hagiwara for their contributions based on actual PVC implementations.

Authors' Addresses

Grenville Armitage
Bell Laboratories, Lucent Technologies
101 Crawfords Corner Road
Holmdel, NJ 07733
USA

EMail: gja@lucent.com

Peter Schulter
BrightTiger Technologies
125 Nagog Park
Acton, MA 01720

EMail: paschulter@acm.org

Markus Jork
European Applied Research Center
Digital Equipment GmbH
CEC Karlsruhe
Vincenz-Priessnitz-Str. 1
D-76131 Karlsruhe
Germany

EMail: jork@kar.dec.com

References

[1] Armitage, G., Schulter, P., Jork, M. and G. Harter, "IPv6 over Non-Broadcast Multiple Access (NBMA) networks", RFC 2491, January 1999.

[2] Heinanen, J., "Multiprotocol Encapsulation over ATM Adaption Layer 5", RFC 1483, July 1993.

[3] Armitage, G., "Support for Multicast over UNI 3.1 based ATM Networks", RFC 2022, November 1996.

[4] Luciani, J., Katz, D., Piscitello, D., Cole, B. and N. Doraswamy, "NBMA Next Hop Resolution Protocol (NHRP)", RFC 2332, April 1998.

[5] "64-Bit Global Identifier Format Tutorial", http://standards.ieee.org/db/oui/tutorials/EUI64.html.

[6] Perez, M., Liaw, F., Mankin, A., Hoffman, E., Grossman, D. and A.

Malis, "ATM Signalling Support for IP over ATM", RFC 1755, February 1995.

[7] Atkinson, R., "Default IP MTU for use over ATM AAL5", RFC 1626, May 1994.

[8] McCann, J., Deering, S. and J. Mogul, "Path MTU Discovery for IP version 6", RFC 1981, August 1996.

[9] ATM Forum, "ATM User Network Interface (UNI) Specification Version 3.1", ISBN 0-13-393828-X, Prentice Hall, Englewood Cliffs, NJ, June 1995.

[10] Hinden, B. and S. Deering, "IP Version 6 Addressing Architecture", RFC 2373, July 1998.

[11] Narten, T., Nordmark, E. and W. Simpson, "Neighbor Discovery for IP Version 6 (IPv6)", RFC 2461, December 1998.

Network Working Group
Request for Comments: 2497
See Also: 1201
Category: Standards Track

I. Souvatzis
The NetBSD Project
January 1999

RFC 2497 1

Transmission of IPv6 Packets over ARCnet Networks

Status of this Memo

This document specifies an Internet standards track protocol for the Internet community, and requests discussion and suggestions for improvements. Please refer to the current edition of the "Internet Official Protocol Standards" (STD 1) for the standardization state and status of this protocol. Distribution of this memo is unlimited.

Copyright Notice

1. Introduction

This memo specifies a frame format for transmission of IPv6 [IPV6] packets and the method of forming IPv6 link-local and statelessly autoconfigured addresses on ARCnet networks. It also specifies the content of the Source/Target Link-layer Address option used by the Router Solicitation, Router Advertisement, Neighbor Solicitation, Neighbor Advertisement and Redirect messages described in [DISC], when those messages are transmitted on an ARCnet.

The key words "MUST", "MUST NOT", "REQUIRED", "SHALL", "SHALL NOT", "SHOULD", "SHOULD NOT", "RECOMMENDED", "MAY", and "OPTIONAL" in this document are to be interpreted as described in RFC 2119 [KWORD].

2. Frame Format

IPv6 packets are link layer fragmented and reassembled according to [PHDS]. A brief but sufficient discussion of this fragmentation method can be found in [ARCIPV4].

The protocol ID (System Code in ARCnet terminology) assigned to IPv6 is C4 hexadecimal.

3. Maximum Transmission Unit

The maximum IPv6 packet length possible using this encapsulation method is 60480 octets. Since this length is impractical because of its worst case transmission time of several seconds, all ARCnet implementations on a given ARCnet network should agree on a smaller value.

The default MTU for IPv6 [IPV6] packets on an ARCnet is 9072 octets.

In the presence of a router, this size MAY be changed by a Router Advertisement [DISC] containing an MTU option. If a Router Advertisement is received with an MTU option specifying an MTU larger than 60480, or larger than a manually configured value less than 60480, that MTU option may be logged to system management but MUST be otherwise ignored.

If no router is available, the local MTU MUST be left at 9072 or MUST be manually configured to the same different value on all connected stations.

Implementations MAY accept arriving IPv6 datagrams which are larger than their configured maximum transmission unit. They are not required to discard such datagrams. If they can not handle larger datagrams, they MAY log the event to the system administration, but MUST otherwise silently discard them.

4. Stateless Auto-configuration

If a node has an EUI-64 which is not used to form the Interface Identifier for any other interface, it SHOULD use that EUI-64 to form the Interface Identifier for its ARCnet interface. If that EUI-64 is in use for another interface attached to a different link, it MAY be used for the ARCnet interface as well.

The Interface Identifier is then formed from the EUI-64 by complementing the "Universal/Local" (U/L) bit, which is the next-to-lowest order bit of the first octet of the EUI-64.

When a node has no EUI-64 available for forming its ARCnet Interface Identifer, it MUST form that identifier as specified in [AARCH], Appendix A, section "Links with Non-Global Identifier". That is, the 8 bit manually configured ARCnet address is appended to the 56 zero bits.

For example, for an ARCnet interface with the configured address of 49 hexadecimal this results in the following identifier:

```
|0              1|1              3|3              4|4              6|
|0              5|6              1|2              7|8              3|
+----------------+----------------+----------------+----------------+
|0000000000000000|0000000000000000|0000000000000000|0000000001001001|
+----------------+----------------+----------------+----------------+
```

Note that this results in the universal/local bit set to "0" to indicate local scope.

An IPv6 address prefix used for stateless auto-configuration [ACONF] of an ARCnet interface MUST have a length of 64 bits.

5. Link-Local Addresses

The IPv6 link-local address [AARCH] for an ARCnet interface is formed by appending the Interface Identifier, as defined above, to the prefix FE80::/64.

```
 10 bits            54 bits                  64 bits
+----------+-----------------------+----------------------------+
|1111111010|         (zeros)       |    Interface Identifier    |
+----------+-----------------------+----------------------------+
```

6. Address Mapping – Unicast

The procedure for mapping IPv6 addresses into ARCnet link-layer addresses is described in [DISC]. The Source/Target link layer Address option has the following form when the link layer is ARCnet.

```
 0                   1
 0 1 2 3 4 5 6 7 8 9 0 1 2 3 4 5
+-+-+-+-+-+-+-+-+-+-+-+-+-+-+-+-+
|     Type      |    Length     |
+-+-+-+-+-+-+-+-+-+-+-+-+-+-+-+-+
|ARCnet address |               |
+---------------+              -+
|                               |
+-     5 octets of padding     -+
|                               |
+-+-+-+-+-+-+-+-+-+-+-+-+-+-+-+-+
```

Option fields:

Type 1 for Source Link-layer address.
2 for Target Link-layer address.
Length 1 (in units of 8 octets).

ARCnet address The 8 bit ARCnet address, in canonical bit order.

7. Address Mapping – Multicast

As ARCnet only provides 1 multicast address (00 hexadecimal), all IPv6 multicast addresses MUST be mapped to this address.

8. Security Considerations

The method of derivation of Interface Identifiers from ARCnet addresses is intended to preserve local uniqueness when possible. However, there is no protection from duplication through accident or forgery.

9. Acknowledgements

Big parts of the new version of this memo are either based on [ETHIPV6] or on Matt Crawford's review of an earlier version.

10. References

[AARCH] Hinden, R. and S. Deering, "IP Version 6 Addressing Architecture", RFC 2373, July 1998.

[ACONF] Thomson, S. and T. Narten, "IPv6 Stateless Address Autoconfiguration", RFC 2462, December 1998.

[ARCIPV4] Provan, D., "Transmitting IP Traffic over ARCNET Networks", RFC1201, Novell, Inc., February 1991.

[DISC] Narten, T., Nordmark, E. and W. Simpson, "Neighbor Discovery for IP Version 6 (IPv6)", RFC 2461, December 1998.

[ETHIPV6] Crawford, M., "Transmission of IPv6 Packets over Ethernet Networks", RFC 2464, December 1998.

[EUI64] "64-Bit Global Identifier Format Tutorial", http://stan≠ dards.ieee.org/db/oui/tutorials/EUI64.html.

[IPV6] Deering, S. and R. Hinden, "Internet Protocol, Version 6 (IPv6) Specification", RFC 2460, December 1998.

[KWORD] Bradner, S., "Key words for use in RFCs to Indicate Requirement Levels", BCP 14, RFC 2119, March 1997.

[PHDS] Novell, Inc., "ARCNET Packet Header Definition Standard", Novell Part Number 100-00721-001, November 1989.

11. Author's Address

Ignatios Souvatzis
The NetBSD Project
Stationenweg 29
D-53332 Bornheim
Germany

Phone (work): +49 (228) 734316
EMail: is@netbsd.org

12. Full Copyright Statement

Network Working Group
Request for Comments: 2529
Category: Standards Track

B. Carpenter
IBM
C. Jung
3Com

March 1999

RFC 2529 1

Transmission of IPv6 over IPv4 Domains without Explicit Tunnels

Status of this Memo

This document specifies an Internet standards track protocol for the Internet community, and requests discussion and suggestions for improvements. Please refer to the current edition of the "Internet Official Protocol Standards" (STD 1) for the standardization state and status of this protocol. Distribution of this memo is unlimited.

Copyright Notice

Abstract

This memo specifies the frame format for transmission of IPv6 [IPV6] packets and the method of forming IPv6 link-local addresses over IPv4 domains. It also specifies the content of the Source/Target Link-layer Address option used in the Router Solicitation, Router Advertisement, Neighbor Solicitation, and Neighbor Advertisement and Redirect messages, when those messages are transmitted on an IPv4 multicast network.

The motivation for this method is to allow isolated IPv6 hosts, located on a physical link which has no directly connected IPv6 router, to become fully functional IPv6 hosts by using an IPv4 domain that supports IPv4 multicast as their virtual local link. It uses IPv4 multicast as a "virtual Ethernet".

Table of Contents

1. Introduction

This memo specifies the frame format for transmission of IPv6 [IPV6] packets and the method of forming IPv6 link-local addresses over IPv4 multicast "domains". For the purposes of this document, an IPv4 domain is a fully interconnected set of IPv4 subnets, within the same local multicast scope, on which there are at least two IPv6 nodes conforming to this specification. This IPv4 domain could form part of the globally-unique IPv4 address space, or could form part of a private IPv4 network [RFC 1918].

This memo also specifies the content of the Source/Target Link-layer Address option used in the Router Solicitation, Router Advertisement, Neighbor Solicitation, Neighbor Advertisement and Redirect messages described in [DISC], when those messages are transmitted on an IPv4 multicast domain.

The motivation for this method is to allow isolated IPv6 hosts, located on a physical link which has no directly connected IPv6 router, to become fully functional IPv6 hosts by using an IPv4 multicast domain as their virtual local link. Thus, at least one IPv6 router using the same method must be connected to the same IPv4 domain if IPv6 routing to other links is required.

IPv6 hosts connected using this method do not require IPv4-compatible addresses or configured tunnels. In this way IPv6 gains considerable independence of the underlying links and can step over many hops of IPv4 subnets. The mechanism is known formally as "IPv6 over IPv4" or "6over4" and colloquially as "virtual Ethernet".

The key words "MUST", "MUST NOT", "REQUIRED", "SHALL", "SHALL NOT", "SHOULD", "SHOULD NOT", "RECOMMENDED", "MAY", and "OPTIONAL" in this document are to be interpreted as described in [RFC2119].

2. Maximum Transmission Unit

The default MTU size for IPv6 packets on an IPv4 domain is 1480 octets. This size may be varied by a Router Advertisement [DISC] containing an MTU option which specifies a different MTU, or by manual configuration of each node.

Note that if by chance the IPv6 MTU size proves to be too large for some intermediate IPv4 subnet, IPv4 fragmentation will ensue. While undesirable, this is not disastrous. However, the IPv4 "do not fragment" bit MUST NOT be set in the encapsulating IPv4 header.

3. Frame Format

IPv6 packets are transmitted in IPv4 packets [RFC 791] with an IPv4 protocol type of 41, the same as has been assigned in [RFC 1933] for IPv6 packets that are tunneled inside of IPv4 frames. The IPv4 header contains the Destination and Source IPv4 addresses. The IPv4 packet body contains the IPv6 header followed immediately by the payload.

```
 0                   1                   2                   3
 0 1 2 3 4 5 6 7 8 9 0 1 2 3 4 5 6 7 8 9 0 1 2 3 4 5 6 7 8 9 0 1
+-+-+-+-+-+-+-+-+-+-+-+-+-+-+-+-+-+-+-+-+-+-+-+-+-+-+-+-+-+-+-+-+
|Version|  IHL  |Type of Service|          Total Length         |
+-+-+-+-+-+-+-+-+-+-+-+-+-+-+-+-+-+-+-+-+-+-+-+-+-+-+-+-+-+-+-+-+
|         Identification        |Flags|      Fragment Offset    |
+-+-+-+-+-+-+-+-+-+-+-+-+-+-+-+-+-+-+-+-+-+-+-+-+-+-+-+-+-+-+-+-+
|  Time to Live | Protocol 41   |         Header Checksum       |
+-+-+-+-+-+-+-+-+-+-+-+-+-+-+-+-+-+-+-+-+-+-+-+-+-+-+-+-+-+-+-+-+
|                       Source Address                          |
+-+-+-+-+-+-+-+-+-+-+-+-+-+-+-+-+-+-+-+-+-+-+-+-+-+-+-+-+-+-+-+-+
|                    Destination Address                        |
+-+-+-+-+-+-+-+-+-+-+-+-+-+-+-+-+-+-+-+-+-+-+-+-+-+-+-+-+-+-+-+-+
|                    Options                    |    Padding    |
+-+-+-+-+-+-+-+-+-+-+-+-+-+-+-+-+-+-+-+-+-+-+-+-+-+-+-+-+-+-+-+-+
|            IPv6 header and payload ...              /
+-------+-------+-------+-------+-------+------+------+
```

If there are IPv4 options, then padding SHOULD be added to the IPv4 header such that the IPv6 header starts on a boundary that is a 32-bit offset from the end of the datalink header.

The Time to Live field SHOULD be set to a low value, to prevent such packets accidentally leaking from the IPv4 domain. This MUST be a configurable parameter, with a recommended default of 8.

4. Stateless Autoconfiguration and Link-Local Addresses

The Interface Identifier [AARCH] of an IPv4 interface is the 32-bit IPv4 address of that interface, with the octets in the same order in which they would appear in the header of an IPv4 packet, padded at the left with zeros to a total of 64 bits. Note that the "Universal/Local" bit is zero, indicating that the Interface Identifer is not globally unique. When the host has more than one IPv4 address in use on the physical interface concerned, an administrative choice of one of these IPv4 addresses is made.

An IPv6 address prefix used for stateless autoconfiguration [CONF] of an IPv4 interface MUST have a length of 64 bits except for a special case mentioned in Section 7.

The IPv6 Link-local address [AARCH] for an IPv4 virtual interface is formed by appending the Interface Identifier, as defined above, to the prefix FE80::/64.

```
+-------+-------+-------+-------+-------+-------+------+------+
|  FE      80      00      00      00      00      00      00  |
+-------+-------+-------+-------+-------+-------+------+------+
|  00      00   |  00   |  00   |      IPv4 Address            |
+-------+-------+-------+-------+-------+-------+------+------+
```


5. Address Mapping — Unicast

The procedure for mapping IPv6 addresses into IPv4 virtual link-layer addresses is described in [DISC]. The Source/Target Link-layer Address option has the following form when the link layer is IPv4. Since the length field is in units of 8 bytes, the value below is 1.

```
+-------+-------+-------+-------+-------+-------+-------+-------+
| Type  |Length | must be zero  |          IPv4 Address         |
+-------+-------+-------+-------+-------+-------+-------+-------+
```

Type:
 1 for Source Link-layer address.
 2 for Target Link-layer address.

Length:
 1 (in units of 8 octets).

IPv4 Address:

The 32 bit IPv4 address, in network byte order. This is the address the interface currently responds to, and may be different from the Interface Identifier for stateless autoconfiguration.

6. Address Mapping — Multicast

IPv4 multicast MUST be available. An IPv6 packet with a multicast destination address DST MUST be transmitted to the IPv4 multicast address of Organization-Local Scope using the mapping below. These IPv4 multicast addresses SHOULD be taken from the block

239.192.0.0/16, a sub-block of the Organization-Local Scope address block, or, if all of those are not available, from the expansion blocks defined in [ADMIN]. Note that when they are formed using the expansion blocks, they use only a /16 sized block.

```
+-------+-------+-------+-------+
|  239  |  OLS  | DST14 | DST15 |
+-------+-------+-------+-------+
```

DST14, DST15 last two bytes of IPv6 multicast address.

OLS from the configured Organization-Local Scope address block. SHOULD be 192, see [ADMIN] for details.

No new IANA registration procedures are required for the above. See appendix A. for a list of all the multicast groups that must be joined to support Neighbor Discovery.

7. Scaling and Transition Issues

The multicast mechanism described in Section 6 above appears to have essentially the same scaling properties as native IPv6 over most media, except for the slight reduction in MTU size which will slightly reduce bulk throughput. On an ATM network, where IPv4 multicast relies on relatively complex mechanisms, it is to be expected that IPv6 over IPv4 over ATM will perform less well than native IPv6 over ATM.

The "IPv6 over IPv4" mechanism is intended to take its place in the range of options available for transition from IPv4 to IPv6. In particular it allows a site to run both IPv4 and IPv6 in coexistence, without having to configure IPv6 hosts either with IPv4-compatible addresses or with tunnels. Interfaces of the IPv6 router and hosts will of course need to be enabled in "6over4" mode.

A site may choose to start its IPv6 transition by configuring one IPv6 router to support "6over4" on an interface connected to the site's IPv4 domain, and another IPv6 format on an interface connected to the IPv6 Internet. Any enabled "6over4" hosts in the IPv4 domain will then be able to communicate both with the router and with the IPv6 Internet, without manual configuration of a tunnel and without the need for an IPv4-compatible IPv6 address, either stateless or stateful address configuration providing the IPv6 address to the IPv6 host.

During transition, routers may need to advertise at least two IPv6 prefixes, one for the native LAN (e.g. Ethernet) and one for "6over4". As with any IPv6 prefix assigned to an IPv6 subnet, the latter MUST be unique within its scope, whether site-local or global addressing is used.

Also note that when a router is handling both native LAN and "6over4" on the same physical interface, during stateless autoconfiguration, there is a period when IPv6 link-local addresses are used, in both cases with the prefix FE80::/64. Note that the prefix-length for these link-local adddress MUST then be 128 so that the two cases can be distinguished.

As the site installs additional IPv6 routers, "6over4" hosts which become physically adjacent to IPv6 routers can be changed to run as native IPv6 hosts, with the the only impact on IPv6 applications being a slight increase in MTU size. At some stage during transition, it might be convenient to dual home hosts in both native LAN and "6over4" mode, but this is not required.

8. IANA Considerations

No assignments by the IANA are required beyond those in [ADMIN].

9. Security Considerations

Implementors should be aware that, in addition to posssible attacks against IPv6, security attacks against IPv4 must also be considered. Use of IP security at both IPv4 and IPv6 levels should nevertheless be avoided, for efficiency reasons. For example, if IPv6 is running encrypted, encryption of IPv4 would be redundant except if traffic analysis is felt to be a threat. If IPv6 is running authenticated, then authentication of IPv4 will add little. Conversely, IPv4 security will not protect IPv6 traffic once it leaves the IPv6-over-IPv4 domain. Therefore, implementing IPv6 security is required even if IPv4 security is available.

There is a possible spoofing attack in which spurious 6over4 packets are injected into a 6over4 domain from outside. Thus, boundary routers MUST discard multicast IPv4 packets with source or destination multicast addresses of organisation local scope as defined in section 6 above, if they arrive on physical interfaces outside that scope. To defend against spurious unicast 6over4 packets, boundary routers MUST discard incoming IPv4 packets with protocol type 41 from unknown sources, i.e. IPv6-in-IPv4 tunnels must only be accepted from trusted sources. Unless IPSEC authentication is available, the RECOMMENDED technique for this is to configure the boundary router only to accept protocol type 41 packets from source addresses within a trusted range or ranges.

Acknowledgements

The basic idea presented above is not original, and we have had invaluable comments from Matt Crawford, Steve Deering, Dan Harrington, Rich Draves, Erik Nordmark, Quang Nguyen, Thomas Narten, and other members of the IPNG and NGTRANS working groups.

This document is seriously ripped off from RFC 1972 written by Matt Crawford. Brian Carpenter was at CERN when the work was started.

References

[AARCH] Hinden, R., and S. Deering, "IP Version 6 Addressing Architecture", RFC 2373, July 1998.

[ADMIN] Meyer, D., "Administratively Scoped IP Multicast", BCP 23, RFC 2365, July 1998.

[CONF] Thomson, S. and T. Narten, "IPv6 Stateless Address Autoconfiguration", RFC 2462, December 1998.

[DISC] Narten, T., Nordmark, E. and W. Simpson, "Neighbor Discovery for IP Version 6 (IPv6)", RFC 2461, December 1998.

[IPV6] Deering, S. and R. Hinden, "Internet Protocol, Version 6 (IPv6) Specification", RFC 2460, December 1998.

[RFC 791] Postel, J., "Internet Protocol", STD 5, RFC 791, September 1981.

[RFC 1918] Rekhter, Y., Moskowitz, R., Karrenberg, D., de Groot, G. and E. Lear, "Address Allocation for Private Internets", RFC 1918, February 1996.

[RFC 1933] Gilligan, R. and E. Nordmark, "Transition Mechanisms for IPv6 Hosts and Routers", RFC 1933, April 1996.

[RFC 2119] Bradner, S., "Key words for use in RFCs to Indicate Requirement Levels", BCP 14, RFC 2119, March 1997.

[RFC 1972] Crawford, M., "A Method for the Transmission of IPv6 Packets over Ethernet Networks", RFC 1972, August 1996.

APPENDIX A: IPv4 Multicast Addresses for Neighbor Discovery

The following IPv4 multicast groups are used to support Neighbor Discovery with this specification. The IPv4 addresses listed in this section were obtained by looking at the IPv6 multicast addresses that Neigbour Discovery uses, and deriving the resulting IPv4 "virtual link-layer" addresses that are generated from them using the algorithm given in Section 6.

all-nodes multicast address
- the administratively-scoped IPv4 multicast address used to reach all nodes in the local IPv4 domain supporting this specification. 239.OLS.0.1

all-routers multicast address
- the administratively-scoped IPv4 multicast address to reach all routers in the local IPv4 domain supporting this specification. 239.OLS.0.2

solicited-node multicast address
- an administratively scoped multicast address that is computed as a function of the solicited target's address by taking the low-order 24 bits of the IPv4 address used to form the IPv6 address, and prepending the prefix FF02:0:0:0:0:1:FF00::/104 [AARCH]. This is then mapped to the IPv4 multicast address by the method described in this document. For example, if the IPv4 address used to form the IPv6 address is W.X.Y.Z, then the IPv6 solicited node multicast address is FF02::1:255.X.Y.Z and the corresponding IPv4 multicast address is 239.OLS.Y.Z

Authors' Addresses

Brian E. Carpenter
Internet Division
IBM United Kingdom Laboratories
MP 185, Hursley Park
Winchester, Hampshire S021 2JN, UK

EMail: brian@hursley.ibm.com

Cyndi Jung
3Com Corporation
5400 Bayfront Plaza, Mailstop 3219
Santa Clara, California 95052-8145

EMail: cmj@3Com.com

Full Copyright Statement

Index